# UNDERSTANDING DRIVING

*For Rosie, who drives me more carefully than I do; my father, who drove me before I drove myself; and Ivan who turned the key*

# Understanding Driving

## Applying cognitive psychology to a complex everyday task

John A. Groeger
*University of Surrey, UK*

PSYCHOLOGY PRESS
ALERE FLAMMAM
Taylor & Francis Group

First published 2000 by Psychology Press Ltd
27 Church Road, Hove, East Sussex, BN3 2FA

http://www.psypress.co.uk

Simultaneously published in the USA and Canada
by Taylor & Francis inc.
325 Chestnut Street, Philadelphia, PA 19106

Reprinted 2001

*Psychology Press is part of the Taylor & Francis Group*

© 2000 John A. Groeger

Typeset in 10/12pt Times by Graphicraft Limited, Hong Kong
Printed and bound in Great Britain by Biddles Ltd, Guildford and King's Lynn

**British Library Cataloguing in Publication Data**
A catalogue record for this book is available from the British Library

*Library of Congress Cataloging in Publication Data*
Groeger, John A., 1959–
    Understanding driving : applying cognitive psychology to a complex everyday task /
John A. Groeger.
        p. cm. — (Frontiers of cognitive science)
    Includes bibliographical references and index.
    1. Cognitive psychology. 2. Automobile driving—Psychological aspects. I. Title. II.
Series.

BF201.G755 2000
153.7—dc21                                                                              00–031086

ISBN 0–415–18752–4

# Contents

**List of illustrations**    ix
**Acknowledgements**    xi
**Foreword: Drivers and the driving they do**    xiii

**1   Assessing distance, speed, and time**    **1**
    Light and the eyes    1
    Depth and distance    3
    Motion and speed    8
    Time-to-collision    17
    Summary    23

**2   Motor responses and behavioural repertoires**    **25**
    Object-oriented actions    26
    Endogenous and exogenous signals: Reactions to expected
       and unexpected events    33
    Summary    38

**3   Combining perceptual-motor skills**    **41**
    Braking to avoid a collision    42
    Following another vehicle    45
    Steering control and gaze    48
    Summary    52

**4    Attention, automaticity, and distraction    55**
    Aspects of attention    56
    Attention as schema scheduling    57
    Routine actions and automaticity    63
    Driving and distraction    69
    Summary    74

**5    Learning, instruction, and training    75**
    Learning curves and practising    76
    Varieties of practice    80
    Stages in the acquisition of skill    88
    Transfer of acquired skill    91
    Instruction and feedback    95
    Summary    96

**6    Memory for driving    99**
    Memories and remembering    99
    Working memory and driving activities    107
    Memory for situational and spatial information    112
    Memory for when and whether accidents happened    114
    Summary    119

**7    When driving is dangerous: Arousal, assessment, and hazard perception    121**
    Physiological consequences of confronting a dangerous situation    122
    Memory for threatening situations    125
    Assessing driving scenes    132
    Hazard perception    136
    Summary    141

**8    Appraisal, efficacy, and action    143**
    Beliefs about attitudes    143
    Assessments of ourselves and others    145
    Developing self-efficacy    152
    Self-efficacy and actual ability    156
    Appraisal, efficacy, and emotion-driven actions    159
    Summary    163

**9    Age, neurological damage, disease, and driving    165**
    Age and driving    166
    Traumatic brain injury and driving    171
    Dementia and driving    177
    Continuing driving with neurological damage and disease    186

**10 Towards a cognitive account of driver behaviour**     **189**

A framework for understanding the driving task     190

Evaluating the four-facet framework     199

The four-facet framework and beyond     202

**References     205**
**Author index     239**
**Subject index     251**

# Illustrations

FIGURES

1.1 Speed assessments under actual and simulated driving conditions    15
1.2 Angular of expansion of 2 m and 4 m targets approached at 45 and
90 kph    20
2.1 Willingham's COBALT model of motor control    28
2.2 Simple reaction time as a function of age, alerting and responding with
hands or feet    34
2.3 Temporal characteristics of gear changes as a function of driving
experience    37
3.1 Temporal characteristics of braking (after van Winsum, 1996)    44
3.2 Tau-dot when following trucks and cars at different speeds    47
4.1 Reductions in ability to detect and add visually and auditorially presented
digits when driving, among experienced and inexperienced drivers    72
5.1 Power function learning curves as a function of differences in initial
performance and rate of learning    77
5.2 Learning and retention as a function of practice regime (after Shea &
Morgan)    86
6.1 Specialist experience and detecting critical events (after Myles-Worsley,
Johnston, & Simons, 1988)    103
6.2 Biases in accident reporting as a function of direction of report    118
7.1 Physiological reactions in difficult and dangerous driving conditions    123
8.1 Assessments of ourselves and others as a function of direction of
report    150
8.2 Assessing others influences self-assessment    152
8.3 New drivers' assessments of own and novice's driving ability as a function of
driving test outcome and driving experience    154
8.4 Self-assessed ability and teacher-assessed ability when learning to drive    158

9.1   Accident involvement as a function of driving experience in the months after gaining a licence    167
9.2   Accident involvement as a function of distance driven in the months after gaining a licence    168
9.3   Accident involvement as a function of experience, age, and gender    169
10.1  Four elements of driver behaviour    190
10.2  Elements of implied goal interruption    193
10.3  Elements of appraisal of future interruption    194
10.4  Elements of action planning    197
10.5  Elements of implementation    198

TABLES

4.1   Brain areas primarily involved in schema control functions    59
4.2   Effects of secondary task on driving performance    70
5.1   Correlations between rates of progress on driving manoeuvres (progress determined by rate of reduction in instructor's comments)    83
6.1   Neuroimaging results and working memory components    108
7.1   Average correlations between objective and subjective measures at each site, and between each site's accident record in the preceding three years    124
7.2   Relationships between assessments of danger, difficulty, arousal, and memory accuracy and quality as a function of delay    130
8.1   Correlations between self- and observer assessments of driving ability    157
8.2   Mood changes pre- and post-test for drivers receiving feedback    161
9.1   Presentation and admission of adults at Accident & Emergency departments with head injury per 100,000    172
9.2   UK driving licence holders aged 60 and over (1997)    178
10.1  Confirmatory factor analysis (all parameters free) oblique factor fit    200

# Acknowledgements

This book takes a complex everyday task and tries to uncover the psychological processes on which its performance is based. In so doing I am deliberately trying to enhance the theoretical basis of research on driving, and to provide a more grounded basis for applying the knowledge we have. I suspect that some will find the theoretical formulations I offer unsatisfactory, while others may find the way I deal with applied issues unconvincing. I would like to have been able to please everyone, and I encourage people to improve on what I offer here. However, I remind the reader of the task I set myself in writing this book—to bring theory and application closer together. Improving theory while ignoring its application, or application without theoretical foundation, is an easier, but short-sighted, enterprise.

I am completing the writing of this book during the 1999 Wimbledon tennis championship, which is an odd sort of anniversary of my involvement in research related to driving. Some 14 years ago, on what seemed an auspicious day at the time, a German qualifier, Boris Becker, knocked out the highly rated if somewhat irascible John McEnroe. That same day I was interviewed for a post at the Applied Psychology Unit, Cambridge, to work as a Research Assistant to Ivan Brown—and I watched that match in an office at the APU while I waited to hear the interview outcome. The quality of the interview panel—Ivan, Roger Watt, John Duncan, and Phil Johnson-Laird—makes clear the breadth of psychological approaches required for, and the investment the MRC then placed in, understanding driving. I learned a great deal from these and other APU colleagues in the nine years I spent at Cambridge. Since then I have largely worked in Surrey, except for a brief period at the University of Leeds. My time in Surrey particularly gave me the confidence and support to attempt to consider some of the more fundamental psychological issues raised by driving.

Throughout my time carrying out research on driving I have been very fortunate to have had the support of a number of outstanding research assistants, including Ben Clegg, Peter Chapman, Gunn Grande, Sarah Brady, David Field, and Jim Whalen, whose common feature seems to have been to do the near impossible at very short notice. Without the support of UK Research Councils (MRC, EPSRC, ESRC), the DGXIII funding of the GIDS, DETER, and ARIADNE projects, and especially of the Department of Environment Transport and the Regions, much of our research reported in this book would not have been possible.

A shared interest in driving research has allowed me to make many very good friends in the UK and beyond, the most constant of whom have been Ivan Brown (Cambridge), Talib Rothengatter (Groningen), and Ray Fuller (Dublin). Without these and other good friends, my family, my wife Rosie Dickson, her parents James and Jean and, when they were alive, my own parents Sylvester and Joan, I would have less joy from where my drive has taken me.

JOHN A. GROEGER
*Guildford, 1999*

# Foreword: Drivers and the driving they do

*A brief overview of the driving task, its history and prevalence, and the dangers it poses for those involved.*

As we sit on the cusp of the millennium, it is an arresting thought that just 100 years ago almost no-one drove a motorised vehicle. In fact, because the fastest horse could run, albeit over a longer distance, only a little faster than the world's fastest sprinter, in both cases about 15 to 20 miles per hour, the human race's experience of travelling at speed was very limited. Because of these boundary conditions on human experience of controlling speed, I do wonder just how well adapted we are to the driving virtually all of us now do. The main chapters of this book will deal with the way different aspects of cognition are intimately involved in driving, but here I review briefly broader aspects of driving and drivers.

Driving is a comparatively recent activity, and a very recent activity for all but a minority of the population. Before the advent of the internal combustion engine, and then only for a relatively brief period of a few decades, steam-powered, solid-wheeled, independently moving carriages were driven on Britain's roads. One of the first of these was "Era", a steam coach taking passengers from Paddington to Regents Park in the early 1830s. The speed at which these vehicles travelled was modest, and legally constrained to 2 mph in towns and 4 mph in the country by the Locomotive Act of 1865. The concerns about the risk of this form of transport were sufficient to merit a pedestrian, bearing a red flag, walking some 60 yards ahead as a safety measure. This requirement was legally enshrined in the same legislation. A few years later the warning distance was reduced to 20 yards (Locomotive Amendment Act 1878). Ultimately, because of the increased controllability of lighter vehicles appearing on the roads, and perhaps the dearth of volunteers to precede these early motorised vehicles (!), the speed limit was raised to 14 mph, and the requirement to warn others of the immanent arrival of the vehicle was met by "an instrument capable of giving audible and sufficient warning" (Locomotive and Highways Act 1896). At about this time the first petrol-driven vehicles began to appear on British roads, the gleaming emergency vehicles made by Dennis Brothers of Guildford being among the first commercially manufactured. Despite the many design, engineering, and mechanical enhancements of the modern vehicle, the car horn has remained ever-present!

By the time The Motor Car Act was introduced in 1903, there were in the region of 5000 vehicles on British roads. The Act made it a legal requirement for vehicles to be registered, displaying a mark of registration in a prominent position, and drivers were required to register on an annual basis. The Act also raised the speed limit to 20 mph, with a limit of 10 mph by the Local Government Boards, and, as offenders could now be identified more easily, introduced heavy fines for speeding and reckless driving. Fines were also introduced for driving unlicensed vehicles. The Roads Act in 1920 saw the introduction of the vehicle registration plate, and 10 years later the Road Traffic Act 1930 abolished the 20 mph speed limit and set a variety of limits for different classes of vehicle. By virtue of this Act there was no speed limit for vehicles carrying fewer than seven persons. The Road Traffic Act of 1930 also introduced new requirements for driving licences, the forerunner of the driving test, which changed little until very recently.

Almost 100 years later, the number of registered vehicles in the UK has risen to 26 million and the number of registered drivers to 38 million. The latter figure is staggering, when considered against the current population of the country (i.e. 59 million), especially against the number of those aged 17 years and older (circa 46 million). It shows that a century after the first motorised vehicles were driven, about 83% of the population hold driving licences of one form or another. The fact that licence holding is much more prevalent in those aged under 45 (circa 88%) than in those aged over 50 (circa 47%) shows the acceleration in licence holding that is to be expected as the 13 or so million teenagers approach licensing age.

Recent government figures[1] show that the road network of Great Britain now extends to about 373 thousand kilometres,[2] of which 3.3 thousand kilometres are motorway. Although it is an unrealistic assumption, if every registered road vehicle took to the road network at the same time, each would have about 14 metres of road space. On British roads, as drivers or passengers, we each travel

---

[1] Government Statistical Services (http://www.statistics.gov.uk/stats/ukinfigs).
[2] This is, incidentally, about 20 times the length of the rail network.

on average about 11 thousand kilometres per year, about 7% of these on buses or coaches. The latter average, about 725 kilometres per year, is about the same as the distance travelled on trains and other urban rail transport systems, and seven times the average distance travelled by air.

One of negative consequences of this explosion in personal mobility is, of course, the increased risk of death and injury.[3] Evans (1991), in his very engaging style, points out a number of truly startling statistics. Over half of teenage deaths occur in traffic accidents. More pre-retirement years of life are lost through traffic crashes than through cancer and heart disease. Across the European Union, despite the increasing number of licence holders and the inexorable increase in registered vehicles, the number of people dying in road accidents has decreased steadily in recent years. Across the 15 EU member states there are 43,000 road deaths per year, and an estimated 3.5 million casualties (ETSC, 1999). The pattern of fatality reduction is similar across EU member states. On average, across all states, road fatality rates per 100,000 population declined by 22% between 1970 and 1980, and a further 12% between 1980 and 1990. For eight member states for which national data were available, fatality rates per billion kilometres fell by 48% between 1970 and 1980, and by a further 48% between 1980 and 1990.

Equivalent figures for the United Kingdom show a fatality rate reduction from just over 6000 in 1984 to 3800 in 1997. When referenced to billion kilometres of road travel, this is a reduction of 50% between 1984 and 1997, and a fatality rate reduction corrected for population shows a decrease of about 41% over the same period. Numbers of accidents that result in serious injury also show substantial reductions, 42% over the same period, uncorrected for travel or population. However, the total number of casualties has risen by 2% to 327,544, because the number of slight injuries has increased. Nevertheless, this increase is considerably less than the 52% increase in road traffic over the period. It is very difficult to get a truly accurate figure for the number of damage-only accidents that occur annually, but the UK Department of Transport's (DETR) estimate for 1996 was 3.6 million.

For the variety of reasons discussed later in this book, not all drivers are equally likely to be involved in accidents. If they were, and purely to try to scale these numbers comprehensibly, about 1 in 10 drivers will have a damage-only accident during the year, 1 in 100 will have a slight injury accident, 1 in 1000 will be involved in an accident requiring hospital treatment, while 1 in every 10,000 drivers will die. Although it may seem morbid to do so, it is important for planning and allocation of resources to attempt to put some financial cost on the trauma that traffic accidents cause. Recently, DETR published the estimated

---

[3] Throughout this book I use the terms "accidents" and "crashes" interchangeably. This does not imply that I believe that accidents or crashes are random events, without cause or blame.

cost of all UK crashes in 1996.[4] For slight and serious accidents and deaths the estimated cost was £9890 m at 1996 prices. The estimated further 3.55 m damage-only accidents that took place were estimated to cost a further £4030 m, bringing the estimated total value of prevention of all road accidents in 1996 to a staggering £13,920 m: about one-third of the UK's then Social Security budget!

For reasons especially discussed in the penultimate chapter of this book (largely the change in age-structure of the driving population) I think it is possible that we will see an increase in crash-risk over the next couple of decades. This will be set against the increased use of public transport, home working, and technological advances which may see a continued reduction in the actual incidence of serious accidents. Because of the newer risks we may face, and the potential for advances in psychological theory that would derive from understanding complex skills, this book seeks to give a cognitive account of how we drive. I do not, quite deliberately, discuss the undeniable role that alcohol and other drugs play in safety, or road safety in general, or the potential for new in-car and road-side technologies. This is not because I see these issues as unimportant; indeed I hope that what I provide here will form a basis for further work in these areas. They are excluded simply because I do not wish these more obvious aspects of driving to distract from my main purpose in this book—to further an understanding of the driving task, by applying cognitive psychology.

---

[4] These figures comprise a number of different cost elements, arising from various sources: loss of output due to injury, calculated as the present value of the expected loss of earnings plus any non-wage payments (national insurance contributions, etc.) paid by the employer; ambulance costs and the costs of hospital treatment, etc.; human costs, based on Willingness To Pay values, which represent pain, grief, and suffering to the casualty, relatives, and friends, and, for fatal casualties, the intrinsic loss of enjoyment of life over and above the consumption of goods and services; costs of damage to vehicles and property (estimated from national survey returns); costs of police and the administrative costs of accident insurance (estimated from national survey returns).

CHAPTER ONE

# Assessing distance, speed, and time

*Perhaps the most immediately apparent aspects of the driving task are that drivers must assess the distance between themselves and other objects, the speed at which both are travelling, and how these might combine to allow the driver to act appropriately in the time available. As will emerge as the book proceeds, I think there is rather more involved in driving than merely combining different sources of visual information with particular motor patterns, but these elements of the task are themselves non-trivial. In this chapter I briefly outline some of the factors that influence distance and speed perception, and the way in which we judge when we may reach another object, or when it may reach us.*

Although engine, wind, and road noise make some contribution, our impression of speed and certainly of distance depends on what we can see. I wish to begin by considering how fundamental the information is that we use as a basis for assessing speed and distance.

## LIGHT AND THE EYES

*How is it that we see something clearly in some situations, but not in others, such as on a foggy day or at dusk? Why is it that some things are easier to see than others? How does our visual system use the light available to help us build the complex visual world we generally take for granted?*

Between ultra violet and infra red, both invisible to the human eye, lies the band of electromagnetic radiation that gives rise to our sense of seeing the world. For most of us this sense of seeing the world consists of the impression that there are "objects" which have a particular shape (i.e. surface, edge, and texture), and colour, the latter comprising the wavelengths of the visible spectrum ranging from violet (390 nanometres) to red (700 nanometres). Light-energy is lost (e.g. absorbed), scattered (e.g. through defraction), bent (e.g. by refraction), and reflected by different media (air, water, etc.) and surfaces (some surfaces reflect some wavelengths more strongly than others; some textures reflect light at different angles). This information, the way our eyes operate, and the knowledge we have of the world, allow us to see what we see.

The light reflected from surfaces across an angle of approximately 150° is directed by the lens of the eye onto the retina, an area of approximately 120–130 million light-sensitive cells at the back of the eye. The extent to which the lens changes in shape—becoming thinner, thus dispersing the light reaching the eye over a greater area of the retina, or fatter, directing the light towards a smaller area of the retina—partly governs the clarity with which we see near and distant objects. The ability of the ciliary muscles to contract or relax, and hence the power of the lens, decreases with age.

The other major factor involved is the nature and concentration of light-sensitive cells in the area of the retina onto which light is directed, whether by lens accommodation or eye movements. Light-sensitive cells comprise cones, which do not respond at low light levels, and rods, which do. Some cones are sensitive to blue, others to green, and others to red. However, because cones respond in bright light (i.e. photopic vision) do not respond in low light (i.e. scotopic vision) conditions, we see colour in reasonably bright conditions, but not in dim or dark conditions. Rods outnumber cones by about 20 to 1 on the surface of the retina as a whole, but the concentration of rods to cones changes over the retina surface, from the cone-rich fovea to more peripheral rod-rich areas. The former provide high-acuity vision in bright light, while rod-rich areas, which comprise the vast majority of the retina, provide considerable sensitivity, but not acuity, in dim light.

As light falls on different areas of the retina, causing some mixture of rods and/or cones to fire, nerve cells beyond the retina in visual pathways to the brain also respond. Which nerve cells will respond depends on the areas of the retina stimulated (i.e. receptive fields), and the periodicity of the pattern of light reaching the retina. The periodicity of this light pattern, usually expressed as the number of cycles per unit of visual angle, is called "spatial frequency".

Imagine, for a moment, that you are a hawk hovering above a zebra crossing. If you are hovering just a few metres above the crossing, the characteristic repetition of black and white stripes goes through just a few cycles for every degree of visual angle of the scene. If you hover, say, twice as high, the same visual angle will comprise more repetitions of the black–white pattern. That is, within the visible range, the higher up the hawk is, the higher the spatial frequency of the zebra crossing. Nerve cells beyond the retina are tuned to respond to different spatial frequencies, thus allowing our brains to build up the complex images, comprising many different spatial frequencies, that guide our everyday behaviour.

In most lighting conditions, telling the difference between the black and white portions of the zebra crossing is relatively easy, because the contrast between adjacent parts of the image is very high; formally, contrast is the difference between the maximum and minimum luminances in a pattern of light expressed as a proportion of the mean intensity or luminance. Telling the difference, under all conditions of illumination, between white and light grey stripes, or black and dark grey stripes, would be a lot more difficult. Where more light is available, assuming the light source does not cause "white-out", discrimination of colour differences, object edges, and textures becomes easier and more accurate.

At midday during a UK summer, the intensity of the light from the unobscured sun is in the region of 10,000 lux. At sunrise or sunset the intensity of this light falls by more than a factor of 10, while by the light of a full moon the light intensity is around 1 lux—still well above the absolute human visual threshold. It is not that we humans cannot see in relative darkness, it is rather a case of *what* we cannot see. Colour information is lost in dim light (i.e. scotopic vision), when cones do not operate. Unless the luminance difference between the colours is very large, as in the case of a white object against a black background or vice versa, contrast discrimination is also impaired as light levels drop. In daylight foggy conditions, the light is sufficient for gross differences in colour to be distinguished, but image-edges are blurred, and the luminance of objects is made more homogeneous, rendering contrast sensitivity much less useful than it would otherwise be. As a result of this reduction in contrast sensitivity, and the blurring of edges and texture information, spatial frequency information is also lost in fog. As we will see later, this renders drivers' ability to assess distance and motion quite inaccurate. Because as we age we tend to lose contrast sensitivity, and our eyes adapt less rapidly to changes in light levels (see Kline & Fuchs, 1993), the elderly driver is especially prone to problems in low light and blurred visual conditions. This, as we shall see, has implications for the visual standards drivers should be required to meet, and also for the driving environment we design.

## DEPTH AND DISTANCE

*As drivers we need to be able to judge reliably how far away objects are, for a variety of reasons, e.g. in order to stop before we reach them, to turn before or after reaching them, or to overtake them. This might involve using some precise measurement in metres, or some more vague approximate subjective scale that allows us to know reliably which things are further away than others, or even some still finer classification of distances into those that permit a certain action (e.g. overtaking before a bend is reached) and those that preclude that action. We may not be able to verbalise these estimates, but nevertheless we reveal consistent use of such estimates in the way we behave. In the second part of this section I review how we estimate distance, but first I want to describe the distance-related information that is available in our visual world.*

Different sources of information are used in making judgements of distance. These partly reflect properties of the object and its environment, such as colour, texture, size, height in the visual field, linear perspective, etc. The information used also partly reflects properties of the perceiver's visual system, such as lens accommodation, blur, eye vergence, and stereopsis. These sources of information are more available and more useful in some circumstances than in others.

Under optimal viewing conditions, a focused image is formed within and beyond certain distances from the eye. This range of distances, referred to as the depth of field, stretches from approximately five metres to infinity, for an eye focused on infinity. For objects closer to the observer than five metres, a clear image is maintained by adjustments of the lens. The requirement to "accommodate", and the extent of accommodation required, provide information on object eccentricity closer than this to the observer. Beyond this range, a single stable image is maintained by turning the eyes towards or away from each other ("vergence"). The amount of vergence and resultant strain provide some cues to distance, but obviously only relate to a single object or distance at a time. Lack of clarity of the image, that is image blur, perhaps arising from inadequate accommodation and vergence, can provide yet another source of depth information (Pentland, 1987). This can be misleading when it arises from environmental conditions such as mist or fog, leading the driver to suppose objects are further away than they actually are. Usually, however, the combination of information from two eyes provides a rather more useful source of information about distance, arising from the difference between the images available from each eye.

Suppose a driver is travelling along a three-lane highway, for the sake of argument in the centre lane. He is following a red car, which is also in the centre lane. Assuming that both of his eyes are focused on the red car, he will have the impression of a stable image of the red car ahead. It is actually a combination of two foveated images. Were he to look at the red vehicle only with his right eye, the image of the car ahead would be displaced relative to the combined image, and to the image he would have if he shut his right eye and looked with his left. Now suppose there is a blue car in the outside lane. Assuming he continues to fixate on the red car, the driver will nevertheless know whether the blue car is closer or further away. Suppose the right eye image of the blue car, which is actually displaced to the right of the point of fixation, is closer to the fovea of the right eye than is the left eye image to the fovea of the left eye. This only arises where the blue car is further away than the fixated red car. If the blue car was closer than the red car, this pattern would be reversed. But the disparity actually yields more information than just relative depth. As disparity depends on the difference in depth between the two vehicles, and change in disparity is closely related to the difference in depth divided by squared viewing distance, the size and sign of relative distance are readily available. Thus, disparity might, in the case described here, provide some information as to whether the driver can overtake the vehicle in front.

Information from one's two eyes remains separate, as it travels along distinct pathways in the lateral geniculate nucleus, until it reaches the observer's primary visual cortex. This is the earliest stage of the visual system, which is responsive to binocular information, and there is evidence that cells here allow disparities to be cortically measured (e.g. Poggio & Poggio, 1984). However, important as disparity is, because similar disparity can arise either from a near object that is close but deep, or from a distant object that has minimal depth, disparity alone would be insufficient for us to negotiate our way around the world. Let us assume, for example, a motorist is following another vehicle, intending to overtake it. In order to ascertain whether the road ahead of that vehicle is clear, the motorist pulls towards, perhaps over, the centre line. A relatively close long articulated vehicle would produce as much disparity as a distant family saloon. Fortunately, there are a range of visual and other cues that generally override this ambiguity, but it is clear that we require some form of scaling to recover real depth or distance.

Beyond the distances where vergence and stereopsis provide veridical distance information, colour and texture may be still be available to the viewer and may provide information useful to the viewer. As there is a correlation between size, which can itself related to colour and texture, and disparity, both can inform inferences about distance. For example, where only coarse texture information is available, sensitivity is best for larger disparities, whereas at much higher spatial frequencies sensitivity is optimal for small disparities (see Smallman & MacLeod, 1994). This and other evidence supports the view that spatial filters, and resulting receptive fields, underlie the correlation between size and disparity.

Far beyond the point at which colour and texture information is unavailable, and perhaps up to several kilometres in optimal viewing conditions, presumably at much lower spatial frequencies, factors such as linear perspective, height in the visual field, relative size, shading, and occlusion may all provide cues to relative, if not actual distance. The first of these, linear perspective, arises where one has the impression that a long stretch of straight road is actually narrowing so that the edges meet far ahead. Objects further away are assumed to be higher in the visual field, and the corollary of this is that slope of regard influences distance estimation, i.e. given the same flat scene, passengers in low-bodied sports cars will tend to believe distant objects are further away than will those travelling in the upper deck of a double-decker bus. Shading can provide a sense that the object has some depth and thus gives rise to disparity, and depending on which parts of an object are seen to be shaded can indicate both the slope of regard and relative distance. Occlusion of one object by another also provides information about their relative distance from the observer, and where known objects are being viewed, the apparent gradient of the image viewed, together with the assumption that light comes from above, can also provide information about relative size, and consequently distance.

As many of these sources of depth- and distance-related information are relatively independent of each other, each can provide different information about how far away an object is, and thus they can potentially conflict. Good evidence is emerging that such cues are combined and some come to dominate more in some situations than others (see Bruce, Green, & Georgeson, 1996 and Cutting, 1986, for more detailed discussion). Having sketched briefly what types of distance information can be available to observers, let us now explore how such information might influence drivers' impressions of how far they are away from other objects they can see.

## Distance estimation

Although it does not necessarily follow, it might be expected that with all of the aforementioned information available, people should estimate distance accurately. A variety of studies show that this is not the case, with people being both lawful and consistent in making judgements, but generally underestimating distance, i.e. assuming objects are closer than they actually are. Teghtsoonian and Teghtsoonian (1970) report that for distances ranging from 5 to 480 feet, estimates are a power function of the actual distance, with an exponent of 0.85. The suggestion that estimates are a power function of the actual distance means that, where the exponent is less than 1, far distances will be underestimated much more than near distances. That is, an object 5 feet away is believed to be just 3.93 feet away, one 480 feet away is thought to be some 190 feet distant. Similar findings are reported by Da Silva and Dos Santos (1982) and Da Silva and Da Silva (1983), although a recent meta-analysis of distance estimation studies shows that the exponent of the power function varies considerably, depending on the estimation task used, the context in which judgements are made, and those making the judgements (Weist & Bell, 1985). Exponents of a similar nature have been reported for driving under simulated conditions (Groeger, 2000), but it is important to recognise that estimates made are also subject to a number of other biases.

Interpretations of the information available may also be biased by previous experience, the context in which decisions are made, and how the person assessing the distance communicates their judgement. This is most clearly seen with respect to the effect of familiarity on judgements of distance, where it is widely shown that known objects are thought to be further away than similar, less familiar objects which are as distant. Thus, for example, Predebon (1990) has shown in relatively free-field viewing that a woman, located at 90, 100, 140, or 150 metres, was always judged to be further away than a similar-sized board 120 metres from the observer. Similar results have been reported under laboratory conditions with smaller objects at shorter distances such as playing cards (e.g. Carlson & Tassone, 1971), and more recently in contrasts between a familiar object (red London bus) and a similar-sized untextured object at much larger simulated distances (range 10–450 m; see Groeger, 2000).

Earlier work tended to encourage comparisons between objects of normal size and off-size versions of the same objects. The emphasis on off-size representations has diverted attention away from the potentially significant issue of whether a normal-size object viewed under naturalistic conditions influences perceptions of extents. In a full-cue situation, the familiar size information provided by a normal-size object does not conflict with visual and oculomotor information, and for that reason might not be expected to influence perceived distance. It certainly appears to be the case that the effect does not occur for unfamiliar objects in the vicinity of familiar objects, and is weakened if the familiar and unfamiliar object are viewed in the presence of a common reference target (see Predebon, 1990).

A further difficulty with some previous research is that the methods used to allow observers to communicate their impressions of distance have ranged from raw verbal estimates to the interposing of other objects between the observer and the target, or other forms of bisection tasks. As not all methods yield similar results, and as one might not expect drivers to rely on verbal estimates but on production estimates to guide their behaviour, it is useful to have it confirmed that the effect of familiarity of the observer with the distant object, such that more familiar objects are thought to be further away than unfamiliar objects at the same eccentricity, occurs whether a verbal or production estimation method is used (Groeger, 2000). Similarly, in the same paper it has been shown with both verbal estimation and production methodologies that where repeated distance judgements are made, a small range in the distances encountered will tend to increase the observer's tendency to underestimate distance (Groeger, 2000; Teghtsoonian, 1973).

It has been suggested by some authors (e.g. Stewart, Cudworth, & Lishman, 1993) that one source of increased accident involvement of child pedestrians is the possibility that they are mistaken for a more distant adult. As will be clear from the foregoing discussion of how depth and distance information are combined, under normal viewing conditions such apparent size illusions will be prevented by the relative size between pedestrians and their surrounds. The research reported earlier implies that where visual information is reduced, e.g. in darkness, fog, rain, very bright light, drivers may well assume objects that are readily identified (e.g. road users, be they pedestrians, motorists, or cyclists), to be more distant than they actually are, and thus drive in such a way as to leave themselves with less time to react than they would intend under normal viewing conditions. Similarly, as discussed further shortly, availability of more environmental information enhances drivers' estimates of when they will reach distant objects (Cavallo, Mestre, & Berthelon, 1997). Another difficulty in reduced cue situations is that the amount of disparity required for detection depends in part on the information available from the objects concerned. Dark objects against gloomy backgrounds, or objects that appear blurred (i.e. where only low spatial frequency information is available), will require far greater angular separation for relative depth to be detected. Where high spatial frequency information is available, very small tolerances in angular separation are sufficient for reliable disparity detection (see Smallman & MacLeod, 1994).

Thus, a wide variety of environmental, perceptual, and cognitive factors underlie our impressions of depth, and hence our sense of distance. Most of this information, it should be noted, provides information on relative distance, rather than absolute distance. Our knowledge of what are the relative sizes of different objects in our world, together with our expectations regarding the clarity with which aspects of an object (e.g. texture) will be seen, allow us to determine a useful scale for when judgements are required. However, it is arguable that drivers never really need to recover actual distance, and the ability to manipulate relative depth information is a sufficient basis for performance of the driving task. Most currently available collision-avoidance systems for cars operate on the basis of inferring from the coherence of radar returns that objects are present, and use the strength of these returns to derive an absolute distance to that object. Arguably such information, which might be essential for some drive-by-wire or automatically driven systems, is more or less irrelevant to the behaviour of driver, unless it can be translated into a more relative form.

## MOTION AND SPEED

*As the previous sections show, the way we perceive and estimate distances is far from veridical. Instead it is a combination of different sources of information, and thus, potentially of error. The driver relies on such information, but ability to use such information, as it changes while he or she moves through the world, is still more important. Here, following the approach adopted for distance, I sketch current approaches to detecting and using motion and speed information. Having done so I review a number of studies that explore drivers' ability to estimate and manipulate speed.*

The visual basis of motion, and hence speed, perception depends on making use of the changes in retinal information that occur as the observer moves, or as the things he or she watches change their position over time. The consensual view is now that this is done by through the operation of motion detectors, linking brain areas V1 and MT, which serve to recover speed and direction of heading information from the retinal image (see Newsome et al., 1995). These motion detectors operate in conjunction with each other such that different resolutions of motion information (i.e. filters) are available to the observer. In effect, what is essentially very localised motion information is combined to yield information about the changes in the spatial structure of the scene as a whole, the observer's own motion, and the movements of other objects in that scene. Regan and Beverley (1978), for example, suggest that looming detectors exist which are specifically sensitive to looming and contracting patterns of optic flow, but that these and binocular information about depth are combined to provide the impression of movement in depth. More generally, Sereno (1993) describes a neurally based connectionist model which demonstrates how the visual system computes the global motion of an object from more local views of its contours.

How do we know that something is actually moving? When watching a single point, realising that what we see is changing depends on our detecting a change in some quality such as spatial frequency, which has an upper limit of 40–50 c/deg for human foveal vision. Such changes in spatial frequency, determining the rate at which, say, luminance fluctuation is changing, give us an impression that the point in space we are watching is "flickering"—the fastest flicker rate being about 40–50 Hz in ordinary viewing conditions. However, flicker is only distinguished from genuine motion when direction-selective motion detectors, comprising cells in V1, fire. This sensitivity to true motion, rather than flicker, information about spatial frequency, and temporal frequency of change underlie our impression of things moving. Our impression that this change is relatively slow or relatively fast depends on contrast (or "opponency") between different sources of information more or less simultaneously available to the observer.

There is growing evidence which suggests that the two main pathways in the lateral geniculate nucleus (LGN) could provide the basis of the information contrasts required for many types of spatial judgement. Parvocellular pathways (P) in the LGN appear to carry information about a broad range of spatial frequencies, luminance contrast at higher spatial frequencies, and chromatic contrast (i.e. wavelength) at lower spatial frequencies. The P pathways also transmit information about relatively slow temporal frequencies. Magnocellular pathways (M), on the other hand, carry information regarding high temporal frequencies, but only lower spatial frequency information (for contrasting views see Livingston & Hubel, 1988, and Merigan & Maunsell, 1993). Roth and Hellige (1998) distinguish between two types of spatial judgement: categorical decisions (e.g. above–below, ahead–behind) and co-ordinate spatial decisions (i.e. whether something might fit between two markers). In a very neat set of studies they show that "coordinate spatial processing is more dependent on the transient/magnocellular pathway than is categorical spatial processing" (1998, p. 472). As such, M pathways may be especially important for drivers when making gap judgements. With regard to motion, the P and M pathways together provide a basis for the comparison of two energy measures whose ratio varies with velocity (see Adelson & Bergen, 1985; Smith & Edgar, 1994).

However, as cells in the LGN do not appear to be selective for motion per se, it is actually in V1 and beyond where cells operate as putative non-directional filters, subsequently combined in pairs to form directional filters. The outputs of such directional filters are combined to assess the degree of motion energy for each direction, with comparison allowing the degree of contrast (i.e. opponent energy) to be assessed. Thus the opponency is crucial in yielding an approximate measure of the movement and contrast in the input, but this same opponency and ways in which the difficulties it poses are resolved, also gives rise to illusory motion in certain circumstances.

For example, constant motion affects the sensitivity of filters that are selective for motion in a particular direction, so that when a stationary scene is subsequently looked at, the impression arises that it is actually moving in an opposite direction. Similarly, because it is thought that variability in local motion in a scene is averaged out, or smoothed, across the scene as a whole (Nawrot & Sekuler, 1990), genuine spatial variations in velocity are sometimes eliminated. Where surfaces of objects are smooth, either in actuality or because of the distance from which they are observed, sudden changes velocity will occur only at occluding edges. Minimising velocity variation, or increasing smoothness, can have surprising effects. Thus, as Hildreth (1984) points out, minimising velocity along a contour in an image yields correct velocities for objects with straight edges, but moving curves can lead to illusory motion. For example, a turning red and white pole, characteristic of ice-cream shops and barber's shops in the past, gives rise to a strong impression of vertical motion even though the vertical position of the pole itself remains stationary. The accounts given of recovery of depth information and relative motion have similarities, such as sensitivity to local stimulation and opposition of alternative sources of energy. Depth and motion also interact in ways that are particularly important in the context of driving.

For example, imagine an observer is waiting to cross a multi-lane highway, with cars travelling from left to right in different carriageways. As they do so, the images caused by these vehicles also travel across the retina, albeit in the opposite direction. This gives rise to a phenomenon known as *motion parallax*, where the image of nearer object travels further and faster across retina than does a distant object, such that the ratio of speeds of the two vehicles is inversely proportional to their distance from the observer. Where the nearer of the two cars is halfway between the observer and the other car, the farther car will appear to be travelling at half the speed of the closer one. This may lead the observer to mistakenly believe that it would be possible to cross the carriageway after the first car has passed but before the other has arrived. In fact, motion parallax and stereo cues represent temporal and spatial samplings of the same 3-D information. Although they would usually be combined, it is important to realise that the depth implied by motion and that implied by stereopsis will not always be weighted equally. Thus, for example, as shown by Johnston, Cumming, and Landy (1994) where disparities in the real world are small, i.e. at larger distances, the weight given to stereopsis is reduced. In the case of the Johnston et al. study, at lower speeds (i.e. by reducing the frame rate of the visual sequence presented), Johnston and colleagues showed that observers' use of stereopsis over motion information increased.

This account of space and motion perception has important implications for how we understand judgements of distance made by moving rather than static observers, and when judgements are made in reduced cue situations, where these arise naturally, such as dusk or fog, or due to laboratory conditions through experimental manipulation. Thus, where driving simulators have a lower than ideal frame rate, which will interfere with veridical perception of motion and speed, it may be possible to compensate by increasing the stereopsis information available. In the real world, the effect that fog has, of reducing the apparent speed of one's own and others' vehicles, might be overcome by increasing the depth information available in the scene (e.g. by using high-visibility roadside markers).

## Speed estimation and adjustment

*Detecting that things are genuinely in motion, i.e. that their spatial position is changing rather than simply flickering, is clearly important for drivers, but knowing what speed you or others are travelling at is still some way beyond this. Here I review studies in which drivers have been asked to estimate or adjust speed to match some criterion. First, some of the more established, but methodologically weak, studies are considered, before I concentrate on two studies, one that took place in a driving simulator, the other on a closed track. The key questions addressed are: Can drivers reliably tell what speed they are travelling at without looking at the speedometer? Can drivers reliably change their current speed to achieve some specified criterion? And, how closely related are verbal estimates of speed and drivers' speed adjustments?*

Milosevic (1986) reports an average underestimation of speed by some 5 kph from a study in which drivers, having driven through a curved section of roadway, were stopped and asked what their speed had been (speed range 20–120 kph). Earlier, Triggs and Berenyi (1982) had subjects estimate speeds between 55 and 100 kph, in the presence of 100 dB of white noise, presumably intended to mask vehicular noise, and found an average underestimation of 10 kph. However, despite the apparent similarity of results in these studies, it is not clear that they give an accurate impression of how absolute verbal and production estimates of speed are related to actual speed. The reasons for reaching this conclusion arise partly because of the methodological limitation of previous work, but also because of findings that have emerged from more recent, better controlled, studies.

### Verbal estimates of speed

Evans (1991, p. 128) concludes that "errors in subjectively estimating speed are sufficiently great that drivers should consult speedometers". Studies in which drivers are stopped by concealed police controls just after negotiating a bend, and asked whether or not they looked at their speedometer, reveal that about 90% of drivers had not done so (Milosevic & Milic, 1990). Studies that have closely examined drivers' visual scanning under actual driving conditions have consistently shown that very little visual attention is directed towards the speedometer (Chapman, 1997; personal communication). On this basis it must be that the vast majority of drivers rely most of the time on environmental information which either conveys an inaccurate impression of speed, or is sufficient to allow accurate perception of speed which, for some reason, the subject does not use adequately. Evans' conclusion is based on a number of studies, but two, one by Denton (1966) and one by Evans himself (Evans, 1970) will be considered in some detail here.

Evans (1970) had subjects driven around a test track, and when the experimenter reached and held one of 11 speeds (10 to 60 in multiples of 5), the subject called out their estimate of what the speed was. Precisely what the instructions were is very difficult to ascertain from the paper, as indeed are the visual aspects of the scene through which subjects were driven. Subjects performed under four conditions: normal vision and hearing, hearing attenuation (unclear to what extent), blindfolded, and both blindfolded and with hearing attenuated. Evans found that as long as engine and other sounds were not attenuated, estimates were as accurate as those given when subjects could see and hear normally. In other words the visual input given to drivers had little overall effect on their performance. In contrast, in a more controlled simulator-based study, Groeger, Carsten, Comte, and Jamson (1999) show that speed estimation is better with visual information alone than with sound alone. The discrepancy in these results stems from a number of methodological problems with the Evans study. First, by requiring verbal estimates, in steps of 5 mph, subjects in the Evans study are likely to rely on canonical points such as 5, 10, 15, etc. As such, the task becomes less one of interval-level speed estimation, and more one of making the appropriate ordinal rankings. Overall, Evans found that lower speeds were believed to be much lower than they actually were, but higher speeds (i.e. in the region of 35 mph and beyond), were accurately perceived. The limitations of the methods used, more of which are discussed next, require that these observations are corroborated.

When tested under real driving conditions, in order to be exposed to a range of speeds which they must judge, drivers inevitably encounter mixtures of faster and slower speeds. Recent studies have shown that a driver's assessment of speed on one trial is systematically influenced by the speeds at which he or she has travelled in the previous trial. In a study in which drivers were driven on a test track, Recarte and Nunes (1996) found that previous acceleration or deceleration influenced verbal estimates of speed, albeit in one study but not in another. This result also emerges from a somewhat similar paradigm, where under simulated driving conditions drivers first estimated the speed, and then went on to "double" or "halve" their current speed. The results showed that if the driver had travelled at a lower speed in the preceding trial their verbal estimates of speed were systematically lower than if the previous trial had been at a higher speed, and systematically higher where on the previous trial the driver had accelerated (Groeger et al., 1999). Importantly, and unlike the Recarte and Nunes study, here drivers watched a stable featureless scene for several seconds between trials, thus limiting the impact of previous impressions of motion, and the speed within a trial was constant until the driver chose to accelerate or decelerate.

One implication from these studies is that previous experience biases drivers' estimates of speed. As the earlier studies just reported seriously confound or give no information about how the speeds to be assessed related to the speeds previously assessed, almost any pattern of assessed speeds might have emerged. Because of this, it is difficult to draw any firm conclusions about drivers' perception and estimation of speed solely on the basis of earlier research. The other and more important implication is that, at least with respect to verbal estimates of speed, people rely on relative, but have little or no access to absolute, speed information.

Verbal estimates, even accounting for the biases which operate, are quite inaccurate, although possibly becoming more accurate at higher speeds. Both the actual driving study by Recarte and Nunes (1996) and the simulator study (Groeger et al., 1999) reveal that verbal estimates of absolute speed show substantial underestimation, the size of the underestimate reducing at higher speeds. In actual driving, Recarte and Nunes show that drivers underestimated actual speeds of 60 kph by 15.2 kph and 20.1 kph when they had previously accelerated or decelerated respectively. In contrast, actual speeds of 120 kph were underestimated by 8.4 and 9.3 kph, again for trials where they had previously accelerated or decelerated. This implies that figures for average underestimation, especially where these arise from so broad a range of speeds, are potentially very misleading.

It is interesting that both the Evans study and the better controlled studies suggest that verbal estimates of higher speeds are more accurate. However, the accurately estimated top speed in the Evans study was the lowest and least accurately estimated speed in the Recarte and Nunes study. It may therefore be that this increased accuracy of higher speeds actually reflects an estimation bias rather like a set size effect, such that top speeds attract the highest estimates a person is prepared to produce—thus leading to an illusory impression of enhanced accuracy at higher speeds. If verbal estimates of speed are likely to be biased and inaccurate, as these studies suggest, then it might be because speed is actually underestimated, or because drivers cannot reliably associate changes in the visual information they see with an absolute numerical scale. Because of this, and because in most instances we are more interested in how drivers *change* their speed rather than what speed they believe they are travelling at, it is worth considering studies in which drivers were required to adjust their current speed.

## Adjustments to current speed

Denton (1966), who was among the first to study drivers' ability to change their speed, had eight subjects drive at one of a number of target speeds. Having reached and held the target speed for some unspecified time, subjects were asked to double or halve their speed. Subjects indicated when they were satisfied that they had reached the target speed. Subjects did not see the speedometer during the task, and drove, without attenuation of vehicle noise, along a straight flat one mile long stretch of roadway (i.e. a closed test track). Denton's main findings show that subjects are much less accurate when reducing speed by half than when required to double their speed. For deceleration, the percentage error remains more or less constant across initial speeds, whereas for acceleration, percentage error increases with initial speed. From these findings Denton concluded that when drivers decelerate they tend to underestimate speed, whereas they tend to overestimate speed when required to accelerate. This seems a rather strange conclusion, as it suggests that the same visual information is interpreted differently depending on whether the driver intends to speed up or slow down. As we shall see, there is indeed something in this.

The Recarte and Nunes study and our own simulator-based work show largely similar results when drivers are asked to adjust the current speed by a certain amount. In both cases having previously accelerated or decelerated has a considerable impact on the speeds drivers produced. Where drivers have accelerated on the previous trial, and that speed is higher than they need to produce for a subsequent trial, they adjust their speed by much more than they should. Where they have decelerated on the previous trial, their acceleration on subsequent trials is greater. Once again this emphasises that drivers are prone to make relative rather than absolute adjustments of speed.

Achieving a target level of speed by slowing down or speeding up give quite different results. Figure 1.1, which amalgamates data from our simulator study and the Recarte and Nunes track study, shows good agreement across the two studies despite the very different visual environments, especially with regard to deceleration. Whether people are asked to halve their current speed or reduce it by 20 kph, they invariably fail to reduce their speed sufficiently. When asked to double or add 20 kph to their current speed they tend not to increase speed sufficiently. Despite the fact that these results are consistent with those reported by Denton over 30 years ago, they remain something of a puzzle. Why should accelerating and decelerating be different?

If drivers were underestimating current speed, as the verbal estimates suggest, then one might expect that when increasing their speed by a particular amount, they would mistakenly produce speeds that are less than the target speed. This would happen if drivers were attempting to double their verbal estimate of the current speed, and also if drivers added less to their speed than a fixed amount specified, which they presumably also underestimate. (It is worth noting that this

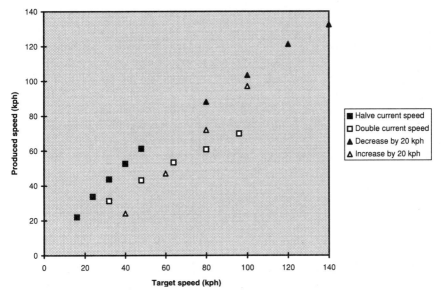

**Figure 1.1.**    Speed assessments under actual and simulated driving conditions.

is inconsistent with the idea that higher speeds are more accurately perceived.[1]) If we assume that drivers believe they are travelling slower than they actually are, when attempting to slow by a particular amount they will seek to decelerate by less than they need to achieve the target speed. This slowing should lead to the target speed being exceeded. This appears to be the pattern or findings in both studies—people slow too little and accelerate too little to achieve the target speed.

This suggests that speed adjustments depend in part on the verbal estimate people may be able to give of their current speed, rather than the visual information drivers have about the speed at which they are actually travelling. This is the suggestion made by Recarte and Nunes, but their study does not allow this to

---

[1] If it was the case that higher speeds are underestimated by less than lower speeds, then attempted acceleration from lower speeds would be less accurate than attempted acceleration from higher speeds. Suppose the current speed was 20 kph, and speed is underestimated by 25%. If the driver attempts to double what he believes to be the current speed, and does so accurately, he will reach an actual speed of 30 kph (i.e. twice the assumed 15 kph), rather than the required 40 kph. If the driver is required to add 20 kph to the current speed, i.e. what he believes to be 15 kph, something more than an actual 20 kph will be added, because speed is underestimated. This will lead the driver to increase his speed to a level closer to the required speed. At higher speeds, which are supposed to be more accurately perceived, speed doubling is more likely to lead to greater accuracy than adding a low speed constant. The latter should lead to greater than required acceleration, leading to speeds above the target level. This suggests that across a range of speeds, the slope of the function relating error to required speed will be steeper in the doubling studies than in the adding a constant studies. The opposite is the case, as can be clearly seen in Figure 1.1. This suggests that higher speeds are not more accurately perceived than lower speeds.

be directly assessed. In their paper they report that the average verbal estimate for each subject and the average speed change are highly negatively correlated, i.e. the higher the error in verbal estimate the lower the error in adjustment. This relationship means that subjects who are more accurate on one task will tend to be accurate on the other task—it does not mean that the same information is being used. Instead it is more appropriate to examine the correlation between verbal estimates and produced speeds for each subject separately, and then average the correlations that result. Doing so, and controlling for the fact that both verbal and production estimates are correlated with the speed drivers initially see, shows that the relationship, while still reliable, accounts for in the region of 10% of the shared variance between the two estimates. This suggests that verbal estimates may mediate speed adjustments, but do so only to a minor extent. Indeed, these analyses show that verbal estimates are most highly correlated with the speed subjects see at the outset, rather than the target speed, whereas speed adjustments are more highly correlated with the target speed than the initial speed.

The relative lack of relationship between subjects' individual verbal estimates and their speed adjustments seriously undermines the notion that both verbal and production estimates of speed rely on largely the same information. Because of this we are still left with the problem of explaining why people are less accurate when slowing to reach some criterion than when accelerating to reach some criterion. The verbal mediation explanation does not offer a satisfactory account of the data. Analysis of the visual information available when slowing and that when accelerating might help to resolve matters, as might studies that focus directly on this issue, rather than include it as an ancillary concern, as was the case in our research.

Both the Recarte and Nunes studies and my own work show clear relationships between the verbal estimates drivers make of speeds they see, and the speeds they produce when requested to change the information they see by some amount. However, both studies also show that verbal estimates and production estimates are also influenced by different variables. Thus, for example, Recarte and Nunes show that similar estimates of speed are given by non-drivers, inexperienced drivers (less than two years experience), and experienced drivers (more than five years experience), and by male and female subjects, but production estimates were more accurate among drivers than non-drivers, and at all levels of driving experience men systematically adjusted their speed more than women. Under simulated driving conditions, having both visual and auditory information available improves verbal estimates of speed, but availability of auditory information actually makes produced speeds less accurate (Groeger et al., 1999). Thus, characteristics of the individuals making the decision and the information available when the decision is being made have different effects on verbal and production estimates of speed, and as such suggest that estimated speed depends in part on the task we require subjects to perform.

In summary, it would seem that where the estimation task is most similar to driving (i.e. where we have drivers adjust their speed) initial speed, whether that speed is to be increased or decreased, driving experience and gender, and the auditory and visual information available will all affect the speed drivers actually produce. A strong implication of this work is that individuals' knowledge of the absolute speed at which they are driving is poor and subject to many sources of bias. Attempts by drivers to reduce their speed to some criterion, after they have been driving at higher speeds for some time, is likely to leave drivers still above the recommended speed. Drivers who have been driving at slower speeds may not increase their speed sufficiently when required to do so. From a practical point of view, this suggests that when (1) leaving motorways and joining lower speed roads, and (2) leaving suburban roads and joining motorways, drivers will have particular problems. Unless they rely on the speedometer, their impression of their current speed is likely to be very misleading.

## TIME-TO-COLLISION

*The distance to a particular object, and the speed at which we are travelling towards it, could be used to calculate how long, at our current speed, it will be before a collision occurs. However, the visual angle of any distant obstacle that we approach at a steady speed will increase gradually, and then very rapidly before we collide. In principle, either an integration of speed and distance information or angular expansion would allow us to decide when to adjust our course or reduce our speed, thus avoiding a collision. This section examines the case for these two strategies.*

The elements of what McLeod and Ross (1983) have called the "cognitive strategy" of time-to-collision elements, i.e. dividing distance to travel by approach speed, have already been discussed in this chapter. Here we concentrate on an alternative strategy: extracting *time-to-collision* information from angular expansion.

### Tau and the processing of target change information

As discussed earlier, when we see objects in the world we have information about their shape, colour, texture, etc. When approaching an object, the edges of the object appear to move further away from each other, and the texture elements on its surface move outwards at a particular velocity from the point we are focusing upon (i.e. the focus of expansion). The ratio of these, i.e. rate of change of angle of the texture elements to rate at which this angle is changing, is what David Lee (1976, 1980) called "tau". The inverse of this specifies the time remaining before the eye and the surface collide, if a constant approach velocity is maintained. This is an example of what Tresilian (1991) terms "global tau", because it relates any texture element to the centre of expansion, in contrast to "local tau", in which time-to-collision is given by the expansion of a coherent subset of the whole optic array—as occurs, for example, with an object approaching a static observer. Here, the angle subtended by the object divided by the rate of change of the angle defines collision time (Lee & Young, 1985). It is useful, for definitional purposes, to distinguish between lamellar flow (i.e. resulting from an object moving across the optic array, maintaining its distance from the observer) and radial flow (i.e. resulting from cases where the object and observer could conceivably collide front to front or front to back) (Hancock & Manser, 1997). This distinction is also supported by empirical findings, as we shall see.

One of the striking features of more popular accounts of this work is the impression it gives of "tau" being used by flies, gannets, pigeons, gerbils, and by implication the whole of the animal kingdom, including ourselves. However, closer reading of the literature reveals a rather different picture. Wang and Frost (1992) have shown from single cell recording studies that pigeons compute tau, and behavioural studies do indeed support the notion that flies (Wagner, 1982) and gannets (Lee & Reddish, 1981) do indeed obtain time-to-contact with surfaces from optic flow, and not distance. However, more recent work in each case (Borst & Bahde, 1988 for flies, and Wann, 1996 for diving gannets), casts considerable doubt on the adequacy of the original studies and on whether such information is actually used in determining time to contact. Sun, Carey, and Goodale (1992) show clearly that while tau may be used by gerbils, it is certainly not the only source of depth information used. In a very clever study, gerbils were taught to approach a food tray placed in front of a television screen which was displaying a circle. During experimental trials, the size of the circle was varied: where the circle expanded the gerbils slowed down earlier on their approach to the food; where the circle contracted, gerbils delayed their deceleration to the food tray. However, the timing of the deceleration, while broadly consistent with the expansion and contraction of the target, was not closely predicted by it, suggesting that other sources of information are used.

As we shall see later, there are many other results, particularly those relevant to driver behaviour, which also serve to qualify considerably the strong interpretation of Gibson's direct perception hypothesis (i.e. the postulation that internal representation and reprocessing of information derived from the external world in unnecessary to account for behaviour). Before considering these, it is worth noting that there is growing physiological evidence that information fundamental to assessing time-to-collision is indeed processed. In a detailed analysis of optic flow patterns, Koenderink and van Doorn (1976) demonstrate that, for textured surfaces at least, the pattern of relative motion within any small region can be fully described as an expansion, rotation, and deformation (see Koenderink, 1986; for discussion of untextured environments). Simpson (1984) has suggested that global motion information is available from the accessory optic system, and that local motion processing may depend in part on the middle temporal area

(MT) of the extrastriate cortex. With regard to flow fields, it has been shown that the lateral supra-sylvian area is sensitive to expanding retinal motion produced by self-motion (Rausecker, von Grunau, & Poulin, 1987), and that areas in the medial superior temporal area of the extrastriate cortex respond to movement of objects towards or away from the observer (Toyama et al., 1985), rotary motion (Tanaka & Saito, 1989), as well as combinations of expansion and rotation information (Duffy & Wurtz, 1991). That is, areas of the brain that specialise in the processing of visual information are indeed sensitive to the types of changes that occur in optical array information, which in principle might specify a driver's time-to-collision with objects on many different trajectories. Empirical evidence that such information is used, or is the only information used, is more equivocal.

## Estimating time-to-collision

Much, if not all, the driving-related research in this area has used a particular paradigm or variants of it. The driver sits and watches as he or she makes a real or simulated radial approach to a distant object and, at some point before the object is reached, it is removed or obscured in some way. The driver's task is to indicate when the object would have been collided with, assuming the previously seen course and speed had been maintained. The difference in actual and estimated collision time, generally expressed as a proportion of the length of time before arrival the object was obscured, is the dependent variable most widely used. If veridically perceived, the distance to the object at the point of disappearance, divided by its approach speed, would veridically specify time-to-collision. Alternatively, given the foregoing discussion, movement towards the object yields global tau, movement of the object towards the observer yields local tau, and both give time-to-collision without access to speed or distance information by dividing the visual angle of the object by the rate of change of that visual angle. An example will help to show how this angular information changes when an object is approached.

Suppose the driver of a Range Rover[2] first notices a flat-backed lorry 300 metres ahead of him on a straight flat road. The back of the truck is 2 metres wide and 4 metres high. When first noticed, the lorry subtends a horizontal visual angle of 0.38° and a vertical visual angle of 0.76°. At 200 metres from the truck, it subtends a vertical angle of a little over 1° (1.15°) and an horizontal angle of 0.57°. One hundred metres closer, the horizontal visual angle of the truck is now 1.15°, the vertical visual angle is 2.29°. As Figure 1.2 shows, this acceleration in the size of the visual angle of the truck continues to increase until it explodes to more than fill the observer's visual field at about 1 centimetre.

---

[2] This is a saloon that has a driving position much higher than normal. I choose it only for ease of explication, because the driver's eye-level would be more or less in line with the focus of expansion.

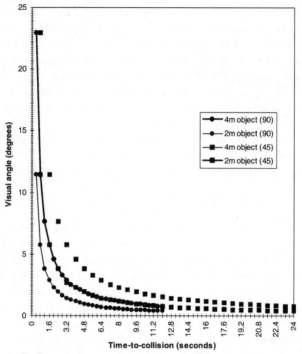

**Figure 1.2.**   Angular of expansion of 2 m and 4 m targets approached at 45 and 90 kph.

Suppose that the Range Rover driver is travelling at 25 m per second, that is, 90 kph. The rate of change in the horizontal visual angle from what it is at 300 m (0.38°) to what it is at 250 m (0.46°), is 0.03° per second. In contrast, between 100 m and 150 m, again at the same speed, the change in visual angle over the two seconds it takes to travel that distance is 0.38°, 0.19° change per second. According to Hoffman and Mortimer (1994), as long as the angular velocity of the lead vehicle was above a threshold of 0.003 radians (0.17°) per second, drivers can make reasonable estimates of time-to-collision.

Notice that over time there are different rates of increase in visual angle (i.e. tau), demonstrating that tau functions are affected by the speed and by the size of the object being tracked. If we consider the two different sized targets (in this case the vertical and horizontal dimensions of the truck), we can see that the line representing a target twice the size approached at half the speed has the same expansion characteristics as a target half the size approached at twice the speed. If time-to-collision were estimated on the basis of angular expansion alone, these two very different situations would be dangerously indistinguishable. Because we have limited the example to a flat road and a driver of a relatively high vehicle (approximately 2 metres eye height), and have assumed that the driver maintains a constant radial heading and speed throughout the approach and the object approached remains stationary, many of the complexities in calculating tau are minimised. It may be that including such complexities, such as contrasting information available from "global" and "local" tau, would reduce the ambiguity of angular expansion in some circumstances.[3] However, it is worth emphasising the complexity of actually using and only using a tau-based strategy in real-world driving. (In Chapter 3 we will explore how tau changes in a real car-following situation, where few of these constraints apply.)

### Factors influencing time-to-collision estimation

As mentioned earlier, the standard experimental paradigm used in time-to-collision research involves an observer watching a distant object, which gradually gets closer. At some point the object disappears from view, and the observer's task is to indicate when they would collide with the object. Viewing conditions ranging from film, video, and computer-generated images to actual driving have all been used, and have generally been shown to yield similar findings (see Cavallo, Mestre, & Berthelon, 1997; Hancock & Manser, 1997 for recent reviews).

A number of findings emerge consistently from the literature. First, time-to-collision is generally, but not invariably, underestimated, usually by 20–40% (see Cavallo et al., 1997; Hancock & Manser, 1997; Tresilian, 1995). The degree of underestimation depends on a variety of factors. The speed at which the approach is made influences estimates, with higher speeds generally leading to greater accuracy. This is true for studies in which the observer moves towards a stationary object (e.g. Cavallo & Laurent, 1988; McLeod & Ross, 1983; Schiff, Oldak, & Shah, 1992; Sidaway, Fairweather, Sekiya, & McNitt-Gray, 1996), and for studies in which the observer remains stationary and the object moves (e.g. Caird & Hancock, 1994; Manser & Hancock, 1996; Schiff & Detwiler, 1979; Schiff & Oldak, 1990). Viewing the target for longer increases the accuracy of time-to-collision estimates (Caird & Hancock, 1994; Groeger & Comte, 1999; McLeod & Ross, 1983; Schiff & Oldak, 1990). Furthermore, Tresilian (1991) has shown that watching an approach over a longer rather than shorter distance also increases accuracy, even when viewing time is taken into account.

Size–distance effects are also apparent in the time-to-collision literature. DeLucia (1991) reports findings which indicate that distant large objects appear to arrive sooner than a nearer smaller object. Similarly, Groeger and Comte (1999) have shown that different sized objects watched for similar amounts of time and approached at similar speeds, and at the same distance from the observer when they disappear, are judged to be arrived at sooner when they are larger. Note that this also undermines the hypothesis purporting to explain the over-involvement of child pedestrians in traffic accidents, i.e. that distance is based

---

[3] How this comparison of global and local tau occurs without reliance on internal representation is unclear.

on familiar size and is consequently overestimated (Stewart et al., 1993). A related effect also suggests that angular size (i.e. distance information) rather than object expansion rate (i.e. local tau) is used, albeit that the importance of this size–distance information is reduced when other environmental information is available. In this study, recently reported by Cavallo et al. (1997), increasing background texture reduces accuracy where observers approach a static object (i.e. leads to greater underestimation). It should be noted that this contrasts with earlier results reported by Schiff and Detwiler (1979), among others, who showed that subjects appear to be able to use the rate of looming of the image of an obstacle to estimate tau (i.e. local tau), and do so with similar levels of accuracy irrespective of whether the approach is judged against a textured or untextured background. Whether this is due to differences between ego and object motion, or to more subtle procedural differences between the studies remains to be seen.

A further influence on time-to-collision estimates concerns the trajectories of approaching objects. Manser and Hancock (1996), for example, show that time-to-collision with vehicles approaching on a radial (i.e. 0°) heading was more accurately and more reliably estimated than where the vehicle approaches on a 40° heading. It is noteworthy that the estimates made with radial motion would actually have led to fewer "collisions" than the 40° trajectory. Earlier, a study by Schiff and Oldak (1990) contrasted "arrival time" estimates of objects moving on radial, transverse (i.e. 90°), and oblique (45°) trajectories. Consistent with the results of Hancock and colleagues, radial events were underestimated, while transverse approaches were more likely to be more accurately estimated, although higher numbers of overestimations were also observed. The arrival time of objects approaching on an oblique trajectory were intermediate on both counts.

Subject variables also influence time-to-collision estimates: older motorists (e.g. Manser & Hancock, 1996; Schiff et al., 1992), inexperienced motorists (Cavallo & Laurent, 1988), and female participants (e.g. Caird & Hancock, 1994; Manser & Hancock, 1996; McLeod & Ross, 1983; Schiff & Oldak, 1990) all tend to estimate less accurately and to have greater variability in estimates.

Together the results reviewed here indicate very substantial inaccuracies in the ways in which people estimate time-to-collision. Whether because of some biologically adaptive "safety margin" (see Schiff & Oldak, 1990), or some characteristic of tau or its variants (see Stewart, Cudworth, & Lishman, 1997; Tresilian, 1997), the usual direction of error in such estimates leads us to expect collisions earlier than they actually occur. The range of variables affecting time-to-collision estimation appears rather larger than would be expected if some adaptive higher-order optical invariant were being directly perceived from the changing optic array (e.g. Gibson, 1979; Lee, 1980). Furthermore, although such approaches have demonstrated very elegantly how, in particular circumstances, tau may provide sufficient information to allow estimation of time-to-collision, the plethora of sources of distortion to such information in a complex environment (e.g. variable speed, angle of heading, obscuration by changes in lighting, contrast, or interpolated objects) seem to me to make it at least as complex and unreliable as lower-order heuristics about distance and speed. This conclusion may be premature as, in the results from the time-to-collision paradigm discussed earlier, it is arguable that requiring subjects to make single explicit estimates of collision is not the best way of assessing how accurately people perform more naturalistic collision-avoidance tasks. Indeed, it may predispose participants to estimate some other parameter, such as the passage of time (see Groeger & Comte, 1999; Tresilian, 1995), rather than the moment of collision. In Chapter 3 we will return to this issue, where tau is said to be used as the basis for adjusting one's position in relation to other motorists.

## SUMMARY

This chapter set out to consider how people derive speed and distance information from their environment, how environmental information may be used to determine whether we are on a collision course with an object, and how long it is likely to be before a collision will occur. This is the primary external information used by drivers, and as such is fundamental for driving. It is clear from the information reviewed that the effectiveness of the visual system's ability to derive this information from the external scene declines with age, and is dramatically affected by neurological damage or disease. This is much more than a matter of static visual acuity, the only aspect of visual processing routinely assessed in drivers. At the very least there is a case for assessing contrast sensitivity, and more dynamic aspects of visual processing. The work reviewed also has implications for the environments we design for drivers to operate in. Inside the vehicle, speedometers are essential for drivers to know their current speed— without such assistance they can neither judge nor accurately adjust their speed to some externally set criterion. Outside the vehicle, inconsistency of signage and road lining, and the use of signs that contain high spatial frequency information, contribute further to drivers' difficulties.

# Motor responses and behavioural repertoires

*This chapter considers the other basic component of the driving task, i.e. the facility with which drivers use a range of car controls. Having placed the task within a general framework of object-oriented actions, the decision and action times associated with accelerating, gear changing, braking, and steering will be described, together with how these are affected by variables such as age, expectancy, and cognitive load. The suggestion that task components performed regularly together form higher-order behavioural repertoires (or schemata), will be discussed, particularly with respect to gear changing.*

Driving is frequently thought of as a perceptual-motor task, in which all that is required is that the driver manipulates car controls so as to track various changes in his or her visual environment. As we shall see, while it is undeniable that driving does involve a considerable amount of motor activity co-ordinated with visual monitoring, one of the consistent theses throughout this book is that driving is quite a lot more than this. The difficulty with advocating this view forcefully is that it may be taken to imply that the perceptual-motor aspects of the task are trivial, and that driving can be studied, or processes involved in driving can be simulated, without reference to motor aspects of the driver's task. This is fundamentally wrong—the way in which we respond, or are allowed to respond, imposes constraints on how we perform the task, and on the task we actually perform. The primary danger with the "driving-as-a-perceptual-motor task" view is that it suggests that driving is a relatively simple task, and in turn that its motor requirements are either trivial or well understood. This chapter has two main purposes, first to review recent developments in our understanding of human movement and how it is produced, and second to consider how this can help us to reconceptualise and regenerate interest in the motor aspects of the driving task.

## OBJECT-ORIENTED ACTIONS

*In recent years understanding of human movement control has been greatly advanced by taking into account the fact that actions are not simply responses or movements that have been initiated, but are attempts to interact with objects in our world. Our movements are constrained by limitations of limbs and the brain structures that control them, but actions are also constrained by the objects with which we interact. In this first section I want to sketch briefly an account of how action is initiated and movement is controlled. I will then use this framework to analyse how an ordinary driving action, such as gear changing, might be controlled.*

### Brain structures in human movement control

As anticipated in the previous chapter, on the basis of extensive neurological studies, it is now believed that humans process aspects of object form in two separate visual systems, one based in the ventral system, which is more concerned with object characteristics such as colour, the other based in the dorsal system, which is primarily concerned with what has been referred to as "dynamic" form (Zeki, 1993). This latter system is "specialized for dealing with all aspects of object-oriented actions, which includes, not only directing action in the proper direction, but also interacting locally with objects" (Jeannerod, 1997, p. 20). Recent research on imagery, particularly motor imagery, makes clear the shared anatomical basis of actual and imagined interactions with objects (see Jeannerod, 1997; Kosslyn, 1994). The fact that actions brought about through imagination or response to an external event share brain structures implies that whether or not a goal originates from the driver's environment, it seems likely that it will substantially involve dorsal visual areas, in order to support spatial representation and control.

Two brain systems are particularly important for the performance of action. These are referred to as the pyramidal system, which comprises the prefrontal cortex, premotor cortex, motor sensory cortex, and sensori-motor cortex, and the extra-pyramidal system, which comprises the cerebellum and basal ganglia (see Jeannerod, 1997). Following the registration of some motivation to act in the limbic system, especially in the cingulate cortex, information passes to the prefrontal cortex, in order to establish intentionality, planning, and general aims for the action. These requirements then pass to the premotor regions, which effect appropriate combinations of motor systems with respect to scale of movements required, alternative ways of achieving the action, etc. The motor programs selected at this stage are then passed to the primary motor cortex, cerebellum, and basal ganglia for effecting the accurate, co-ordinated, smooth implementation of the actions that should achieve the goal established earlier. These systems are approximately organised front to back, with an even more approximate allocation of planning to frontal regions and execution to posterior regions.

The prefrontal cortex is now widely regarded as the primary structure involved in complex supervisory and executive functions (Bradshaw & Mattingley, 1995). Alone or in consort with other brain structures, "It manages behaviours sequentially in space and time and it organises goals, intentionality and anticipatory set, which it maintains or changes as appropriate. It plans, prepares, formulates, and oversees the execution of action sequences; it monitors the strategic aspects of success or failure, the consequences (including social) of actions, it applies both foresight and insight for non-routine activities and provides a sustained and motivating level of drive" (Bradshaw & Mattingley, 1995, p. 253). It is thought that the premotor cortex is involved in the motor aspects of spatial orientation, choice and operation of action plans, preparatory movements, and postural adjustments, and is especially involved where movements are made in response to external cues (see Rizzolatti & Craighero, 1998). The adjacent supplementary motor area is more concerned with running-off movement sequences, moving control from one element of a sequence to the next, and is thus more involved in internally cued movements, and bi-manual co-ordination. The primary motor cortex is highly organised, with areas specific to limbs, arms, hands, fingers, legs, feet, toes, face, eyes, lips, etc., and is largely responsible for the operation and modulation of the activity of individual muscles in these body areas. In the parietal cortex more forward regions encode sensory and muscular input topographically, while more posterior regions of the parietal cortex integrate information from head, eyes, and hand, thus allowing retinotopic to be translated into spatiotopic co-ordinates, establishing the location of events with respect to the body itself, or leading to "visuo-spatial neglect" where such structures are damaged (see Doane, Alderton, Sohn, & Pellegrino, 1996). Recently di Pellegrino and colleagues have reported evidence of the existence of a visual peri-personal space centred on the hand in humans, and have shown how it modulates tactile perception (di Pellegrino et al., 1992).

The cerebellum appears to operate as a general timing mechanism, being involved in discrimination of different durations but especially the temporal control of activities (see Mangels, Ivry, & Shimizu, 1998). It serves as an integration and predictive control system for a vast array of sensory, motor, and limbic systems, improving the performance of all parts of the brain to which it is reciprocally connected. It does so by feed-forward and feed-back which assists behaviour regulation, but non-consciously, in contrast to the parietal cortex. The cerebellum receives most of its input from the sensory and motor cortices, and outputs mostly to the premotor and motor cortex and spinal cord. It is thought to regulate co-ordination of multiple joints, posture, and movement execution, especially visual-based aiming and tracking (i.e. direction, intensity, aim, timing, and smoothness). The basal ganglia (i.e. caudate, putamen, globus pallidus, and

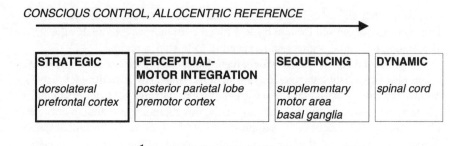

**Figure 2.1.**   Willingham's COBALT model of motor control.

substantia nigra and sub-thalamic nucleus) receives much wider cortical input, outputs via the thalamus to the prefrontal, premotor, and motor cortex, and the supplementary motor area. It is thought to regulate higher cognitive planning and non-motor cognitive behaviours, and the planning and execution of more complex motor strategies (see Hayes, Davidson, Keele, & Rafal, 1998). The basal ganglia operate in the context of well learned semi-automatic behaviours, rather than where novel, unfamiliar, or difficult tasks require conscious and controlled monitoring (but see Jueptner et al., 1997, who report frontal involvement in the former case).[1] Cerebellar damage affects the execution of each response, and dysfunction of the basal ganglia is reflected in dysfluencies between successive responses, characterised by slow, deliberate non-fluent behaviour.

Willingham (1998), in an ambitious and thoughtful review, has recently proposed an alternative conception of how motor performance is regulated, focusing in particular on neuropsychological aspects of motor skill acquisition. Willingham proposes that there are four motor control processes: one that selects environmental goals which are to be met by action, one that selects spatial targets for movement, one that sequences these target movements, and one that transforms them into muscle commands (see Figure 2.1).

The first of Willingham's processes operates on the external world in terms of its spatial organisation (i.e. has an allocentric frame of reference) and is solely under conscious control. The second and third processes can also be brought under conscious control and can be allocentrically based. More usually the second and third processes, i.e. selection of spatial movement targets and sequencing, are non-conscious and operate on a frame of reference that is based around the body of the performer (i.e. egocentrically). This is always the case with regard to

---

[1] This may arise because previously well-used responses are re-mapped as responses to new stimuli in these responses, i.e. the learning is not wholly new.

the final process, which transforms the selected sequences of target movements into action. The first process, which Willingham calls "strategic", involves the dorsolateral prefrontal cortex. Suppose the driver decides to travel faster: The decision to shift to a higher gear or simply accelerate will involve the first process. The second "perceptual-motor integration" process is based in the posterior parietal lobe and premotor cortex. Here the simple actions required for gear changing are selected. The third "sequencing" process is based in the supplementary motor area and basal ganglia: It would serve to compose and tune the simple actions into one that will support changing gear. The fourth "dynamic" process, based in the spinal cord, controls the spatial and temporal patterns of muscle activity, and will carry out the actions determined by the other processes.

While constituted very differently, and dealing much more effectively with issues of the representations on which movement is based, Willingham's COBALT (control-based learning theory) differs more in surface than in substance from the account presented earlier. Later, when I go on to address skill learning (Chapter 5), I will return to Willingham's theory. Even at this level, the work of Jeannerod and Willingham offer important insights into how movement is produced and controlled. These may seem a very long way from being of importance to driving researchers. Next I want to illustrate the importance of this framework by considering more closely one apparently very simple action—changing gear.

## Gear changing as an object-oriented action

Suppose a driver, with both hands on the steering wheel, is moving along at a relatively slow speed, say in second gear. He decides to change gear—because the engine begins to labour through over-acceleration, as he is travelling more slowly than he expects to be given his pressure on the accelerator, or because he "simply" decides to, in the absence of more external action-cues. Having determined, be it consciously or unconsciously, to shift gears, a goal is established. Note that although this internal goal may have arisen because of some external stimulus, or through some internal desire, the actions to be performed are similar, probably identical, irrespective of whether the origins of the intention lie in the individual or in the environment. Because of this, it is more likely that the action-plan that must be fulfilled is an internal goal, rather than some external target state of the world, as it overcomes the difficulty of explaining how non-environmentally determined goals arise and are dispatched. Furthermore, were goals to be wholly environmentally determined, too much of the complexity of the external world would need to be monitored or its redundancy established in each situation. For similar reasons, at this top level of an action-plan, the requirement that must be met should be specified in terms of a goal state, or an "intention", rather than the performance of a particular movement or action. This goal state need not map onto some change in the driver's relationship with the external environment, although it often will. It may also relate to some internal state, such as feeling excited or more in control. Jeannerod (1997) proposes a way in which these high-level action-plans may refer to, or connect with, more "local" aspects of the action requirement.

For the gear change, the action-plan may be further broken down into components, or chunks of motor activity,[2] such as re-locate hand, move left foot, etc. These in turn are composed of smaller components: *release* grip on steering wheel, *remove* hand from steering wheel, *reach* to gear lever, *grasp* lever knob, *pull* towards and across (when foot has depressed clutch), *release* grip, *reach* to steering wheel, *grasp* steering wheel, *remove* foot from clutch (when hand returns to steering wheel). These component activities can be thought of as motor schemas—that is, well-learned, relatively invariant, complexes of activity, which are generic in the sense that they may feature as parts of many different, but related, action plans (i.e. those involving the release, reach, grasp, and removal activities might feature in gear shifts from first gear to second, or fourth to third, but the "pull" activity is specific to second to third). If I am correct about equating conception of the act of moving the hand towards the gear level (and steering wheel) as reaching, and gripping the gear lever and steering wheel as grasping, then we can be more specific about the neural activity we would expect to occur when gear changing takes place.[3]

Let us suppose that the gear change is determined by the fact that clear roadway ahead, which is established partly by processing in the infratemporal lobe, and a consequent motivational change (towards increasing the energetic level) is registered in the limbic system. The information that action is desired signals to the prefrontal cortex that an action-plan for meeting the requirement should be initiated. It establishes the broad parameters for the desired change (e.g. simple acceleration or gear change and acceleration). Information then passes to the premotor cortex to establish which of a number of alternative ways of effecting gear changes will be embarked upon (e.g. hand is already on gear lever versus hand being on steering wheel), and which arrangement of the motor synergies is required to bring this about. At this point the primary motor cortex assumes primary responsibility for realising the now well-formed action-plan —arm to move the hand from the steering wheel to the gear lever, change from second gear to third, and return the hand to the steering wheel. Now right hemisphere activation of the region of the primary motor cortex specialised for the left leg, left foot and left arm, left hand and fingers of the left hand occurs. In the left hemisphere, the region of the primary motor cortex responsible for

---

[2] Verwey (1994) defines a motor chunk as "an integrated representation of one or a series of elementary movements which can be selected and retrieved from long term memory as a whole and which is subsequently loaded in the motor buffer" (p. 41).

[3] Jeannerod (1997) himself actually uses transporting the hand, before an act of grasping, as an example of reaching.

activation of the right arm and hand is presumably already activated in order to continue with steering. The aspects of the prefrontal and cingulate cortex that make them highly relevant to more global aspects of the organisation of an action are particularly what Barone and Joseph (1989) refer to as "context neurons". Further back, what Taira and colleagues (1990) call "motor dominant" neurons encode more elementary aspects of an action, and are not much influenced by what happens before or what happens next, such as making a reach or a grasp. These are located in the inferior parietal lobe and premotor cortex, and are reciprocally connected with the prefrontal areas.

At a further level of specificity, the elements of gear changing that comprise reaching and grasping movements are themselves likely to involve neurologically distinct subsystems (see Jeannerod, 1997; Zeki, 1993). Thus, as the ballistic movement of the arm proceeds without the need for visual control, if similar to other co-ordinated reaching and grasping, we would expect the hand to open maximally (wider than the gear knob), when it has travelled 60–70% of its original distance to the target, well before impact with the target (e.g. Wallace & Weeks, 1988; Wing, Turton, & Fraser, 1986). Interestingly, this maximum grip size depends on biomechanical factors, e.g. maximum grip size is increased where the variability of the reaching movement is larger (e.g. Wing & Fraser, 1983), and on visuo-motor factors, such as the size of the object to be gripped (e.g. Wallace & Weeks, 1988), where an object is in space (e.g. single object moved about, Stelmach, Castiello, & Jeannerod, 1994; objects in peripheral visual field, Sivak & MacKenzie, 1992), and whether it is visible or unseen (e.g. Wing et al., 1986). Together these results indicate that action control moves from an ego-centred to a more object-centred frame of reference, even within a simple gear change. These results suggest that grip formation may differ depending on which gear the car is in, as the gear lever will be in a different place. If this is achieved without actually looking at the gears, then it would suggest further that drivers "remember", presumably implicitly, which gear the car is in, or are "reminded" or deduce this from more general visual or auditory aspects of the driving task. This suggestion is purely speculative, of course, but if supported would demonstrate a remarkable degree of cross-modal priming of spatial memory.

Finally, although gear changing is well practised, because it becomes a bi-manual task when combined with steering, the supplementary motor area will also be involved. Because the task is well practised, it is likely that motor schemata exist to allow performance of aspects of the task—these are implemented, timed, and co-ordinated by the joint action of the cerebellum (probably the cerebro-cerebellar structure) and basal ganglia.

Although gear changing is a rather more complex motor act than has been formally studied hitherto, I believe the account just given is neurologically plausible; except that for clarity that it has been presented as far more serial than it is likely to be. Jeannerod's (1997) view of object-oriented action extends to include not only the initiation and production of motor acts, but also their control and co-ordination. It is useful to rehearse his description here, and apply it to the gear-changing task.

## Motor control and representation

It is envisaged that at each level representations are built on sustained neuronal discharge arising in structures relevant to the various stages of the preparation of motor acts. Taken as a whole, the enhanced activity across the brain is specific to the task to be performed and the way it will be performed. This selective activation persists until the action, or a component of the action, is completed. Thus, at the action-plan level, the sustained activation will last until the driver's goal is achieved, whereas elsewhere the "duration of the sustained activation will be determined by the hierarchical position of that unit in the network . . . upstream in the sequence of events that lead to the final goal will remain activated as along as the full action has not been completed, a more local unit will remain activated for only a short time, sufficient to complete the immediate step of the action encoded by that unit" (Jeannerod, 1997, p. 164). When the "completion" signal is received, by an upper level in the hierarchy, the enhanced activity is no longer sustained, and it returns over time to some resting level, which would not be sufficient for it to influence behaviour. Thus information flowing upwards, a reconceptualisation of re-afferent input, largely comprises completion signals; downward flow is essentially concerned with specifying the requirements that must be met.

This implies that performing a well learned action involves both transitory memories, which specify and control the current task, and more enduring motor schemata, which the driver establishes through experience and which in the healthy driver remain quiescent, but available for use, until the appropriate behavioural specification is received. This echoes the suggestion of Schmidt (1975, 1982), but is considerably extended with several advantages, not least that it does not constrain us to the rather unlikely assumptions Schmidt makes about memory. By envisaging that as many transitory memories are created as there are elements within the motor representation, the memories thus represent a distributed system for controlling the unfolding of the action. Re-afferent input serves to document the current state of the action, and the difference between this input and the transitory memories can serve to summarise its degree of completion. If the desired action has been completed, the re-afferences and the current content of memories will coincide, and the latter will be erased. That is, at the action-plan level, this might be "be in third gear". At a more intermediate level this might be "hand grasping gear lever knob", while at the motor schema level it might specify the efferent pattern that must be met for that to be true. If the action is incomplete, residual activity will persist in the memories, which will reactivate the downward stream, which would then serve to generate corrective actions. Thus, an additional advantage of these distributed transitory motor requirements is that errors detected at a given level can generate appropriate corrections without interfering catastrophically with the operation of the whole system. In doing so, this model also affords an alternative to notions of an internal "comparator", which are especially prevalent in models of risk that characterise behaviour as homeostatic (see Chapters 7 and 8).

Although the description proposed by Jeannerod is hierarchical, he is careful to limit what this means, stressing that it concerns the nature of the information that flows between levels, rather than the timing or direction of information flow. As he points out, cortical connections are numerous and most are reciprocal, which implies that information circulates in both directions and can be simultaneously available in many areas (i.e. activation is simultaneous rather than serial). It is also important to recognise that within Jeannerod's framework, motor representations are dynamic, and are reassembled *de novo* for each action. This is so because the external constraints on each action may differ and the context in which the action takes place changes, so that the same action will rarely be repeated identically in exactly the same way. That is not to say that the behaviour which results will necessarily be highly variable, quite the contrary in fact—the customisation of action to the particular circumstances of a given performance can achieve a high degree of regularity, albeit at the cost of a more complex but more neurologically plausible account than is afforded by previous models of motor behaviour.

## ENDOGENOUS AND EXOGENOUS SIGNALS: REACTIONS TO EXPECTED AND UNEXPECTED EVENTS

*The foregoing account suggests that, once initiated, actions proceed similarly whether they were initiated by some external occurrence or by some volitional change independent of external events. Of course, this cannot be the whole story, because some action initiated in response to an external occurrence is likely to be monitored in relation to the extent to which it meets that externally derived goal, whereas when a goal's genesis is endogenous, while it will still presumably cause some monitoring of external events, this monitoring is likely to serve different purposes (see Willingham, 1998, for further discussion of this issue).*

In this section we continue to explore this theme, examining actions that are performed in response to some external signal (i.e. from exogenous, allocentric signals), and those that arise within an action sequence, and are thus initiated from within the driving task itself, as the individual has learned to perform it (i.e. from endogenous, egocentric signals).

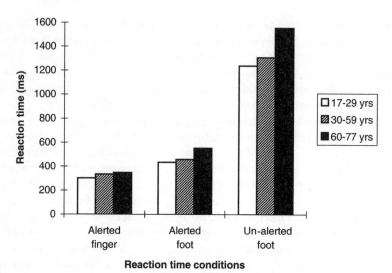

**Figure 2.2.**   Simple reaction time as a function of age, alerting and responding with hands or feet.

## Exogenous signals: Simple reactions with hands and feet

As part of a project exploring psychological aspects of risk, funded by the Department of Environment, Transport and the Regions, David Field, Sean Hammond, and I collected a considerable amount of data on reaction times of various sorts (see Figure 2.2).

Around 400 drivers, aged between 17 and 77 years, were tested on a batch of reaction time trials, during which, forewarned, they moved their finger from a resting position to a target position on the other side of a keyboard. The average time taken for the whole response, from onset of the cue on the computer screen to pressing the response key, ranged from 230 ms to 730 ms, with the average reaction time being 320 ms (standard deviation = 50 ms). This average was substantially affected by age, with drivers under 30 (300 ms) being reliably faster than drivers aged between 30 and 59 (333 ms) and those aged 60 and above (346 ms). We also assessed reaction time to identical stimuli, but this time the response had to be made by the driver moving his or her foot from a resting position to a foot pedal. The average reaction time for the forewarned block of trials here was 450 ms (standard deviation = 120 ms; range: 240–1020 ms), but when responding with feet drivers aged 30 to 59 were significantly slower (459 ms) than drivers under 30 years of age (434 ms), but were significantly faster than those aged 60 years and over (552 ms). Once people had practised these reaction time tasks throughout the computerised testing session, at the beginning or end of some of the other tests drivers had to perform an un-alerted foot reaction time task. Now we found the average reaction time was 1280 ms, with drivers under

30 years of age reacting to this surprise task faster (1239 ms) than those aged between 30 and 60 (1307 ms). Both of these groups were significantly faster than those aged over 60 (1552 ms). These results, collected under strict laboratory conditions and from a large representative sample, indicate that the speed with which people react will depend on the limb used, their age, and whether or not they are expecting to have to react. As such, they neatly parallel data available from studies closer to the driving task.

Olson and Sivak (1986) have shown that accelerator to brake movement times are relatively unaffected by age, the movement taking about 200 ms. The movement time is similar whether it is initiated by a typical (brake light) or an atypical (piece of yellow foam on the carriageway) stimulus. Where drivers were not alerted to the fact that a reaction time would soon be required, the accelerator to brake movement time was substantially longer, about 440 ms (i.e. 15 m when travelling at 110 kph). Olson and Sivak (1986) also measured the time drivers took to detect objects (a piece of foam rubber on the carriageway or a red brake light on the hood of the driver's own vehicle). The time that elapsed from the first appearance of the signal to the first measurable reduction of pressure on the accelerator depended on object familiarity—detection of brake lights was about 430 ms, whereas detection of the foam object was about 700 ms. Detection also took longer for older than for younger subjects, even though both groups were comparable when reacting to a stimulus they knew was present. In other words, although it physically takes about 100 ms to move your foot between the accelerator and the brake, when moving as quickly as possible and initiating the movement whenever you choose (Kroemer, 1971), making the same movement in response to some signal takes longer, even when you are expecting it. Detecting a stimulus you are not expecting takes much longer, especially if it is unfamiliar in that particular context, and movement time is also affected by stimulus familiarity. Finally, detection and movement time to unexpected signals is affected by age, just as we showed in the laboratory work described earlier. Overall the total response time for un-alerted foot reactions, at approximately 1200–1300 ms, is very similar in both studies. Translating this back into a situation where a driver is travelling on a motorway at around 120 kph, the driver will travel over 40 metres between detecting that there is some debris on the carriageway ahead, and putting his or her foot on the brake. Applying the appropriate force, the braking reaction time of the vehicle will further determine whether the driver can successfully stop before hitting the obstacle. We return to the controlling of braking and obstacle avoidance in the next chapter.

Another way in which the driver is required to react quickly, using hands this time, is where a sudden alteration of course is required, such as when a sudden gust of wind blows or threatens to blow the vehicle off course. This is precisely the situation explored by studies reported by Wierwille, Casali, and Repa (1983). These assessed, under simulated conditions, how long steering-wheel reactions to the onset of a sudden gust of wind take. Despite procedural differences between the two studies, the results obtained are very similar, being 440 ms and 500 ms respectively. It is also clear from the Wierwille et al. (1983) studies that such reaction times are likely to be longer where the centre point of the wind pressure is closer to the centre of gravity of the vehicle. Thus, even when buffeted by an expected gust of wind, sensory factors that should affect the time taken to detect a stimulus, such as gust strength and point of greatest pressure, alter the time taken to correct steering.

In both studies, the reaction times measured were effectively alerted reaction times, and the data presented tell us about when the reaction occurs rather than whether or not the steering correction would have been sufficient to restore the vehicle to its course. Although it might be argued that the close visual coupling between steering and vision (e.g. Land & Lee, 1994; see Chapter 3), and con-sequent clear expectations about heading may render any differences between alerted and un-alerted detection times negligible, it should also be noted that Summala (1981) reports the results of a field experiment which show that the typical driver/vehicle steering response latency, to a light stimulus on a dark road in a fully unexpected situation, was approximately 2.5 seconds. As the hands are already on the steering wheel, movement time is also minimised, and the applica-tion of directional force should be sufficient to make the required adjustment. Repeating these studies, attempting to manipulate the extent to which drivers may expect where buffeting may occur, perhaps also exploring the extent to which different steering tolerances influence the time taken to react and the extent of any reaction, would help to clarify whether the reactions made are merely reflexive or are informed by some model of the vehicle's steering characteristics.

## Endogenous signals: Components within action sequences

Gear changing, although likely to be initiated for some external reason, comprises components with well-learned inter-relationships. Thus, a gear change will always be preceded by a movement of the left foot to the clutch, and the disengaging of the engine, brought about by depressing the clutch. The left hand will always locate and grip the gear lever, probably before this second phase occurs, and at some point after the engine is disengaged, the hand will move the gear lever, through neutral, to the target gear. Release actions will then follow, with either the gradual reduction of pressure on the clutch, thus re-engaging the engine, or the presumably faster release of grip on the gear lever. Although doubtless we have all noticed and been embarrassed by some error that may occur in gear changing, for the most part the gear changes we perform faultlessly on so many occasions go unnoticed.

An excellent study reported by Duncan, Williams, and Brown (1991) sheds some light on how these components are related to each other (see Figure 2.3). In the study drivers repeatedly drove around corners on a quiet suburban road.

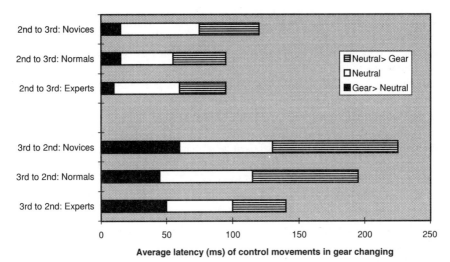

**Figure 2.3.**    Temporal characteristics of gear changes as a function of driving experience.

Doing so necessitated a gear change from third to second, and a gear change from second to third.[4] This study shows that to shift gear from third to second (i.e. to depress the clutch, shift the gear lever from third gear, through neutral, to second gear, and release the clutch) took close to 1950 ms, which was more than twice the average time taken to change from second gear to third (950 ms). When shifting down, clutch depression to neutral occupied less time (approximately 450 ms) than did neutral to target gear (approximately 700 ms), while target gear to clutch release was considerably shorter (about 800 ms). When shifting gear from second to third, where the total time taken was about 950 ms, the initial phase (i.e. clutch depression to neutral) took about 150 ms, but remaining components occupied similar amounts of the remaining time (i.e. about 400 ms each).

It may be that pushing up (shift-up) and pulling down and across (shift-down) motions may not be equally easy or fast to perform. This might account for some of the difference between the times spent in neutral in both cases (i.e. 400 ms versus 700 ms). However, it is rather more difficult to account for the time taken over the first phase of the gear change, i.e. depressing the clutch and moving the gear lever to neutral (i.e. 450 ms versus 150 ms), and especially differences in the final phase of the gear shift, from the point at which the gear lever leaves neutral to releasing the clutch (i.e. 800 ms versus 400 ms). One possibility is that motor schemata are formed which can be assembled *de novo* for each gear change. In such a situation it would be reasonable to assume that

---

[4] I am grateful to John Duncan for providing me with copies of the raw data which have greatly helped this re-analysis.

similar components, e.g. target gear reached, release clutch, might take similar amounts of time, irrespective of what the gear was changed to or from. The data reported by Duncan and colleagues demonstrate that this is not so. An alternative possibility is that a schema develops which combines the component activities within a particular gear change, such that the component activities initially modify until each is performed in a regular fashion within that gear change, but is performed differently when part of a different gear change. Thus, individual gear changes (e.g. second to third) would take similar amounts of time, as would their component activities, but different gear changes (e.g. third to second) would also last for a consistent, but different, length of time, the time taken to change gear presumably being a function of practice.

At first sight, other data reported by Duncan et al. (1991), support this view. They also contrast the performance of these "normal" drivers with two other groups who were age-matched: "novices" (who had been driving for less than a year) and "experts" (who undergone an advanced driving course, but had held their driving licences for as long as the normal drivers). As with normal drivers, "shifting-down" took longer than "shifting-up" both for the experts (950 ms versus 1400 ms) and for novices (1200 ms versus 2250 ms). Thus, experts and normal drivers take the same amount of time to change from second gear to third gear, but novices take longer, while the three groups take different amounts of time to change from third to second gear. This is consistent with the view that shifting-down is the more complex task. Driving ability is reflected in the way in which the task is performed, as well the time taken to perform it. Where the task or its components are more difficult, the novice differs from the normal driver. For the expert, however, the time spent in neutral and the time taken to release the clutch is equivalent in both tasks, and the difference in the time taken to perform the two tasks is almost entirely due to the initial component, i.e. the lag between depressing the clutch and entering neutral. This encourages the view that individual schemata are formed for each type of gear change, and become more internally consistent as a function of practice. Later, in Chapter 4 where I discuss automaticity and driving, we will return to these data, and show that even these highly practised sequences of action are not internally temporally consistent, which strongly argues against the suggestion that even aspects of driving such as gear changing are not automatic.

## SUMMARY

By looking very closely at the actions involved in very simple components of the driving task, I have tried to show the complexity of the task with which we are dealing. This complexity manifests itself in terms of (1) the number of brain areas that must be co-ordinated to allow even the simplest of driving tasks to be performed, and (2) the difficulty of specifying what type of information is processed in order to activate these brain areas. There are clear indications from the modern motor control literature that goal determination, selection of appropriate actions, assembly or sequencing of these actions, and implementation of these assemblages, all rely on activity in quite distinct regions of the brain. Because very little research is available on how well brain-injured people might drive, I feel it is more defensible to be pessimistic as to the impact on driving skills, even those that have been very well learned, of damage to the premotor cortex, primary motor cortex, supplementary motor areas, and cerebellar regions. It is clear from the research that has been done that factors such as age will cause even simple reactions to slow very substantially and become erratic. These problems of age and neuropsychological dysfunction will be still more evident where the driver is required to deal with something unexpected.

# CHAPTER THREE

# Combining perceptual-motor skills

*This chapter examines how the visual processing and motor actions described in previous chapters might be combined to allow us to perform the tasks we routinely consider comprise driving—headway control, braking, and the inter-relationship between steering control and gaze direction. These will be used to introduce the distinction between closed- and open-loop control, which affords a reasonable description of how lower elements of the driving task might be combined in order to control performance. However, as will be made clear, this view is internally inconsistent and neglects aspects of the driving task that must form part of any adequate description of how tasks as complex as driving are performed. Together, these inadequacies severely limit the theoretical gains to be made from considering higher- and lower-order aspects of the driving task separately. These higher-order aspects of the task are considered in the subsequent chapters.*

Most of the time when driving we are not simply looking ahead or around, or accelerating or braking, or steering right or left, but performing each of these actions concurrently, as part of some larger task—such as, for example, when following another vehicle or turning a corner. Indeed it is one of the difficulties in understanding driving that so many relatively complex human activities must be performed together in order to achieve what seem like the most trivial of driving tasks. Here I want to consider what might be involved in these tasks, partly in order to reveal some of their inherent complexity, and partly in order to open another issue—how the interplay of complex activities that comprise driving might be controlled.

## BRAKING TO AVOID COLLISION

In discussing earlier how people might make decisions about when they might reach a distant object towards which they were travelling, the issue of how they might use such information to brake was deliberately finessed. Assuming that the driver's intention is to stop close to but without colliding with a target object, a wide variety of factors influence performance, including: current speed, the point at which the driver decides to commence braking, the severity of braking of which the vehicle is capable, and the severity of braking and extent of braking modulation the driver will tolerate, the friction that can be achieved between road surface and tyres, and the margin of error with respect to the ultimate proximity to the target, etc. Lee (1976) provided an elegantly economical resolution of how these influences might interact by proposing that the detection and regulation of two aspects of how targets expand as we approach them is sufficient to control braking. It is worth taking a closer look at this framework, as it is also implicated in ideas about how drivers control the way they follow other vehicles.

Let us suppose that a driver is approaching, at say 30 kph (8.3 m/s), a set of traffic lights at which a vehicle (1.4 m wide) is already stationary. At 100 metres, the stationary vehicle will subtend a visual angle of 0.80°, one second later (at 30 km/h), the visual angle of the vehicle will be 0.88°, and one second from the vehicle (at 30 km/h) it will subtend a visual angle of 9.64°. In Chapter 1, Figure 1.2 shows how the change in visual angle varies with different constant speeds, to objects of different sizes. Obviously, as speed increases, the rate of change of this visual angle will also increase. According to Lee (1976), time-to-collision, as specified by optical variable tau (the rate of change of the visual angle subtended by the vehicle[1]), serves to initiate braking, while tau-dot (the rate of change of tau) is the basis on which the amount of braking is controlled.

Lee's analysis shows that if people were to apply a constant force to the brakes, the rate of change of the visual angle of the approached vehicle would fluctuate during the approach. Alternatively, by changing the force applied during braking, the rate of change of the visual angle of the approached vehicle can be held constant. Where tau-dot is held at some value between 0 and −0.5, the driver will stop close to, but not hit the vehicle ahead. Constant values of tau-dot between −0.5 and −1.0 will result in a collision, whereas between 0 and +1 will result in a stopping position some way short of the vehicle. Data from the work of Spurr (1969), re-analysed by Lee (1976), show that drivers brake hard initially and ease off brake pressure subsequently, as Lee's theory, based on the driver's attempt to maintain tau-dot, rather than braking pressure at a constant, would predict. However, the paucity of empirical data on which it is based, and

---

[1] Note that time-to-collision, as determined by dividing distance remaining by speed, and tau, derived from the rate of change of visual angle, are negatively correlated.

the fact that some but not all of Spurr's subjects actually show the desired pattern, raises the question of whether or not tau-dot is actually the critical variable used by drivers to control their braking. Data from studies by van der Horst (1990) and van Winsum (1996) help to address this issue more satisfactorily.

Van der Horst (1990) reports a study carried out on an airfield, in which a driver drove towards a styrofoam plate, representing the shape of the rear end of a car, at one of three constant speeds (30, 50, and 70 kph), and then braked hard, or braked normally, at the latest moment where stopping in front of the object would be possible. Although the object approached in each case was identical, the point at which drivers began to brake, in the normal braking condition, was reliably influenced by approach speed, being 2.2 s, 2.5 s, and 2.7 s at 30, 50, and 70 kph respectively. At these points, the angle subtended by the target would have been 4.37°, 2.31°, and 1.53°. Over the preceding second, the rates of change of the stationary vehicle's visual angle for each approach speed would have been 1.45, 1.39, 1.37 respectively, that is similar to but certainly neither identical to nor independent of speed. In the hard braking condition, approach speed similarly influenced the point at which braking began, although drivers delayed responding until closer to the target and applied more force. Repeating the analyses for visual angle and angular velocity for the hard braking condition reveals a broadly similar pattern. Van der Horst also reports in each case the minimum time-to-collision (TTC) reached during braking with, once again, reliable differences between approach speeds (normal braking: 1.4 s, 1.2 s, and 1.0 s; hard braking: 1.00 s, 1.05 s, 1.10 s). These figures, recalculated from those reported by van der Horst, appear to show that neither the time-to-collision to the target, the angle subtended by the target, nor the angular velocity of the target determine the point at which braking is initiated. There is some evidence that visual angle influenced the point at which the minimum time-to-collision to the target was reached, but only where drivers were attempting to brake as hard as possible.

The possibility that time-to-collision may be used to control braking, albeit not in the way envisaged by Lee, also gains some support from van Winsum's (1996) simulator-based study of drivers' reactions to the braking of a lead vehicle. Figure 3.1, adapted from van Winsum's work, shows how 500–600 ms after a lead vehicle's brake lights go on, the driver begins to reduce pressure on the accelerator, a process completed some 400 ms later. About a tenth of a second later the driver's foot moves from the accelerator to the brake (note here the temporal similarity to the data reported by Kroemer, 1971, see Chapter 2). Braking pressure is not evenly applied; as Figure 3.1 shows, there is a discontinuity after 200–300 ms, where pressure is maintained, before it is steadily increased, reaching its maximum force about a second after the brakes are first applied, after which braking pressure is gradually reduced. The minimum TTC is more or less coincident with the maximum brake pressure, but increases much more rapidly than the reduction in brake pressure. Unfortunately, van

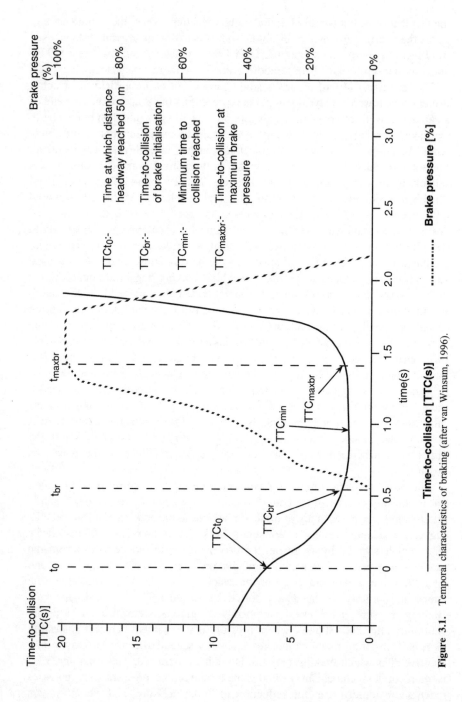

**Figure 3.1.** Temporal characteristics of braking (after van Winsum, 1996).

Winsum does not provide sufficient information to allow us to calculate the angular velocity of the lead vehicle at any of these points, and thus it is unclear what visual information drivers were using to control their behaviour, but the pattern of brake application does not immediately appear consistent with Lee's model.

The foregoing paragraphs review studies that bring Lee's account of braking behaviour into question. However, in fairness to the theory, Lee's account has not been formally tested under driving-like conditions. In the main these are observational studies, which do not dissociate tau-based or tau-dot-based information from other information available in the testing situation. Under controlled laboratory conditions, where computer-generated chequerboard targets approached observers, Yilmaz and Warren (1995) showed that direction and magnitude of brake adjustments were regulated using tau information, and not ground surface or object size. This study is very convincing and shows, just as Lee suggests, that mean tau-dot during braking was −0.51, and critical values for brake adjustment were −0.44 and −0.52 respectively. However, the task used is quite some way from actual driving, and somewhat lacking in the ecogoical validity so prized by many neo-Gibsonian theorists, and it remains to be seen whether the tau-dot hypothesis with regard to braking control is sustained in the face of more exacting testing circumstances. Further studies, based in driving simulators or on closed tracks with good control over the visual information available to drivers, are needed before any firm conclusion can be reached.

## FOLLOWING ANOTHER VEHICLE

While highway codes suggest or require that drivers keep a safe distance from other vehicles they may be following, doing so is a non-trivial task in perceptual terms. Drivers can reliably assess the point at which they will collide with stationary objects that are within two seconds, the temporal separation suggested by the UK Highway Code, but there is ample evidence that prospective or retrospective estimates of two seconds are subject to considerable distortion. An alternative to this would be assessing the speed of one's own vehicle, that of the vehicle ahead, and the distance between both, manipulating these to determine a stable following position. The adequacy of accounts of how drivers maintain and modify their following behaviour is considered further here.

Although a number of studies demonstrate that drivers do not preserve a two-second margin, and that the aggregate margins drivers observe can be lengthened or shortened given additional information, for example from an in-car device (Fairclough, May, & Carter, 1997; Groeger, Chapman, & Stove, 1994) or by marking the roadway in various ways, there are scant data that consider the longitudinal control of vehicles and its stability over time in sufficient detail to allow formal tests of the psychological assumptions made in various models of following behaviour.

Engineering models of car following rely on the driver's ability to operate within a particular time period, on the distances, speeds, and accelerations as they see them, to regulate following behaviour. Models such as the GHR, Linear, or Helly models, which originated in the 1950s and 1960s, make such assumptions (see recent review by Brackstone & McDonald, 2000). However, despite the impressive mathematical formulations that characterise such models, they are implausible from a psychological point of view for a variety of reasons. First, a number of studies have shown that observers are insensitive to acceleration when it is perpendicular to the line of sight, being unable to distinguish reliably between accelerated and unaccelerated motion unless it is viewed for several seconds (e.g. Gottsdanker, 1956; Gottsdanker, Frick, & Lockherd, 1961; Runeson, 1975). As pointed out earlier, most of the traditional models of following assume that drivers are sensitive to changes in acceleration and alter their behaviour according their perception. Second, as shown in Chapter 2, both verbal estimates and production estimates of distance and speed are prone to very substantial error and bias, and thus it is unlikely that following behaviour based on subjective speed or distance would be either stable or reliable.

A further model of following behaviour is the "action point" model (see Brackstone & McDonald, 2000), in which following is determined by the apparent size of the vehicle ahead, until this apparent size exceeds a critical value. At this "action point" following is determined by inter-vehicular spacing. One such theory, albeit without the dependence on spacing per se, is that proposed by Lee and Lishman (1977), who extended Lee's theory of controlled braking. In doing so, they show the rate of change of visual angle of the vehicle ahead (tau) and the acceleration or deceleration of this quantity (i.e. tau-dot), might be used in order to allow the driver to keep up with the vehicle ahead, while maintaining a safe distance.

The Lee and Lishman account suggests that backward force, either through deceleration or braking, will occur when the rate of change of the visual angle subtended by the vehicle ahead is greater than 0 and when the rate of change of this information is less than −0.5. Speed will be allowed to increase if tau is greater than 0 and tau-dot is greater than −0.5. Thus, for example, at an initial distance of 200 metres from a vehicle 1.4 metres wide (i.e. subtending an angle of 0.007 radians), the driver would have to be travelling almost 216 kph faster than the lead vehicle for the change in its visual angle to be perceptible (i.e. 0.003 radians $s^{-1}$, see Hoffman, 1994). That is, when viewed from 200 metres, for most intents and purposes, the lead vehicle would need to be stationary for us to detect closure with it. At an initial longitudinal separation of 100 m the threshold for detecting closure of the visual angle would require a speed differential of 64 kph, which is perhaps more plausible. Assuming the speeds of the two vehicles remain constant, tau (rate of change of angular velocity per second) will first become less than −0.5 about 2.3 seconds later, when the time-to-

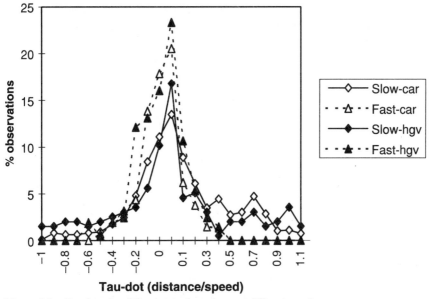

**Figure 3.2.**    Tau-dot when following trucks and cars at different speeds.

collision is about 2.3 seconds. At which point the driver will decelerate, according to the Lee and Lishman theory, so that tau is maintained at a "safe level".[2]

Groeger and Brady (in press) analysed data collected from an instrumented car study of driving under real road conditions. The instrumentation included both a radar system, capable of determining the distance to vehicles ahead, and a video, which could be used to subsequently determine the precise make (and hence size) of the vehicle followed. Those cases in which a vehicle was detected in the distance and could subsequently be identified, were extracted from the data set, together with information about the driver's current speed, pressure on the accelerator and brake, and location. Together these should allow us to determine the point at which drivers reach a stable state when following behind another vehicle, and specifically whether tau, tau-dot, or some other parameter is the basis on which this stable state is maintained and regulated.

As Figure 3.2 shows, the percentage of time spent with tau-dot values higher than the theoretical change point of −0.5 suggested by Lee and Lishman (1977) is not at all what we might expect from the tau theory of car following. In addition, as the Groeger and Brady study shows, the consistency with which different values of tau are held varies as a function of speed and the size of the

---

[2] Tresilian (1991) points out that this level is based on the time-to-collision at the driver's eye, rather that at the front of his or her vehicle, making collision much more likely, and requiring a correction for bonnet size which is problematic for the theory.

vehicle being followed. Neither of these effects would be predicted by the theory. Equally damaging for the theory is that the level and amount of change in tau before and after acceleration actions are very similar. This suggests, contrary to the tau theory, that the change in tau over time is not the basis on which drivers decide to accelerate or decelerate—leaving us unfortunately no closer to understanding how drivers regulate their following behaviour.

## STEERING CONTROL AND GAZE

After a hiatus lasting something in the region of 20 years, We have recently seen a renewed interest in the role eye movements may play in driving. However, although the theoretical and methodological sophistication of eye-movement research in other domains, especially reading, seems likely to exert a positive influence on eye-movement studies in driving research (see Underwood, 1998), we are some way short of having reliable and generalisable answers to the key questions of how steering is controlled, and whether and how drivers' scanning strategies play a role in guiding this behaviour.

One of the widely accepted accounts of drivers' visual strategies is that as we become more experienced we gradually look further away from the front of the vehicle we are driving. This view is based on the pioneering research of Mourant and Rockwell (1970), and it has an attractive coherence with work which clearly shows that as the skills of professional typists improve, their tendency to look further ahead in the passage than the words they are currently typing also increases. This resonates with the idea that as skill increases, look-ahead or anticipatory skills, and hence tactical appreciation of task performance, improve. Unfortunately, while the synergy between these accounts is pleasing, it is much less clear that it is actually supported by the data. In the Mourant and Rockwell study, four experienced drivers and six people who had only ever driven for 15 minutes prior to the study, took part. The results show that novice drivers tended to have a narrower lateral scanning pattern for the road ahead than experienced drivers, although merely repeating the same route on a couple more occasions reduced this novice–experienced difference. Novice drivers did indeed display reduced longitudinal scanning, but only in one of the nine scenarios studied. As we will see, these rather sparse data, with all their inherent artefacts, still play something of a talismanic role.

Models of steering behaviour had no more auspicious beginnings—the widespread assumption being that the "driver acts as an error-correcting mechanism with continuous attention allocated to the steering task" (Godthelp, 1986, p. 211). The suggestion from almost all well-elaborated models of steering behaviour (e.g. Donges, 1978; see also Reid, 1983), is that two processes combine to allow us to accurately guide our vehicles through curves. The first is a long-range process, which relies on preview and prediction of the curvature of upcoming sections of the road, perhaps allowing the establishment or activation of some pattern of likely future gross steering movement requirements. The second is a short-range process, which operates in a corrective fashion, allowing the driver to modify slightly the current heading as a function of proximity to the road edge. The assumption made in many of the models proposed prior to the mid-1980s, was that both the short- and long-range processes operated in parallel.

Since then, elegant research by Godthelp (1986) has shown that while there is good evidence for there being two processes of the form just described, they operate serially rather than in parallel, anticipatory movements being made in the time available before a short-range correction is possible (what he calls "time-to-line-crossing"). Godthelp has shown further that reducing the time available for looking at the road ahead, by temporarily shutting off visual input for 500 ms, has a small but not catastrophic effect on the longer-range process. Godthelp shows that drivers are well able to take account of curvature and speed effects when generating the anticipatory steering action on entering a curve, the errors they make being strongly related to the inaccuracies of the anticipatory steering action rather than short-range corrective actions. The fact that these inaccuracies increase with the road curvature, whether people are allowed to continue or interrupted in viewing the road ahead, leads him to suggest that "experienced drivers have a rather good internal representation of the vehicle characteristics. By consequence, it may be expected that drivers use this knowledge during curve negotiation to rely on internal feedback processes, thus allowing a temporary loss of external, visual feedback" (Godthelp, 1986, p. 219).

Recently, Land and colleagues have reported findings that patterns of gaze direction map neatly onto just such a long-range–short-range distinction in steering models. Land and Lee (1994) show a remarkable regularity of gaze pattern among three drivers, driving along a curved road. Summarising their results, they report that the distributions of fixations "are centred within a degree of the tangent point itself on both left and right hand bends. As with straight driving, they are horizontally elongated. With roughly exponential decline from the central peak . . . Gaze is directed to the tangent point, with a rather obvious saccade 1–2 s before the car enters each bend, and remains there with relatively few excursions for ~3 s into the bend. Half a second after the car has entered the bend, the gaze of all three drivers is directed to the tangent point for about 80% of the time" (1994, p. 743). This might seem to imply a clear requirement for drivers to fixate the tangent to the upcoming curve in order to steer competently.

This conclusion is broadly confirmed by another small-scale-study by Land and Horwood (1995), of how two experienced drivers obtained visual information from two sections of their view of the road ahead, while maintaining their lane position as they drove around a series of curves. They report that road sections 0.75–1.00 seconds ahead of the driver are used to predict the road's future curvature. These sections are said to contain the tangent point, and serve as input to a feed-forward anticipatory mechanism which allows the driver to match the curvature of the road ahead. The drivers also made use of nearer sections of the road ahead, about 0.5 seconds ahead of the driver. These, it is suggested, are used by a more reactive, feedback-based system, to "fine tune" the driver's position in lane.

These findings echo suggestions in much earlier studies, such as those where drivers' fixation patterns on straight roads are described as dwelling on a point near to the focus of expansion, presumably the point from which patterns of optic flow emanate, with occasional fixations on items of road furniture and road edge markers (e.g. Helander & Soderberg, 1972; Mourant & Rockwell, 1970; Shinar, McDowell, & Rockwell, 1977). This resonance between earlier and more recent studies serves to obscure, rather than make, what seem to me to be the crucial points about gaze direction and its role in vehicle control. It is not easy to reconstruct from earlier studies precisely what the visual conditions were when data were collected. However, Land's studies are rather better specified—especially if this is extended with some local knowledge. In particular, the Land and Lee study was carried out on a section of Edinburgh roadway known as Arthur's Seat, which is a heavily banked, undulating, twisting narrow track. Although it would be very demanding to drive this route quickly, there is relatively little of what one might consider the normal visual demands on the urban driver (e.g. oncoming traffic, roadside pedestrians on the pavement, shop fronts, road signs and furniture). Similarly, the rudimentary black-and-white display that presumably sought to simulate key aspects of the driver's perceptual motor task in the Land and Horwood (1995) study, offered little by way of the visual richness drivers routinely encounter. Thus, with little else to distract him, the driver in the Land studies does indeed fixate the tangent to the curve, one of the few sources of visual information available, and which might be used as a basis for controlling behaviour.

These studies nevertheless raise some very important issues. First, there probably are certain relatively simple sources of visual information that can be used to guide vehicle control. These include the tangent to the curve and the focus of expansion. Use of the tangent point is reasonable in the light of the fact that the tangent point direction relative to the car's heading is a very good predictor of the curvature of the road ahead. On the basis of Land's work it appears that it is the part of the curve that has most impact on fixations which would first require the driver to modify a straight trajectory (i.e. near side on a bend in the road to the driver's left, far side on a bend to the driver's right). This may reflect a general strategy on the driver's part to maximise the preview of any approaching object. On a blind bend, the tangent point, in addition to providing course-control information, would also be the first possible moment at which an oncoming vehicle would (re-)appear from behind the bend that may partially obscure it. Where the driver's eye height is such as to allow any obscuration by the bend to be overcome, it seems unlikely that drivers would simply ignore early preview information about upcoming obstacles or hazards. This would explain why own and other sides of the road are fixated on approaches for left- and right-hand bends—although it is also clearly the case that the tangent reflects the most rapidly changing portion of the curve, and may be the best source of course information available. Similarly, use of the focus of expansion, while it provides excellent information about heading, which would seem to be crucial for vehicle control, also maximises the preview available.[3] Indeed recent preliminary research from Nissan's CRB lab in Boston suggests that a point on the road surface some way into the carriageway adjacent to the tangent point is crucial (see Hildreth, Beusmans, Boer, & Royden, 1998).

The second issue that these studies raise is what happens when scenes are more visually complex. The hardly unexpected suggestion from the early and recent literature is that increasing complexity of visual scene increases the number of eye movements made and decreases the mean fixation duration on individual objects (Chapman & Underwood, 1998; Erikson & Horberg, 1980; Luoma, 1986; Miura, 1990; Rutley & Mace, 1968). That is, where there is more to look at, drivers look at more things, consequently reducing the amount of time drivers fixate on each—given that the time they spend confronting any scene is limited by their speed. If studies were available in which new visual information was systematically added, while also monitoring aspects of the visual scene such as whether the focus of expansion and the tangent point were still fixated, we could begin to get a better idea of the relative importance and redundancy of certain types of information. A simulator study by Liu, Veltri, and Pentland (1996; reported in Liu, 1998), which was itself an attempt to replicate an on-road study by Olson, Battle, and Aoki (1989), comes close to allowing us to do so.

In the Liu et al. study, four experienced drivers drove on a simulated single-lane unmarked road comprising alternating straight and curved sections. In one condition, drivers were told to follow a lead vehicle at a comfortable following distance, and in another condition, where there was no lead vehicle, simply to stay in the middle of the road. In the first case, the speed of the lead vehicle was controlled, while in the second case the driver's own speed was kept constant. When not following another vehicle, 37% of fixations were to points on the road beyond 2 seconds, with 31% of fixations being on the road ahead but within 2 seconds; a further 18% and 12% were to the left and right sides of the road respectively—with minimal numbers of glances to in-car instruments. As in the on-road Olson et al. (1989) study, following a lead car substantially influences the pattern of fixations, with more than a third of all glances now being to the vehicle being followed (< 2 s: 17%; > 2 s: 35%; left: 9%; right: 4%; lead car 34%). However, what Andy Liu's data allow us to do is to exclude the lead vehicle from consideration, and see whether the precedence given to different

---

[3] It is worth noting in passing here that the focus of expansion has been equated by some with the point at which hazards are likely to be first visible, but this clearly neglects the many hazards that stem from objects or people intersecting the driver's path, e.g. children crossing between parked vehicles, cyclists wobbling about in the road, cars emerging from side roads.

parts of the road is changed by the task of following. Doing so we find that the near road ahead is fixated less often (25%; i.e. 17% divided by 66%), and the far road ahead proportionally more often (53%), with less attention paid to the sides of the road (left: 14%; right: 6%). Thus, it is not only that following another car changes the way drivers inspect the road near that lead vehicle, which is hardly surprising, but also other aspects of the roadway. Because in the following condition the driver was required to control his or her own speed, it may be that the increased tendency to look further ahead may be the result of the driver's attempt to predict what upcoming alterations in road characteristics may influence the vehicle ahead—thus providing early warning of ways in which their own vehicle's performance may need to be adapted.

Liu's results (1998) provide another caution. While it is true that changing the task from "following" to "leading" caused a similar order of reallocation of the proportion of fixations away from the roadway to the lead vehicle in both his and Olson et al.'s study, the visual inspection of the roadway in the simulated and actual driving studies is rather different. While actually driving, drivers do allocate an albeit small proportion of fixations to in-car instruments (about 2–3%), and look at the sides of the road proportionally more frequently, but the largest change occurs when following, where the drivers drastically reduce the amount they inspect the road a long distance ahead (from 25% to 2%). Thus, even with very sophisticated simulation, gaze patterns and the aspects of the road that influence them, may be quite different between actual and simulated driving. A similar point is provoked by Cohen's (1981) contrasting of visual inspection of slides and a very similar roadway when actually driving. With slides he found far longer fixations than on-road, suggesting that on-road subjects adopt more task strategies relevant to actual driving. As Chapman and Underwood astutely observe, "it may be that long fixation durations in situations with low visual complexity tell us little about the information that is being extracted from the scene and more about the low subjective workload imposed in such situations" (1998, p. 371).

The amount of gaze duration and its pattern of allocation that subserves vehicle control, and how much is required for other aspects of the driving task, remain unclear. However, what is clear is that where we look in a driving scene depends on what is in that scene, what we are required to do in response to it, and what we may have intended to do. As such, we need to recognise that an account of driving that focuses purely on perceptual-motor control, although quite complex, is actually very limited indeed.

## SUMMARY

The focus in this chapter, in contrast to that in the previous chapter, is on how drivers adjust their speed or heading in relation to the external environment. Braking to avoid collision, following behind another vehicle, and steering so as to follow the road ahead, all require the driver to detect and monitor changes in objects some way distant in the external world. While in close physical contact with the car controls that are used to bring change about, this "egocentric" control must be interfaced with the "allocentric" frame of reference in which are represented those objects to which the driver must react (see Chapter 2). This in itself suggests that these activities will increase activity in the prefrontal cortex. There are other reasons to think that braking, following, and curve driving require more selective and deliberate action than is possible without attention.

The early models of steering assume that attention is continuously deployed to support steering. If such models are correct, then manipulating proximal and distal position simultaneously, by manipulating the steering wheel alone, would certainly be attention-demanding. If instead, the long- and short-range steering processes are not performed simultaneously, but switched between as time and external stimuli permit, then attention is once again implicated. Liu's Markov[4] modelling of the scanning strategies adopted by drivers when leading or following demonstrates that in the highly visually complex environment in which drivers usually operate, the time available for detecting and monitoring relatively simple optical parameters such as the tangent to some curve the driver is about to enter, will change considerably from one circumstance to another. It may be that there is much more attention available for supervision and switching than driving routinely requires—that is, that the attentional requirements of driving tasks are quite minimal. This issue will be the main focus of the next chapter, but a final point should be made here. The claim that driving requires minimal attention is frequently supported by claims that simple optical parameters such as tau and tau-dot are available from the driver's changing visual world without the need for (much) further processing. It is hard to see how this claim can be sustained for cases where the time-derivative of some directly available information is required (e.g. tau-dot). In any case, the evidence for the actual use, rather than the availability, of such information is far from established. The findings in relation to braking and car following presented earlier convince me that integrating perception and action in driving requires much more than the sole use of such optical variables.

---

[4] Markov modelling assumes that the position of the eyes at one time depends on their position in the immediately prior epoch and not on positions before this.

CHAPTER FOUR

# Attention, automaticity, and distraction

*The fact that much of what we do when driving is repetitive, and hence predict-able, has given rise to the view that much of driving is an automated skill. Indeed, driving is described as the quintessential example of an everyday automated task by most of the major attention/automaticity theorists (e.g. Anderson, 1995; Shiffrin & Schneider, 1977). Where there has been any detailed exploration of the concept of automaticity and the extent to which components of the driving task might be automated, this has been premised on naturalistic observations such as being able to pursue a conversation without a noticeable decrement in driving performance, or the fact that what appears to be an adequate level of performance can be achieved without any recollection of the intervening events. However, while a range of studies demonstrate that secondary tasks have little effect on driving performance, others show that driver performance deteriorates when attentional load increases. The issues to be discussed in this chapter will include: meeting and resolving the attentional demands of the driving task, the criteria for determining automaticity including the extent to which these are met by some or all aspects of the driving task, and the implications of how these issues are resolved within driving for mainstream theories of attention and automaticity.*

Previous chapters have sought to detail how various aspects of the driving task might be carried out, but the fundamental problem is how all of these things might occur together, what might determine which of a range of poss-ible alternative tasks is performed, and how the initiation and cessation of the many tasks that seem to have to be performed in parallel are controlled.

55

Building on these earlier discussions, it would seem that quite different aspects of what might broadly be termed attention appear to play a role in normal driving. These will be considered, somewhat casually at first, but then, more formally.

## ASPECTS OF ATTENTION

One of the ways in which attention is typically thought of is in terms of vigilance, where the driver may have to *sustain* attention over long periods of time, maintaining a readiness to react to events that may occur only occasionally. An example of this might be where the driver is travelling a long distance on a particular motorway, and needs to take a particular exit in order to reach his or her destination. At the same time, suppose the driver is on a busy stretch of motorway, and may need to *concentrate* carefully when following closely or where traffic ahead is weaving between lanes. Perhaps the driver is also talking to a passenger, or on a car-phone, and in doing so may need to *share* attention between their primary task (driving) and the secondary task of maintaining a coherent conversation. When having this conversation the driver might wish to, say, take a note of something that is said, or even more naturally, turn and face the person being spoken to, thus reducing what can be seen of the road ahead. This desire to have eye-contact has to be *suppressed*. *Switching* attention, for example from monitoring the traffic ahead to checking the traffic behind in the rear-view mirror, is also typically required when driving, as are the *preparing* actions, as when the sign for the required motorway exit is seen and the driver prepares to begin an exiting-motorway manoeuvre. Throughout, of course, the driver has *set* and maintained a goal, such as getting to a particular destination, and in this sense too attention is required when driving. It is striking that these seven aspects of attention, recently identified by Stuss, Shallice, Alexander, and Picton (1995), i.e. sustaining, concentrating, suppressing, switching, sharing, setting, and preparing, may all be concurrently deployed during driving. This framework can be mapped onto the three-function account of attention proposed by Posner and Petersen (1990) which suggests that the major functions of attention are to orient to sensory stimuli, engage in executive control (including target detection and response selection), and maintain an alert state (see also further developments and further description in Posner & Raichle, 1994 and Posner, DiGirolamo, & Fernandez-Duque, 1997). However, I believe the broader range of functions suggested by Shallice and colleagues takes us further in understanding the nature of attentional demands in driving. In the next section I characterise this view of attention as a way of scheduling operations that have become routine by virtue of being frequently performed under similar circumstances. The characteristics of this "proceduralisation" or "schematisation" is something to which I return later.

## ATTENTION AS SCHEMA SCHEDULING

The framework advanced by Stuss et al. (1995), builds on earlier work, especially by Shallice (Norman & Shallice, 1980, 1986; Shallice, 1982) and Stuss and Benson (1983, 1986). The original Norman and Shallice (1980) framework identified two basic "control" mechanisms which determined how we monitor our activities. The Contention Scheduler operates when environmental events, whether thought about or actually occurring, directly prime stored knowledge. The Supervisory Attention System reflects conscious thoughts about internal states, and is used to prioritise action in the absence of, or different from, that which might readily be made to environmental stimuli. This separation of automatic and implicit functioning from controlled explicit functioning accounted for a great deal of data regarding attention and action failures in normal and clinical populations, and both echoes and has influenced many other conceptualisations of memory and cognition (e.g. Baddeley's 1986 Central Executive is modelled directly on Shallice's Supervisory Attention System). Because the framework is articulated in a way that I hope illuminates the driving task, and because of its acceptance of the need to separate executive and non-executive control, I will consider the Shallice and Stuss framework in more detail in the following pages.

### Schemata and architecture

Stuss and colleagues use the term schemata as a way of referring to routine programmes for the control of over-learned skills, even those of considerable complexity. Stressing that "even when complex, schemata are still standard and routine . . . hierarchies of schemata allow component schemata to be recruited into complex routine activities" (Stuss et al., 1995, p. 192), a schema is seen as a network of neurons that can be activated by sensory input, by the Supervisory Attentional System, or by other schemata. According to this account, a schema contains multiple internal connections, some to other functionally related schemata, some that provide feedback to the Supervisory Attentional System about its level of activity. Different schemata compete for the control of thought and behaviour by means of contention scheduling, which is "probably mediated by lateral inhibition" (Stuss et al., 1995, p. 194). Inhibition is also used by the Supervisory Attentional System, where contention scheduling fails to yield a single highly activated schema, that is, where specific selection between schemata is required or where a schema's influence needs to be suppressed. Activation is used where the schema is weakly activated or where there is no known solution to the task at hand.

Having briefly sketched the architecture of the system, and some elements of its operation, the task control functions, as they might operate in the motorway driving example used earlier, can now be considered more closely.

## Setting overarching schemata

Where somebody is consistently engaged in a particular activity, there is a sense in which the goals that comprise that activity, determine or "set" the way attention is allocated. Setting of attention, according to the Stuss and Shallice framework, relates to the "consistent mobilisation of the most appropriate schemata across testing sessions" (p. 197). This is equivalent to the driver's determination to, say, drive along a stretch of busy motorway, rather than, say, park on the hard shoulder, or to think primarily about what they may do at the end of their journey or some aspect of what may be on the radio. This "driving along the motorway" schema, once initially activated, will tend to remain selected with consistent use. Activation of this schema makes available, as a consequence, representations of how the task was carried out in the past. These may serve as a guide for current activity, and, as a result, any discrepancies from these expectations result in feedback as to how well the task is being executed. Stuss and colleagues point out that tasks that depend on such intention-driven performance (i.e. top-down processing) pose particular difficulties for head-injured patients, especially those with damage to their dorso-lateral prefrontal cortex. Schemata that operate in this way can usefully be thought of as continuous with performance of the whole activity, overarching and limiting the influence of others.

## Sustaining preparedness to respond to occasional events (Vigilance)

Although attention may be "set" to support some generally specified activity, e.g. driving along a motorway, a driver may also need to sustain his or her preparedness to respond to relatively rare events (i.e. remain vigilant). Dramatic examples of this such, as responding to unexpected hazards, will be discussed later in this book but, for present purposes, a more mundane event, such as continuing along a motorway until a desired exit is reached, will suffice. The Stuss and Shallice framework implies that the schema that would operate to allow the recognition of the appropriate motorway exit would gradually lose activation over a period of seconds, and thereby lose its power to activate the component schemata that will facilitate the driver's checking for following traffic, signalling, changing lane position, and adopting the different driving behaviours appropriate to taking a motorway exit. Alternatively, the reduced level of activation of the "leave motorway" schema may allow it to be replaced by some other schema inappropriate to the driver's intended actions, e.g. taking the opportunity to overtake just as the junction is approached. In order to overcome this reduction of activation and the difficulties it may lead to, the supervisory system must continually reactivate either the target required for detecting occasional stimuli (e.g. reminding oneself about what the exit sign might look like) or, in other cases, for initiating the motor acts that might be required. This form of sustained attention is suggested by some authors, e.g. Posner and Petersen (1990), to involve

TABLE 4.1
Brain areas primarily involved in schema control functions

| Schema control function | Brain areas primarily involved |
|---|---|
| Setting | Dorsolateral prefrontal cortex |
| Sustaining preparedness (Vigilance) | Right lateral mid-frontal regions of the brain, possibly involved in vigilance monitoring, or continual activation/inhibition of target |
| Maximising activation of current schema (Concentration) | Anterior cingulate with reciprocal connections to dorsolateral frontal cortex, or circuit comprising connecting midline thalamo, cingulate, and supplementary motor areas |
| Suppressing associated irrelevant schemata | Bilateral orbitofrontal areas |
| Sharing across schemata | Orbitofrontal and anterior cingulate regions |
| Switching | Dorsolateral frontal regions of either hemisphere, also more diffuse areas |

right lateral mid-frontal regions of the brain, although it is unclear whether this brain region is implicated in the monitoring that is required for vigilance, or in the continual activation or inhibition of target and incorrect schemata.

## Maximising activation of the current schema (Concentration)

While sustaining attention, remaining prepared to respond to some rare event, and continually allocating the attention required to perform the task set at the outset, the system must also ensure that other schemata do not capture behaviour, and is said to do so by monitoring the output of other schemata and inhibiting these schemata as they become active. Colloquially we might refer to this as "concentration". According to the Stuss and Shallice framework, concentration is maintained in one of two ways. The first of these arises from contention scheduling's property of inhibiting other related schemata, thus leading to reduced distraction. The second occurs where infrequently used combinations of schemata may require co-ordination and triggering by the supervisory system (which obviously must then maintain activation of more than a single schema). The anterior cingulate has been associated with concentrating attention, and maintaining activation of multiple schemata (e.g. Pandya, van Hoesen, & Mesulam, 1981), through the operation of two cerebral mechanisms. The first of these relies on the extensive reciprocal connections of the anterior cingulate with the dorsolateral frontal cortex, the second involves the anterior cingulate in a circuit comprising connecting midline thalamo, cingulate, and supplementary motor areas, which, for example, might be involved in maintaining motor activation (see Table 4.1).

## Suppressing associated irrelevant schemata

Sometimes, because of their intensity, recent occurrence, reflex, or prolonged learning stimuli elicit strong automatic responses—that is, have schemata that are rapidly and strongly triggered. Thus, a driver who has been determinedly overtaking other traffic throughout his motorway journey, may be drawn to another overtaking opportunity as he approaches his intended exit junction. Ensuring that behaviour is not captured by such task-inappropriate alternatives requires the suppression of schemata that are inappropriate to the task requirements. Patients with dorsolateral frontal lesions show patterns of Stroop interference similar to normals (i.e. attending to one salient target dimension but suppressing responding to another—see Stuss et al., 1981), but those with bilateral orbitofrontal leucotomies are not impaired in this respect (Richer et al., 1993). This suggests that orbitofrontal connections facilitate the combination of stimulus attributes that, although otherwise important for everyday functioning, pose difficulties for performing tasks where one attribute rather than another related attribute should be the basis of selection. One implication of repeatedly inhibiting material is that the individual subsequently finds it considerably more difficult to attend to or retrieve this information (for example see Fisk & Jones, 1992) leading to the phenomenon of retrieval-induced forgetting (Anderson, Bjork, & Bjork, 1994), in which repeated retrieval of related material serves to render the retrieval of different related material less likely.

## Sharing across schemata

While maintaining concentration, sustaining attention for rare events, and holding attentional set, in the case of driving at least, tasks irrelevant to the currently activated schemata may also be carried out. Suppose, as in the driving along a motorway example, the driver is also talking to a passenger. Because the two tasks would be carried out by unrelated sets of schemata, less inhibition would be present than where attention is being concentrated on a single task. This comparative lack of inhibition would allow two or more unrelated tasks to be carried on simultaneously, but the schemata controlling both tasks would, as a result of being simultaneously activated, be less highly activated than where just one schema was active. Thus, in order to allow performance of both tasks to proceed successfully, an activation-augmentation or energising process within the supervisory system would be required. The supervisory system may also be implicated where the input streams do not naturally lead to frequent triggering of each set of schemata (suppose the other person talks garrulously). People who have had frontal leucotomies and aneurysms of the anterior communicating artery (ACoA), have difficulty in holding facts in memory while performing a second task (e.g. Moscovitch, 1995). A PET study by Vandenberghe and colleagues (1997) demonstrates how attending to a single feature of an object (e.g. length or texture), differs from attending to two features of the same object, or different features of different objects appearing in different hemifields. When participants attended to a single feature, PET activity increased in the parietal, premotor, and anterior cingulate cortex, particularly in the right hemisphere (irrespective of whether the object attended to was in the right or left hemifield[1]). Activity in these areas increased further when two features of the same object were attended to. When participants had to attend to opposite hemifields, activity in occipital and frontal regions was similar in both hemispheres, reducing to levels midway between those observed with single objects appearing to the right or left. Additionally, again in a brain-imaging study, researchers have shown that a list learning and concurrent encoding and retrieval task increased anterior cingulate activation in a difficult compared with an easy dual-task condition[2] (Shallice et al., 1995). Together these findings suggest that the orbitofrontal and anterior cingulate regions are implicated in sharing attention.

## Switching between schemata

Let us suppose, for the purposes of exposition, that steering behaviour and speed control are distinct tasks. Clearly, within many driving manoeuvres these would both need to be performed over a period of time. One alternative might be that both would be performed in parallel with each other. This seems unlikely in the light of the open-looped nature of components of both tasks, and perhaps it makes more sense to assume that both are switched between as circumstances determine—the requirement to switch between operations is taken as evidence by some theorists for the absence of parallellism within the system (e.g. Pashler, 1998). In clinical situations, attention switching has been studied using the Wisconsin Card Sorting Test (WCST),[3] in which the subject is required to change an established way of classifying materials in response to an external stimulus, instead processing more or less the same information for a different purpose. Those suffering damage to the dorsolateral frontal region of either hemisphere appear to have most difficulty in performing WCST, although performance on this task is also sensitive to more diffuse brain damage (see Lezak, 1995). Tasks that principally require only the detection of a task-shift also show a frontal

---

[1] Note that occipital and frontal activity was influenced by direction of attention. With a right-ward object, activity changed in the right lateral frontal and left occipital areas. When attending to an object on the left, activity increased in the left lateral frontal and right occipital areas.

[2] What concerns us here is what happens when the requirement to share attention increased. More generally Shallice and colleagues showed that acquisition was associated with activity in the left prefrontal cortex and the retrosplenial area, whereas retrieval was associated with activity in the right prefrontal cortex and precuneus.

[3] WCST comprises cards that vary on a number of different dimensions, e.g. colour of objects, number of objects, etc. The subject's task is to sort cards into a pattern previously established by the experimenter. Having learned to sort on the basis of one criterion (e.g. sequence of red, green, blue, yellow), the subject is required to sort subsequent cards in response to a different criterion of the same experimenter-established set (e.g. sequence of one, two, three, or four objects on the card sequence).

localisation, and it remains to be determined if this is also the case where subjects know in advance the basis on which attentional set must be shifted. Where tasks require different stimulus–response mappings, it is frequently observed that it takes longer for subjects to switch from one task to another task within a block of trials than when the subject performs the same task over the whole trial-block. That is, task switching takes time (e.g. Rogers & Monsell, 1995). This is so, although the time-cost is lower, where the subject is forewarned that a switch is required. In such situations, where the subject knows about the upcoming task ahead of time by means of a warning cue or the ordering of stimuli, it is almost as if upcoming performance cannot be fully reconfigured until the new stimulus occurs (see Stuss et al., 1995, p. 202). This point is well demonstrated by a number of studies by Rogers and Monsell (1995) who had subjects alternate between two simple tasks (i.e. determine whether a number is odd or even, or whether a letter is a consonant or a vowel). The cost of switching, in terms of time, was highest where there was a delay between the subject's response and the presentation of the next to-be-categorised item. As the lag increased, participants showed clear evidence that they could partially reconfigure their task expectations, as response time fell as the lag increased to in the region of 600 ms. Nevertheless, even when the lag was 1200 ms, subjects were not fully able to respond as quickly on the categorisation task as they did when task-switching was not required. Rogers and Monsell (1995) attribute this residual task-switching cost to a component of reconfiguration that is triggered only by a task-relevant stimulus (i.e. exogenously). In theoretical terms, successfully switching control of behaviour between two schemata relies on augmenting the activation of the schema that is less activated, a function assumed to be performed by the supervisory system, with contention scheduling reducing the activation level of the current schema through inhibition. The extent of this inhibition must be carefully monitored, as complete inhibition of the newly deactivated schema would render a subsequent return to this schema more difficult.

## Preparing for upcoming action

Returning to our example of driving on a motorway, the driver must be prepared, somehow, to initiate a "leaving a motorway" schema when the intended exit junction is reached. According to Stuss and colleagues, this may occur through submaximal activation of the later-to-be-used schema, so that when the critical stimulus subsequently arrives, the driver is ready to respond optimally. They point out that deficits in preparing a response for later use seem to occur maximally after dorsolateral lesions of either hemisphere, or their connecting regions (1995, p. 202). An alternative way of thinking about how this advance preparation may be achieved is through initiation of the desired activity once the sustaining attention operation described earlier has been triggered by the stimulus for which the performer was remaining vigilant. This would predict that where people perform an action earlier than is appropriate, it would be preceded by some event that would be sufficient to meet the requirements of the vigilance system, i.e. what Norman (1981) or Reason (1984) might term loss of place errors or anticipatory errors.

## Section summary

The Stuss and Shallice framework has been used here as a basis for describing the range of ways in which "attention" or task control may need to operate even within relatively simple driving tasks. Because of their attempts to identify the neurological basis for the functions described, the framework offers real promise for furthering our understanding. The framework envisages that contention scheduling is sufficient to effect satisfactory control over routine activities, while the supervisory system monitors levels of schema activation, energises some, inhibits others, responds to stimuli in a contingent fashion (i.e. IF then >>>, ELSE >>>), and exercises control over contention scheduling. However, this assumption of a bifurcation between what might casually be referred to as unconscious and conscious activities or processes is more controversial than it might at first seem. The notion of a schema, which is fundamental to their framework, also requires scrutiny, not least in terms of what and how specific the contents of a schema might be, how schemata are acquired and modified, etc. These are both issues that have substantial implications for driving and the way we research it.

## ROUTINE ACTIONS AND AUTOMATICITY

*The foregoing parts of this chapter have tried to sketch a framework within which the numerous ongoing tasks that drivers must perform might be scheduled and controlled. However, the regularity of the tasks performed, and the fact that so many appear to be carried out without an obvious decrement in performance, raises the possibility, frequently suggested but rarely demonstrated, that driving skills are "automatic". In this section I discuss routine activity and the notion of automaticity as a way of addressing the issue of which, or whether, driving skills can reasonably be considered automatic.*

### Routine actions and everyday errors

The framework outlined earlier "follows the basic tenet of other theories of executive abilities—the separation between routine and non-routine activities" (Stuss et al., 1995, p. 192). No account I am aware of would suggest that non-routine matters can be adequately dealt with by non-conscious or automatic processes, however they are described. It is more questionable whether what might be characterised as executive, conscious, or controlled processes have no involvement in routine processing. There are eminent antecedents of this position. Luria (1966), for example, in his book *The Higher Cortical Functions in*

*Man*, describes patients who, when called upon to perform a familiar action (light a cigarette), behaved in a disorganised and fragmented fashion. When called upon to perform a similar but less familiar action (light a candle), one patient, having lit the candle, "would put it in his mouth, or perform the habitual movements of smoking a cigarette with it, or break it and throw it away". Luria continues, "The plan of the action, formed in response to the instruction, readily disintegrated and was replaced by isolated, fragmentary acts. Comparison between the effect of the completed action and its intention was also lost" (Luria, 1966, pp. 237–238). Luria's analyses of these patients, who were suffering from extensive damage to their frontal lobes, have been criticised on the basis that the brain damage extended beyond frontal regions and, partly because of this, the notion that routine behaviours impose some processing requirement on the frontal lobes has received little support. Among the exceptions to this is the work of Myrna Schwartz (1995), who has investigated errors in everyday actions and, more intensively, the performance of routine activities by patients with frontal damage.

In the former case, Schwartz, as have many other authors (e.g. Heckhausen & Beckmann, 1990; Norman, 1981; Reason, 1984; Sellen & Norman, 1992), identifies errors in everyday actions that reflect the following: capture of part of a sequence of action by a similar more familiar action (e.g. driving past the entrance to the university on a Saturday, on the way to seeing a colleague at home, you drive into the university and park where you normally would); omission errors (e.g. getting out of the car at night without turning off the headlights); exchange errors (e.g. applying force to the accelerator before releasing the clutch when changing gear); substitution errors (e.g. turning on the windscreen wipers rather than the indicators); addition errors (e.g. indicating a turn when the road ahead merely sweeps sharply to the right or left); anticipation errors (e.g. releasing the clutch before the car is properly in gear); and perseveration errors (e.g. failing to release the clutch once the car is in gear). In many cases, these errors suggest that two plans were simultaneously active and competing, somehow, for control of what the performer finally did.

The fact that elements of these plans can replace or corrupt each other gives some insight into how crudely the constituents of these plans are specified. Presumably, if when intending to make a left turn at a particular crossing, I take up a road position to make a right turn, with the subsequent realisation before I make the turn that I am about to go wrong, then two things are implied. First, that direction of turn is loosely specified in whatever schema is controlling my behaviour, and second, that what I am doing is being monitored for error and subsequently corrected. Schwartz (1995, p. 324) summarises the position thus:

> routine action production involves a more highly constructed process, with greater potential for error, than appeared at first blush. The requirement is for the constituents of action plans—for example goal, action and argument schemas—to be bound together in temporary assemblies; but for competition at each level of constituent

structure the potential for faulty selection within each level and erroneous or rapidly fading linkages across levels. . . . Here then is the key point: If routine action production is as prone to error as this, and if it falls to supervisory attention to monitor for errors and correct them before they are overtly expressed, then the supervisory attention system is playing a more active role in routing action production than is generally appreciated.

Studying people with traumatic brain injuries, Schwarz notes that patients suffering from what she terms Action Disorganization Syndrome (ADS), tend to have complex neuropsychological profiles, exhibiting abnormal performance on tests of both frontal and posterior cognitive functions, but performance profiles that are not characteristic of global dementia or confusion. ADS patients show substantial variability in how they go about routine activities (such as making a pot of coffee or preparing to post a letter), with little correspondence between the errors made in such activities from day to day. She also finds that the errors made are in part dependent on the task at hand, with substitution errors characteristic of some tasks, and sequencing activities characteristic of others. Noting that all the types of errors that are observed in our own routine daily activities can also be found in patients with ADS, albeit that there are differences of severity and quality in such errors (e.g. they are made even when deliberate attention is being paid; they persist for long periods without being corrected), Schwartz stresses the need to recognise the integrated role that both supervisory attention and what Shallice and colleagues term contention scheduling play in controlling routine performance. "The point is not to deny" she writes, "that routine tasks are less demanding of prefrontal executive functions; rather, it is to argue that there is no clear demarcation of novel and routine that justifies attributing executive functions to one but not to the other. The routine activities of everyday life are certainly low on the continuum of executive demands, but they are represented on that continuum nonetheless" (Schwartz, 1995, p. 325).

In short, the view is that what we are observing, even in our everyday activities, is the product of a single continuum of control, rather than separate control systems, separately involved in routine and non-routine activities. If this is so, then for me at least it raises questions about the extent to which conscious control is required for driving, and in particular the extent to which driving, or elements of driving, can be seen as "automatic".

## Automaticity of routine driving actions

Driving, or at least elements of driving, are widely regarded by cognitive psychologists and driving researchers alike as "automatic" (e.g. Anderson, 1995; Baddeley, 1990; Brown, 1982; Grafman, 1995; MacKay, 1982; Michon, 1985; Schmidt, 1982; Welford, 1986). I have been suspicious for some time about what we mean by this term, and sceptical about the claims made for elements of driving meeting any reasonable requirements for being regarded as automatic.

## Criteria for automaticity

Shiffrin and Schneider (1977), for example, describe how automaticity develops as a function of consistent reactions to a particular stimulus—using driving towards a signalised junction as an example of how their laboratory-derived principles might extend to everyday life (see Grafman, 1995, p. 340 for a similar example). Driving is also characterised, by those working on human factors and psychological aspects of driving, as a largely automatic task, also being seen as "self-paced", because the driver chooses the manner and speed of his or her interaction with other traffic (Brown, 1982).[4] Driving is also portrayed as "automatic" because there is little recollection of specific elements of the task, because it can be performed alongside other tasks (e.g. talking, listening to the radio), and because it relies on open-loop control (i.e. sequences of actions that do not rely on feedback from the results of preceding actions before subsequent actions are performed, see Anderson, 1995; Brown, 1982; Underwood & Everatt, 1996).

As implied several times earlier, it is common practice to make a distinction between automatic and controlled processes. Thus for example, Sellen and Norman (1992, p. 318) point out that:

> There are two main modes of control: an unconscious, automatic mode best modelled as a network of distributed processors acting locally and in parallel; and a conscious control mode acting globally to oversee and override automatic control. Automatic and conscious control are complementary: the unconscious mode is fast, parallel, and context-dependent, responding to regularities in the environment in routine ways, whereas the conscious mode is effortful, limited, and flexible, stepping in to handle novel situations.

Automatic processing is "a fast, parallel, fairly effortless process that is not limited by short term memory (STM) capacity, is not under direct subject control, and is responsible for the performance of well-developed skilled behaviours" (Schneider, Dumais, & Shiffrin, 1984, p. 1). Most theories assume that it develops only when subjects process stimuli consistently over many trials. Consistent practice is assumed to occur when the stimuli and responses are consistently mapped, that is, across training trials the subject makes the same overt or covert response each time the stimulus occurs. This is contrasted with controlled processing, which "is characterised as a slow, generally serial, effortful, capacity-limited, subject-regulated processing mode that must be used to deal with novel or inconsistent information. Control processing is expected when the subject's response to the stimulus varies from trial to trial" (Schneider et al., 1984, p. 2).

---

[4] Note that this use of "self-paced" does not map onto self-paced as used by others in the engineering literature, in which it is seen as the opposite of "fixed-paced", where performance is required at a pace that is fully determined by factors outside the operator's control (e.g. Wickens, 1992).

Automatic processing also leads to stereotyped responses and activity (McLeod, McLaughlin, & Nimmo-Smith, 1985; Naveh-Benjamin & Jonides, 1986), which are unavailable to conscious awareness (Marcel, 1983). Processes and performance become automated after very substantial amounts of practice, generally several thousands of trials, where the same mapping relationship is repeated between stimulus and action (Shiffrin & Schneider, 1977). Practice does not necessarily result in automaticity or skill, as "skill does not develop from practising the skill per se, but rather from practising consistent components of the skill. Consistent practice develops automatic component processes that exhibit fast, accurate, parallel processing" (Schneider et al., 1984, p. 2). Moreover, and importantly for the discussion to follow, increased automaticity not only leads to reduced error and performance speed-up, but also to substantial reductions in variability as determined by the amount of practice (McLeod et al., 1985; Naveh-Benjamin & Jonides, 1984). Together these findings form the cornerstones of most theories of automaticity, which are based on linkage strengthening between stimuli and responding, although despite what appears to be a rigorous set of criteria, automatic processing has been claimed to occur where only a subset of these have been met (e.g. Bargh, 1992; Logan, 1988). Other researchers have adopted still less demanding criteria, i.e. that automatic processes are those that proceed without the need of conscious monitoring (Bargh, 1992; Tzelgov, 1997), or as the result of direct priming of schemata (Stuss et al., 1995).

### Automaticity and gear changing

The flavour of these accounts of automaticity is well captured by Welford (1988, pp. 458–459), describing gear changing:

> Changing gears involves, in succession, ungraded movement by the feet to release the accelerator and press the clutch pedals; a more or less complex movement that is neither too fast nor too slow with the one hand on the gear lever; and then a graded release of the clutch pedal simultaneous with a graded pressing of the accelerator . . . Presumably, for most car drivers, the separate actions of changing gear are integrated into a "higher unit" of performance . . . Such integration means that the transitions between actions become established so that the degree of choice involved in each action is greatly reduced . . . It also means that the observation and monitoring of each action following its completion is cut out.

The parallel between this account of gear changing and that of open-loop control offered 20 years earlier by Keele (1968, p. 387), where actions "structured before the movement begins and allow the entire sequence to be carried out uninfluenced by peripheral feedback", is striking, but misleading.

A number of recent studies have explored gear changing, with, at first sight, conflicting results. Duncan, Williams, Nimmo-Smith, and Brown (1992) report a study that focused particularly on the effect of performing a centrally loading secondary task (i.e. random generation, having to say aloud a single digit every one second which is unrelated to those previously said) on the performance of different driving manoeuvres. The study is discussed further later, but is considered here because of the fact that Duncan et al. report that the time taken to complete a gear change (i.e. from leaving current gear to clutch release following selection of target gear) without simultaneously performing a secondary task (594 ms) and while performing a secondary task (611 ms) are very similar. This encourages the view that lower-order tasks such as gear changing are indeed performed automatically. However, another study by Duncan and colleagues gives some pause for thought.

Duncan et al. (1991) reported that when changing from third gear to second gear, experts (mean = 550 ms; standard deviation = 130 ms) change gear significantly faster than normal drivers (mean = 710 ms; standard deviation = 150 ms) and novice drivers (mean = 730 ms; standard deviation = 150 ms), the latter two groups changing gear equally quickly. When changing from second gear to third gear, however, experts (mean = 440 ms; standard deviation = 130 ms) and normal drivers (mean = 430 ms; standard deviation = 110 ms) change gear equally fast, both performing the gear change significantly faster than novice drivers (mean = 530 ms; standard deviation = 120 ms). According to theory, additional practice should indeed influence performance. This would imply that experts and normals should not differ, as the number of years of driving experience of both groups, and presumably the total number of gear changes performed, did not differ. On the other hand, novices should have had substantially less practice, and thus should be slower than both normals and experts. Advanced driver training, which was the respect in which experts and normals differed, has relatively little focus on lower-order elements of the driving task, and thus should not lead to a difference in task performance at the level of gear changing. Even though the strength theory view (see next chapter), advocated by people such as Shiffrin and Schneider, Anderson, and MacKay, would predict differences due to task experience, it is very hard to see how any of the strength theory views would predict different effects of task experience and task training on changes of gear from second to third and third to second!

A study by Ben Clegg and myself (Groeger & Clegg, 1998) addresses another aspect of the claimed "automaticity" of gear changing—the degree of internal variability of the timing of gear-changing components when individual subjects repeatedly performed second to third and third to second gear changes. Reanalysing the data of Duncan and colleagues (1991, 1992), we found that (1) changing-up (i.e. second to third) and changing-down (third to second) differ in their variability; (2) components of gear changes, such as the time taken to depress the clutch and shift out of current gear, or to move from one gear to another, do not predict each other; and (3) within a gear change, although the first component is correlated with the second component, neither is related to the variance in time taken to complete the gear change, i.e. reach target gear and

release the clutch. These results clearly undermine the notion that through extensive practice subsets of the components of a gear change become closely tied
to each other, and show a level of variability and contextual sensitivity that is
inconsistent with the most widely accepted views of automaticity.

The view that even something as routine as gear changing when driving is not
automatic, and thus has some measurable cognitive cost, was tested recently in a
field study by Shinar, Meir, and Ben-Shoham (1998). This involved studying the
driving of two groups of drivers: novices, who had about one year's driving
experience, and experienced drivers, who had had eight or so years of experience. They drove either an automatic or a manual shift car over a fixed route.
Their task was to signal when they detected either of two types of road sign.
Shinar et al. report a fascinating set of results, such as that novices detected
fewer signs than experienced drivers, and drivers driving automatic vehicles rather
than manual shift vehicles also correctly detected more target signs. These main
effects interacted, such that the difference in road sign detection performance
for experienced drivers when driving manual shift and automatic shift cars was
less than for novice drivers. Shinar and colleagues conclude from this that gear
changing in manual vehicles has a cognitive cost, albeit one that is lessened with
experience.

Although each of these studies has its weaknesses, they remain the only ones
that have examined gear changing with respect to the concept of automaticity. I
believe they show that gear changing is a learned ability which, even after a
very great deal of practice, reduces the driver's ability to attend to their external
environment, and which varies considerably in terms of how long it takes to
perform, as a whole and with respect to its individual components, from one
occasion to another. These findings are contrary to the notion that gear changing
is an automatic process, if we are to retain any meaningful conception of what
automaticity is. The fact that Duncan and colleagues show no effect of performing a demanding secondary task on total gear change time is particularly interesting, but it does not invalidate this view, because people may have been
switching between tasks, and in any case arguing from a null result is not a
particularly empirically strong position. Although I cannot defend this assertion,
I believe that gear changing offers the most likely opportunity for automaticity
to be demonstrated in the driving task. The fact that the evidence is that gear
changing is not automatic implies to me that very little, if any, of the driving
task is—and beyond that, that we should seriously question the utility of strength-
based accounts of automaticity.

## DRIVING AND DISTRACTION

A view more widespread than the notion of automaticity is that there is a single
general, central, or intellectual capacity, which has been equated with supervisory
attention or executive processes by some (see Bourke, 1997; Bourke, Duncan,

TABLE 4.2
Effects of secondary task on driving performance

| Driving performance measures | Single task | Dual task |
| --- | --- | --- |
| Mirror checks: Total on urban circuit | 15.8 | 19.2** |
| Mirror checks: Probability at intersection | 0.46 | 0.40 |
| Mirror checks: Checking at less appropriate times | 0.76 | 0.94* |
| Roundabouts: Right looks per approach | 2.62 | 2.59 |
| Overtake: Probability of left look during pass phase | 0.21 | 0.27 |
| Overtake: Probability of rear look during pull-in phase | 0.97 | 0.90 |
| Intersections: Time of braking on entry (s) | 4.77 | 4.50* |
| Intersections: Time of acceleration on exit (s) | 1.26 | 1.33 |
| Intersections: Divergence from kerb (early : later points) | 1.08 | 1.05 |
| Intersections: Consistency of path (cm) | 11.3 | 11.7 |
| Gear changes: Duration of movement (ms) | 611 | 594 |
| Overtaking: Following distance (m) | 62.5 | 59.8 |

After Duncan, Williams Nimmo-Smith, & Brown (1992). Differences reliable at *p < .05; **p < .01.

& Nimmo-Smith, 1996; Duncan et al., 1991). Taken to extremes, the notion that driving is largely or completely automatic would imply that there is little or no cost of driving to executive or supervisory attentional processes. Thus, we should expect to see virtually no reduction in driver performance, or in the performance of secondary non-driving tasks, where driving and other tasks are performed simultaneously—except perhaps where there is some relatively trivial competition for hands, feet, eyes, or ears.

Over 30 years ago, Brown, Tickner, and Simmonds (1969), showed that when driving towards posts that formed gaps along a test track, speed and steering were unaffected by having to perform a concurrent logical reasoning task. However, drivers' ability to select those gaps through which their vehicle would pass safely was significantly impaired. This was one of the first studies in which the possibility was put forward that higher-order aspects of the driving task, such as those requiring some explicit decision making, also draw on some form of executive or supervisory attentional process. A quarter of a century later, Ivan Brown was again involved in a study that seemed to show similar effects.

The study Duncan et al. (1992) report focused particularly on the effect, on various components of the driving task, of performing a task that should disrupt supervisory attention or executive processes (i.e. random generation, having to say aloud a single digit every one second which is unrelated to those previously said; see Baddeley, Emslie, Kolodny, & Duncan, 1998 for detailed consideration of the random generation task). Table 4.2 shows the impact that concurrent random generation has on driving in the 24 drivers taking part, bearing out the point made earlier with regard to how at least some elements of the driving task are indeed influenced by concurrent performance of a secondary task. Thus, drivers brake later approaching intersections when also carrying out a secondary task, and tend to check their mirrors more, but especially at inappropriate times.

It might be argued that this study, although it does show some decrements in performance, does so in only three of twelve comparisons, and that if driving really was demanding of attentional resources then more widespread effects should be observed. However, as the discussion of the Stuss and Shallice framework at the outset of this chapter indicates, executive processes are many and varied, and supposing that one task known to be demanding of executive processes would necessarily affect all others, and thence the performance of any other task making similar sorts of demand, is overly simplistic. There is, however, another difficulty with this study. We do not know whether subjects maintained their driving performance by reducing the rate or randomness of their performance of the secondary task, or indeed switched between the primary (driving) and secondary (random generation) tasks as demands changed.

A study reported by Verwey (1991) makes this point clearly. Drivers who were either classed as experienced (licence held for at least 5 years and drive more than 10,000 km per year) or novices (licence held for less than 1 year and drive less than 10,000 km ever), performed a number of paced tasks, saying when a number appeared on a screen on the dashboard, saying what the sum was of successive pairs of numbers displayed on the same screen, or reporting aloud when the same numbers were heard rather than seen. They did this before driving, and while performing six driving manoeuvres (merging or exiting a motorway, driving straight ahead on a motorway, turning at a two-lane roundabout, performing a complex turn across oncoming traffic, turning—not across oncoming traffic, i.e. left in UK or right in Netherlands—driving straight ahead on a rural road).

Verwey's results show that visual detection, visual detection plus addition, and auditory detection plus addition place different loads on the driver, but more importantly, the extent to which the driving task interferes with ability to perform the secondary task depends crucially on the manoeuvre underway. As Figure 4.1 shows, Verwey's study makes clear that driving situations differ in the extent to which they are demanding of visual attention. Even when not being occasionally visually distracted from where they might wish to look at the road, experienced drivers' capacity to carry out the (auditory) serial addition task is reduced where turning rather than driving straight ahead. What is more evident, however, is the way in which novice drivers' capacity is sharply reduced from baseline performance across all, but especially the more complex, manoeuvres. Contrast the performance of the visual and auditory versions of the addition task. In each case the requirement to maintain a visual code or re-code a visually presented number into a speech code, rather than maintain an auditory/speech-like code, has an effect over and above the difficulty imposed by simply adding the two numbers together. Paced auditory and visual serial addition has been shown by Natasha Merat and myself, among others (Merat & Groeger, 1999),

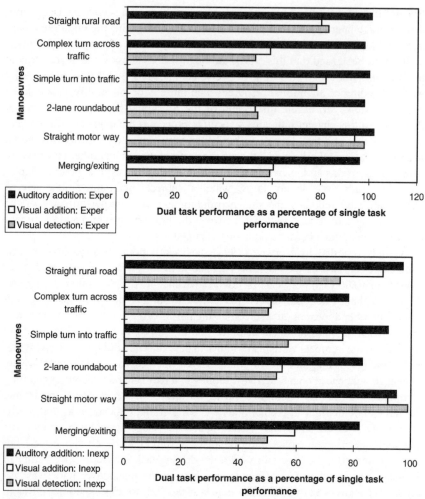

**Figure 4.1.** Reductions in ability to detect and add visually and auditorially presented digits when driving, among experienced (top) and inexperienced (bottom) drivers.

to be very demanding of what are generally seen as executive processes. What this study additionally shows is that the presentation of the addition task, and the addition task itself, are separate sources of competition for the resources that are also used to differing extents when driving in different situations. This implies that different information processing resources are required by different driving manoeuvres, and in doing so also serve to echo a debate in the wider attention literature.

The results just considered add emphasis to Navon and Gopher's (1979, p. 247) suggestion that "many findings would embarrass the strict model of central capacity interference". In part, these findings reflect cases in which interference between tasks is predicted not by their difficulty, as one might expect from a simple single-central resource hypothesis, but by "structural" overlaps between the structure of the two tasks (e.g. the codes in which stimuli are presented or processed, modalities of processing or responding). This is demonstrated in findings by Wickens (1976) among others. Studies are also reported in which, under dual task conditions, an increase in the degree of difficulty in one task does not degrade performance of the other task (e.g. Wickens, Sandry, & Vidulich, 1983). A study by Allport, Antonis, and Reynolds (1972), which showed that skilled pianists could sight-read music and engage in verbal shadowing without any discernible decrement in the performance of either task, exemplifies another class of findings that posed difficulties for the unitary view, in that they appear to show perfect time sharing between tasks.[5]

In order to account for these and other findings, Wickens (1980, 1984) proposed that resources can be defined by three simple dichotomous dimensions: "two stage-defined resources (early versus late processes), two modality-defined resources (auditory versus visual encoding), and two resources defined by processing codes (spatial versus verbal)" (Wickens, 1992, p. 375). Wickens's multiple-resource view, in arguing that people have a number of different relatively independent performance capacities, is consistent with a very broad range of data. Thus, where two tasks performed together require different resources, time sharing will be more efficient, increases in the difficulty of one task are less likely to affect performance of the other, and decreases in the difficulty of one task are less likely to lead to an improvement in the other.

As a counter to the multiple-resource position, which has been criticised as "fuzzy" in respect of its definition of resources, Cowan (1994) has suggested that two positions may be adopted. First, "one may propose that one or both tasks have become automatized and no longer require attention" (Cowan, 1994, p. 208). Second, "one may propose that subjects are able to learn to use efficient time-sampling and attention-switching strategies to carry out both tasks simultaneously" (Cowan, 1994, p. 208). As is probably evident from my earlier discussion of automaticity, I doubt whether any rigorous account of automaticity can be extended beyond laboratory tasks, especially to tasks such as driving. The fact that people can indeed become better at task sharing, especially after extensive practice, seems to underline the basic tenets of the multiple resource view, rather than undermine it. Wickens's account of processing resources may be rather dated, and takes insufficient account of modern theories of working memory (see Baddeley, 1990; Logie, 1995) which might profitably be used to extend the multiple resource framework, but the basic point that separate capacities

---

[5] It should be noted that this issue may not be resolvable empirically as total available capacity of the system cannot be assumed to be constant, because it depends on the subject's motivation and arousal (Kahneman, 1973).

underlie task performance, at least at its initial stages, seems to emphasise that such different capacities exist.

At the outset of this chapter I presented in some detail the framework advanced by Stuss, Shallice and colleagues. They write "if we are correct that there is no central executive, neither can there be a dys-executive syndrome. The frontal lobes (in anatomical terms) or the supervisory system (in cognitive terms) do not function (in physiological terms) as a simple (inexplicable) homunculus" (Stuss et al., 1995, p. 206). This approach is based on Shallice and Norman's work, whose notion of executive functioning has been seen as a strong candidate for the single central attentional resource (e.g. Cowan, 1994, p. 223). The fact that Shallice and others now recognise the need to fractionate executive functioning emphasises the need for some form of multiple resources account of how people perform complex tasks or combine the performance of simpler ones.

## SUMMARY

Driving is demanding of what we generally refer to as attention. Certainly the level and nature of this depend on the level of experience of the performer, the nature of the driving manoeuvre underway and how it is measured, and the nature of the secondary tasks we use to assess remaining capacity. As such, I believe it also encourages us to treat rather sceptically a number of conceptions we as cognitive psychologists have cherished: the notion of a single limited-capacity central processor, the notion of automaticity, and the clear separation of what are usually referred to as executive or controlled and automatic processes. Instead, it seems more reasonable to assume that a broad range of activities and capacities comprise what was previously seen as attention, and while this serves to exercise conscious control, it, along with well practised routines, is part of a single control architecture. Except for its echo in the previous sentence, the notion of schema, so crucial to the Shallice and Stuss framework described earlier, may appear to have been abandoned. Readers with stamina will notice it receives rather more attention in the next chapter.

# CHAPTER FIVE

# Learning, instruction, and training

*This chapter focuses on two related issues: what factors influence the learning of simple and complex ability to drive and progress made when learning, and the implications of these for understanding the acquisition of driving skills. The first issue considers the implications of recently reported findings that, when learning to drive, the instruction given to learning drivers reduces as a power function of the amount of practice the pupil has had (Groeger & Clegg, 2000b). This approach is extended to other indices of skill acquisition, as well as treating the issue of whether learning of tasks of this level of complexity should be regarded as involving implicit or explicit learning. Having described the basis of learning in the driving tasks, this chapter will go on to consider the issue of whether skills are acquired in a particular order, whether there are hierarchies evident in the acquisition of skill, and why the power law of practice should be evident in complex everyday skills, just as in the simple laboratory skills in which it is usually demonstrated. This discussion will also seek to clarify how the traditional distinction between massed and distributed practice contributes to the rapid acquisition of some skill components and the relatively slow acquisition of others.*

Driving is among the most complex skills we ever acquire, and one that, if performed without some measure of proficiency, raises the risk of an accident to oneself or others to an unacceptably high level. Several years ago, along with Ivan Brown and Bernard Biehl, I concluded that there was little convincing evidence that formal training actually reduced accident risk (Brown, Groeger, & Biehl, 1987). This claim has been over-interpreted by some as suggesting that formal driver training is ineffective, and that as many more accidents would surely result were no-one to be formally trained, our conclusion must obviously be false (see Elander, West, & French, 1993). The intervening decade or so has still not provided any convincing evidence of a safety benefit from training, and the original case made, that a safety benefit of professional driver training is "not proven", is one to which I still adhere. Since that review was published, other reviews have reached a similar conclusion (e.g. Horneman, 1993; Williams, 1997). However, a far more substantial point is made in the second part of the Brown, Groeger, and Biehl review, that we really knew very little about how drivers are taught, and how they learn. The admirably detailed task analyses of driving by McKnight and Adams (1970), although they provide an exhaustive description of the actions that must be performed, offer little insight into these critical aspects of driver training. Over the past ten years, research has moved some way to address these issues. Before considering this research in detail and what it implies about how we might teach people to drive and about complex skill acquisition in general, this chapter considers some general properties that emerge from analyses of skill acquisition in less complex situations.

## LEARNING CURVES AND PRACTISING

Since the work of Snoddy (1926), reports in the literature on skill acquisition have frequently suggested that the rate at which proficiency on a task develops is a function of the amount of practice the performer has had. Earlier, Thurstone (1919) used a related type of function to describe cumulative errors. Newell and Rosenbloom (1981), summarising a wide range of research albeit largely from relatively simple tasks, suggest that skill develops as a power function of practice. That is, the gain from practice is considerably greater early in learning than it is later in learning—the reducing benefit of training being evident even after millions of trials (see Crossman, 1959). Let us look briefly at the power function and some of the alternatives that have been proposed.

### Alternative forms of learning curves

The standard form of this power law relationship, for a task in which performance is measured by the number of errors committed is:

Power[1]: Number of Errors = Initial Level $*$ Amount of Practice$^{-\text{Rate of Learning}}$

Power functions have a number of important properties. The speed at which the curve flattens is effectively similar to the slope or a straight line, and thus readily

---

[1] Initial Level is performance on the first trial. Amount of practice is measured in time on task or number of trials. The minus sign preceding the rate of learning reflects the fact that learning will be reflected in a reduction in errors over time, as it might be were time taken to complete the task measured, but not where, say, the percentage correct was the index of performance used.

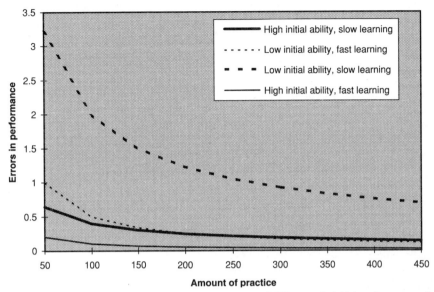

**Figure 5.1.** Power function learning curves as a function of differences in initial performance and rate of learning.

provides a "rate of learning". Thus, for example, for power functions, the amount of learning on each trial is a constant proportion of what remains to be learned. The way power functions work, if the number of errors halves over the course of 100 trials, it will take N times N−1 trials (i.e. 9900 trials) for the number of errors to reduce by half as much again (see Figure 5.1).

A power relationship between practice and performance is not the only relationship that has been observed. Hull (1943) suggested that learning and what he called "Habit Strength" develops exponentially with exposure, i.e. an equation that also yields a negatively accelerated curve, but tends to overstate the level of performance achieved, given a similar rate of learning, level of initial performance, and amount of practice. This can easily be seen by realising that if learning follows an exponential function, where the number of errors in performance halves after 100 trials, it will halve again after 100 further trials—a stark contrast with the estimate of 9900 where learning is a power function.

Exponential[2]: Number of Errors = Initial Level $* e^{-\text{Rate of Learning}*\text{Amount of practice}}$

Others authors, such as Mazur and Hastie (1978), but as early as Thurstone (1919), suggest that skill and practice are related by a hyperbola, which is a special form of power function that leads to slower acquisition initially, with

---

[2] Here $e$ refers the natural or Naperian logarithm (i.e. 2.718..).

a rapid increase in performance level after a period of practice, followed by a period in which the rate of growth in skill declines again.

Hyperbolic[3]: Number of Errors = Initial Level/Amount of Practice

The hyperbolic function is simpler, and produces a curve that changes in slope at each trial such that changes between trials follow the ratio of $n/(n+1)$. Mazur and Hastie (1978), reviewed over 70 studies and demonstrated that in the vast majority of cases, hyperbolic functions provided better fits to the data than did exponential functions, whether the tasks involved the acquisition of perceptual-motor skills or verbal learning. As the hyperbolic function is a special case of the power function, this supports the conclusion reached later by Newell and Rosenbloom (1981) that the power function family offer the best description of the relationship between practice and performance.

Occasionally, researchers have found that logistic functions fit learning data, especially where performance assessment is based on ratings by experts (Spears, 1983, 1985). Usually, perhaps in part because of biases in ratings,[4] the logistic function produces a sigmoidal curve, which rises slowly in early trials, accelerates rapidly in mid-portion, and levels off becoming progressively flatter. The rate of learning in the logistic function is more complex, reflecting both the percentage of learning that still remains to be acquired, but also a quantity that reflects the amount which has already been learned. This leads to an acceleration in learning. This is usually represented as a single constant ("k" in the equation given below) which is the Rate of Learning/[Current Performance * (Asymptotic Performance–Current Performance)].

Logistic: Number of Errors = Asymptote/[1 + (Initial Level –
Asymptote) * $e^{-k*\text{Amount of practice}}$]

If the initial slower learning portion of the function were not present, as in the case where prior experience of some similar task successfully "transfers", then the logistic function would also show the negative acceleration and single inflection point characteristic of the other functions described earlier. The logistic function is the only learning function which incorporates the notion that skill develops as a succession of periods of rapid progress and periods of little progress

---

[3] Note that a learning rate of −1 is implied.

[4] Schneider (1985) suggests that experts apply a moving expectation when rating performance, such that early in performance there is a tendency to underrate performance to reinforce the need for perfect performance, whereas as practice proceeds and performance improves, experts tend to over-rate performance so as to motivate learners to further effort, with very high ratings given at the end of the learning period. There is obvious scope here for the operation of self-enhancement and downward comparison biases to operate (see Chapter 8).

(i.e. plateaux). We will return to this issue later in this chapter where theories of skill acquisition are considered in more detail.

The evidence from simple and relatively complex skills, in which actual performance is measured, seems to me to clearly favour the power function account. That is not to deny that some situations may produce performance that appears more like one of the other functions, but I believe the evidence and theoretical support very much favours the proposal that skill develops as a power function of practice. Before concluding, it is worth noting that the standard form of the power function can be extended in order to more easily identify contributions from past experience and task difficulty. This allows a number of points to be made more obviously than might otherwise be the case.

$$\text{Power: Number of Errors} = \text{Asymptote of Performance} +$$
$$\text{Performance on first trial (Practice + Prior Experience)}^{-\text{Rate of Learning}}$$

First, by including specifically a term to reflect prior experience, the function makes clear that learning curves reflect individual, rather than group, performance—because two individuals are unlikely to have had similar prior experience. The inclusion of a constant to reflect asymptotic performance in the function points to the level of error (and hence task difficulty) that would be expected when the individual reaches their optimal level of performance. Once again this may vary across individuals, because there is unlikely to be sufficient practice for all individuals to reach optimal performance. Notice also that when considering performance in terms of errors, this asymptotic level may be zero, but were we instead to measure performance in terms of time, this would not be zero, but closer to the maximum speed of the muscles and limbs involved in performance. Finally, the power function need not be based on performance on a single trial, but may also be used with cumulative data. Stevens and Savin (1962) suggest using cumulative data more appropriate for continuous response tasks where division into trials is arbitrary and performance is measured on a momentary basis. There other advantages, especially where one wishes to compare across individuals or acquisition of sub-tasks within a larger task, as taking the slope and intercept of cumulative data reduces variability. Given these advantages, it is reassuring that Newell and Rosenbloom (1981) show that cumulative power function is a conventional power law equation.

## Implications and interpretations of power law learning

Mazur and Hastie (1978) suggest that it is the accumulation of segments of performance that is the basis of how learning proceeds. A point worth making is that this accumulated segmented or "episodic" knowledge of task performance may reflect performance that is good or bad, appropriate or inappropriate. The strong implication of accounts of learning which suggest that it is "exponential" is that new task knowledge "replaces" old task knowledge, while power- or hyperbolic-function accounts assume that previous histories of positive and negative outcomes remain available (see Restle & Greeno, 1970, for contrast between exponential and hyperbolic accounts of learning by Hull, 1943, and Tolman, 1919, respectively). Among other problems, the notion that previously unsuccessful attempts are replaced, does not allow behaviour to revert to a less sophisticated level of performance where the performer is under stress, fatigued, or otherwise in a sub-optimal state.

The fact that a power law relationship between amount of practice and level of performance has been widely demonstrated, especially for relatively simple skills, has encouraged researchers to offer a variety of explanations of why this relationship exists. One account suggests that performance as it becomes more practised gradually reflects not the improvement of single components but the grouping (or "chunking") of performance, leading skilled behaviour to be based on larger organisations of components than unskilled behaviour (e.g. Newell, 1990; Newell & Rosenbloom, 1981). Another account suggests that with practice knowledge is converted from a slow format (declarative knowledge) to a faster format (i.e. procedural knowledge), the usability of procedural knowledge itself speeding up with practice (Anderson, 1993). Others suggest that increased practice provides the performer with a greater range of experience from which to select the appropriate behaviour subsequently (e.g. Logan, 1988). These and other explanations of why power law relationships between skill and practice are observed have implications for how we should train. Before considering these implications and other explanations of the power law relationship, it is worth looking more closely at practice and how differences in the way it is comprised influence learning and retention.

## VARIETIES OF PRACTICE

Extensive practice is an essential prerequisite for developing expertise on a task. Detailed analyses of skills such as chess playing, ballet, and piano playing among many others show that what was once thought to be due to a superabundance of some particular talent, in reality results from an unusual degree of commitment and extended and highly deliberate practice over more than a decade (see Ericsson & Charness, 1994, and Ericsson & Lehmann, 1996 for extended reviews). It is important to recognise that practice is more than merely repetition of some activity previously performed. However, matters are more complicated than that, as the distribution and difficulty of practice are also variables that influence the skill level people attain. Since the early work of Ebbinghaus (1885/ 1964) researchers have distinguished between situations where repetition of to-be-learned items in which identical items are adjacent to each other within practice episodes (i.e. "massed" practice), and situations where encounters with identical items are separated by interpolated to-be-learned items, or time (i.e. "spaced" or "distributed" practice). Although the effects have not been consistently observed in every study, it is generally thought that massed practice leads to more rapid acquisition, but also less durable retention and extension or transfer beyond those trials encountered during training. Distributed practice, on the other hand, usually results in less rapid improvements in performance during training, but, ultimately, learning that is both more durable and more likely to positively transfer to other situations (see Groeger, 1997). As with Schmidt and Bjork (1992), I suggest that what really reflects learning is what we retain from training, not how well we do during training (i.e. rate of acquisition is less important that quantity/quality of retention).

## Massed, spaced, and distributed practice

In the studies reviewed by both Mazur and Hastie (1978) and Stevens and Savin (1962), those that had breaks in performance tended to show intercepts, slopes, and asymptotic values which suggest more effective learning than studies where practice was continuous—even when the numbers of practice trials were similar. Within-session periods of respite from performance also lead to improvements, as has been shown by Kolers and Duchnicky (1985). They found, in a task where subjects had to read aloud geometrically transformed text from pages, that subjects' reading increased in speed, page on page, irrespective of the page length.[5] In contrast, improvements on a line-by-line basis were not evident within pages. This was the case irrespective of whether people read one page of each of several kinds of transformation each day, or read several pages of a single transformation. Actual pause duration (0–36 seconds) had no effect on performance, and indeed although Kolers and Duchnicky do not make the point explicitly themselves, the log–log slopes where subjects read pages of inverted text within a single session (−0.353) and where subjects read similar material over successive days (−0.400) were very similar. This suggests that the size of intervals between practice of particular tasks has little effect. To me this implies that neither fatigue nor boredom underlie these effects—that is, spaced practice allows something other than, or as well as, recovery to take place.

In the cases where subjects read pages of transformed text on successive days, each daily session involved reading text in a range of different orientations. The mixed nature of the text transformations subjects performed also seemed to have little effect on the speed of reading. This implies that there is relatively little benefit (or indeed handicap) of interleaving periods of practice of similar but different skills, a matter that, as we shall see later, has important implications

---

[5] It is worth noting that Kolers and Duchnicky's data fit well to a straight line where the time taken to read a page and the page number are transformed into logarithms, and thus reflect yet another example of power law learning.

for learning to drive. Overall the Kolers and Duchnicky (1985) results imply that the benefit of practice of reading transformed text in a particular orientation is confined to that orientation and not to reading of transformed text operations in general. Kolers and Duchnicky suggest that improvement occurs on a page-by-page basis, but not within pages, because "skill was acquired in a continuous way as a direct function of exercise, but the enhanced skill was expressed discontinuously" (1985, p. 668), and that "the effects of practice do not accrue directly or automatically to a skilled action, rather, the effects of practice cumulate and then as a separate event are transferred for application to a previously segmented task unit" (p. 672). The period of respite, whether it is filled with some other operation (i.e. distributed practice), or not, allows what has already been learned to be applied to an upcoming situation. But it is only applied when what has been learned is similar to what has to be done in that upcoming situation. Thus the Kolers and Duchnicky study helps us to clarify a number of issues, but leaves others tantalisingly unresolved.

The Kolers and Duchnicky work suggests that the benefit from pauses in practice comes about, not because it allows a period of rest or recuperation (although of course in massed practice situations it may also have this benefit), but because it "segments" experience and allows what has been learned in one segment to be applied in another. Second, the power function relationship of performance to practice holds where performance is continuous or discontinuous, and more surprisingly, whether this discontinuity in practice is caused by a pause or by performance of some other task matters little to the shape of the learning function.

## Continuous, distributed practice and the development of driving skill

Our own analyses of the rate at which driving skill is acquired (as indexed by the reduction in instruction provided by an accompanying teacher, Groeger & Clegg, 2000a, or the errors made in observed lessons, Groeger & Brady, 1998), appear to make similar points.

First, it is clear that, whether the index used is the number of comments delivered by an accompanying instructor (Groeger & Brady, 1998; Groeger & Clegg, 2000a) or the number of errors the pupil is observed to make during lessons (Groeger & Brady, 1998), the level of skill of the pupil is determined in part by how much driving experience the pupil has had up to that point. Second, this relationship between skill and practice is a power law, again irrespective of the skill-index used. Third, as Groeger and Clegg (2000a) show, in their observational study of the complete learning-to-drive experience of some 20 teenagers, each individual driver's skill level at any point depends on how much practice they have previously had. Fourth, this power law relationship between skill and practice is also seen at the level of individual manoeuvres. The relationship between previous practice and performance of a particular manoeuvre is more

TABLE 5.1
Correlations between rates of progress on driving manoeuvres
(progress determined by rate of reduction in instructor's comments)

| | AC | LC | RC | AR | LR | RR | AT | LT | RT | AB | AP |
|---|---|---|---|---|---|---|---|---|---|---|---|
| Ahead at crossroads (AC) | — | | | | | | | | | | |
| Left at crossroads (LC) | .60** | — | | | | | | | | | |
| Right at crossroads (RC) | .66** | .83** | — | | | | | | | | |
| Ahead at roundabout (AR) | .58** | .78** | .70** | — | | | | | | | |
| Left at roundabout (LR) | .73** | .70** | .81** | .82** | — | | | | | | |
| Right at roundabout (RR) | .25 | .51* | .68** | .43 | .66** | — | | | | | |
| Ahead at T-junction (AT) | .30 | .51* | .50* | .49* | .52* | .49* | — | | | | |
| Left at T-junction (LT) | .56* | .87** | .85** | .81** | .78** | .74** | .49* | — | | | |
| Right at T-junction (RT) | .68** | .82** | .90** | .69** | .78** | .65** | .40 | .89** | — | | |
| Ahead on bend (AB) | .40 | .20 | .25 | .35 | .39 | .22 | .17 | .31 | .18 | — | |
| Ahead near others (AP) | .29 | .27 | .30 | .49* | .32 | .07 | .18 | .36 | .27 | .60** | — |

evident where the number of previous manoeuvres of a particular type (e.g. turning right at a roundabout), rather than the amount of driving in general, is used as the index of prior practice. This suggests rather limited transfer of learning between manoeuvres of different types—a suggestion borne out by the correlations between rates of skill acquisition for various manoeuvres[6] (see Table 5.1).

The rates of learning of individual manoeuvres, such as turning right at various types of junction, are quite high, but not very reliably related to driving ahead at those junctions or elsewhere. This suggests transfer may be taking place between and within turning at different types of junction, but learning to drive ahead at these junctions and driving ahead in other circumstances are quite separate. Thus driving not only requires multiple functions (e.g. steering, speed control, gear changing, interpreting the road ahead, navigation, etc.) to be performed, but there is a continuous stream of quite different tasks to be performed from one situation to another as we drive along.

The nature of the driving task is such that two identical manoeuvres will virtually never follow each other directly, thus the pupil is performing under conditions more akin to Kolers and Duchnicky's distributed practice conditions. Extrapolating from their results, because the task is continuous, what is learned on one manoeuvre within a lesson will probably not be applied very reliably to another manoeuvre within the same lesson. It would be fascinating to study empirically the development of driving skills where each manoeuvre was punctuated with a brief rest period, and theoretically important to assess whether in a continuous distributed practice situation learning does actually transfer within

---

[6] These are correlations between each individual driver's learning rate for the manoeuvres concerned.

sessions, rather than merely across sessions as Kolers and Duchnicky's results imply. Because driving tasks do not all impose the same level of demand on the driver (as discussed in the previous chapter), it is unlikely that one complex driving manoeuvre will immediately be followed by another difficult but different manoeuvre—usually there is a period of simpler driving ahead between the two (e.g. driving straight ahead between junctions). It is conceivable that simple tasks function as "pauses", allowing more time for learners to set themselves for the next difficult task, and thus parse and store the results of complex "segments" of a complex stream of activity. This suggests that interspersing practice of easy skills between practice of difficult skills, rather than actually pausing, might allow the latter to progress more rapidly than if all of the skills practised are difficult.

Picking up a point made earlier with regard to the shape of the learning curve observed when pupils learn to drive, our extensive study of the instruction given to pupils when learning to drive shows that the amount of instruction given reduces as a function of the number of times a pupil has performed a particular manoeuvre, and on the task as a whole as a function of the amount of driving done (Groeger & Clegg, 2000a). If instead we assess performance by noting the errors pupils make, we again observe the power function relationship (Groeger & Brady, 1998). This demonstrates that even with highly complex skills like driving, which are acquired over a long period of time with distributed but virtually randomly constituted practice, the power law of learning holds. Before this research, Mazur and Hastie (1978, p. 1258) concluded that:

> In the replacement model the replacement process is assumed to occur at a constant rate, and in the accumulation model the size of t (i.e. amount of training) is assumed to be a constant function of the amount or duration of study. This constant-rate condition implies that the models will not apply when learning to perform the experimental task which involves mastering several distinct subtasks (e.g. stimulus learning, response learning, and stimulus–response hook-up in paired associate learning [McGuire, 1961] or the change from receiving words to receiving phrases in telegraphy [Bryan & Harter, 1897]). The constant-rate condition also seems to rule out application of the models in the cases where subjects' motivational levels can be expected to fluctuate significantly.

Our research on driving forced a revision of this conclusion, demonstrating the robustness and ubiquity of the power law relationship.

Our findings also indicate that, just as Kolers shows for reading transformed text, progress on individual tasks proceeds as a power function of the experience the pupil has had of each task or manoeuvre, albeit at different rates depending on the intrinsic difficulty of the sub-tasks concerned, but overall progress in driving ability across the whole task is also a power function, despite its being composed of elements that change at different rates.

This raises an issue of what is happening when the same training experience is repeated, and how these accumulated experiences facilitate our performance in novel circumstances. That is, we need to know about both the progress made during learning, and the transfer to different tasks. Issues of transfer will be returned to later. But before doing so, I want to examine another way of addressing the massed–distributed practice issue, which since the work of Shea and Morgan (1979) has been termed "contextual interference".

## Contextual interference

In a laboratory study, Shea and Morgan (1979) had people touch each of six blocks in one of three sequences—the sequences being shown to subjects in diagrammatic form before each trial began. During each session subjects performed 18 trials of each sequence. These trials were either blocked, so that the 18 trials for one sequence were performed before trials with the next sequence were begun (low contextual interference), or mixed, so that trials with each sequence were randomised across the session (high contextual interference).

Shea and Morgan's findings are represented in Figure 5.2, taken from Groeger (1997). Subjects performed the task more quickly where the sequences were blocked, although by the sixth session both groups were performing equally well. Retention of what was learned was also assessed, having subjects perform the same sequences, either in blocked trials with the same sequences, or intermixed trials of the same sequences. Those who learned with blocked trials of the same sequence performed better when tested with blocked trials than when they were confronted with mixed trials at test. Those who learned in mixed conditions performed well when tested in mixed conditions, just as we might expect on the basis of the transfer-appropriate processing principle. However, those who learned under mixed trial conditions also performed very well when tested under blocked conditions, suggesting that these subjects were better able to generalise what they learned to new test situations. As Figure 5.2 also makes clear, in general, retention deteriorates as the time between learning and testing increases. Once again, however, there is an exception to this general rule: Those who learn under blocked trial conditions, who are initially tested under blocked trial conditions, and who are then tested again, ten days later, under blocked conditions appear to improve. It may be that what is happening here is that people actually become better at being tested, given practice, where the tests used are consistent, but not where trials are randomised. It would be intriguing to re-run this study, but this time varying and controlling the order of blocks between learning and testing to see how robust the effect of being re-tested actually is; and also to extend testing for those who learned under mixed conditions to still more demanding test circumstances (e.g. using novel but similar stimuli) to assess the limits of the increased generalisability of knowledge acquired through distributed practice. Two explanations for these contextual interference results have been proposed.

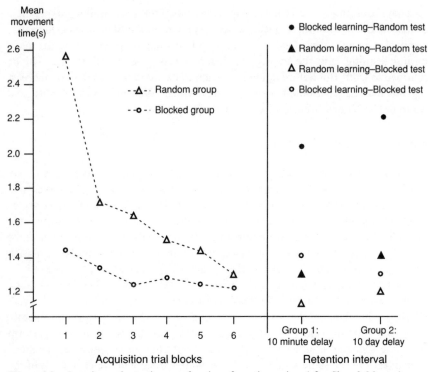

**Figure 5.2.**   Learning and retention as a function of practice regime (after Shea & Morgan).

On the one hand, authors such as Einstein and Hunt (1980) and Shea and Zimny (1983, 1988) favour what is termed an "elaboration hypothesis". They suggest that practice can make use of intra-task knowledge, which does not make reference to extant knowledge structures, or inter-task knowledge, which enables the learner to incorporate new task information with existing knowledge. Blocked, massed, or uninterrupted repetitions of the same action or event, i.e. low contextual interference, discourages use of inter-task knowledge. During high contextual interference learning, learners encode what is learned in a more elaborate fashion, integrating it with knowledge previously acquired in other circumstances.

An alternative explanation is that during blocked practice, the same working memory representation of the task is used, with the result that learners gain less experience at switching between tasks and/or rapidly retrieving the responses appropriate to different tasks. Random practice, on the other hand, allows extensive retrieval practice that occurs as a result of a continual interchange of task information in working memory from trial to trial (Schneider, Healy, Ericsson, & Bourne, 1995). To perform under such circumstances, the learner must reconstruct an action-plan from the information available from long-term memory and information currently available from the current context. This practice at "reconstructing" the task confers benefits when retention is assessed (Lee & Magill, 1985).

Immink and Wright (1998) have recently sought to test these hypotheses. In their studies subjects were required to type each of three sequences 18 times. Sequences were either practised in 18 trail blocks, where one and only one sequence was performed within a block (blocked practice), or performance of six of each sequence was required with each block (random practice). Acquisition was tested 24 hours later, by requiring a block of three of each sequence to be typed. Immink and Wright's results showed that people who experienced random or mixed practice used more study time between responses during acquisition, and when free to use as much study time as they wished, performed as well as subjects whose acquisition practice was blocked. These results support the idea that more time is required when acquisition occurs within a mixed or distributed practice regime, in order to reach a particular criterion, rather than more practice per se. The results also suggest that the widely reported benefit to retention of distributed practice acquisition (or high contextual interference) stems in part from the additional practice people have had at response retrieval and planning.

However, although their account of their results is very plausible, Immink and Wright do not test the reconstruction hypothesis directly, in that they do not show that the additional time required is actually used for response planning, nor that improved retrieval skills, rather than more a elaborate knowledge base, underlie the retention advantage of those who learn under random practice conditions. Nevertheless, these and other results discussed here show that amount of practice alone does not account for the rates at which skill is acquired.

## Section summary

Practice is fundamental to acquiring skill, and to the competence with which we perform tasks once training has ceased. What the foregoing text makes clear is that practice is much more than the simple repetition of the same activity, and differences in practice regimes can have profound effects on how quickly we learn, and how well we retain what we have learned. The circumstances under which practice occurs, in terms of gaps between repetitions or the interpolation of other activities, are also important factors. Spacing, i.e. "pauses" or gaps between iterations, leads to more rapid learning, and on the basis of the current evidence at least, it appears that this is more effective than simply changing the task people do. However, interpolating a variety of to-be-learned tasks, while of dubious value in terms of the rate of acquisition, appears to confer real advantages when we assess how well people have retained the knowledge gained during training. Why this is so is much less clear, and an important issue for further study. However, the fact that the power law relationship between amount of practice and rate of acquisition holds, almost however that practice is built up, suggests that quantity of practice is the more important determinant, and may imply something very fundamental indeed about what skill acquisition actually involves.

## STAGES IN THE ACQUISITION OF SKILL

Two of the most cited accounts of how people develop skills stress a tripartite separation of "stages". Fitts (1962), and later Fitts (1964) and Fitts and Posner (1967), refer to these stages as "cognitive", "associative", and "autonomous", whereas Anderson (1982) refers to very similar stages as "declarative", "knowledge compilation", and "procedural". An excellent recent article by Posner et al. (1997) has sought to explore the neurological bases of such differences in levels of skill.

Both approaches see the initial stage as heavily dependent on expressible or expressed verbal accounts of what is required. Performance is relatively unstable as possible strategies are tested and discarded, and easily interfered with where distractions are present. The second stages envisaged by Fitts and Anderson differ considerably in the language used to describe them, but the common characteristic is that verbal mediation of performance is much reduced, and that associations strengthen between eliciting conditions and the actions they require. Performance is still subject to disruption through distraction or consideration of alternative sources of action, but is faster and more reliable. The final stage is "automatic", according to Fitts, in the sense that verbal mediation of performance, even accurate verbal description of performance, is no longer required or possible. It is also effortless, and highly consistent. The original Fitts framework has been a useful heuristic for researchers and trainers alike for the best part of four decades, but I consider that it is Anderson's framework, as well as rather different conceptions offered by Logan (1988) and MacKay (1982), that merit more close consideration here.

Anderson's (1983) ACT* theory, and the revised account ACT-R (see Anderson, 1993), specifies a fixed computational architecture that applies to all cognitive tasks. Within ACT* skilled behaviour is seen as procedural in nature, and assumes that the procedures used are derived from declarative or factual knowledge of a domain. Declarative knowledge is a semantic network of facts about items within a domain, which an individual learns when he or she first encounters a new domain. In order to perform tasks within this domain, the learner must use this knowledge together with general problem-solving strategies. Productions, i.e. condition–action rules, are formed on the basis of the outcomes of the application of these general strategies to domain-specific knowledge. The same declarative knowledge and the same general strategies, applied to different circumstances, will result in different productions being formed which support the different uses of the same knowledge. The derivation of such productions though association of declarative knowledge and general problem-solving strategy is the main purpose of the Knowledge Compilation stage. Once formed, procedures are triggered, and thoughts or action result, only when certain highly specific criteria are met. The outcome of repeated use of the same production is proceduralisation. The original assumption was that the declarative knowledge acquired was initially used to support performance, but became independent of actual performance, and changed minimally as the performer became more skilled.

Anderson himself concedes that as originally presented the ACT* version of his theoretical framework appeared to suggest that "all knowledge first came into the system in a declarative form" (Anderson & Fincham, 1994, p. 1322). As originally envisaged, declarative memory for instructions was the essential feature of the declarative stage. Anderson and colleagues now suggest that what is important is declarative memory for examples of how the procedures should be implemented. The point is also now made that what is required is that this is active in working memory, not that the declarative knowledge is permanent and retrievable in long-term memory. As we shall see later, when discussing transfer of learning, Anderson's revision of ACT*, ACT-R, also emphasises rather more the suggestion that declarative knowledge actually changes, becoming more elaborate, during learning (Anderson, 1993).

Anderson's view assumes that repeated use of particular productions serves to strengthen that production, the strengthening being reflected in the rapidity with which the production's eliciting conditions are detected, and the ease, i.e. consistency and speed, with which the production is implemented. The framework advocated by MacKay (1982) shares with Anderson the notion that repeated practice leads to strengthening, but differs in that MacKay assumes a hierarchical organisation within skilled activity. That is, an activity can be decomposed into constituent units, activities that comprise some or all of the same constituents, are associated with each other, and more or less independent of activities comprising different components. Repeated use of certain components results in their connections to superordinate activities being strengthened. As a result, activities that share some components also increase in strength, even though the whole activity was not itself performed. Similar principles operate at higher levels of the system, such that future use is made more likely, and performance made more consistent, of related elements and activities. MacKay's formulation shares much with the multi-layered network models of (cognitive) activity advanced by Rumelhart and McClelland (1986).

Within MacKay's framework, the consistent strengthening of particular element combinations would result in the formation of higher-level units, which are responsive to high degrees of consistent information, and relatively impervious to small amounts of incidental departures from the higher-level unit. Such higher-level units would be almost indistinguishable from the common notion of a schema. More complex units are also formed as a function of repeated practice in Anderson's framework, but these reflect combinations of productions that are consistently used together, but which are increasingly tuned to operate in specific circumstances, rather than becoming involved in an increasingly broad range of circumstances. It is worth contrasting the implications of MacKay's view of what constitutes a hierarchical system. Some, for example Broadbent (1977) and Sternberg, Knoll, and Turock (1990), when theorising about differences between hierarchical and non-hierarchical systems, have proposed that in truly hierarchical systems changes in elements at one level will not affect elements at a different level of a hierarchy. In contrast, MacKay's view is that levels of the hierarchy strengthen each other. Thus there is a sense in which his is not a hierarchical framework. Anderson's ACT*, on the other hand, originally recognised a discontinuity between changes at the procedural level and at the declarative level—ACT* is a hierarchical system. Both seek to explain the negatively associated gain from practice as the learner gains experience of a domain, in MacKay's case through hierarchical strengthening, and in Anderson's case through composition of productions.

Be they hierarchical or not, both the Anderson and the MacKay frameworks assume that repeated exposure to the same circumstance leads to the strengthening of some representation, or a change to a new representational format, rather than to the formation of separate or distinct representations, which is the basis of Logan's (1988) instance theory.[7] For Logan, as indeed for Anderson, performance in some new domain or on some new task depends on the use of generic problem-solving strategies, which Logan refers to as "algorithms". The outcome of the application of the algorithm leads to the formation of a memory trace (an "instance"). The next time a similar situation is encountered, the algorithm is again initiated, but a search also ensues for some instance of past experience that is appropriate to the task at hand. Whichever operation delivers a result first will form the basis of the action taken. This race between retrieval and algorithm will always occur, but increasingly, as experience is gained, instance-retrieval, rather than *de novo* resolution of some demand, will be reflected in behaviour. Adding of instances through practice increases the likelihood of this occurring, but the return from doing so diminishes—the average amount of reduction in response time with added instances progressively declines, resulting in a power-function change in response time. Logan's theory is essentially one of how episodic memory supports skilled behaviour. Although he does not deal much with whether or how instances are organised, I presume this must follow what we understand about the organisation of episodic memory in general. As such, even though he assumes that memory retrieval is parallel and automatic, organisation must surely contribute to retrieval efficacy. It is worth noting that Pashler supports this view,

---

[7] I assume here that some segmentation of experience is essential for the formation of separate instances, be these "pauses" in otherwise continuous experience, or interpolation of different experiences.

up to the point where Logan advocates parallelism within the system, suggesting that the latter is not a necessary aspect of instance theory (see Pashler, 1998). This, and the issue of what is stored in an instance will be returned to in Chapter 6.

Thus, there are at least three dimensions along which we can consider the development of skill: (1) the extent to which behaviour relies on specific performance episodes or generic knowledge formed from such instances; (2) the extent to which performance relies on previous outcomes or some amalgam of previous outcomes of performing in a similar situation, or instead on the application of generic (i.e. non-domain-specific) procedures; and (3) the amount of prior experience the performer has had. Posner et al. (1997) offer a different perspective on differences between people with different levels of skill. Seeing practice and priming as different sides of the same coin, they propose four alternative accounts of what differs between skilled and unskilled performers. Skill acquisition may result in better connections between the brain areas required to perform the task; the brain areas involved may be increased in size or number; different brain areas are activated in the novice and expert when performing the "same" task, resulting in more efficient performance; and there may be differences in the brain circuits activated when performing familiar and unfamiliar tasks. More prosaically, these suggestions imply that skilled and unskilled performers differ because the former are: doing the same task but in a more automated and co-ordinated fashion; performing the same task but with improved efficiency of components of the task; performing the same task but in a different way; and performing a different task. The exciting aspect of this proposal is that Posner and colleagues claim that these alternatives should result in different brain activity, and thus should be distinguishable using brain imaging. As yet there is little decisive evidence as to which view best accounts for the data, but we may be at a point where skill researchers can move on from a re-working of the ideas Fitts and Posner presented over three decades ago.

## TRANSFER OF ACQUIRED SKILL

Thorndike (1906) among others argued that an individual in a new situation will benefit from previous experience to the extent that the new and old situations share stimulus–response associations. In contrast, early Gestalt theorists (Judd, 1908) suggested that transfer occurs to the extent that situations share a "deep structural relationship". Anderson's (1983) ACT* and ACT-R (1993), which is deeply associationist, is the overwhelmingly dominant view. Based on this account, Singley and Anderson (1989) proposed that transfer depends on "common elements", i.e. that a procedure learned in one part of a domain will not be used in another part of the domain unless the conditions of use of the procedures are identical in the two cases. Anderson (1987), amplifying his earlier view, stresses that what is learned with training and practice is not knowledge per se, but a particular use of that knowledge, i.e. acquired knowledge is "use-specific".

Even though sub-skills within a complex task rest on the same body of declarative knowledge, this theory predicts that there will be little or no transfer between the sub-skills of a task where the knowledge on which both are based are used in different ways, and that transfer will depend almost entirely on overlap in constituents of the productions that have been compiled (Anderson, 1987; Singley & Anderson, 1989). However, while there is substantial evidence in favour of this position, there is a small but growing body of research that does find transfer between dissimilar tasks (see for example the similarity and dissimilarity of learning rates for different driving manoeuvres presented in Table 5.2).

## Verbal mediation versus production similarity

A number of studies suggest that verbal mediation, rather than production similarity, mediates transfer. For example, little learning and transfer occurs in physics and programming problem solving unless the student "self explains" from examples presented during the acquisition of declarative knowledge (Chi & Van Lehn, 1991),[8] while Meyer (1989) found that a "conceptual model" increased creative problem solving by 64% transfer. Similarly, Brown (1990) and Lewis (1988) conclude that conceptual understanding of the domain is essential to flexible and creative transfer. To some extent, these conclusions were somewhat premature, as it is not clear that transfer could have occurred in any way other than on the basis of some declarative or generic problem-solving strategies, because it is unclear whether the acquired and transfer tasks actually did share the same underlying declarative knowledge.

Summarising the position, Pennington, Nicolich, and Rahm (1995, p. 219) conclude that:

> when tasks share overlapping goal structures and many production rule elements, production rule analysis of overlap does a good job of predicting transfer of training. However, then [sic] tasks do not share overlapping goal structures or many production rules, production rule analysis does not do a good job of predicting transfer, but there is still transfer.... feedback and the declarative knowledge which results from feedback will be critical in determining the amount of sub-task transfer.

Transfer therefore is not simply limited to situations in which the same actions, processes, or productions are required, although the basis for transfer at higher levels does appear somewhat different. Indeed, in the absence of a procedural similarity, the application of inappropriate declarative knowledge may help to account for negative transfer, which otherwise the Anderson framework has difficulty in dealing with.

---

[8] There is a possible parallel here with the "commentary drive" technique used by some driving instructors.

## Experience during practice and limits on generalisation

Masson (1986) reports a study in which people were required to read typo-graphically transformed text. Subjects were given training with words composed of one half of the alphabet, the other letters not being used during training. In order to assess learning, subjects were presented with words that had occurred earlier in the training phase, new words composed of previously encountered transformed letters, and words not previously encountered made up from letters that had not been encountered in their transformed form. New and old words made up from previously encountered transformed letters were read faster than words made up from previously unseen letters, with previously read words being read faster. Words made from previously unseen letters were read slowly, and showed no evidence of transfer from the training session. Masson interprets this result as supporting the instance view, which assumes that transformed letters and words were individually represented. Although previously encountered text was indeed read faster, the fact that new words made from familiar letters were read more slowly than previously seen words suggests to me that both letter- and word-based information was stored. As only words were encountered, only words should have been stored as instances. However, what Masson's study does show is how limited transfer actually is—people were not developing some general competence at reading transformed text, but only a facility for re-reading what they had already encountered. It is unlikely that the transfer is mediated by changes at a declarative level.

The way that practice is constituted also has a considerable impact on transfer. Koh and Meyer (1991) report a study in which subjects were required to produce temporal judgements which reflected the separation of two visually presented stimuli. In all, subjects experienced 12 different separations of the visual stimuli, but only received feedback on the four smallest and four largest separations. The estimates for the transfer points fell directly on the same power function as those more extreme points that had been encountered during train-ing. It thus seems as if participants were able to generalise beyond the specific examples encountered during training, at least when the new examples encountered during the test phase were from the same range as those encountered during training.

An earlier study by Catalano and Kleiner (1984) showed similar effects, and helps to isolate the conditions under which such transfer might be expected. In this study, subjects watched an object moving at the equivalent of 5, 7, 9, 11 mph. The task was to press a button when the object reached a particular point. Some subjects trained on just one speed (i.e. constant speed training), while another group made decisions about each of the four speeds during the learning phase (i.e. variable speed training). By the end of the learning session, the con-stant group were responding significantly more accurately than the variable speed group (average error of interception times: 38 ms versus 52 ms). However, when both groups were tested on a new set of speeds not encountered during the learning phase (i.e. 1, 3, 13, 15 mph), those who encountered more speeds during training were able to respond more accurately (50 ms) than those who had practised on just one speed (60 ms). These results suggest that what subjects learn in the constant speed training group is rather more restricted than what is learned by the variable speed group. This gives the latter group an advantage when the performance required of them lies outside the range of experiences they have had during learning. Taken together, these two studies show that transfer of training depends on the composition and variability of prior practice, as predicted in Schmidt's (1988) schema theory (but see van Rossum, 1990).

The difficulty of what is practised also impacts on learning and transfer. Doane, Alderton, Sohn, and Pellegrino (1996) report a series of studies which investigate the development of visual discrimination skills. Those who encounter easy discriminations early in training perform better than those who are required to make difficult discriminations early in practice. However when, later in training, more difficult discriminations are required of those participants who had only made easy discriminations, performance deteriorated considerably, whereas the other group performed very well on easy discriminations. Doane and colleagues interpret these results as showing that "initial difficult discrimination leads to the development of a precise comparison strategy . . . this strategy can be compromised if participants are exposed to easier discriminations, but will return again when the task becomes more difficult . . . in contrast easy-first discrimination training leads to the development of a less precise comparison strategy, which can be modified if completely new difficult discrimination stimuli are viewed" (1996, p. 1240). This modification requires practice, and even after substantial practice performance was still inferior to those whose first training session required difficult discriminations. However, while initially demanding training is beneficial, this is not necessarily the case for all tasks. In a further study, Doane and colleagues showed that when asked to judge the familiarity of familiar and unfamiliar figures, the hard discrimination group were much more likely to falsely recognise slightly altered figures as familiar.

Together these studies suggest a degree of use-specificity in what is being learned, albeit that there is transfer a little beyond the events that took place during training. They also raise the possibility that well learned skills can negatively impact on new tasks. This partly bears out Lane's (1987, p. 15) surmise that "too much training time results in inefficient training but rarely to a loss of retention; too much practice and the associated over-learning of task-specific skills can actually reduce transfer".

With regard to driving, and especially learning to drive, the findings from studies of transfer of training suggest that training drivers on actual roads, rather than under more simplified track or simulator conditions, offers the best chance of learners transferring what they have learned during training to the situations they will later encounter when driving alone. The variety of sub-tasks that comprise driving lead to a level of difficulty that results in slower acquisition than might be possible were components practised separately, but this difficulty may actually result in far greater transfer across situations. Finally, the frequent instructor available from an accompanying instructor may, almost accidentally, provide the verbal mediation that is required for transfer where two manoeuvres are rather dissimilar in terms of the operations, activities, or what Anderson would term "productions" required of the pupil.

## INSTRUCTION AND FEEDBACK

Declarative knowledge occupies a crucial place in Anderson's ideas of how skills develop. In the case of driving, which most pupils learn in declaratively rich circumstances, instruction provides both a broad description of the tasks to be performed, action-specific "how-to" information, and feedback, some of which serves a motivational function and some of which fine-tunes actions. How pupils would progress without the scaffolding and guidance this provides is impossible to know. A range of different types of study can help us appreciate how instruction and feedback can influence the acquisition of driving skills.

Thorndike (1932) noted that the reinforcing effects of knowledge of results (i.e. KR) in strengthening the stimulus–response bond were best served when KR was provided as close to the relevant response and on as many occasions as possible. In actual fact, it was subsequently shown that strict temporal contiguity between performance and feedback can be violated without detrimental effects on learning, provided that the interval between response and feedback is not filled with other activities (Lorge & Thorndike, 1935). Bilodeau and Bilodeau (1958) independently varied the interval between response and KR and post-KR delay. They demonstrated that delay of KR as such was of no consequence, and also that rate of learning was directly proportional to the absolute number of trials on which KR was provided. More recent research has served to qualify these general principles.

For motor skills, when performance is evaluated by a long-term retention test, individuals who received more or better KR perform best during acquisition, but typically perform worse during retention than individuals who receive less useful KR or have KR gradually withdrawn during practice (see Schmidt, Young, Swinnen, & Shapiro, 1989). The explanation for this is that less detailed KR, and the gradual withdrawal of KR, encourage the performer to rely more on task-intrinsic feedback for the remainder of the training period. As observed by Schmidt et al. (1989), these results suggest that KR is essential for initial guidance, but at some point during learning it can produce a kind of dependency. Much earlier, Annett and Kay (1957) pointed out that the provision of temporary KR is only of value if the trainee can subsequently get all the information needed from cues that are intrinsic to the task.

Another of the drawbacks of extensive immediate feedback is that it may mask, or distract the learner's attention away from the task-intrinsic cues that can continue to be used to guide behaviour long after formal training has ended (see Boldovici, 1987; Kincade, 1963). Recent work suggests that it is very important to consider what we are expecting the learner to learn from the feedback we provide. Studying subjects' ability to make sinusoidal movements, Wulf, Schmidt, and Deubel (1993) distinguish between how feedback influences the development of a more general understanding of a whole movement pattern, and what they refer to as parametrerisation; that is, the "tuning" of specific aspects of performance. They show quite conclusively that learning the general movement was better with intermittent feedback (63% of trials), but learning of the timing and force of movements was better when feedback was given after each trial. Identifying ways of systematically removing such feedback, without reducing the level of performance, is the key issue in research on "fading". However, this is an area where there is relatively little human research. On the basis of animal learning models, it would seem that making feedback unpredictable, but not removing it completely, could be sufficient to maintain performance. By increasing the lag between feedback, the learner can be weaned away from knowledge of results on which they would otherwise become dependent (see Patrick, 1992, for further discussion).

A final point that must be made regarding the acquisition of driving skills is that the purpose of formal training is to produce people with a minimum level of proficiency. It is thus criterion-referenced, rather than specifically related to the progress or speed of progress pupils make. As such, it is akin to "mastery level training" (Bloom, 1974), in which the time taken to acquire the skill, rather than the level of proficiency achieved, is the primary concern of the trainer. This is also probably true of driving as a whole, where people drive well enough to accomplish their task but do not strive after continual improvement towards some "gold standard" or "mastery" (see Hancock & Scallen, 1999).

## SUMMARY

When people learn to drive, they develop a measure of proficiency at a number of different skills, rather than one single skill: "driving". They do so as a function of the amount of practice or supervised experience they have. There is a degree of transfer between what is learned from one situation to another, and that which is observed appears to be based on the similarity of functions or sub-tasks drivers must perform in those situations. However, because a substantial amount of instruction given in these situations is not specific to these situations, actually being almost indistinguishable between certain manoeuvres, it is possible that this transfer occurs through declarative similarity rather than functional similarity. Despite the transfer that is observed, the major factor underlying progress is the amount of experience the learner has of that particular type of situation, rather than of driving in general. This has clear implications for the way we train drivers: we must ensure that learners gain sufficient time-on-task experience in all the aspects of driving at which we wish them to be proficient. We must also realise that drivers may be closer to competence on some manoeuvres rather than others, simply because some tasks are easier than others. Continually practising those that the pupil does well, and neglecting those on which he or she is improving more slowly, is obviously detrimental.

There is another implication from these results. The nature of the driving task, being continuous and composed of a sequence of driving manoeuvres of different levels of difficulty and which make different requirements of the driver, means that the practice regime that normally operates when people learn to drive is one of highly distributed practice of mixed-difficulty operations. On the basis of the literature reviewed earlier, this is actually a very powerful, if slow, way of acquiring a complex skill, and retaining what has been learned. However, this method of learning to drive, in which the vast majority of time during training is spent on the road, which is more common in Europe than in the US, has developed by accident, rather than by design. There is scope for improving the effectiveness and efficiency of training, by increasing the amount and breadth of practice drivers have (e.g. at different times of the day and in different weather conditions, with and without passengers) and by making this practice more systematic (e.g. by systematically varying routes driven to optimise the mixture of demands and difficulty levels, graduated reduction of feedback and instruction, more pauses between manoeuvres or sequences of manoeuvres to allow application of what has been learned). Some of these issues are discussed in more detail in Groeger and Maycock (1999).

# CHAPTER SIX

# Memory for driving

*Although people readily attest to the experience that they have no recall of particular parts of a journey, the conclusion that performance of complex tasks depends on remembering is inescapable. In this chapter, issues such as the dependence of performance on implicit memory, recognition, and categorisation of stimuli encountered when driving are discussed. In particular, the role working memory may play in different driving tasks, more enduring memories of spatial information, and situational models are considered. So too is the fact that people forget that they have been involved in accidents, and that those not forgotten are mis-dated. This is used to illustrate the phenomenon of "temporal telescoping", and to discuss the limitations of current accounts of why temporal telescoping occurs, and memory biases can be minimised in questionnaire-based studies of accident risk.*

## MEMORIES AND REMEMBERING

Whether we remember something depends on a wide variety of factors, including the attention paid to the event, how we attempt to learn it, our previous experience of similar things, and the requirements we have for deciding that something is "remembered".

### Intention, attention and memory

Even if we are unaware that an event is occurring, suppose for example we were anaesthetised on an operating table, we may later still have isolated recollections of what occurred, or the conversations the medical team were having (see Andrade, 1995 for review). In such situations people are not merely guessing, but the wealth of exposure to hospital situations and operations on television, as well as discussion and rumination on what it will be like, all serve to establish quite specific verbal and visual memory traces which endure over long periods. Some surviving fragmentary awareness of events during the operation integrates with experience gained prior to the operation that matches these temporary memory fragments most closely. This redintegration, i.e. integration of temporary memory traces with enduring memories (e.g. Nairne, 1990), gives rise to a more complete, and sometimes reportable memory. What is reported, however, may reflect more about what was previously known than it does about the most recent experience. Nevertheless, it is clear from studies of memory and anaesthesia, as it was from laboratory-based studies in which people encountered words with or without the instruction to remember them (e.g. Hyde & Jenkins, 1973), that intention to learn something or the realisation that memory will later be tested, is not a prerequisite for remembering.

## Learning strategies and memory

Despite the fact that we can learn without intending to, learning and memory operate more effectively when the learner-rememberer has the opportunity to apply different strategies to the activities involved in learning and remembering. The systematic application of strategies requires intention, and thus attention. Mere exposure alone is unfortunately no guarantee of learning, as former colleagues Bekerian and Baddeley (1980) showed when, prior to the changing of national radio frequencies, people were unable to report the new frequencies despite what were estimated to be several thousand exposures to the new frequencies in the media and public postings (see also Hintzman, Curran, & Oppy, 1992, who showed that additional exposures to information do not necessarily benefit memory). Processing the to-be-learned information in a variety of ways, especially considering its meaning and relevance to particular aspects of the individual's life and concerns, generally leads to more durable and effective retention, i.e. levels of processing (Craik & Lockhart, 1972), as long as the way in which learning proceeds maps onto the way in which memory for that information or task is later assessed, i.e. transfer-appropriate processing (e.g. Morris, Bransford, & Franks, 1977). We have seen in the previous chapter that practice, i.e. repeated exposure to similar experiences, is a fundamental requirement for learning. The way in which this practice accrues, whether it is massed or distributed, the variety of things practised, and pauses between episodes of learning, all contribute not only to learning but to successful retention. Arguably, the benefits of distributed practice, contextual interference, and difficult-first training, all arise because of the need to attend to what is being learned where the task at hand changes, and the increased opportunity for practising retrieval of what has been learned in a variety of circumstances. Despite this emphasis on deliberate and repeated practising of learning and retrieval, it should also be borne in mind that single distinctive experiences can also be very well remembered, such as in the von Restorff effect, a matter that receives much more attention later.

## Prior experience and skilled memorising

Turning to the importance of prior experience in enabling us to learn effectively, a range of studies across different skill domains have demonstrated superior performance on the part of those skill performers. Some of the earliest findings of this sort emerged from the early work of de Groot (1966) on chess expertise. Expert and relatively unskilled players were contrasted in a number of ways. Experts, for example, shown a chess board position taken from a game for just five seconds, were able to remember 90% of the positions of pieces. Average club players, on the other hand, remembered only about half as much in the same period, and required four more five-second glances to reach the level experts achieved in a single four-second glance. Later, Lane and Robertson (1979) showed that knowing or not knowing that they would have to recall the position of pieces on the board did not affect the accuracy of recall, as long as these expert chess players had first decided on their next move. However, when the experts were performing some other task which also encouraged them to look at all the pieces and their position, such as counting the number of pieces whose colour matched the colour square on which they sat, incidental learning of chess piece position was minimal. In another study, where subjects were instructed that a recall test would follow (i.e. an intentional learning task), but where the orienting task was more or less irrelevant to the game of chess (i.e. number of pieces on matching squares), recall was substantially better (see Lane & Robertson, 1979). Similarly, incidental memory for data on patients after a medical review and diagnosis is far greater for medical experts than for medical students (Norman, Brooks, & Allen, 1989). The suggestion that incidental memory occurs where the orienting task being done mirrors some of the activities in which the learner has developed some proficiency, is further supported by a study by Chase and Simon (1973). They found that chess experts' advantage in remembering where pieces were placed is limited to those situations in which the positions of pieces were non-random and legitimate within the context of the game, and perhaps even where they were non-random. Similar results also reported for games such as Go (Reitman, 1976) and Bridge (Charness, 1979); activities such as electronics (Egan & Schwartz, 1979), computer programming (McKeithen, Reitman, Rueter, & Hirtle, 1981), and medicine (Norman et al., 1989); as well as sports and pastimes such as dance, basketball, and hockey (Allard & Starkes, 1991) and even figure skating (Deakin & Allard, 1991).

These and similar results have been interpreted within the "skilled memory" framework, proposed by Chase and Ericsson (1981) and developed further by Ericsson and Kintsch (1995). The theory attempts to explain the exceptional memory performance of both task-experts and people with exceptional memory performance (i.e. mnemonists) by claiming that such exceptional abilities reflect the use of more enduring memory rather than an expanded transient memory, but the capacity to do so is limited to specific tasks or domains. Specifically, "individuals can acquire memory skill to accommodate expanded demands for working memory in a specific task domain" (Ericsson & Kintsch, 1995, p. 232). The key elements of their proposal are as follows: (1) material is encoded meaningfully, using pre-existing knowledge, (2) encoding involves attaching retrieval cues to some specified structure built on existing knowledge, (3) doing so becomes progressively faster with increasing practice, (4) retrieval involves the reinstatement of earlier mental states together with the retrieval cues associated with information in long-term memory (LTM).

As Ericsson and Kintsch make clear in their excellent recent paper, this skilled memory facility is attainable only under very restricted circumstances. First, "subjects must be able to rapidly store information in LTM; this requires a large body of relevant knowledge and patterns for the particular type of information involved" (Ericsson & Kintsch, 1995, p. 215). Second, "the activity must be very familiar to the experts because only then can they accurately anticipate future demands for retrieval of relevant information" (Ericsson & Kintsch, 1995, p. 215). Together these allow more enduring selective storage of information. Third, "subjects must associate the encoded information with appropriate retrieval cues. This association allows them to activate a particular retrieval cue at a later time and thus partially reinstates the conditions of encoding to retrieve the desired information from LTM" (Ericsson & Kintsch, 1995, p. 216). Sets of retrieval cues can become organised into stable structures, which are equivalent to what they term retrieval schemata. The extended skilled memory theory appears to cope well with a broad range of empirical findings, and offers a useful new perspective on skilled behaviour, which we will consider in the next chapter. The restrictions placed on this use of long-term memory to support well practised activity may also offer another way of thinking about the selective decrements that occur with various types of neurological dysfunction (e.g. the preservation of some procedural knowledge in dense amnesia).

For reasons that will become apparent shortly, a study by Myles-Worsley, Johnston, and Simons (1988) is worth considering carefully. Myles-Worsley and colleagues compared radiographers with different levels of radiological experience in terms of their ability to recognise previously seen faces, and equal numbers of clinically normal and clinically abnormal chest X-ray films (see Figure 6.1). Recognition memory for faces was uniformly high across all levels of radiological experience. X-ray films with clinical abnormalities were better recognised as a function of degree of radiological experience and, for the most experienced radiologists, was equivalent to memory for faces. However, recognition memory for normal films actually decreased with radiological experience from above chance to a chance level. Thus, radiological expertise allows clinically relevant stimuli to be better detected and remembered, but very similar stimuli,

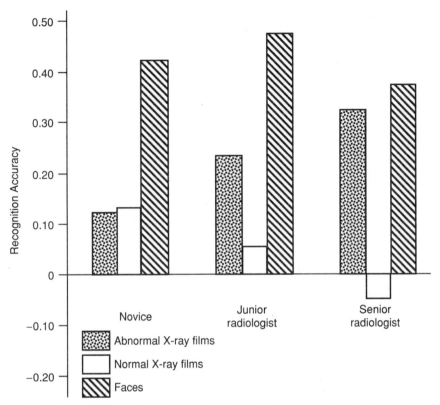

**Figure 6.1.** Specialist experience and detecting critical events (after Myles-Worsley, Johnston, & Simons, 1988).

which may not be relevant to clinical diagnosis, seem to be forgotten. Arguably, for the expert radiographer, stimuli without clinical abnormalities form, and later reinforce, notions of what inconsistencies are not associated with clinical abnormality. With such material experts also make significantly fewer false alarms. In the less experienced radiographer, who may possess less differentiated schemata, many more clinically normal and abnormal X-rays will seem inconsistent with each other, and thus are more likely to be remembered. In short, by virtue of repeated exposure to a particular domain of experience, we can classify very complex stimuli as familiar (i.e. consistent with most of what we have seen before) or unfamiliar. For a sub-class of unfamiliar events we may have additionally learned that certain configurations are indicative of, for example, danger. As experts in the domain we will recognise these particularly well, although other familiar stimuli will not be as well remembered. Later I will review some studies by a former colleague of mine, Peter Chapman, which can perhaps be interpreted within this framework.

## What counts as memory?

Typically, when we speak about "remembering" something, we mean being able to recall something, perhaps with little more to go on than a question such as "How do I get to the University from here?", or being able to "recognise" something we have previously encountered, such as realising that a car we are following is one that we previously overtook. These "direct" ways of accessing particular stored knowledge contrast with circumstances in which we can only infer that someone has learned something because of the way in which they perform. This distinction between *direct measures* and *indirect measures* of memory has been made most clearly by Richardson-Klavehn and Bjork (1988). *Direct measures* at test refer to specific target events, while *indirect measures* require that people engage in activity that shows change in performance, and requires no specific reference to previous events. Thus, for example, an "amnesic" patient such as TR, who has been shown to be performing at chance in a simple recognition test of words, in contrast to normals who performed almost at ceiling, responds as much as normals on a measure of galvanic skin response (i.e. decreased skin resistance due to slight "sweating") when new and old words are presented—responding reliably more to previously unpresented words, just as non-patient controls do (Verfaellie, Bauer, & Bowers, 1991). Such effects have been reported to be maintained even for periods of over a year, for example Sloman et al., (1988) have shown repetition priming effects can be observed up to 16 months later, while Hayman, MacDonald, and Tulving (1993) have shown evidence of repetition priming in an amnesic patients some 12 months after the original learning episode. The evidence for such long-term retention is less clear with regard to sequence learning (see Willingham, 1998).

The distinction between implicit and explicit memory relates, in part, to the distinction between "direct" and "indirect" measures. "Implicit memory is revealed on tasks that do not require reference to a specific episode" or "when performance on a task is facilitated in the absence of conscious recollection" (Graf & Schacter, 1985, p. 501). Explicit memory requires conscious recollection of prior experiences (Graf & Schacter, 1985) and even "awareness of the learning episode" (Roediger & Blaxton, 1987, p. 351). Explicit remembering may occur voluntarily (i.e. trying to remember) or spontaneously (i.e. being reminded of something, or having intrusive thoughts as the result of, for example, post-traumatic stress disorder).

There is growing evidence, largely from brain-imaging studies, that implicit and explicit memory systems are neuropsychologically distinct (see Posner et al., 1997). The typical paradigm in such studies has been to assess brain activity in tasks where participants first study a list of words, and then participate in one of two "recall" conditions: complete a word stem (usually the first three letters) with the first word that comes to mind, or complete a word stem with a word from the original list. In the former case, although not instructed to do so, participants frequently complete the word stem with words from the list originally learned. Under such conditions, part of the right posterior visual system shows reduced blood flow when words have been presented previously, whereas this reduction is not evident for word stems that require a new word to be generated. Studies using auditory presentation of the original word list find a similar alteration in blood flow for previously presented items within the auditory system (Schacter et al., 1996a). When explicit instructions are given there is activation in both frontal and hippocampal areas at least under some conditions (Schacter et al., 1996b).

Badgaiyan and Posner (1996) have replicated these results using high-density electrical scalp recordings. Their results show that there is no appreciable difference over the last few hundred milliseconds before production between words from the original list when used as stem completions, and when words not from the original list were used. However, the primed and unprimed completions did indeed differ in electrical activity in about 100 ms after the three-letter cue was presented, suggesting that the use of information about the learning list is not under conscious / deliberate control. As with the studies of Schacter and colleagues, using PET scanning, a right posterior reduction in blood flow was found irrespective of instructions. When the explicit instructions were followed, i.e. participants deliberately tried to recall a word from the original list, electrical brain activity differed from the priming instruction mainly in frontal areas that have been previously associated with semantic processing, as well as in the hippocampus, which has been linked with episodic recall (e.g. Schacter & Tulving, 1994). When subjects were given implicit instructions and the word had been presented previously in the list, there was no frontal or hippocampal activation. Thus these brain areas appear to be associated with volitional efforts to search the prior list or determine a related word, and show clearly the separation between these multiple memory systems.

There are numerous demonstrations that amnesic and other specific clinical populations show little evidence of the capacity to access previous experience when require to access it through direct tests such as recall or recognition, but nevertheless demonstrate both the capacity to access previous experience and to acquire new information, where indirect tests are used (see Schacter, 1996; Groeger, 1997 for review). This dissociation between the knowledge that people can report, and the knowledge that their performance reveals they do indeed possess, also emerges from a procedural learning study by Nissen and Bullemer (1987), which has subsequently spawned many other such studies. In the standard condition, normal subjects are merely instructed to press a key under the position where an asterisk appears. The asterisk appears in one of four positions. When the sequence of positions in which the asterisk appears repeats, even with a periodicity of 15 or more trials, the time taken to press the key under the asterisk reduces steadily. In contrast, where asterisks appear randomly in the four positions, response time was effectively flat over hundreds of trials. Following a minor change in the procedure, i.e. requesting participants to press the key under the position in which the asterisk would next appear, there was little evidence that subjects were explicitly able to predict the sequence. Thus, while people were unable to explicitly show any knowledge of the sequence, they clearly acquired implicit knowledge about the sequential nature of the position of the asterisk, as evidenced by their behaviour (i.e. procedural knowledge). For a more detailed review of this work and its implications see the excellent review by Ben Clegg and his then colleagues (Clegg, DiGirolamo, & Keele, 1998).

Following an earlier proposal made by Kolers and Roediger (1984), Fendrich, Gesi, Healy, and Bourne (1995, p. 87) concluded that "retention depends on the degree to which procedures executed, and thereby exercised, at study are reinstated at test." A range of evidence is presented to support this proposal, but one example, of what Fendrich and colleagues call "procedural reinstatement", serves to illustrate the proposal. Subjects read or typed a series of four-digit numbers during the learning phase of the study. Those who typed the sequences used either the numerical keys on the top row of a standard keyboard, or used the numerical keypad. In the test phase, one week later, all subjects typed four-digit sequences, this time some of the subjects who had initially used the keypad typed the digits using the row of numerical keys and vice versa. Subjects who simply read the digits at study used the keypad or row of numerical keys at test. Overall the results demonstrated evidence of learning using both an implicit test (shorter typing times for sequences of digits that had been typed during the learning phase) and an explicit test (recognition of previously encountered sequences). With regard to performance on the implicit test, it was shown that the time taken to enter the digit sequences in the "same" condition (i.e. in which both perceptual features of the display and movements made in response to it were repeated) were faster than in the "different" and "read" conditions (where only perceptual processing was repeated). Explicit recognition judgements were more accurate when they were entered in the same manner at study and test than when the entry methods differed. Thus, repetition of the movements made from study to test enhances recognition memory. Second, adding movements to the study task only improved recognition when that processing was reinstated at test.

Together these studies indicate that very complex, and highly durable knowledge of the relationships between elements of a complex task can be acquired through practice, and that while people may be unable to report on or introspect on such knowledge, the way in which they perform the same and similar tasks clearly demonstrates that learning has occurred, and that memory is supporting performance. The results from Fendrich and colleagues' procedural reinstatement paradigm further suggests that responding differently to stimuli for which we already have practised reactions influences both our recognition of those stimuli, and our ability to respond quickly and appropriately to them.

## WORKING MEMORY AND DRIVING ACTIVITIES

Baddeley and Hitch's (1974) model of what they term "working memory" has dominated the literature on what I have called elsewhere "transitory memory" (Groeger, 1997) over the past couple of decades.

### Overview of working memory (after Baddeley, 1986)

Although the model has changed little in fundamental conceptualisation over the years, the regular frequent updates that Baddeley has made (e.g. 1986, 1998), have ensured that it provides a coherent account of a far broader range of findings than any competing model. Certainly there are difficulties with some elements of the framework, which are readily conceded by those who work Within and those outside the working memory framework (e.g. Gathercole, 1996; Merat & Groeger, 2000), but its breadth and coherence make it very useful as a way of exploring the dependence of a task such as driving on transitory memory.

In essence, I see the central concern of the working memory model as to account for how people acquire and maintain sufficient information to guide their performance in the tasks they perform. The model assumes that there are two systems, the phonological loop and the visuo-spatial scratchpad (or sketchpad), which are specialised for dealing with (1) phonological information (although there are arguments for assuming it deals with a broader range of auditory information, see Brown & Hulme, 1995; Merat & Groeger, 2000; Merat, Groeger, & Withington, 1999; Salame & Baddeley, 1989) and (2) visuo-spatial information (which includes both imagery and movement control, see Logie, 1995). Both of these systems are composed of two elements: a passive store dedicated to storage of information of that particular type, and an active rehearsal or translation process, which serves to maintain the level of activity of items in the passive store, and to translate information from one format to another. Thus, for example, the "articulatory control process", which is the active maintenance element of the phonological loop, is involved in the transformation of text into speech. A third and overarching system, the central executive is essentially a collection of processes that come into operation when the individual becomes involved in some goal-directed strategic activity. It serves as a quasi-attentional system, being involved in selecting what will be attended to, maintaining attention, switching attention between two or more things that might be attended to, inhibiting undesired activities, effortful or strategic encoding or retrieval, the co-ordination of how the two "slave" systems operate, and co-ordinating activities in dual task situations. This is a rather long list of functions, which are now readily recognised (see for example the account of Shallice's work in Chapter 4), and Baddeley now concedes that the central executive can no longer be sensibly regarded as a single entity (Baddeley et al., 1998).

TABLE 6.1
Neuroimaging results and working memory components

| Working memory component | Brain areas involved | Function/task |
|---|---|---|
| Phonological loop | Brodmann's Area 44 (Broca's area) | Articulatory control process, involved in remembering letters and rhyming (Paulesu, Frith, & Frackowiak, 1993) |
| | Areas 44 & 45, left hemisphere | Remembering pseudo-words (Fiez et al., 1996) |
| | Supplementary motor area | Rehearsal (Smith & Jonides, 1997) |
| | Cerebellum | Rehearsal (Smith & Jonides, 1997) |
| | Superior temporal gyri (BA 22/42) | Phonological storage area |
| | Supramarginal gyri (BA 40– LH) | |
| Visuo-spatial sketchpad | Right occipital cortex | Creates image, of dots on screen (Jonides et al., 1993) establishes spatial co-ordinates of dots (Jonides et al., 1993) |
| | Right parietal | Retention of image of dots (Jonides et al., 1993) |
| | Right prefrontal | Retention of image of dots (Jonides et al., 1993) |
| | Right posterior parietal | Rehearsal or motor preparation (Jonides et al., 1993) |
| | Right premotor | Rehearsal (Jonides et al., 1993) |
| | Right frontal parietal | |
| | Occipitotemporal ventral pathway, fusiform, parohippocampal, inferior frontal, & anterior cingulate cortex | Object recognition, was face seen before (Courtney et al., 1996) |
| | Occipitotemporal dorsal pathway, superior and parietal cortex & frontal sulcus | Space/location based system, were faces previously in particular location (Courtney et al., 1996) |
| Central executive | Dorsolateral prefrontal cortex | Activated in dual task situations, with spatial or semantic primary task, not in single task (D'Esposito et al., 1995), Wisconscin Card Sort (Ragland et al., 1997), Tower of London task (Rogers et al., 1994), random generation (Petrides et al., 1993) |

In addition to accounting for many of the difficulties encountered by earlier conceptualisations of short-term memory (see Groeger, 1997 for review), the working memory model is largely based on two types of evidence. One type of evidence has been gained from studies of memory disorders and, more recently from studies of imaging of intact brains. These have helped to identify a neuropsychological basis for most of the components of the working memory model (summarised in Table 6.1). The other type of evidence, and in essence the empirical bedrock of the theory, comes from studies of the patterns of interference that occur when two tasks (at least one of which is known to require the involvement of one component of the working memory model) are performed concurrently.

In addition to formally testing the model, this approach also allows us in principle to quantify the extent and nature of the memory demands that might be involved in any task. In essence, this sort of approach is similar to that employed by Wickens (1992), although the greater explicitness of working memory, its established neuropsychological basis, and breadth of empirical support, has convinced me that as an approach to measuring task demand, it offers more than the multiple resources approach. I will now briefly try to show how the framework can be used in this way to good effect.

## Working memory requirements of driving

Suppose you are driving along, and your car telephone rings. It is very likely, because the telephone sound is different from any others you are currently hearing, that you will notice it immediately. That act of noticing the telephone ringing will "capture" some of your attentional capacity, and activity in the frontal areas of your brain will increase. We could in principle detect the increased blood flow in brain tissue, using fMRI (functional Magnetic Resonance Imaging). You will have to decide whether to answer the phone or not. Multitasking will increase activity, but differently depending on the difficulty of secondary tasks (Shallice et al., 1994). Part of this decision may be based on your assumptions about who might be telephoning. Part of the decision will also hopefully involve an assessment on your part of whether the current situation is dangerous, difficult to drive in (e.g. currently changing across several gears, moving off on a hill, etc), or likely to become so. The decision to answer the telephone will maintain or increase the demand on central executive resources, because retrieval from more enduring memory (in order to guess who is phoning), assessing likely difficulty and danger, or indeed dealing with it are also, I suggest, likely to be demanding of central executive resources. In particular, assuming the load from the driving task is relatively low, there will be increased involvement of the Dorso-Lateral Prefrontal Cortex (i.e. DLPFC) reflecting deliberate attempt to retrieve from episodic memory. If you decide to answer the phone, the planning and preparation of any movement involved will also require spare frontal capacity. Unless the driving task is difficult at the point when the decision is being made, and assuming that the phone call is the subsidiary task, such deliberate retrieval activity is unlikely. The period between the telephone ringing and the decision being made to answer it is thus quite demanding. Obviously, if it is a call you are anticipating or dreading, contemplation of the implications of the call will serve to increase this demand still further. If you are currently engaged in some difficult driving manoeuvre, which might reasonably be expected to be demanding, the level of demand imposed on the driver might prove greater than that which the driver can meet safely. For example, in circumstances where you were overtaking a large truck on a narrow road with limited preview, or approaching a signalised junction when the lights change to amber and you wonder whether to stop or go, or if you were fatigued or preoccupied with something other than driving, the distraction of the telephone ringing, and your deciding whether to answer it, might be disastrous.

You have decided to answer the phone, and made whatever movements are required for you to do so. Doing so has increased demand on the areas of your brain responsible for motor activity. Obviously these are already active because of the movements you need to perform in order to drive (see Chapters 2 and 3). Speaking will also serve to increase activity in Broca's area (i.e. Brodmann's Area, BA 44), superior temporal gyri (BA 22/42), supramarginal gyri (BA 40), and frontal operculum (BA 44 & 45) (Fiez et al., 1996; Paulesu, Frith, & Frackowiak, 1993; see Table 6.1). As none of these areas might ordinarily be expected to be involved in driving, multi-tasking listening and speaking should cause little difficulty. However, once again fatigue and other preoccupations will make combining two tasks more difficult, and as a result will make performance more effortful and perhaps more dangerous. Obviously, the nature of the call itself, or elements of the call, may also serve to increase cognitive load. If the quality of the line deteriorates, and more effort is deployed to try to identify what is being said, if the matters discussed are intellectually demanding or emotionally arousing, then additional demand on central executive resources will result. Quite some time ago now, Ivan Brown and colleagues showed what might result in such situations.

Brown, Tickner, and Simmonds (1969) had 24 drivers approach gaps on a flat roadway. The gaps were created by positioning two 4ft high, 1.75 ft wide hardboard covered frames at various distances apart: 3 inches less than the car width; the car width (5 ft); and 3, 6, and 9 inches wider than the car. Drivers drove through 20 gaps, composed of random arrangements of four of each type. Before confronting each gap, the driver had to determine whether or not he could pass through it without colliding; if the latter was the decision, there was sufficient space for him to pass by the obstacles with a slight alteration in course. Drivers also performed a verbal reasoning task (i.e. saying "true" or "false" to sentences such as "A follows B – BA", "B precedes A – AB", "A is followed by B – AB", "B is not followed by A – BA", "B is preceded by A – BA", "A does not precede B – BA", etc., previously used by Baddeley, 1968). When both tasks were performed concurrently, drivers drove through more impossible gaps (–3 inches: 47.2%; 0 inches: 93.0%) than when driving without performing the verbal reasoning task (–3 inches: 28.0%; 0 inches: 70.8%), and rejected more possible gaps in the concurrent condition (3 inches: 81.2%; 6 inches: 39.2%; 9 inches: 18.5%), than in the single task driving condition (3 inches: 79.5%; 6 inches: 28.5%; 9 inches: 7.7%). Speed was slower in the concurrent task condition (approximately 14 mph over the 1.5 mile circuit) than in the single task driving condition (15 mph), which was a reliable reduction in speed. Drivers did not collide with more of the obstacles when driving through possible gaps in the concurrent task condition, suggesting that steering accuracy per se does not deteriorate. Performance on the sentence-checking task was also worse in the concurrent task condition, taking on average 800 ms (1.81 seconds versus 2.60 seconds) longer and with almost twice as many errors (23.8% versus 45%).

Obviously, hearing sentences lasting a couple of seconds and maintaining some representation of the order in which the letters were said, and uttering a monosyllabic response while driving towards narrow gaps, hardly represent a normal telephoning while driving situation, but this study by Brown and colleagues clearly demonstrates that decision making will be severely decremented by a difficult, attention-demanding telephone conversation. The way in which the data are analysed and reported does not really allow us to be sure that steering control is unaffected, as the slight reduction in speed over the circuit as a whole does not make clear whether subjects slowed dramatically when driving through gaps, thus making the steering task substantially easier than it would otherwise be. Nevertheless, given that the average speed as a whole is relatively low, the study hardly encourages much confidence that having a difficult telephone conversation while driving is unlikely to compromise safety.

To return to our main theme here, we know from working memory research that verbal reasoning is demanding both of the phonological loop, if only to maintain the sentence in memory, but also the central executive. Interestingly, we have also used Baddeley's (1968) verbal reasoning task recently, and found that performance on the test predicted reliably the assessments made by driving examiners of some 100 drivers' skill levels and tendency to adopt a speed appropriate for the real road conditions in which they drove (see Groeger, Hammond, & Field, 1999). This strengthens the suggestion that the central executive plays a role in adapting behaviour to the particular demands of a situation. Interestingly, in the dual task study of driving by Duncan et al. (1992) discussed earlier (Chapter 4), concurrent performance of a demanding secondary task was associated with later braking on entry to intersections, a result that perhaps corroborates the suggestion that suiting speed to the conditions in which we are driving is demanding of central resources.

Unfortunately, there has been very little research that has explicitly examined the role the visuo-spatial sketchpad may play in driving. This may in part reflect the supposition that interfering with drivers' visual attention would drastically disrupt performance and would be inherently dangerous. Certainly we know from studies carried out outside a driving context that ability to learn or indeed to recollect a well-known route is interfered with if people are required to perform a reasonably simple tracking task at the same time (see Baddeley, 1986). There is also substantial evidence that constructing and maintaining visual images has a negative impact on perception (e.g. Craver-Lemley & Reeves, 1992; Farah, 1988). Furthermore, the close association of movement control with spatial memory processes (see Logie, 1995), and the fact that movement control is clearly vital to driving, might further suggest that steering control would be interfered with by the imposition of an additional visuo-spatial task. Thus, being asked during a telephone conversation while driving, where in one's room one left some papers, or where one might meet up so that one can reasonably expect to park while waiting, might also be expected to disrupt steering, when steering is already demanding (e.g. making a rapid and precise lane change, weaving between parked cars). A final speculation is that, as Natasha Merat and I have recently shown, localising sound in space is particularly demanding of spatial working memory (Merat & Groeger, 1999), and I thus wonder whether deciding where a car horn has sounded from (i.e. "was he blowing his horn at me?"), or determining whether a siren-blaring emergency vehicle is behind you or ahead, may also lead to steering disruption. Obviously, a requirement for fine motor control of an in-car display, or non-hands-free phoning, would also be expected to impact on motor control, and indeed, as reported earlier (Chapters 2 & 3), there is also evidence that requiring drivers to perform a complex spatial judgement has a negative impact on their ability to assess when they will arrive at a distant object towards which they are travelling (Groeger & Comte, 1999).

In summary, what I have tried to do here is to illustrate the ways in which different aspects of the working memory framework may subserve performance of different aspects of the driving task. A formal analysis of the effects of different secondary tasks, which have known demands on working memory, on components of the driving task would be fascinating. However, it would also be of practical use, as determining which new in-car devices will impact on different elements of the driving task, or how interfaces to current devices might be redesigned, remains a rather atheoretical and somewhat arbitrary research and development enterprise.

## MEMORY FOR SITUATIONAL AND SPATIAL INFORMATION

Providing an account of how more enduring memory might be involved in driving is rather more difficult. In earlier chapters, I have discussed how skills develop and thus, procedural memory. Beyond this, memory for directions and where places are, together with memory for complex dynamic events, seem the most appropriate issues to consider. Later I will consider what is by definition "episodic memory", that is, whether and when accidents occur, and in the next chapter, memory for risk-related events.

Memory for spatial relations is subject to a variety of biases: alignment, landmark distortion, perspective, and grouping. When choosing between maps that showed correct and incorrect alignments of continents, Tversky (1981) found that subjects selected maps that showed continents more aligned than they actually are, and perhaps more relevantly, remembered roads as being more aligned than they are, a result confirmed by research reported by Byrne (1979, 1982).

Distances between towns or within urban environments is also subject to distortion. For example, a study by Sadalla, Burroughs, and Staplin (1980) had students estimate distances between buildings on their university campus. Some of the buildings were regarded as good "landmarks", generally because of their central-ity, being better known, or their size. Estimates of distances from landmarks to non-landmark buildings were generally higher than from ordinary buildings to landmarks, suggesting that a metric model of space is not being used, and that landmarks in some way "organise" the other elements in their vicinity. A study by Hirtle and Jonides (1985) had one group of students group various buildings in their university town together, and another group estimate distances between pairs of buildings. Typically, students grouped campus and town buildings sep-arately, and when distances between pairs of buildings that featured in the same group or different groups were estimated, within-group distances were thought to be shorter than between-group distances, even when in fact the actual distances were identical. Distance estimation is affected by the estimator's current per-spective, or assumed spatial location. Holyoak and Mah (1982), for instance, report a study in which students had to imagine themselves to be on the east or west coast of America, and to estimate distances between cities on the Atlantic or Pacific coast. The results showed that distances estimated were closer for those cities on the same coast as the subject imagined, while greater estimates of distance were given between pairs of cities on the other coast.

Recently, Radavansky and Zacks (1997) have described a framework for how such spatial information might be incorporated within what they call a "situation model". Situations models are functional analogues of a situation in a real or imaginary world, simulating a unique set of circumstances in that world. Situa-tion models contain tokens that represent any meaningful object or abstract idea (which Radavansky & Zacks call "entities"), the properties associated with them, and the relationships between these entities. Thus a situation such as car-following would comprise entities standing for the car ahead, the bonnet of mine, and my wondering whether the driver ahead will brake. The properties of these entities might include the colour of the car ahead, its speed and general condition, the relative shortness of the distance, and my slight apprehension were the driver ahead to brake. The relationships between entities would also be in the situation model, such as the distance between our two cars. It might also repres-ent where in the world this following incident is occurring, the time of day, etc. Unlike a schema, a situation model can represent novel sets of circumstances, as well as more mundane circumstances (in which case the model's construction might be heavily influenced by the structure of more schematised knowledge). According to Radavansky and Zacks, situation models need not rely on a per-ceptual code, need not be constrained by the properties of perceptual codes, and are not concerned with the representation and organisation of categorical or gen-eral world knowledge, although they may contain "pointers" to such information represented elsewhere in enduring memory. Situation models can represent either dynamic or static situations, and thus can in principle extend to include ongoing circumstances, in which the course of events change, with different locations, changes in the properties of the entities included, and their inter-relationship.

A situation model "is a representation of the situation as it is comprehended by the individual" (Radavansky & Zacks, 1997, p. 176), and situation models are created only where individuals have the goal of understanding the situation in which they find themselves. As such, requiring an intention for their formation, situation models are not created automatically (Graesser, Singer, & Trabasso, 1994; Zwaan, 1994), depending on working memory for their creation and updating, and being stored as separate traces in long-term memory. Only one situation model can be active in working memory at a time, but having that model active in working memory makes available the entities, properties, relations, and location that comprise the situation, although people can only retrieve specific information from situation models when motivated to do so. As with many other accounts of retrieval from long-term memory, situation models are accessed from memory though a content-addressable search, which includes the degree of commonality between what is being searched for (which might be dictated by some new circumstance the individual is trying to understand) and the situation models that have been laid down previously (see also Hintzman, 1986, for a similar account of parallel activation of memory traces and feature matching). In this way, a person can access the appropriate memory on the basis of knowing the objects in a situation model (e.g. cars being ahead), the properties of the entities involved (i.e. colour, size, make of vehicle), the relations between objects (i.e. close following), and where it might have occurred (e.g. on a motorway). However, while a situation model might be retrieved on the basis of similarity with any or all of these features, the precise configuration of these properties is not available until the model has been brought into working memory. Thus, you might retrieve a "close following on a motorway" model, but it might reflect following a car rather than the truck that is currently ahead.

The attraction of this albeit sketchy account of how ongoing and completed situations are represented in memory, is that it copes with dynamic situations in a more satisfactory fashion than any other account I know of. In the next chapter, I will use this framework as a basis for trying to account for how drivers might interpret driving scenes, ascribe danger to elements of those scenes, and act appropriately in order to remain safe. Before I do so, I want to consider briefly circumstances that have turned out not to be safe, and how accurately people remember such episodes.

## MEMORY FOR WHEN AND WHETHER ACCIDENTS HAPPENED

Given the pain, personal trauma, and financial penalties that result from accidents, not to mention the unfortunate artificial retrieval aid of a dented vehicle, it is, at first glance at least, surprising that people might forget being involved in a road traffic accident. Nevertheless, that is precisely the conclusion that Maycock, Lockwood, and Lester (1991) draw from a study of accident reporting which sampled several thousand drivers. Drivers were asked to report the accidents they had had in the previous three years (a widely used reporting period in road accident research), and to give the date on which the accident occurred. Analysing the number of accidents reported in each month of the three-year period, Maycock and colleagues found a highly systematic fall-off in the number of accidents reported, the longer time had elapsed since the accident was reported to have occurred. The negative relationship between accident frequency per month and time since accident is, interestingly, a negative exponential with an exponent of −0.29, suggesting that about a quarter of accidents are forgotten per year. This in spite of the fact that accident rates were stable, if not falling, across the period in which the research was carried out.

Confronted with a task that requires estimating the frequency of an event over a period of time, and dating the events making up that estimate, there are a number clear sources of error. First, participants may simply forget that an event occurred. Applied to the data reported by Maycock et al., this would require that the longer ago an event took place, the more likely it is to be forgotten. Although this both accords with intuition, and with a wealth of data (see Groeger, 1997), it is obviously not the case that we forget everything that happened a long time ago. Particularly important experiences, or what were at the time mundane experiences that in hindsight turned out to be important, are relatively well remembered over time (see Conway, 1990). Consequentiality is thus important, which might in this case be roughly equated with the extent of damage or injury that occurred. Whether this is because of their intrinsic memorability, or the fact that we revisit them frequently in conversation or thought, i.e. the amount of rehearsal or practice at retrieval the memory receives, is another factor that might mitigate forgetting. The period of one's life in which the experience occurred is also thought to influence its retrieval, as with the so-called reminiscence bump, where events that occurred between the ages of 10 and 30 are better remembered that those from earlier or later in life (see Rubin, Wetzler, & Nebes, 1986). A second source of error is that a memory for the accident might be retrieved, but misdated. Assuming that people can accurately report on very recent events, a tendency for, say, more vividly remembered events to be misdated as more recent would result in an increased number of accidents being dated as recent. It seems clear that dates are not "remembered" in the strictest sense, but estimated or reconstructed from whatever else is recollected of an experience.

Brown, Rips, and Shevell (1985) showed that dates are estimated rather than remembered, finding that accuracy in dating events over the previous five-year period depended on the amount of knowledge the rememberer could retrieve about the events in question. Where more was remembered about the events, these were thought to be more recent, by an average of some +0.28 years. Low-knowledge events were dated as being less recent, by an average of −0.17 years from their actual date of occurrence. The dating of events as more recent, or less recent, refers respectively to "forward" and "backward" telescoping. As Brown and colleagues show, the telescoping tendency is in part determined by the knowledge one has about events.

In general, more attention has been paid to forward telescoping, as it appears to be the more prevalent phenomenon. There are systematic biases which may underlie both its apparent prevalence and actual occurrence. Bradburn, Rips, and Shevell (1987), for example, suggest that the target events that are generally used in dating studies are often more salient. As a result of this, the greater detail that can be retrieved about the events concerned causes them to be judged as more recent. The relative salience of target and non-target events offers an explanation of why forward telescoping occurs. Thus, if we were more likely to forget minor accidents over time, accidents dated as recent would reflect accidents, both minor and more serious, that had occurred recently, and less recent serious accidents.

Thompson, Skowronski, and Lee (1988) and Huttenlocher, Hedges, and Prohaska (1988) suggest that people judge when an event might have occurred by using an estimate of the number of events intervening between it and the present. Where more time has elapsed, more intervening items are forgotten, leading subjects to report distant events as more recent, simply because they do not recollect things happening in the interim. This would suggest that where people report several accidents, earlier ones are less likely to be misdated. However, as with other explanations regarding the salience or memorability of certain episodes, this too runs into the difficulty that memories that are rated as very clear or vivid are not necessarily displaced towards the present. A number of studies, as well as that by Brown, Rips, and Shevell cited earlier, report backward telescoping of events (e.g. Rubin & Baddeley, 1989; Tzeng, 1976). How might we resolve such conflicting interpretations? To do so we need to consider some of the ways in which the questions we ask subjects lead to certain biases in answering the question that we, as researchers, would *wish* they answered.

Requiring that events are dated in relation to the present is one of the reasons why backward telescoping is less frequently observed. Obviously events that are yet to take place cannot be dated as having already taken place, thus only forward slippage in dating is possible. Where the end point is not the present, both types of error can and do apply. Baddeley, Lewis, and Nimmo-Smith (1978), for instance, carried out a study in which panel subjects at the Applied Psychology Unit were asked to identify the date on which they last served as a subject. They found that there was a striking relationship between the recency of the event and the standard deviation of the estimate given. It increased by 19 days for each 100 days of elapsed time, thus showing that dating accuracy becomes more variable with increases in intervening time. This can partly be overcome. Studies in which people have been asked to date or locate events with respect to temporal landmarks (e.g. "before Chistmas", "since your last birthday"), have generally shown far less forgetting of events, and greater accuracy in dating (e.g. Loftus & Marburger, 1983; Means, Mingay, Nigam, & Zarrow, 1988). These "landmark" studies make it unlikely that telescoping can be explained solely in terms of the ages of events, or the relative accessibility of memories for the events in question.

The range of events to be considered also exerts an influence on dating accuracy (e.g. Huttenlocher et al., 1988), while telescoping is reduced still further if analysis is restricted to events that the subject is confident of remembering (Thompson et al., 1988). Together these findings suggest that telescoping is not caused by vividness of memory codes, or by progressive shortening or lengthening, but by imprecision in the way time is represented and the way subjects try to solve the dating tasks with which they are confronted (Huttenlocher et al., 1988; Rubin & Baddeley, 1989). Huttenlocher and colleagues suggest that temporal representations are essentially metric, but events are represented at several different levels of precision based on calendar time (i.e. in terms of hours, days, months). If information at one level of the hierarchy is lost, the boundaries arising from the more gross temporal units systematically bias the estimate produced. There is good support for the Huttenlocher proposal. More recent studies extend the model and point to two sources of error that may also underlie forward telescoping (see Huttenlocher, Hedges, & Bradburn, 1990).

One source of error is subjects' imposition of an upper boundary on reports, based on their notion of what would constitute reasonable answers to the question asked. This boundary truncates the distribution of reports, yielding systematically biased estimates. In part this can be overcome by telling the subject that they should report about events within a restricted period, e.g. the last three years. However, in doing so, we may implicitly request a search backwards in time, rather than from "three years ago until now". If we assume that people will gradually run out of events they can report, this direction of recall will result in a systematically biased sample of events. The surface form of the question may thus also introduce bias: temporally marked questions (e.g. "how *long* ago was it?" also systematically bias the direction of error in people's estimates, see Yarmey, 1990). The other factor is subjects' use of rounded (prototypic) values when estimating: Thus, when using day-based ranges people plump for values such as 14, 21, 30, 60, etc. days ago. As the temporal distance between rounded values increases as the temporal categories become larger, dating of more distant events in this way will be subject to systematic biases (see Huttenlocher et al., 1990). This suggests that asking for an actual calendar date, although it may be intrinsically subject to error, may lessen biases due to rounding, and in any case may allow us to test whether rounding has occurred.

In a recent study, Geoff Maycock, Graham Grayson and I asked over a thousand drivers who had been driving for less than 10 years to describe the first accident they had as drivers, or their most recent accident, in terms of its location, weather, time of year, lighting conditions, etc. All drivers were then

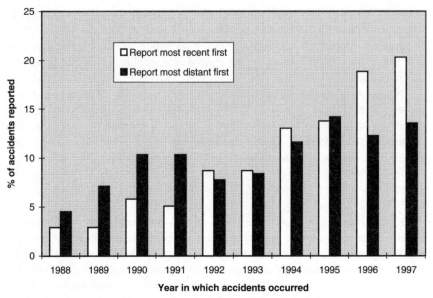

**Figure 6.2.**    Biases in accident reporting as a function of direction of report.

asked to report the date and details of any accidents they had had in the preceding 10 years. A number of important results emerged. The purpose of the study was to test my assumption that encouraging people to think in detail about a particular accident, before going on to record details of other accidents, would make retrieval of other accidents easier, and thereby reduce forgetting. I also hypothesised that by thinking of their first or more recent accident, and then reporting accidents from past to present or present to past, people would report increased numbers of "older" accidents.

As Figure 6.2 shows, the results provide striking support for these hypotheses. First, significantly more accidents dating back more than five years were reported by those doing past to present recall. As allocation to conditions was random, and both groups were similar in terms of the factors that would usually be related to accident involvement (i.e. age, exposure, gender, pattern of driving), this difference is likely to be due to direction of recall. If we simply compare accidents in the most recent five years, the people doing past to present recall report fewer accidents than those doing present to past recall. This reflects a similar direction of recall bias. However, what is striking is that over this period the reduction in accidents reported per year is similar for both directions of recall, again showing an exponential decline. However, in contrast to the "memory loss" exponent reported in the earlier study by Maycock and colleagues (i.e. $-0.29$), in the present study the exponent was $-0.16$. Unfortunately, we did not include a condition in which people simply reported and dated the accident they had had, without our attempt to think in detail about an accident, and thus the much slower forgetting, almost half the rate in the earlier study, cannot be unequivocally attributed to an effect of "context reinstatement", although this does offer the best explanation of what went on.

Thus it does seem that manipulating the direction of recall allows people to retrieve accidents they otherwise do not report, and that the forgetting effect in accident reporting can be partly overcome by having people think in detail about their own involvement in a particular accident. As such, these results help to clarify the "forgetting effect" previously reported by Maycock et al. (1991), in that people do indeed fail to report "older" accidents as often as they report more recent accidents, but they can do so where reporting conditions are adapted to take account of this bias. As such, accidents may not be reported, but they are not "forgotten" in the sense of being lost or unreportable. This serves to address in part the puzzle of why people would "forget" something as consequential as an accident. From a more practical point of view, the results of this study also imply that questionnaires that assess accident involvement using more tradi- tional methods, i.e. questions such as "how many accidents have you had in the past five years?", probably lead to an underestimation of accident frequency, and that requiring recalls over shorter periods is preferable.

## SUMMARY

Although most of us remember nothing of the mundane journeys we make, this is certainly not an indication that our memory systems are either defective or have not been operating while we have been driving. The fact that we do not remember in part reflects the operation of implicit learning and memory, and the fact that driving is a heavily proceduralised task and thus not necessarily readily accessible to ways of remembering that serve us very well in other tasks (e.g. remembering your telephone number, where you live, or what make of car has just three wheels). In this chapter I have tried to show how an understanding of the model of what used to be called short-term memory can help us to under- stand the added complexity of using a telephone while driving. I believe that this approach, which not only relies on well-established empirical results but also has been shown to depend on a number of distinct brain systems, will be ex- tended to an analysis of the compatibility of a range of different new in-vehicle technologies and the driving task as we have learned to perform it. Beyond such transitory task-related memory systems, I have also tried to show how the dependence on procedural or action-oriented memory, in the previous chapter, is supplemented with more enduring memories for facts, places, time, and events. In the next chapter one particular aspect of episodic memory is examined, i.e. how knowledge of what has been dangerous in the past may be acquired and used.

# CHAPTER SEVEN

# When driving is dangerous: Arousal, assessment, and hazard perception

*Across the world a range of attempts to measure "hazard perception" are currently underway. Although early detection of upcoming hazards has considerable face validity, most approaches are bereft of any theoretical basis. In addition to evaluating current attempts to measure such higher-order driving skills, an approach is made towards integrating "hazard perception", task-induced arousal, scene perception, and theories of episodic/autobiographical memory, specifically Logan's (1988) Instance Theory. The chapter considers how these might relate to each other, and to the development of drivers' appreciation of risk (see Groeger & Chapman, 1996).*

Over the last couple of decades, driver behaviour researchers have debated, often with some vitriol, whether drivers seek to avoid threat (e.g. Fuller, 1984), attempt to achieve a zero level of accident by adjusting their behaviour (e.g. Naatanen & Summala, 1972) or, most controversially, adjust their behaviour so as to maintain the level of accident risk at some subjectively acceptable, non-zero, target level (Wilde, 1982; Wilde, Gerszke, & Paulozza, 1998). The purpose of this chapter is not to rehearse the positions people have adopted in this debate, but to attempt to move away from what are essentially motivational accounts of behaviour, towards one that considers what cognitive operations might be involved in assessing whether some danger is present, and in deciding what to do in the face of it. These are issues that are not adequately addressed by any of the aforementioned theories, although obviously fundamental to any satisfactory account of risk assessment and behaviour. In the next chapter, I will return to the debate on what underlies risk taking, as I too find it hard to allow this rather tired old dog to sleep!

## PHYSIOLOGICAL CONSEQUENCES OF
## CONFRONTING A DANGEROUS SITUATION

*In the face of danger, as is widely reported in a variety of literatures, a number changes occur which partly reflect the changes in subjective arousal experienced by the individual. It seems obvious that driving varies in the level of what we might conventionally call fear or stress. Here I want to explore the relationship between subjective and objective measures of these in the context of driving.*

I believe that feeling in danger has much in common with other stressors—stress being a process whereby environmental demands ("stressors": e.g. heat, noise, fear of death) evoke an appraisal process in which perceived demand exceeds resources and results in undesirable physiological, psychological, behavioural, or social outcomes (Salas, Driskell, & Hughes, 1996). This interactionist view of stress and the one particular stressor that concerns us here, danger, considers that physiological changes (endocrine and autonomic response), emotional reactions (fear, anxiety, frustration), cognitive effects (narrowing of useful field of view), and changes in social behaviour will result from exposure to danger.

These changes have been quantified in a variety of ways. Autonomic responses that have been widely taken to reflect stress responses include: skin conductance, pulse rate, heart rate variability, P300 evoked potential response, muscle tension, eye blink and eye blink duration, and respiration rate. Several of these are used in other contexts as indices of attention, and in memory research as indices of encoding and retrieval effort. The link between these physiological consequences of stress and their impact on subsequent cognitive processes will receive much more attention later.

Endocrine responses would be reflected in measures of epinephrine and norepinephrine secretion, blood glucose level, because it rises after epinephrine and cortisol secretion, and salivary cortisol (see Kirschbaum & Hellhammer, 1994, for review). Emotional appraisals also change, leading, obviously, to increased feelings of fear and anxiety, but less obviously to feelings of annoyance, tension, and frustration. In social contexts these feelings may be manifested by a reduced tendency be co-operative and assist others, increased interpersonal aggression, and neglect of social conventions and interpersonal cues.

Figure 7.1 shows how some of the autonomic parameters change when driving. These data are taken from a study Peter Chapman, Ben Clegg, and I did some time ago in which drivers drove along a route comprising some 20 miles of urban, suburban, and motorway driving. As they drove, the subjects' heart rate and skin resistance was measured, and at 20 junctions along the route the driver was asked to rate the "danger" and "difficulty" they were currently encountering. As the figure shows, at the outset, heart rate and skin resistance reflect the level of effort and involvement of the individual in the task underway, and both are regular and flat. In that circumstance the driver, asked to assess the

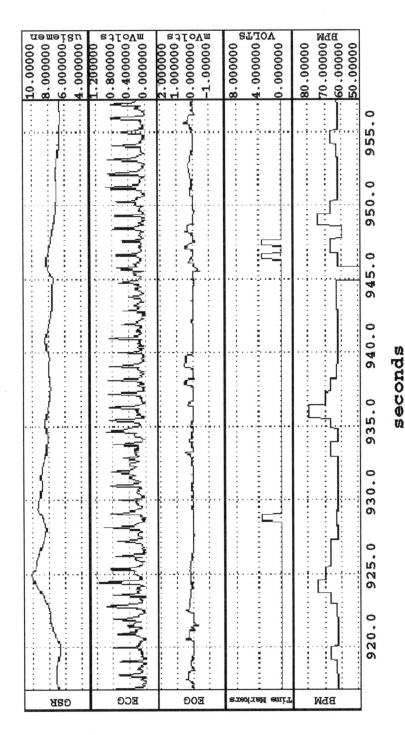

**Figure 7.1.** Physiological reactions in difficult and dangerous driving conditions.

TABLE 7.1

Average correlations between objective and subjective measures at each site, and between each site's accident record in the preceding three years

| | Ratings | | Skin conductance | | | | Heart rate | |
|---|---|---|---|---|---|---|---|---|
| | *Danger* | *Difficulty* | *No.* | *No./s* | *Mean* | *SD* | *Mean* | *SD* |
| *Ratings* | | | | | | | | |
| Danger | | | | | | | | |
| Difficulty | *0.61* | | | | | | | |
| *GSR* | | | | | | | | |
| Number (no.) | *0.21* | *0.30* | | | | | | |
| No. per sec. | *0.12* | *0.16* | — | | | | | |
| | | | *0.87* | | | | | |
| Mean | *0.16* | *0.19* | *0.41* | *0.40* | | | | |
| Stan. Dev. | *0.18* | *0.32* | *0.54* | *0.43* | *0.49* | | | |
| *Heartrate* | | | | | | | | |
| Mean (BPM) | *0.19* | *0.29* | *0.32* | *0.23* | *0.38* | *0.41* | | |
| SD | 0.11 | *0.22* | *0.25* | *0.18* | *0.15* | *0.40* | *0.26* | |
| *Accidents* | | | | | | | | |
| All | −0.01 | 0.03 | 0.09 | 0.08 | 0.05 | *0.17* | *0.17* | *0.18* |

These correlations were calculated by correlating each individual's data for each of the 20 locations, and then averaging these correlations using Fisher's transformation. This procedure is much more sensitive to individual testing conditions and is thus more powerful statistically.

Italicised entries significant at 1% level, with $df > 500$; $r > .115$.

danger inherent in driving at that location in the circumstances pertaining at that time, rated the danger relatively low. When these circumstances change, heart rate, heart-rate variability, and skin conductance level also change. Asked to rate the danger in this circumstance, the same driver produced a higher rating. In the same two situations, the difficulty of driving was rated as similar. In other circumstances, the rating of danger changed relatively little, but the ratings of difficulty and physiological indices changed (see Table 7.1).

A number of aspects of these data are worthy of comment, but three are of particular relevance here. In the first place both difficulty and danger ratings are closely correlated with each other. Second, both appear to be correlated with many of the physiological indices. Thus, drivers who report higher levels of difficulty in driving at a particular location are likely to exhibit increased electro-dermal activity (i.e. numbers of GSR responses, highest level of GSR, standard deviation of GSR), increased heart rate and heart-rate variability, and greater numbers of eye movements. Partial correlations which control for the relation-ship between danger and difficulty show that the relationship between the level of danger experienced and the physiological indices is due almost entirely to the relationship between these measures and the level of difficulty experienced. It is therefore clear that danger and difficulty assessments can be physiologically distinguished, and that standard physiological measures of what might be termed mental load can be measured subjectively, albeit with less precision. It is of particular interest that drivers' judgements of "danger" and "difficulty" are physiologically underpinned, especially in the light of how such judgements can successfully discriminate between drivers of different ages and with different levels of traffic experience (see Groeger & Chapman, 1996, discussed further later).

A third important result also relates to accident frequency; that is, the total number of accidents of all types occurring at the sites studied is reliably correlated with the variation in electrodermal activity and the mean heart rate which occurs as the location is driven through. As noted earlier these indicators are also generally taken to reflect increased workload. If taken as such the present results show that increases in workload are predictive of increased accident involvement. Thus this replicates Taylor's (1964) seminal work which appeared to show that changes in galvanic skin response were related to the accident history at particular sites. What the data reported later show is that such relationships are not due to subjective feelings of danger, per se, as Taylor concluded, but to the perceived difficulty in driving at certain locations—this turns out to reflect in part the speed environment and presence of other traffic.

Finally, drivers were only required to provide ratings at designated locations, but of all the 600 or more junctions studied across all locations and drivers, discernible physiological changes in heart-rate or skin conductance were rarely accompanied by ratings of danger or difficulty that were low for the subject concerned. That is, physiological changes were almost always reflected in an increased subjective rating of danger or difficulty. Higher ratings of danger or difficulty were also, almost invariably, accompanied by discernible changes in the physiological record. We are not in a position from these data to say that every actual increase in danger or difficulty was spotted by subjects, but drivers were certainly sensitive to physiological changes. Whether the subjective awareness of an increase in danger or difficulty precedes, mediates, or follows the physiological reaction, is also not possible to determine from the present data. However, the data do allow us to conclude that subjective interpretations of danger and difficulty when driving are closely coupled with physiological changes.

## MEMORY FOR THREATENING SITUATIONS

*The previous section shows that arousal, which people interpret as difficulty or danger, changes as we drive through the world. Here I want to consider how changes in arousal, especially where this is due to some form of threat, affects what we remember.*

Everyday intuition suggests that situations in which individuals experience fear or threat, or rather some aspects of situations in which they experience fear or threat, should be well remembered. However, expert opinion is rather different. Kassin, Ellsworth, and Smith (1989) report that the majority of memory experts surveyed considered that violent and stressful events are less well remembered than non-stressful events. However, considering the empirical evidence now available, I would suggest that within certain limits this expert opinion is wrong, as would authors such as Christianson (1997) and Heuer, Reisberg, and Rios (1997).

## Recall and recognition in emotionally arousing laboratory tasks

For the most part, the studies on which all must rely to reach their conclusion are situations in which events are simulated that would be expected to be threatening and to change arousal level. With Heuer et al., I wonder "whether the quality and intensity of the emotions aroused in these studies are comparable to the emotions experienced in real life" (1997, p. 118), but studies that expose people to real risk, and have sufficient objective information about the events that transpired, and subsequently assess how well those events have been remembered, are fraught with operational and ethical difficulties. As we will see later, memory for events while driving may actually serve to break this log-jam. Before considering this evidence, however, I want to briefly highlight some of the expectations we might have on the basis of better controlled, albeit artificial, laboratory studies.

Although there is some degree of disagreement about the actual shape of the relationship between arousal and remembering, it does seem clear that the relationship is non-linear. Many authors have suggested that the relationship follows the inverted U-shaped curvilinear relationship between arousal, task difficulty, and performance described first by Yerkes and Dodson (1908). Others, such as Deffenbacher et al. (1994), suggest that the relationship between arousal and memory is itself moderated by other variables, such as anxiety, which would also undermine the familiar Yerkes-Dodson law. The Yerkes-Dodson position has itself been subject to considerable criticism (see Teigen, 1994). These criticisms, together with the difficulty of comparing across arousal levels measured from different individuals, equating different materials for the change in arousal each will provoke, and the additional complexity that arises where an individual repeatedly attempts to retrieve details of the same event (i.e. "hypernesia", see Payne, 1986), leave me very sceptical about claims regarding the relationship between memory and arousal, beyond those that suggest that it is positive and non-linear.

A variety of laboratory-based studies, largely using slides that were either neutral or emotionally arousing, show that those elements that are emotionally provocative are both recalled and recognised better than neutral elements, even when these are within the same slide. It is also clear that details *linked to* these threatening elements are also better remembered than details of neutral elements (see Christianson, 1992b, 1997 for reviews). Heuer et al. (1997) present evidence that suggests that we need to be careful about how we interpret "linked to". They separated out those aspects of the emotion-inducing slide that were within or beyond 4° of visual angle of the threatening element, or physically linked to each threatening element. They found that recognition memory was better for threat-attached than for non-threat-attached items, that memory was better for near-threat than for far-threat elements, even when both were linked, and also that memory was also good for neutral items close to but not physically joined to the threat. Thus, in remembering details of a criminal brandishing a gun, the gun is remembered better than the face or feet of the person holding the gun, and separate objects near the gun are remembered better than separate objects far from the gun, the latter being remembered less well than the criminal's face or feet. Studies also make clear that neutral events prior to the threatening event are remembered less well than the threatening event (i.e. retrograde amnesia), and that neutral events subsequent to the threatening event are also poorly remembered (i.e. anterograde amnesia).[1] This gives rise to something akin to a von Restorff effect (see Christianson, 1997; Wallace, 1965 for review), in which distinctive events are generally better remembered than less distinctive events. Three other points should be made arising from this and similar research.

First, the increased likelihood of certain elements of a threatening experience being well remembered persists over time. The rate at which forgetting occurs for traumatic experiences is slower than that for neutral events (see Groeger, 1997; Heuer et al., 1997). This is also true for the consistency of what is remembered (e.g. Bohannon & Symons, 1992; Christianson, 1997).

Second, it is clear that where an evident threat is present, people spend more time looking or look more often at that threat (i.e. weapon-focus, see Steblay, 1992 for review), than they do at a similar scene that does not contain that threat (see Loftus, Loftus, & Messo, 1987). Where slides of scenes are presented so rapidly that eye movements would be rendered useless, essentially the same results emerge (Christianson, Loftus, Hoffman, & Loftus, 1991). It therefore seems that although threat is likely to attract attention, continually seeing or looking at the threat is unnecessary for the effects of central/plot relevant–peripheral/plot irrelevant difference to emerge. Speculating somewhat, it may be that this curious pattern of results can be resolved by proposing that people continue processing some visuo-spatial image of the briefly seen threatening stimulus after it has disappeared. If so, repeating the Christianson et al. (1991) study using rapidly presented slides, but separating each with visual or spatial interference, should cause the original effect to diminish.

---

[1] It must be stressed that in cases where the trauma inherent in an event causes it to be forgotten, i.e. "psychogenic amnesia", the event itself, and events leading up to and following it, are all at least temporarily forgotten (see Christianson & Nilsson, 1989). This is also the case in circumstances where organic decay or damage result in "organic amnesia" (see Christianson, Nilsson, & Silfvenius, 1987).

Finally, although there is ample evidence that increased arousal through fear makes successful retrieval less likely, a number of caveats limit this generalisation. As has emerged from a number of studies of people about to make parachute jumps, ability to concentrate well enough to read numbers (Somonov, Frolov, Evtushenko, & Sviridov, 1977), and to remember numbers in the order in which they were presented, is reduced (Idzikowski & Baddeley, 1983, 1987). This shows that although encoding is enhanced in threatening situations it is so only for threat-related learning, and learning otherwise within the capacities of individuals is much reduced. Retrieval of highly learned, but essentially irrelevant material (i.e. parachutists' own telephone numbers), is also quite poor where the individuals trying to remember feeling at risk (Loftus, 1980). However, where the arousal at retrieval matches arousal at learning, then remembering is greatly facilitated (Fisher & Geiselman, 1992; Geiselman & Fisher, 1997). Thus, as with many other demonstrations of context-effects in memory research, re-experiencing during retrieval the emotions felt at learning improves remembering. Where the emotions experienced at learning and retrieval are different, remembering may be inhibited, even where the physical surroundings are similar (see Groeger, 1997 for overview).[2] As suggested earlier, not all elements of the original experience may be retrieved. Indeed it may even be that very little of the original experience itself is remembered, but an emotional reaction to being in similar circumstances nevertheless results. This has led Tobias, Kihlstrom, and Schacter (1992), among others, to suggest that emotions are essentially implicit memories. I believe that such a process underlies the feelings of danger and risk most of us experience when driving.

## Memory for driving situations and arousal

Over the last few years, Peter Chapman and I have investigated the relationships between risk encountered while driving and memory for those risky events. Some of Peter's doctoral work required drivers to evaluate videotaped driving scenes, in terms of the risk the driver would feel were she or he to be driving in those situations. The scenes themselves were carefully matched, such that the same driving situations and manoeuvres appeared in a number of different films. Having rated a subset of the available films, the driver then had to watch some of these again, along with other films of the same manoeuvres at the same junctions. The driver had to decide which films had been seen before, and which had not. Drivers readily recognised driving scenes that they had previously rated as risky, but they tended to also report that they had previously seen risky exemplars of low-risk films they had previously seen and rated. This same result

---

[2] It is worth noting that this facilitation through context re-instatement may be because a sufficiently similar physiological state occurs at encoding and retrieval, or because fear causes a specific type of attention (i.e. processing operation) to the situation at hand.

emerged from a range of other similar studies in which the assessments made of the films at the outset were in terms other than the risk the driver would feel in those situations. It seemed as if the presence of risk in a film was sufficient for the driver to claim they had seen that film before, whether or not they had actually done so.

At the time, we believed that these results showed something akin to "weapon-focus", (i.e. a tendency for attention to be attracted to and dominated by threat-related material in a scene). The presence of something evaluated as threatening was sufficient to ensure that it would be recognised in future, but also sufficient to impoverish encoding of background information. Such "background information" was encoded in low-risk films, but was no longer accessible where a similar film was encountered, which now contained some risky event. This led to false recognition. Unfortunately, when these studies were originally carried out, we relied on drivers' subjective evaluations of risk, and did not corroborate this with physiological measures. Later, when we monitored skin conductance and heart-rate activity among other drivers watching the same films, there was very little evidence of the fluctuations in arousal levels so characteristic of real driving.

Thus, although these studies tend to support ideas that emerge from the broader eyewitness testimony literature, it is not clear that either our own studies, or indeed those slide-based laboratory studies considered earlier, adequately simulated actual feelings of threat, danger, risk, etc. In the studies that take care to assess the impact of the stimuli used (and surprisingly many did not), and our earlier work, people make deliberate assessments of threat, although they may experience very few actual feelings of being endangered. In situations where people feel endangered, there are accompanying physiological changes. In such situations people can also make risk or danger assessments, which may well correlate, as we have shown, with objectively measurable changes in arousal. Unfortunately for our own and most other studies in the literature, the influence on memory of cognitive assessment of threat without such physiological changes may not be the same as when fear is genuinely experienced.

The study described earlier in which drivers drove along a fixed route making occasional subjective assessments of danger and difficulty while having various physiological measures taken, can help to address some of these issues. When the drivers completed the route, they returned to our laboratory for a debriefing. During this they were asked, by experimenters who did not accompany them on the drive, to remember as much as they could of the events that had occurred at six specific locations. Having done so they were asked a series of questions relating to their own actions and the presence of particular types of road users. One week later they returned and were put through the same memory exercise, again by different interviewers. We were subsequently able to assess the accuracy of their recall, and its relationship to our subjective and objective indices of danger and arousal, by examining a videotape of each of the actual drives made. The results of this study, which is perhaps unique in the literature on incidental

TABLE 7.2
Relationships between assessments of danger, difficulty, arousal,
and memory accuracy and quality as a function of delay

| | Immediately after drive | | | 1 week after drive | | | |
|---|---|---|---|---|---|---|---|
| | Overall accuracy | Vivid detail | Rest of memory | Overall accuracy | Vivid detail | Rest of memory | Stability over time |
| Difficulty | 0.18** | 0.21** | 0.40** | 0.16** | 0.43** | 0.11 | 0.01 |
| Danger | 0.43** | 0.02 | 0.55** | 0.17** | 0.57** | 0.25** | 0.05 |
| Ngsr | 0.16** | 0.03 | 0.27** | 0.10 | 0.39** | 0.32** | 0.16** |
| SDgsr | 0.12 | 0.17** | 0.08 | 0.14 | 0.06 | 0.01 | 0.03 |
| BPM | 0.14 | 0.15** | 0.13 | 0.08 | 0.08 | 0.08 | 0.03 |
| Variance | 0.19** | 0.28** | 0.05 | 0.19** | 0.04 | 0.03 | 0.04 |

Ngsr: Number of GSR responses at junction. SDgsr: Standard deviation of GSR activity at junction. BPM: Heart rate, Beats Per Minute. Variance: Standard deviation of BPM.
** Statistically reliable correlations at $p < .01$.

memory and arousal, are presented in full in Groeger, Chapman, and Clegg (2000). They can briefly be summarised as follows.

Drivers remembered whether or not they stopped at particular junctions. They also reliably remembered whether or not there was a vehicle ahead of them as they drove through the junction, and whether or not other vehicles crossed their paths. They did not remember whether or not there were vehicles parked at or near the junction, nor did they remember whether there were pedestrians or cyclists present. The answers to these questions were highly consistent across time. Although drivers reliably remembered when a vehicle was ahead of them at the junction, they provided as many accurate as inaccurate details about its make, the type of vehicle it was, and its colour. They correctly remembered its location, i.e. inner or outer lane, and its actions, although these details became less reliable by the second recall. There is thus some reasonably reliable recollection of things the driver might have had to interact with, or considered interacting of, but not of, as it were, more irrelevant or peripheral information. Even with those objects that were reliably remembered, attributes of these objects (e.g. shape and colour) were not well remembered. These might also be regarded as irrelevant to how the driver might interact with them. As Table 7.2 shows, both subjective measures and objective indices of arousal relate to the accuracy, durability, and stability of memories for driving at the six locations in question, but perhaps not in the way one would have expected from the literature.

Immediately after the drive, if the driver had rated the junction as difficult to drive through, the overall accuracy or his or her memory for events at the junction was more accurate. If, according to the driver, the drive through the junction had been difficult, the driver considered the most important detail of what they remembered was vividly remembered. The remaining details remembered were also rated to be vividly remembered (i.e. "background"). The more dangerous the junction was rated, the more accurate recall was, and the more vividly remembered were the background details, but not the most important detail. The number of discernible galvanic skin responses was also related to overall accuracy of memory. GSR activity across the junction and mean heart rate were reliably correlated only with the vividness with which the most important detail was remembered, while heart-rate variability was also related to overall memory accuracy.

A week later, danger and difficulty ratings made while driving through the junction were both related to the overall accuracy of memory for events at the junction, and to the vividness of the central detail, but no longer to the vividness of the background details. Number of GSRs related to the vividness of both the central detail and background of the memory, but was no longer related to accuracy. When memory for events was assessed one week later, heart rate at the time of driving through the junction was no longer related to the accuracy or quality of memory, although heart-rate variability still related to accuracy, but not to vividness. Thus, in general, increased physiological arousal at encoding is actually related to better memory for details, although this relationship weakens over time, except for the change in heart rate across the junction.

Finally, comparing the stability of the account of events immediately after the drive and one week later, only the number of GSRs when driving through the junction was related to stability. Because of the pattern of relationships observed between physiological activity and lack of accuracy, this means that those events that are correctly remembered are remembered for longer where the individual is under stress. Subjective assessments of danger and difficulty were not associated with stability.

In summary, these results indicate that drivers' incidental memory for traffic conditions is good, but primarily for objects with which they might have to interact. Memory for details of these events is unreliable. Experiencing danger and difficulty promotes more vivid and more durable memories—experiencing danger perhaps more so than experiencing difficulty. The tendency to remember details is promoted by arousal at encoding, and some aspects of arousal are related to the stability of recall over time, if not its accuracy. It thus seems that increased arousal, at least at the levels encountered in normal traffic, has positive consequences for memory accuracy. This may in part be because drivers were also required to make subjective assessments of danger and difficulty. Whether events that promoted the same physiological changes but were not attended to directly in order to provide ratings would have the same consequences is an open but very interesting question. These relationships parallel the findings that have emerged from laboratory-based studies using materials that serve to simulate arousal, albeit that a clear dissociation between differential remembering of "central" and "peripheral" details was not observed. However, this use of driving as a means of assessing the relationships between arousal and memory is rather preliminary, and would benefit from replication.

# ASSESSING DRIVING SCENES

*There are many ways in which drivers might judge or assess the situations in which they drive. Our research has shown that assessments of "danger" and "difficulty" relate to driving experience and to how safely people drive. I describe this research in more detail here, and reconsider some issues to do with scene perception.*

## Danger and difficulty assessments when driving

Our interest in distinguishing danger and difficulty in driving stems from some research that was carried out in order to explore how drivers assessed driving scenes. This showed that individual pieces of video, rated across various dimensions after they had been watched, were largely considered in terms of two broader dimensions. Judgements of traffic scenes (JOTs) related to the "risk" driven would have felt, their proximity to other vehicles in the scene, the amount of concentration required, the normality or usualness of the situation, how stressful it would be to drive in such circumstances, and the seriousness of the consequences that would result from an accident which occurred in the circumstances depicted. We termed this factor "danger", when it consistently emerged in every one of the principal components analyses of the 24 scenes studied. The other factor that emerged consistently across films was a composite of the chances of something unexpected happening, the amount of control the individual would have, the skill required of the driver, the number of accidents that might occur in such circumstances, the speed at which the cars appeared to be travelling, and the business of the scene. We termed this factor "difficulty". The fact that these dimensions reliably emerged for each of the scenes studied suggested to us that these were indeed aspects of the ways in which drivers judged scenes, at least under laboratory conditions. The other finding that encouraged our earlier efforts was that drivers with similar amounts of driving experience, but who differed in age, assessed scenes differently in terms of danger and difficulty, and drivers of similar age, but with different amounts of traffic experience, also differed. It has proved notoriously difficult to isolate what ought in principle to be separate effects of age and experience in driving tasks (see Groeger & Chapman, 1996).

Since then, greatly assisted by Sean Hammond's statistical wizardry, we have developed an index of how well individual drivers distinguish between danger and difficulty. This has allowed us to show that understanding of the danger and difficulty of traffic scenes develops as a function of the amount of driving experience young drivers report. This study, conducted with Ben Clegg, involved the testing of 180 teenage qualified drivers, using the JOTs task (see Groeger & Clegg, 1999). The goodness of fit to the predicted danger–difficulty dimensions improved not as a function of chronological age, but as a consequence of each driver's self-reported distance driven since passing the state practical driving test, suggesting that the differentiation of danger and difficulty is something that develops as a function of task experience.

Under real traffic circumstances danger and difficulty ratings have been made by drivers and have been shown, in the study discussed earlier, to be differently related to the physiological changes that occur while driving. Recently, in a study reported by Grayson (1998), drivers were accompanied by a state driving examiner, and were asked to make ratings of the danger and difficulty of the situations they drove through. The results showed a clear relationship between the rating the driver made of the situation and the driving examiner's rating of that driver's ability to drive safely.[3]

These results suggest to us that assessing danger and difficulty in driving scenes is an important part of learning to be a safe driver, and that these concepts of danger and difficulty develop and differentiate as a function of task experience. But what is actually being learned from the experience we gain while driving? How are the scenes seen evaluated and used as a basis for future action? In attempting to answer these questions we need to return to some issues raised in Chapters 4 and 5, in relation to scene perception. This is a way of laying down some further building blocks, but also a way of introducing consideration of another issue, that of hazard perception.

## Scene perception revisited

Henderson and Hollingworth (1998) suggest that scene perception is initially driven by visual features of the scene, whereas later in scene inspection, allocation of gaze is more influenced by what they refer to as "semantic" properties of the objects in the scene. Where people will look in a scene is thought to depend on the formation of a "salience map", which is a representation of potential saccade targets generated from an early parse of the scene into regions of potential interest. The initial parse is based on low-frequency information which is subjected to a fast early analysis, with the salience of different regions initially determined by information such as luminance, contrast, texture, colour, contour density, etc. The positions of regions of potential interest are coded in a representation of the visual space and are assigned a priority or "saliency weight". This saliency weight and the combined spatial positions of such weights form the saliency map (Mahoney & Ullman, 1988). As we will see, salience may also be influenced by the viewer's task. Such influences might include having the subject search for particular objects, requiring them to produce global semantic analysis of the scene, or constraining the likely position of semantically consistent targets, or may arise from the evaluation the person is seeking to make

---

[3] As these two scales do not reflect all of the different aspects of danger and difficulty that are tapped by the individual judgements which make up the composite danger and difficulty factors, these may be less discriminable than when measured using the full form of the JOTs task.

of the scene (e.g. Yarbus, 1967, which shows that the same scene is scanned differently depending on the nature of the judgement being made).

The whole retinal image is not fully analysed by visual systems in order to yield a complete representation of the whole scene (e.g. see Churchland, Ramachandran, & Sejnowski, 1994; Grimes, 1996). Instead, driven by the salience map, aspects of the scene are successively subjected to detailed analysis. Henderson and Hollingworth (1998) provide a convincing account of how this might be achieved. First, visuo-spatial attention is allocated to the scene region with the highest saliency weight (Koch & Ullman, 1985), with further attentional resources being deployed in order to keep the eyes fixated on the attended scene region (Henderson, 1992; Henderson & Ferreira, 1993). The eyes remain fixated on the selected element of the scene until perceptual and cognitive analysis is completed, or until the rate at which information is gained about that region slows markedly. In the first case, the saliency weight for that region is reduced and attention will be released and allocated to the region that now has the highest saliency, and the eyes are programmed to move to that region (Henderson, 1992). Where analysis of the current region is slow, perhaps because of a scene's complexity, a within-region re-fixation will occur, in order to acquire additional information, or simply because of occulo-motor factors.[4] Henderson and Hollingworth (1998, p. 290) further suggest that:

> as individual scene regions are fixated and cognitively analysed, saliency weights will be modified to reflect the relative cognitive interest of those regions. In other words, the source of the saliency weight for a given region will change from primarily visual to primarily cognitive interest as regions are fixated and understood ... as scene viewing and understanding progresses region salience will become heavily determined by factors such as semantic informativeness ... eyes then sent to regions of cognitive salience rather than visual salience leading to greater fixation density and total fixation time on semantically interesting objects and scene regions.

One of the key factors in such cognitive salience and semantic informativeness is the extent to which the scene conforms to expectations we might have. Many researchers have reported advantages for the processing of objects in their expected context. Thus, for example, objects fixated in a scene in which they are likely to appear are easier to identify than the same objects fixated in an implausible context (Boyce & Pollatsek, 1992; DeGraef, 1992; Henderson, 1992), and plausible objects exhibit shorter first-fixation durations (DeGraef, Christiaens, & d'Ydewalle, 1990), shorter gaze durations (Antes & Pentland, 1981; Friedman, 1979), and shorter naming latencies (Boyce & Pollatsek, 1992) than implausible

---

[4] It seems to me that detecting the rate of gain of information asymptotes would provide a simple but reliable basis for re-allocation of attention.

objects. Importantly, perceptibility of objects, even prior to fixation, in a real-world scene is enhanced when they belong in that scene (Wolfe & Bennett, 1997). The first region fixated, and the detection of implausible objects, depends in part on how well the situation is understood (i.e. the degree to which it is interpretable within past experience). In poorly understood scenes, implausible objects may be discriminated without being fixated, and may be subsequently fixated sooner than plausible objects. In well understood scenes populated by plausible items, these perceptual advantages for unexpected items may disappear or reverse. In such cases it may be that extra-foveal detection of schema-specified object features allows superior pre-fixation identification of plausible objects, or that the scene is more efficiently segmented, separating the plausible object from its background, thus providing a more salient target for attention shift.

These findings suggest that the way a scene will be analysed and inspected will depend on why the observer is looking at it, e.g. looking for a direction sign, rather than looking for something with which one will collide. Knowing what to expect in such circumstances will allow more efficient searching, but it may also serve to make deviations from what might otherwise be expected less detectable, and less easily selected for further analysis. Thus, we might expect novice drivers and experienced drivers to differ in how they analyse and interpret traffic scenes, but differences may be observed for a variety of reasons. The experienced driver, having encountered many dangerous situations previously, is likely to do better when asked to perform a task in which they have to detect hazards. This knowledge effect might be expected to generalise to any explicit search and detect task (e.g. looking for a traffic sign). However where, say, the hazards to be detected are very unusual, experienced drivers' knowledge may "lock in" their expectations of what an appropriate answer will be. This would result in unusual objects being detected later, in very familiar situations. In less familiar circumstances unusual hazards may be more detectable. For the novice, not only will knowledge of what constitutes a hazard be more limited, but because their exposure to different driving situations will also be more limited, expectations of what unusual event might plausibly occur will also be less strong. Following this logic, we might expect novices to be better than more experienced drivers at detecting certain types of hazards in some situations, although overall the experienced driver should be better able to perform the task with familiar types of hazard in a broader range of situations. This way of thinking about how hazard detection will vary with the degree of exposure to particular events in specific situations, also predicts that the extent to which hazards will be noticed, even where the driver is not intentionally searching for them, will vary as a function of driving experience, and what that experience comprises (i.e. the range and degree of familiarity with different driving situations). Thus, experience confers a general benefit in detecting unusualness, and thus hazards, but finding evidence of this benefit will depend very much on what the hazard is, where it is in the scene, and what the nature of the scene is. This may account for the lack of positive effects of experience when people are directly asked to rate the dangers in a scene (see Kruysse & Christie, 1992). It is important to keep in mind what I have discussed here with regard to scene perception and assessment when considering hazard perception in the next section.

## HAZARD PERCEPTION

*Encouraged by face validity, rather than any particularly sophisticated psychological theorising, for several decades researchers have pursued the reasonable idea that people who are safer drivers will be better able to perceive the hazards in their environment. Here I want to examine the evidence for this assumption, and seek to set the test within a theoretical context which arises from the foregoing sections.*

Many research have sought to develop tests of drivers' hazard-perception abilities, (e.g. Hull & Christie, 1992; McKenna & Crick, 1991; Pelz & Krupat, 1974). Many of these tests require individuals to sit and watch a video display of traffic scenes and indicate, by pressing a button, when a hazard is visible. It is assumed that the earlier the driver detects the hazard, the safer that person will be on the road. Generally, experienced drivers, whose a priori likelihood of being involved in an accident is low compared with a newly qualified driver, have been found to show better anticipatory skills (but see Chapman & Underwood, 1998). This assumes that absence of accidents while holding a licence is a surrogate of some cognitive, emotional, or motivational qualities that will generalise to risks and hazards which are encountered in the future. However, there must surely be limits on this transfer. I consider some of these limits next.

### Assumptions underlying hazard perception tests

First of all it must be assumed that hazard perception is a learned rather than an innate ability—an assumption common to every hazard perception test. Otherwise we would see no difference between experienced and novice drivers. That is not to say drivers must experience every possible hazard in order to be able to detect such a hazard again in the future. We might reasonably expect some acquired knowledge of hazards to generalise to quite similar circumstances. As discussed earlier, the transfer of training to untrained stimuli is limited to those that bear some functional relationship to the trained set (see Chapter 5). Tests of hazard perception will thus be effective or not in discriminating between drivers depending on the relationship between the hazard experience of the drivers tested and the films included in the test battery. This is, of course, true of any test—but as we know little about what hazard-perception ability is in theoretical terms, it is wise to remind ourselves of what any resultant classification of drivers is based upon.

There is another, more fundamental, problem which also relates to successful transfer of acquired knowledge. People who in traffic anticipate hazards and respond to them appropriately by, for example, decelerating, braking, changing their course, or even accelerating, are likely to learn associations between particular types of hazard or event and particular ways of responding. Just as in the studies of procedural reinstatement by Fendrich et al. (1995; see Chapter 5), quite mundane stimuli responded to in a particular way, will be responded to slower where the response requirements are changed. Attempting to relearn a new way of responding to a particular stimulus becomes more difficult the stronger or more established are previous relationships between these stimuli and some response (see Fisk & Jones, 1992; Fisk, Lee, & Rogers, 1991). This means that people who really do respond safely when confronted by hazards in actual driving conditions, may actually respond more slowly in hazard perception tests, because they have learned, for example, to decelerate rather than press a button in response to hazards. It also follows from this, that simply detecting hazards when watching video tapes, while it may well reveal strong anticipatory skills, will only confer a real safety advantage in traffic where the additional time available to such people is used to choose the appropriate way of responding to the hazard.

## Hazard perception: Training, memory, and automaticity

It has been suggested that hazard-perception abilities can be trained and it does seem that people who receive rather general road safety training perform better on tests of hazard-perception ability (e.g. McKenna & Crick, 1991, 1994). Precisely what is learned from such training, and how it may generalise to hazard perception or actual driving, remains unclear. It is possible that what can be gained from such training is a general idea of what unexpected events may occur, and what the consequences of these might be, or that people are motivated to become more responsible or cautious. How one controls for false positive responding (i.e. indicating that a hazard was present when none was) thus becomes critical, and unfortunately these data are rarely reported in studies in this area. The issue remains of what people are doing when performing in hazard-perception tests.

It seems clear that experience of driving is required to perform well on tests of hazard perception. This suggests that the knowledge required is more than simply determining that one is on a collision course, or that something is heading towards us, of which adults and older children are equally capable (see Hoffman & Mortimer, 1994). A test simply made up of determining whether one's course was obstructed would be unlikely to discriminate between drivers and non-drivers. Instead the items included in the test must relate to previously encountered hazards, or information acquired indirectly about hazards from public education campaigns. Our own in-depth analysis of the instruction actually given to drivers shows that there is too little formal teaching from professional instructors about risks, hazards, or dangers, and in most cases driving instruction will have been received too long ago for it to provide a reliable basis for discriminating between dangerous and safe situations (see Groeger & Clegg, 2000).

Hazard-perception tests, and indeed real driving, require that some element of the scene "reminds" the driver of this previously acquired road knowledge. Thus, except in the case of imminent collision scenarios, detecting hazards is based on what is retrieved from memory. The driver is not required to provide an account of what is hazardous, nor why it is so, but either to determine that it is sufficiently similar to some past circumstance which was understood to be dangerous, or alternatively that it is sufficiently far from his or her previous experience that some caution should be exercised. As such, determining that a hazard is present is more similar to recognition than to recall. It should be noted that effects of schemata, particularly with respect to typicality and familiarity, while influential in recall or reproduction of past experience, have different effects in recognition. Barbara Tversky summarises thus: "schemas may be useful both in construction at encoding and retrieval, but they do not seem to be operative at recognition. In recognition, on the other hand, atypical features may have an advantage because of their very distinctiveness. Unusual features that are easy to recognize are at the same time more difficult to integrate into a schema" (Tversky, 1997, p. 266). A similar point emerges from studies of memory for faces, which show that caricatured faces are identified or recognised more rapidly (Benson & Perrett, 1992). Hazards, by virtue of the fact that they are unfamiliar, and perhaps distortions of usual traffic situations, might then be expected to have a similar advantage in terms of identification and recognition, among those with enough experience to have accumulated sufficient "safe" experience to allow hazards to be recognised as unusual. That is not to say all hazard-perception responses will be based directly on previous driving experiences. For example, so many warnings are given to children about safe crossing procedures (e.g. not emerging from between parked cars), that the presence of parked cars in a video may be readily identified as a hazard, on the basis of declarative, rather than episodic memory. It may be that such knowledge is foregrounded more when people participate in a direct test of hazard perception (i.e. in an explicit test—can you think of anything that might be hazardous about driving here?). I suspect that under normal driving circumstances, the determination that there is danger ahead spontaneously interrupts some other primary task (e.g. way finding, day dreaming, etc). In such a case it cannot be due to intention-driven search and retrieval from memory.

This raises another issue: whether hazard perception is an "automatic" or a "controlled" process. Viewed simply in the way in which these terms were originally operationally defined by Shiffrin and Schneider (1977), exposure to hazard is probably too rare and too inconsistent for automaticity to result—as

extended consistent mapping of stimuli to responses is very unlikely. An alternative account of automaticity is offer by Gordon Logan. According to Logan's
theory, two processes are set in train at the outset of any (classification) task.
One is an algorithmic, effortful search for a solution to the problem at hand;
the other is an automatic search of previous solutions to determine which of
those previously encountered best matches the current requirement. The process that delivers an answer first is the one that impacts on behaviour. In
his view, with increasing task experience, performance will result more from the
automatic retrieval of past instances than from the effortful algorithmic search.
If hazard perception were to be due to retrieval of past experiences, in order to
determine unfamiliarity or distinctiveness, hazard-perception abilities should,
in general, be better in experienced than in novice drivers. Hazard-perception
processes should be less disrupted in experienced drivers, who might be expected
to rely on automatic retrieval from past experience, than in novices, who have
insufficient experience for the memory-retrieval-based process to yield an
answer. As absence of automaticity is frequently equated with amount of disruption from some concurrent activity, this seems to lead to a clear prediction.
Hazard perception will be more slowed in inexperienced drivers than it is in
more experienced drivers when performed at the same time as another attention-
demanding task—as the latter are relying on automatic retrieval of past experiences
while the former will be more affected because they are engaged in an effortful
algorithmic processing. Of course, if we do not accept the Logan view of automaticity, and instead rely on a more traditional account which sees automaticity
as a result of extended practice, experienced drivers should also show less impact
on hazard perception of a concurrently performed task than inexperienced drivers.
This is exactly the question Frank McKenna and colleagues posed a few years ago.

They found (McKenna & Crick, 1994) that newly qualified drivers' simple
reaction times were slowed while performing a letter-monitoring task, in which
participants were required to detect a target letter among letters presented at one
per second. They also found that time taken to detect hazards was also reliably
slowed, by about 200 milliseconds. Unfortunately, it is not clear whether this
effect would remain reliable were the change in reaction time taken into account.
My calculation of the two effect sizes suggests that the reaction time effect is
substantially larger, and thus the position is rather inconclusive for younger
inexperienced drivers. Summarising the results of other studies, McKenna and
Horswill report that "in two experiments we found that experienced drivers'
hazard perception scores suffered more than those of inexperienced drivers. From
these results it seems clear that hazard perception is dependent on higher order
cognition" (McKenna & Horswill, 1997, p. 80). Unfortunately, this study of
experienced drivers, although it used a secondary task that would have imposed
considerable demands on attention, i.e. random generation, did not include a
measure of simple reaction time, and thus we do not know whether the slowing
of hazard perception found in this study reflects a reduction in ability to detect

hazards, or to generate a response. If we take it that the impact of a concurrent task really was on hazard perception, rather than on reaction time or response generation, McKenna's results suggest that hazard perception is an attention-demanding task, rather than an automatic one. Frank favours the view that hazard perception depends on the building, maintenance, and modification of a mental model of the driving situation, which relates both to the discussion of situational memory (see Tversky, 1997; and Chapter 6 here), and concepts such as situational awareness (Endsley, 1995). Unfortunately, in the studies carried out, while they appear to rule out the possibility that hazard perception is an automatic process (i.e. unaffected by other ongoing cognitive demands), it is not clear that the bottleneck occurs both at the stage at which some determination of "hazardness" is made, or only at the point when the participant generates a response to indicate their assessment. Until this is clear, say from studies where physiological activity is scrutinised for evidence of risk detection rather than from studies where overt responding is required, theorising about the nature of the psychological processes involved is fraught with opportunities for misdeductions.

## Validity of hazard-perception tests

A final point regarding hazard-perception tests, but one that is very important, is that validations are few and far between. The study most widely cited as demonstrating a link between hazard perception and accident involvement, by Watts and Quimby (1979), made use of a continuous response, in which drivers continually adjusted a lever as the level of risk encountered changed, rather than seeking a single discrete response. The drivers in question also sat in a vehicle, and watched a screen providing near actual size projections of traffic events. The fact that people have subsequently failed to replicate the Watts and Quimby findings with other stimulus arrangements (personal communication G. Grayson, 1998), should give us pause for thought. Recent failures to find relationships between level of accident involvement and hazard-perception time, or differences between the hazard-perception time of accident-involved and accident-free drivers, with samples vastly exceeding the size of the original study (Chapman & Underwood, 1998; Groeger, Field, & Hammond, 1998) also bring into question the assumption that button-pressing time in response to hazards will serve to identify safe and dangerous drivers.

A different approach to the issue of validating hazard-perception tests is reported by Grayson (1998, p. 11), who describes a study in which 100 drivers who had previously been tested on the computerised assessment of drivers' skills (see Groeger et al., 1998) and reports that "shorter response times to the filmed hazard were assessed as being attentive, safe and skilful drivers, and as having good anticipation and good speed setting abilities". However, as each of these assessments made by an accompanying driving examiner is strongly influenced by age, as is hazard-perception score, it is unclear whether the examiner was merely assessing older drivers more positively, or whether hazard perception really was predicting how people drove during the assessment drive. Similarly, the extent to which an individual driver actually drove faster or slower than all of the drivers taking part, was related to hazard-perception ability $[r(100) = -.21; p < .05]$, but importantly also to age $[r(100) = -.34; p < .01]$. When age was statistically controlled, the relationship between relative driving speed and hazard-perception ability was no longer statistically reliable. Thus, although tests of hazard perception may relate to the individual's actual driving, and the assessments experts might may of his of her driving, it is at best unclear whether these relationships merely reflect broader relationships between age and the measures taken. Nevertheless, studying the relationships between actual driving and off-road measures offers considerably more promise for assessing driving aptitude, rather than accident involvement or accident history, because of the "noise" inherent in such measures of relative safety.

## SUMMARY

This chapter has attempted to consider in detail the ways in which we change physiologically when we confront danger, and how these changes and the way we appraise them might subsequently be used to allow us to determine whether situations we later encounter are dangerous or not. The determination that something is or is not dangerous proceeds, I suggest, from a rather unspecific feeling that something about the environment one is in has previously been encountered and is associated with high arousal. Events that are associated with high arousal have an advantage in terms of the vividness and durability of the memories they create. The fact that memory for certain types of detail is rather unreliable, even when these are associated with threat, may serve to show that some types of detail (e.g. the colour of a vehicle) are irrelevant when the driver determines that something is dangerous. In principle, this would allow a broader range of situations to be regarded as "similar" to the previously threatening situation— facilitating greater transfer of previously acquired knowledge. It needs to be borne in mind that the techniques that have been used, by ourselves and other researchers, only assess what subjects can report. Were memory for past events, especially with regard to their emotional implications, to proceed on an implicit basis, these suppositions might well be incorrect. Whether memory for danger is implicit or explicit, the determination that something is dangerous must proceed from an analysis of the visual scene. Initially, it seems reasonable to assume, this is based on features of visual interest in the scene, and only subsequently is there inspection of the aspects of this saliency map that have cognitive or emotional implications. I doubt whether tests of hazard perception using video can tap into these processes in a meaningful way but they have enabled us to come closer to posing what I regard as the more crucial questions.

# CHAPTER EIGHT

# Appraisal, efficacy, and action

*This chapter explores the attitudes people have towards driving, how these relate to their evaluations of their own ability, and how these attitudes and self-evaluations influence actual performance of the driving task. In doing so the chapter provides a cognitive interpretation of attitudes, and the relationship between attitudes, behavioural intentions, and actual actions. The basis of this approach is an extension of Groeger and Grande's (1996) account of the development of task-related selves (in this case a driving self or self-schema which summarises one's own driving experiences), as well as Bandura's conception of self-efficacy (1997) and the role of self-evaluation in reactions to being threatened, and the subsequent impact on performance.*

As has probably become clear, I have a very broad conception of what cognition is, and a very strong belief in the contribution cognition can make. This extends to the attitudes we have and the appraisals we make of ourselves and others. In the first part of this chapter I want to make clear the relationship between cognition, attitudes, and behaviour, as I see it. Having done so, I will devote rather more attention to the attitudes and beliefs we have about our own and other drivers' ability.

## BELIEFS ABOUT ATTITUDES

As I understand from the social psychological literature, attitudes reflect evaluative experience which refers to specific objects, events, people, or issues, and which frequently carries an implication about how one ought to act with respect to that object or event. As such, although somewhat more complex than the types of memory I have considered up to now, I do not see that we need to assume that attitudes are anything more than complexes of self-relevant memories, with some evaluative or affective content, which endure over time. There is abundant evidence in the literature on autobiographical memory, and that concerning the relationship between emotion and memory, that self-related materials are remembered more accurately and more durably, and exercise a broader influence on how situations and events are interpreted, than materials that are not interpreted as personally relevant (see Conway, 1990; Groeger, 1997; Rogers, Kuiper, & Kirker, 1977; Slameka & Graf, 1978). Because we are also more likely to remember actions we ourselves have produced, and are more likely to repeat these consistently than those we have merely witnessed, it seems to me that the suggestion that attitudes tend to be associated with particular forms of action can also easily be incorporated within the conception of cognition that is fundamental to the earlier chapters of this book. This is not to deny the importance of work that seeks to understand how different attitudes relate to each other, why different attitudes are held by different people, or how attitudes might be acquired or changed. Instead, it is a recognition that while reportage of one's own or evaluations of others' behaviour can be very illuminating, fundamentally, a satisfactory understanding of behaviour requires an account based in individual cognition—that is, in terms of the processing abilities and biases we inherit, and the experiences we retain from our exposure to the environments we imagine and inhabit.

This position, although one that will doubtless upset many friends and colleagues who are social psychologists, does avoid some of the infelicities of more social accounts. For example, if we adopt the view that attitudes are in fact organised memories of events and experiences, we do not need to assume that such structures will yield some "consistency". Nor is there any need to assume some minimum amount of instability (Heider, 1946), nor some intrinsic balance (Newcomb, 1981). The issue of the relationship between reported attitudes and behaviour can also be seen in a different light.

Wicker (1969), on the basis of an extensive meta-analysis, reported that only in a minority of studies was there any close relationship found between verbally expressed attitudes and overt behaviour. Others have objected to this suggestion, and instead claim that when attitudes and behaviour are measured at the same level of specificity or generality, correlations between attitudes and behaviour are higher (Ajzen & Fishbein, 1977). It is unsurprising that supplying greater contextual detail would allow a greater consistency to emerge especially if, as I believe, experiences are episodically encoded. First, it is important to recognise that the importance of attitudinal and normative factors in the determination of intention may vary depending on the context. Second, that tighter specification within the measures of both attitude and subjective norm of the precise target and context (when and where) of the behaviour in question, improves the relationship. Both points are suggestions made by Ajzen and Fishbein (1980) and

Bentler and Spechart (1979) and are entirely consistent with the view that consistency depends in part on episodic memory encodings. Although I am uncomfortable with some of the less cognitively oriented phrasing, I support Fazio's (1986) account of "evaluative beliefs", in which attitude influences behaviour by selectively activating various thoughts stored in memory. By activating memory, "beliefs" lead to a selective perception of the subject of the attitude. Fazio's suggestion that attitude is dependent on previous positive or negative experiences, and that it influences decisions made prior to embarking on a course of action, is again consistent with the current position.

Finally, the fact that self-reports regarding affective, cognitive, and behavioural components are more highly intercorrelated than are self-reported attitudes, actual measures of heart rate, and what people do (see Breckler, 1984) may simply reflect the difference between explicit or more direct measures of remembering and more implicit or indirect measures of remembering (see Chapter 6 and Richardson-Klahven & Bjork, 1988). The fact that we can bias the attitudes people express, and indeed their impressions of themselves and other people, through simple manipulations of the information currently available, as reported later and by Eiser and van der Pligt (1988), is all grist to this particular mill.

## ASSESSMENTS OF OURSELVES AND OTHERS

In this section I want to consider one particular complex of attitudes, that beliefs we have about our own and others' abilities. There are two reasons for doing so. First, some conceptions of why people engage in risky behaviour (e.g. Brown & Groeger, 1988) assume that risky behaviour depends on the dangers considered to be inherent in a situation and the person's beliefs about their ability to overcome these dangers. A second reason for concentrating on assessments of ourselves and others is that I believe they demonstrate how the cognitive principles outlined earlier shed light on what might be regarded as more "social" phenomena.

### Comparisons with "typical" unknown others

A widely held belief among some driving researchers is that we, as drivers, all believe we are better than average. This impossible belief was first reported by Svenson (1981), on the basis of a study in which drivers were asked to identify where on a 10-point scale they rated their skill and safety. Svenson found that the majority of people rated themselves above the mid-point (i.e. 50%), and some time ago now Ivan Brown and myself replicated this effect (Groeger & Brown, 1989). Unfortunately this finding, if not spurious, is very misleading, and conceals issues that are far more important than those it reveals.

A number of studies in the wider psychological literature show that when asked to do so, people rate their adherence to ethical principles (Baumhart, 1968), their health (Larwood, 1978; Weinstein, 1980, 1982), and their leadership, athleticism, interpersonal skills, and personality (see Dunning, Meyerowitz, &

Holzberg, 1989) more positively than when making similar ratings for an average person. With a few exceptions, psychologists have rarely been able to collect data on how well these people actually perform on the tasks they themselves consider they carry out with "above average" success, and have in general simply concluded that people tend to have an overly positive view of their own abilities.

A number of studies report similar findings in the driving domain. McKenna, Stanier, and Lewis (1991) showed that over a range of 20 driving skills, drivers consistently rated themselves higher than they rated "an average driver" on a 0–20 scale. Finn and Bragg (1986) and Mathews and Moran (1986) have also reported studies that were taken to indicate that drivers had an overly positive view of their own ability. These studies depend on the assumption that the driver assessing him or herself can make equally reliable assessments of the "average driver". However, as many have suggested that "average" is a negative term (e.g. Dunning et al., 1989; Groeger & Grande, 1996), and thus encourages the subject to claim they are "better", these studies may have unwittingly biased subjects towards making more positive assessments. In the studies reported by Dunning et al. (1989) students rated the extent to which various personality traits applied to them. Dunning et al. consistently showed that their subjects made "apparently impossible self-serving assessments to a greater degree when the traits were ambiguous . . . when considering unambiguous traits, people exhibited hardly any self-serving pattern whatsoever. That is, once the criteria are clearly established, people have the ability to assess their own standing in relation to their peers accurately" (1989, p. 1085).

The study reported by McCormick, Walkey, and Green (1986) is interesting in this respect. McCormick et al. asked drivers to assess themselves with respect to "the average driver" and "a very good driver". They found that drivers rate themselves as better than average, but not as good as "a very good driver". One might thus conclude that while drivers tend to have a positive view of their own ability, such a view may not be exaggerated (i.e. they do not consider themselves to be "very good"). However, there may be an additional source of difficulty lurking in the McCormick methodology, in that although the study at least sought to "anchor" the judgements made, subjects were effectively asked to judge themselves with respect to two ambiguous standards. In other words, what constitutes the "average driver" is very ambiguous—what the "very good driver" is may be clearer, but it is still ambiguous. In a study of some 300 drivers of different ages and experience levels, we showed that the tendency to believe oneself to be better than another driver the day after passing their driving test was highly prevalent, but was much more likely in drivers who were older and more experienced (Groeger & Grande, 1996). The more unlike you someone is in terms of their level of experience, the more negatively is your evaluation of them. It may be that once again, what this shows is that the less direct knowledge you have of "the other" and thus the more unclear is the standard against which you are judging yourself, the more self-serving will be your judgement, which was the position reached earlier by Dunning et al. (1989), in their study of students' assessments of their own and others' personalities. However, I believe we are in a position to say rather more than that the overly positive view of own ability which emerges from these studies is simply due to the ambiguity of the judgements people are asked to make. In the next section I consider the primary theories that purport to account for how we assess ourselves in relation to others.

## Self-enhancement and downward comparison

According to Brown's (1986) "self-enhancement" theory, when engaged in self–other comparisons, people tend to over-attribute positive attributes to themselves, and simultaneously over-attribute negative attributes to others. This not only leads to a positive view of self, but an active devaluation of the other. In contrast, "downward comparison theory" (e.g. Wills, 1981) suggests that this positive view of self is actively maintained by choosing less able others against whom to compare oneself, or where this is not possible, by actively derogating the attributes of the other. Perhaps simplistically, the two theories differ in terms of the extent to which one's assessment of one's own abilities changes over time. Downward comparison theory suggests that once established, self-assessments will remain more or less stable, while self-enhancement theory suggests that self-assessment will change as a function of what level of ability we would expect the other to have. Self-enhancement theory also suggests that the view of the other will be actively changed, especially where the evaluation is perceived as threatening to self-esteem. Downward comparison also assumes the view of the other will be altered by the one making the assessment, with downward adjustments in assessments of ability being made in order to preserve one's self-esteem. McKenna and colleagues (1991) suggest that the findings of McCormick et al. (1986) that drivers considered themselves more reliable, more considerate, wise and relaxed than the average driver, indicate "that there are many areas where drivers are willing to attribute a positive characteristic to themselves" (p. 46). This is considered to be evidence for self-enhancement being the mechanism underlying overly positive self-assessments. It is perhaps worth noting, however, that the fact that drivers do not consider themselves to be as good as a "very good driver" suggests that self-enhancement is not the whole story. McKenna et al. took their own results to indicate that drivers "when judging their own skills . . . have a positive estimation. The results are, therefore more consistent with a self-enhancement bias rather than with downward comparison" (1991, p. 50). However, it should be noted that most conceptualisations of self-enhancement require that the rater both increase the positive *and* decrease the negative aspects of his or her own performance. In the McKenna et al. study, people were required to compare themselves simply with "an average driver". It is impossible to say whether the same "average driver" was used as the basis of comparison in each case by each subject, on each question. Thus a "better" or "worse" average driver might easily have been used when the driver felt variously secure or insecure about his or her ability to perform a particular manoeuvre. Therefore, the design used may not have been sensitive to the operation of "downward comparison". Previously we have found that self-assessments are stable over time, as indexed by the low variability in how questions were answered, while assessments of a novice driver show greater variability, which we interpreted as showing active adjustment of assessments of the other (Groeger & Grande, 1996). Our more recent work on the consistency of self–other assessments causes me to doubt whether either of these two theoretical positions is correct.

## Consistency of assessments of driving ability

Before considering why we might have comparatively positive views of our own ability and a relatively poor view of that of some other person, I want to first consider some of the factors that influence the consistency of the assessments we make.

In the Groeger and Grande study, a subset of 24 drivers also assessed their own driving performance in an actual test drive, during which they were silently assessed by an accompanying driving instructor. The correlation between their assessments of their ability on the two occasions, several months apart, was highly significant. The driver's assessment of how he or she had performed did not correlate with the rating made by the instructor. Another group, again a subset of those from the original study, also assessed their performance on a test drive, this time receiving feedback from the instructor who accompanied them. Again, when they assessed their actual driving on a set route, drivers' assessments were very well predicted by assessments they had made of their ability some months earlier. This relationship between how they previously assessed themselves and how they assessed their driving was present in spite of the fact that their performance rating was in part due to the amount of criticism and praise the accompanying driving instructor provided. The severity of faults corrected by the instructor was negatively related to the assessment the driver made of his or her performance, and positively related to the number of comments made en route that praised the driver. When drivers receive feedback on their performance, the ratings made by the driver and the instructor are reliably correlated. These results indicate that there is considerable consistency over time in the way drivers assess their ability, indeed the consistency between the two assessments is positively related to the amount of driving people have done in their lives. The results also suggest that although these assessments can be tempered somewhat by feedback, they may not be a particularly reliable guide to how drivers actually perform.

The consistency of one's impression of one's ability over time suggests to me that for tasks we engage in repeatedly we develop a stable and durable sense of self. This is not simply a function of people making reliable judgements on identical measures, as the assessments to be made in each case were quite different. This is similar to what Markus and Nurius (1986) have referred to as a "possible self", i.e. a consistent way of viewing ourselves and the world which serves to identify that which we aspire to avoid or to achieve. What the present data suggest, which is not explicitly part of the framework laid out by Markus and Nurius, is that repeated performance of a task may be one of the reasons why such selves develop. Markus and Nurius also suggest that possible selves are distinct from what they see as a highly labile "working self-concept". Arguably, it is this that suffers from criticism or enjoys praise, and this that tempers the established view we have of our ability with knowledge of results from other sources (such as the instructor in the study considered earlier). This suggestion was made at the end of the Groeger and Grande (1996) paper, but recent results allow it to be both confirmed and extended.

As part of our recent study of the processes that might influence drivers' responses to risk, we again used a version of the self-assessment and novice-assessment scales, this time using computerised presentation (see Groeger, Field, & Hammond, 1998). First, and not surprisingly, most drivers considered their ability to drive in the specified situations to be better than that of novice drivers. Of the 400 drivers taking part, about 10% considered themselves equal to or worse than novices. Because of the computerised presentation of the materials, which were identical for the novice and self judgements, we were able to both control the order in which assessments were made, and assess the time taken to make the judgements. Drivers took about the same length of time (about 5.5 seconds) to make decisions about themselves as they did about the novice driver. They took longer to make their first set of judgements than they did to make their second set of judgements, irrespective of whether the first judgements were about themselves or about the novice. However, the order in which judgements were made did make a considerable difference. Drivers always viewed themselves as better than a novice would be in similar circumstances; but the difference was considerably larger where drivers judged themselves before they judged the novice (see Figure 8.1). Planned comparisons revealed that when rating their own ability first, drivers evaluated their driving less positively than if they had first considered a novice's ability to drive under similar circumstances, but they evaluated a novice more positively when they had previously considered their own ability. These results are contrary to those we would have expected on the basis of our previous findings. To appreciate why this may be we need to step back to review some theoretical approaches that have sought to describe how we assess ourselves in comparison with others.

Considering these data in the light of the two theories of self–other assessment introduced earlier, it appears that both theories gain some support, but both also fail to account for the findings observed. When rating own ability, and not expecting to have to rate anyone else, drivers assess themselves as being slightly

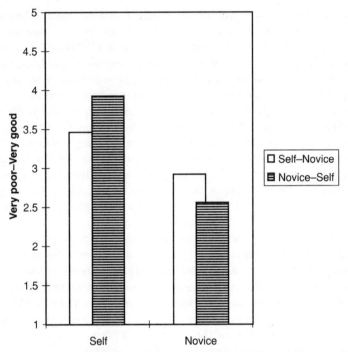

**Figure 8.1.**    Assessments of ourselves and others as a function of direction of report.

above the mid-point on a number of scales. One might expect, if either "downward comparison theory" or "self-enhancement theory" results were operating, that having rated oneself and then unexpectedly being required to rate another by definition less able driver, the ratings made should reflect a more negative assessment of the other's ability. This is what happened. On the other hand, when required to assess a novice first, because self-comparison is not explicitly invoked, the novice might be seen as less negative than where we had rated our own ability first. The opposite happened—when judged first the novice was seen as less able than when judged after rating own ability. Again, where the novice is assessed first, one would anticipate that a positive view of own ability would be asserted by exaggerating judgements of own competence—this indeed happened. Self-assessments were even more positive than among those drivers who were first called on to rate their own ability. This evidence supports self-enhancement as an explanation. However, the uprating of the other, having assessed oneself, is not predictable from either theory.

It is possible that having rated oneself, ensuring there is a gap between self and other, thus preserving self-esteem, can be done reliably, simply because self-assessments are more stable over tasks and time. It may also be that we do indeed have a positive view of our ability on tasks we repeatedly perform, and because this is reassuringly high to begin with, we can tolerate having a positive view of others. In contrast, how one previously rated a novice's ability may be less memorable, and thus, in order to ensure that we maintain an acceptable difference between self and other, we exaggerate our own capabilities. The uncertainty of how one rated the other may itself pose a possible threat to self-esteem, which in turn may encourage us to self-enhance.

This interpretation is predicated on the idea that with a sufficiently large sample the absolute assessments of different groups are directly comparable. This assumption may or may not be warranted, but it would lead to the suggestion that we might all have a somewhat negative conception of the ability of the "average" driver. We would expect, having made that judgement, to consider an "expert" driver to be substantially better than average, and a "novice" driver to be substantially below average. The argument I have been trying to make, i.e. that we self-enhance partly when we have no other option and partly to protect our self-esteem when we have already assessed others less positively, predicts what will happen when multiple assessments are made. If we first rate an average driver, then our own driving, and then that of a novice driver, the assessment of our own ability will be more positive than if we first rate an average driver, then rate an expert driver, and then ourselves. We tested this in a study of over 1000 motorists (see Grayson et al., 1998).

Some 20% of drivers considered themselves below (11%) or of average (9%) ability; 90% of drivers considered themselves better drivers than novices, with 6% considering themselves worse than novices and 5% considering themselves as able as novice drivers; 64% of drivers considered themselves worse than expert drivers, 11% as able as expert drivers, and 25% as better than expert drivers. We found that drivers who rated their own ability having first rated an average and then a novice, gave themselves a higher rating than those who rated their ability having rated an average and then an expert driver (see Figure 8.2). The prediction made at the outset, that assessing less able others leads us to inflate our view of our own ability, was thus borne out and, reassuringly, this emerged from a study in which the two groups of drivers had very similar views of how well the average driver would perform.

To summarise, most drivers do indeed consider that they perform better than would average drivers in similar circumstances. The average driver appears to be placed slightly but reliably above the mid-point of the 5-point scale (2.87 versus 2.5). Rather strangely, so too is the novice driver (2.56 versus 2.5). We assess ourselves similarly over time, and in different circumstances, but these assessments may be inflated where we have already assessed the ability of someone we consider less able. Contrary to what one might expect on the basis of the reportage of similar results in the literature, we do not all consider ourselves above average, or even better than novices: Between 10 and 20% of drivers make unfavourable assessments of their own ability. Three questions emerge from this tendency to be overly positive about one's own ability, some of which

**Figure 8.2.**    Assessing others influences self-assessment.

have already been touched upon. How does such belief in our own ability develop? Is our view of our own ability borne out by more objective assessments? Does the way we assess ourselves contribute to how we assess driving situations and our ability to cope in different situations? These questions are addressed in the next section.

## DEVELOPING SELF-EFFICACY

The previous sections lead to the conclusion that the difference between our assessments of how we ourselves will perform and how we expect others will perform, reflects something real about our confidence or feelings of efficacy. For this to be so we would expect the strength of these beliefs to be related to the experience we have of the task on which the assessments are based. Over the past few years we have explored this in a variety of ways.

### Self–other differences and amount of driving experience

In our study of drivers' assessments of their own and other drivers' abilities, Gunn Grande and I reported highly reliable relationships which showed that the more experienced a driver was, the greater the difference they suggested there was between their own driving and that of a novice (Groeger & Grande, 1996). The computer-based study by Groeger, Field, and Hammond (1998) reveals similar relationships between amount of driving experience and the perceived difference between a novice's driving and one's own.[1] In our large-scale survey, years of driving experience and average distance driven in the previous three years were related to the extent to which people assessed themselves as better than the novice, but also the extent to which they assessed themselves as better than the average driver. Older drivers were also found to be more likely to consider themselves more like expert drivers (see Grayson et al., 1998). There are two implications of these results. First, contrary to the usual assumption, it is not young inexperienced drivers who tend to present themselves as much better than other drivers. Whether the standard judged is a novice, an average, or an expert driver, the tendency to be better than the standard against which you are judging yourself increases with amount of driving experience. The pattern for male and female self–other assessments was similar, which also confounds the stereotype of the young male with too much misplaced confidence in his own ability. In fact, the studies consistently show that the average ratings of self and self–other difference are reliably lower for young drivers than those of older motorists. Second, demonstrating that the tendency to assess oneself as being better than others depends on driving experience, especially the distance said to have been driven in the recent past, underlines the claim that self-assessments develop as a function of actual task experience. That is, self–other differences in the way driving is assessed reflect something quite real about the driving experience we have had. We have been able to investigate the way impressions of one's own ability develop in our recent longitudinal study of learner drivers.

## Changes in self-efficacy while learning to drive

The learner drivers in our longitudinal study were asked to rate their own ability and that of a novice driver on a number of occasions throughout their training. Assessments were made on four occasions: two weeks after they began to drive, approximately mid-way between this point and when they took their first practical driving test, immediately after that test, and several weeks after they finally qualified for a full driving licence. The results are summarised in Figure 8.3. Statistical analysis showed that while the ability of the novice to perform the manoeuvres described in the questionnaire was stable across these four occasions, the L-driver's view of his or her own ability was initially substantially below that of the novice. Midway through their period of learning to drive, L-drivers assessed themselves more positively, but still less positively than they assessed the novice's ability. At the point at which they took their first driving test, their assessments of their own and the novice's ability were similar, whereas a few months after passing their driving test they considered themselves better than the novice (described as a driver the day after passing their driving test).

---

[1] This is especially strong where the novice driver is assessed before the driver assessed themselves.

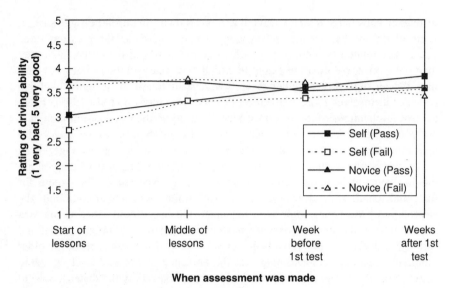

**Figure 8.3.** New drivers' assessments of own and novice's driving ability as a function of driving test outcome and driving experience.

These data show, more clearly than any others I know of, that drivers' beliefs about their own ability develop as their actual ability does. They also show that new drivers have considerably greater realism about their ability than has hitherto been supposed.

## Test outcome influences what drivers believe about themselves and others

The longitudinal study of drivers' assessments of their own ability and opinions of that of others shows an increase in self-efficacy with increasing experience—they see themselves as being similar to novice drivers as they are about to take their first driving test. The study suggests that the outcome of this test greatly affects how learners see themselves.

A final piece of evidence in this jigsaw of relationships between growth of driving experience and development of a view of one's competence as a driver, comes from a survey Sarah Brady and I recently carried out on almost 1000 drivers taking their driving test (see Groeger & Brady, 1998 for details). This was based on a large survey of new drivers which used a similar methodology to many of the studies referred to earlier. Drivers were given a questionnaire by the examiner in their practical driving test on the day that test took place. On average, new drivers rated expert drivers at 4.36 on a 5-point scale, the average driver at 3.42, and a novice driver at 3.09. They rated themselves more highly than both the novice and the average driver. These ratings were greatly affected by whether the test candidate failed their driving test, or had failed a driving test previously.

Drivers opinions of their own ability were unaffected by whether they were taking the driving test for the first time or had previously failed, nor did whether they passed or failed the current test influence their assessment of their own ability. In contrast to this, drivers taking their first test tended to believe the average driver was better than those who were taking their test for at least the second time (i.e. had previously failed). Test candidates who failed the current test also tended to believe that the average driver was better than did respondents who passed their driving test. These results suggest that when drivers receive negative information (e.g. failing their driving test), it has little impact on how they see themselves, and instead influences how they see the relative abilities of other drivers. Where the candidate has previously failed, they tend to judge the standard of other (average) drivers more negatively, thus preserving some self-respect. Where they themselves pass their driving test, they see the average driver as worse, thus emphasising their achievement. Thus, as pointed out previously by Groeger and Grande (1996) we protect our sense of self-worth by altering our view of other people rather than by altering our view of ourselves.

The respondent's experience of test failure has an interesting effect on these assessments of the other driver. Those taking their driving test for the first time and those who have previously failed a driving test share similarly high views about the abilities of experts, but those who have previously failed tend to believe novice drivers are worse than those taking their test for the first time. Thus, while we tend to protect our sense of self-worth by downgrading others, we seem to do so by picking targets that are more vulnerable, such as novice or average drivers, rather than those who have achieved the high standards of performance we ourselves have failed to achieve. This seems to show a clear effect of "downward comparison", but again in a situation where "self-enhancement" would not be a credible way of maintaining self-esteem.

The studies reported here show clear relationships between the amount of experience one has of a task, and one's sense of efficacy in performing it. Important negative experiences, such as failing an assessment or having an accident (Groeger & Grande, 1996), temper this view of one's own ability, and in circumstances where this view of self is threatened, drivers generally attempt to downgrade others rather than revamp their assessment of themselves. Certainly some of the studies reported earlier can be interpreted as showing evidence of self-enhancement, but these seem limited to situations in which the scope for altering assessments of others is limited. These adjustments appear to be made to protect one's view of self, but the assessments made are not as unreasonable as might be expected from studies that suggest that the majority of drivers believe they are better than average. We too find that people tend to believe they are better than they are likely to be, but overall the picture is a more complicated one than is usually recognised. In particular, it should be noted that these studies show very little evidence that young drivers are especially different in confidence levels from people with similar levels of driving experience. The implications of this are important: If young drivers are not actually overconfident, which these results strongly indicate, seeking to undermine unwarranted "overconfidence" through training is likely to be counterproductive. More generally, accounts of risk taking in young drivers frequently cite overconfidence as a basis for young drivers' dangerous driving. If they are not more overconfident than other drivers, some alternative explanation of why young drivers appear to expose themselves to greater risk is required.

## SELF-EFFICACY AND ACTUAL ABILITY

It seems as if drivers' opinions of themselves and others reflect in part the experiences they themselves have had as drivers. But are drivers' self-assessments accurate in any sense?

The work I originally did with Gunn Grande, described earlier, was at that stage one of the few studies that looked at whether the assessments drivers make of their own ability relate to their capacity to perform. The findings of this research suggested that where an instructor, travelling with the driver, gave feedback on the driver's performance, the assessments of behaviour made by the instructor and the driver were highly correlated. The ratings made by drivers some weeks before were weakly correlated with the instructor's assessment, at about the 10% level. However, it may have been that the drivers actually drove differently from the way in which they normally would when being given feedback, and so this is not particularly strong evidence that the way in which we rate our behaviour necessarily predicts the way we drive. Recently, in a study carried out with Graham Grayson, discussed earlier (Grayson et al., 1998), some 100 drivers drove a 10-mile route with an experienced driving examiner alongside. He remained silent except for providing information about direction of travel, etc. A few weeks earlier these same drivers assessed their ability to drive using the computerised self-assessment driving questionnaire described earlier, along with a range of other computer-based tests of drivers' skills (Groeger, Field, & Hammond, 1998). The examiner assessed the driver on a range of 5-point scales: safety, speed (i.e. fast to slow), anticipation, speed setting (i.e. appropriateness of speed for setting), attentiveness, driving skill. In practice these assessments are highly inter-correlated, such that re-analysing the data using principal components analysis reveals a single factor which accounts for about 68% of the variance in ratings. This suggests that the examiner's ratings reflect a single general driving ability factor, rather than a carefully differentiated assessment of a range of different driving indices. Table 8.1 presents the Pearson correlations between the ratings made by the driving examiner and the self-assessments originally made by the 100 drivers who took part. As the table shows, driving ability as assessed by an experienced objective expert is

## TABLE 8.1
### Correlations between self- and observer assessments of driving ability

| | Original driver rating | | Rating by driving examiner | | | | | |
|---|---|---|---|---|---|---|---|---|
| | Self-rating | Self–Novice | Safety | Speed | Anticipation | Speed setting | Attentive | Skill |
| Self–Novice | .770** | | | | | | | |
| Safety | .165 | .191 | | | | | | |
| Speed | .089 | .096 | -.400** | | | | | |
| Anticipation | .238** | .172 | .688** | -.078 | | | | |
| Speed setting | .183 | .241** | .729** | -.281** | .636** | | | |
| Attentiveness | .232* | .234* | .790** | -.203 | .801** | .723** | | |
| Skill | .196* | .249** | .794** | -.159 | .765** | .733** | .804** | |
| General ability | .215* | .230* | .909** | -.326** | .856** | .857** | .919** | .910** |

Correlations reliable at $*p < 0.05$, $**p < 0.01$.

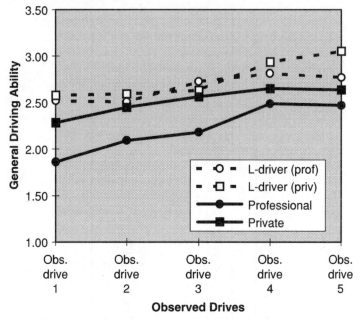

**Figure 8.4.**   Self-assessed ability and teacher-assessed ability when learning to drive.

reliably correlated with how the individuals assessed their driving ability several weeks before.

Our longitudinal study of L-drivers yields results that are similar to these. After each of the L-driver's five observed lessons, given as usual by a professional instructor or their parent (whoever was the designated main teacher), L-drivers and teachers were asked to assess how well the L-driver was capable of performing in a range of common driving situations.[2]

Figure 8.4 shows the mean across item score for the 11 driving situations, for both teachers and pupils. In all cases subjective ratings of ability improve across the learning period. Professional instructors provide a more negative assessment of performance than do parents. While L-drivers are considerably more positive about their own performance than are their teachers, who they drive with makes little difference to their assessments of their general ability. Contrasts between the mean ratings made by teachers and their pupils indicated that L-drivers rated themselves as significantly more competent than did their teachers, whether these teachers were professional driving instructors or parents. Interestingly, a significant correlation between pupil and teacher ratings was only found between professional instructors and their pupils, but not between parents and

---

[2] The items used were a subset of those originally used in studies by West, Elander, and French (1992).

pupils. Given that professional instructors actually speak twice as much as do parents, it is unsurprising that, although more positive, L-drivers' views of their ability are in line with those of their accompanying professional instructor. This suggests that parents who teach people to drive either make too few comments for the teacher and pupil assessments to be brought into line with each other, or that what parents say is discounted by their children!

In summary, the assessments that experienced and inexperienced drivers make of their own ability are in line with those made by experienced observers who have the opportunity to witness some of the driver's actual driving performance. Despite this correlation, it is clear that people do indeed assess themselves more positively than their actual ability justifies, even when they possess only rudimentary competence and are being provided with substantial feedback on their performance.

## APPRAISAL, EFFICACY, AND EMOTION-DRIVEN ACTIONS

If drivers' self-assessments genuinely reflect self-efficacy, as the results just described strongly suggest, then when feelings of self-efficacy are under threat, drivers' emotions should reflect this. In this section I want to assess this suggestion in the light of relevant empirical data.

In the previous chapter I described some of the ways in which arousal changes as a consequence of the dangers and demands that are intrinsically part of the driving task. Emotions are regarded, by many authors, as abstract, high-level descriptions of the relationship between a person and his or her environment (e.g. Lazarus & Smith, 1988). According to Schacter (1964) experience of emotion requires both a subjective feeling, which reflects some level of physiological arousal, and the availability of a label for that arousal, derived from a cognitive appraisal of the source of that arousal. This labelling is likely to be mediated by basic emotion terms such as "anger", "disgust", "fear", "happiness", and "sadness" (see Ekman, 1973; Oatley & Johnson-Laird, 1987). Within Schacter's account, physiological arousal was considered to be non-specific, while cognitive appraisal was said to be determined by interpretations of proximal stimuli on the basis of the memories we have relating to those stimuli (see Schacter, 1996 for the view that "emotion" is a form of implicit memory). An idea worth considering is that our assessments of our own ability reflect the structure inherent in such memory. My rationale for believing so is as follows.

Lazarus (Lazarus & Folkman, 1984; Lazarus, Kanner, & Folkman, 1980) in his transactional account of emotional processing suggests that "emotion arises from how a person construes the outcome, actual or anticipated, of a transaction or bit of commerce with the environment" (Lazarus et al., 1980, p. 192). This construal depends on the appraisal of any environmental event, which continues as the event unfolds, in terms of (1) whether it is irrelevant to an individual's sense of well-being, as benign, or as stressful, and (2) the likely success of the personal or environmental resources that might be deployed to deal with the event. Lazarus distinguishes three ways in which stressful events are evaluated, i.e. in terms of their past history of harm or loss, the threat of future injury or loss, and something that Lazarus calls "challenge", which is related to a potential for gain given successful coping or mastery. Within this framework emotions are regarded as a complex of cognitive appraisals, action impulses, and patterned somatic reactions, with much of the cognitive appraisal based on our beliefs in our own ability, or what Bandura (1997) would refer to as self-efficacy.

## Emotional changes when experienced drivers take a driving test

This proposed linkage between emotional reactions and self-efficacy would suggest that people who assess their ability to drive very positively will react differently to the prospect of having their driving assessed than those with less positive views of their own ability. I reported data relevant to this issue recently (Groeger, 1997). The subjects whose self-assessments of ability and actual driving ability were reported in the study by Gunn Grande and myself reported earlier, made ratings of their current mood when completing the self-assessment questionnaires, as well as immediately before and after the test drive. Mood was assessed using Zuckerman and Lubin's (1985) Multiple Affect Adjective Check-List (MAACL), which as well as measuring amount of positive and negative affect currently being experienced, also assesses current feelings of anxiety, depression, and hostility.

When the MAACL was completed at home, at a time of the individual's choosing, the levels of anxiety, depression, and hostility for this sample were close to what would be expected for a sample of this type and age. A few weeks later, sitting in their own vehicle about to have their driving assessed, they completed the MAACL again. As might be expected, faced with a test of their driving ability, drivers became more significantly more anxious, but their levels of depression and hostility were no different from those when they previously completed the MAACL at home at a time of their choosing. Only two of a wide range of variables investigated correlated with the change in anxiety level. As would be predicted on the basis that confident people are less affected by the prospect of being tested, it was found that the larger the difference between their assessment of themselves and their assessment of a novice driver, the less anxious they became when facing an assessment of that ability. What may be a little more surprising was that the extent of increase in anxiety before the test was strongly negatively correlated with the level of anxiety experienced in the baseline (i.e. measurement at home) condition. That is, overall people become more anxious: Those who were less anxious to begin with grow more anxious

TABLE 8.2
Mood changes pre- and post-test for drivers receiving feedback

| Emotion | Base-line | Pre-test | Post-test | Statistical outcome |
|---------|-----------|----------|-----------|---------------------|
| Anxiety | 6.71 (3.15) | 7.78 (2.87) | 8.21 (3.03) | Baseline < Pre-test < Post-test |
| Depression | 14.47 (5.60) | 14.21 (4.44) | 15.45 (4.48) | Baseline = Pre-test < Post-test |
| Hostility | 8.33 (3.64) | 7.90 (2.77) | 8.02 (2.93) | Baseline = Pre-test < Post-test |

than those who probably consistently experience high levels of anxiety (see Table 8.2).

More detailed analysis revealed that people who were in the top 25% of reported anxiety at baseline actually experienced lower levels of anxiety immediately before the driving test, while those in the lowest quartile of reported anxiety at baseline became significantly more anxious when confronting the driving test. Interestingly, there is no relationship between self-efficacy and change in anxiety before test in the high anxiety group. For this group what predicts pre-test anxiety is baseline anxiety level, whereas for those in the lowest anxiety group, baseline anxiety is less important than belief in own ability, with those who are more confident becoming less anxious. These results show that those who experience consistently higher levels of anxiety may have a more generalised conception of what they consider threatening, and their domain-specific feelings of efficacy are less relevant to how they will feel when evaluated. On the other hand, those less confident in their driving abilities are more likely to perceive a driving test as threatening, and become more anxious as a result.

The feedback given during the drive has a substantial impact on mood change. For those who receive no feedback during the drive, mood does not change on any of the dimensions studied. Given feedback, however, the events of the drive have a very substantial negative effect on mood, with anxiety, depression, and hostility all increasing reliably from pre-test levels. The extent of change in anxiety or depression is not reliably correlated with the actual proportion of feedback given by the instructor that is critical, that praises the driver, or that is merely advisory. On the other hand, greater increases in hostility are strongly associated with reduced praise from the assessor, while greater hostility is also associated with a higher incidence of feedback that is critical.

Level of hostility also appeared to be related to the attributions people made about positive and negative events. As part of the baseline phase of the study, in order to assess attributional style, we used the Attributional Style Questionnaire, which distinguishes between the extent to which positive and negative events are "explained" by the individual as resulting from their own or others' actions (i.e. "internal–external", Peterson, 1991); whether such events are likely or unlikely to recur in the future (i.e. "stable–unstable", Peterson, 1991); and whether the causes of such events are likely to influence only that specific situation, or are likely to have more widespread effects (i.e. "specific–global", Peterson, 1991). Changes in hostility, but not depression or anxiety, were found to be related to the attributions drivers had made in the baseline phase of the study. Hostility increased for those who tended to believe themselves to be responsible for positive events, and for those who tended to believe others to be responsible for negative events. People believing that negative events are specific to a particular situation, and those who believe that such negative events are unlikely to recur in that situation, also become more hostile when criticised for making some error. This does not happen when they are praised or simply given advice.

There are parallels between the driver's attributional style, the changes in hostility, and the amounts of different types of feedback on the way drivers assessed how well they had driven. The more the driver was praised during the test drive, the higher the assessment they made of how well they drove during the test drive, but this had no impact on their assessment of how a novice driver would have performed under identical circumstances. The opposite pattern was found with criticism: There was no reliable relationship between the amount of criticism received and the driver's assessment of his or her own ability, but amount of criticism was negatively related to the driver's assessment of how well a novice driver would have performed, such that the more his or her own driving was criticised, the worse he or she claimed the novice would have performed in similar circumstances.

Finally, attributional style for positive and negative events clearly influences our mood, and the way we appraise ourselves and others. Neither mood at the beginning or end of the drive, nor the extent to which it changed during the course of the drive, influenced the assessment of performance made by the assessor, except in the case of hostility. The more hostile the driver became, the worse the driver's performance was rated by the accompanying examiner. Whether this is because the accompanying assessor considers the person more unpleasant, or their driving worse, is unfortunately not possible to deduce on the basis of this study.

## Aggression, hostility, and rage

In so far as studies have sought to measure aggression and anger, they show that, contrary to popular opinion, gender and age differences in driving anger and aggression are minimal or non-existent (e.g. Deffenbacher, Oetting, & Lynch, 1994; Groeger, 1997; Shinar, 1998). This poses something of a conundrum with regard to the media phenomenon that has had so much coverage over the last decade (i.e. "road rage"). There is beginning to be some well conducted behavioural research in relation to anger and driving (e.g. Shinar, 1998; Underwood, Chapman, Wright, & Crundall, 1999), which helps to supplement attitudinal studies such as those by Deffenbacher et al. (1994) and Parker, Lajunen, and Stradling (1998). However, we are a long way from understanding why or whether driving gives rise to increased amounts of anger or rage. Reported emotion, particularly after some delay, is so unreliable (see Groeger, 1997) that I believe such indices are at best a temporary basis on which to build understanding. Fundamentally, it is behavioural evidence we need, i.e. measures of subjective feelings, more objective indices of arousal, personality, and driving performance, before, during, and after incidents have taken place.

It seems to me possible that the peculiar cocktail of personal challenge, threat to own safety and self-esteem, stress induced by time pressure, lack of control over events, and frustration of goals that comprises the driving task in the modern world, does indeed have all the ingredients that might give rise to increased levels of anger and hostility. However, it may equally be that the people involved would be aggressive or hostile in situations beyond driving—with driving being an opportunity for, rather than a cause of, the display of aggression. Until we resolve these and other issues satisfactorily, I do not think it does us much professional or scientific credit to give credence to anger or rage as a phenomenon confined to, or more prevalent in, driving.

## SUMMARY

Especially where the activities concerned are perceived as being important, or take extensive amounts of time, we develop a consistent way of assessing our own and others' ability to perform. Our sense of self-efficacy, while neither universally positive across all tasks, nor necessarily positive with respect to driving, is probably more positive than is warranted on the basis of our actual ability. This may in part be because of the dearth of tangible and authoritative feedback on how well we normally drive—but it also reflects a tendency to make self-serving judgements. We protect ourselves from the anxieties involved in constantly placing ourselves at risk by developing confidence in our ability which we are rarely likely to be forced to realise is misplaced. There is very little convincing evidence that young inexperienced motorists are more prone to this, indeed the reverse may be closer to the truth. Threats to these feelings of self-efficacy are either forgotten, or explained by emphasising the role others have played in how such events arose—an effortful re-appraisal that causes us to become more hostile, and perhaps even to drive less well and behave more aggressively. There may well be links between such hostility, overconfidence etc. and accident involvement, but we seem to be some way short of understanding how the link is manifested and maintained. It is possible the re-prioritisation of goals that occurs in anger, and the restricted way in which attention is deployed when we are frightened, offer a way of understanding why driving when emotionally aroused may well be different, and less safe.

# CHAPTER NINE

# Age, neurological damage, disease, and driving

*This chapter focuses on the cognitive deficits that are thought to accompany ageing and particular types of neuropsychological damage, specifically traumatic brain injury and cortical and subcortical dementias. In considering the extent to which the driving task depends on such cognitive operations, the chapter will address the questions of whether certain cognitive deficits might exclude people from driving, and how such the impacts of deficits on driving should be assessed.*

Driving is a purposeful activity—it meets one's goals for travelling to, or forms part of, many work or leisure activities. While the way in which we carry out the task may depend on the purposes of particular journeys, and the circumstances we encounter en route, I believe there is considerable truth in the suggestion, originally made by Tillman and Hobbs (1949) that "a man drives as he lives". At the time, the number of female drivers was relatively small, and this, together with the insights gained over the past 50 years of driver behaviour research, would lead me to revise their suggestion as "we drive as we have driven, and as we currently live". That is, there is a consistency in our behaviour, after initial learning, over time and across situations, and this past is a primary determinant of behaviour in any situation. However, gradually over time the way in which we engage in the task may change, as the result of a growth of experience and decline in functioning which accompanies old age. Our performance capabilities, if not our desire to perform, may change more abruptly as the result of disease or neurological damage. Together, past experience and current capacity determine how ably we perform. In this penultimate chapter, I consider how normal ageing, acquired brain injury, and the cognitive dysfunction that may accompany ageing, may influence ability to drive.

# AGE AND DRIVING

It has become almost axiomatic that young drivers are at greater risk than any other sector of the motoring population. At the other end of the age distribution, the evidence may be a little more equivocal, but there is now broad agreement that although drivers over 60 years of age are involved in fewer crashes, they drive so little that their risk of being involved in an accident per unit distance driven is comparable to that of the young inexperienced driver. Why should age matter?

## Young drivers

There is very little reason why any psychologically "normal" teenage driver should find the cognitive operations involved in driving problematical. The caveat to this sweeping statement is that the weight of practice more experienced drivers have makes much of what they do routine, and as such, allows many otherwise incompatible tasks to be performed together. Allied to this, increased experience usually, although not always, implies the driver has had a broader variety of driving experiences, such as driving at different times of the day or days of the week, with different weather conditions, journey lengths, passenger distractions, different vehicles, etc. As experience grows, the motorist is less likely to encounter situations very different from those they have encountered before. Despite their cognitive strengths, the fact is that young inexperienced motorists are both involved in more crashes, and more crashes per unit distance driven, than any other grouping within the normal motoring population.

Usually, it is the presumed overconfidence and risk-seeking characteristics of young, particularly male, motorists that is cited as the reason for the overinvolvement of young drivers in crashes (e.g. Evans, 1991; Jonah, 1997). In earlier chapters I have questioned whether the young are any more overconfident than others (see especially Chapter 8). While I accept that overconfidence can contribute to crash-involvement, I believe the effects of inexperience are far more powerful.

The evidence recently reported by Sagberg (1998) demonstrates this point very clearly. A sample of almost 60,000 drivers was drawn from the Norwegian register of driving licence holders. About half of those who agreed to participate in the study were aged between 18 and 20 years of age, and had held their licences for between 1 and 18 months (N = 17,400). The others were a control sample of 24-year-old drivers, with at least five years of licence holding behind them (N = 13,200). The groups differed markedly in the number of crashes they reported having been involved in in the previous month: 651 for the novice group and 259 for the others; that is 37.4 per thousand and 19.6 per thousand respectively. Among the novice group, after 18 months of licence-holding, 45% of males and 32% of females had been involved in an accident. This gender difference is almost entirely explained by the difference between the distance driven by males and females during that period.

Etching

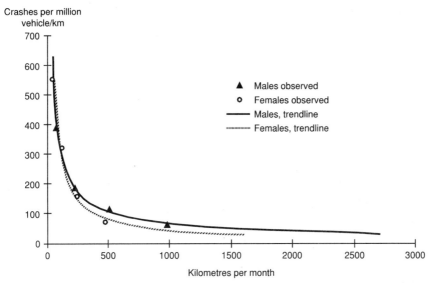

**Figure 9.1.**  Accident involvement as a function of driving experience in the months after gaining a licence.

However, the data that really serve to make the point about the role of inexperience in crash involvement which Sagberg reports are presented in Figure 9.1. Respondents were asked to report the number of crashes, if any, they had had in the previous month, and how far they had driven in that time. As the graph shows, the number of crashes per million kilometres driven reduces as the time for which a licence has been held increases. The rate at which this change occurs slows over time. In fact the relationship between experience and risk reduction is a power function (crash risk = $102.82*$ number of months licence held$^{-0.327}$), which accounts for some 60% of the monthly accident risk variation.

This is not simply a maturational effect, as Sagberg makes clear, showing that accident risk reduces with the distance driven per month (see Figure 9.2), the accident risk for male and female drivers driving similar distances per month being slightly lower for women, a result also reported by Maycock et al. (1991). These results show that whatever the many differences between young and older drivers, they learn to be safe as a function of practising their driving skills—an enormous amount of accident risk variability is accounted for by distance driven. It is still possible that personality differences, propensity to expose oneself to risk, and cognitive abilities compromised by inexperience, also play a role in accident risk, perhaps even being the mechanism by which practice has its effect. That recognised, for me the case for safety increasing as a function of task experience seems overwhelming.

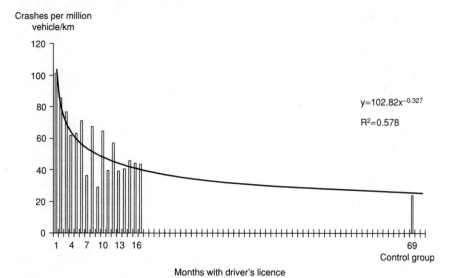

Crashes per million
vehicle/km

$y=102.82x^{-0.327}$

$R^2=0.578$

Months with driver's licence

**Figure 9.2.**   Accident involvement as a function of distance driven in the months after gaining a licence.

## Older drivers

Drivers of 60 and older have fewer crashes that young drivers. However, there are far fewer older drivers than there are young drivers, largely because of the social and economic changes that hugely enhanced the importance of the motor vehicle in the later decades of the twentieth century. For example, as of spring 1999, the United Kingdom had 6 million driving licence holders over 60 years of age, but 22 million between 30 and 59 years of age and 9 million under 30 years of age. When corrected for the age structure of the population as a whole by using an index such as accidents per 100,000 people, accident rates, having reduced systematically decade on decade from the highest point when drivers are in their teens, rise again as drivers reach their sixties (e.g. McGwin, Owsley, & Ball, 1998). If, on the other hand, we correct for distance driven by different motorists, then elderly drivers are as likely to be involved in crashes are drivers some 40 or 50 years younger (e.g. McGwin et al., 1998; see Figure 9.3). Why are drivers beyond middle age more likely to have crashes per unit distance driven?

Uncomfortable a fact as it is, we simply must recognise that most of us grow less able as we grow older. Reports of perceptual, motor, and cognitive changes in old age are legion (see Craik & Anderson, 1999; Schwartz, Park, Knauper, & Sudman, 1998). Declining perceptual abilities, e.g. reduction in accommodation and vergence, macular degeneration, and decreased light adaptation, are among the visual changes that often accompany old age (see Chapter 1, and Owsley &

Accident-free miles (log)

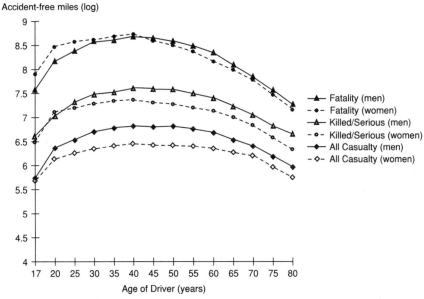

**Figure 9.3.**  Accident involvement as a function of experience, age, and gender.

McGwin, 1999). Cognitive changes in the efficiency of working memory and the formation and retrieval of episodic memories, and reductions in ability to sustain and switch attention (see Chapter 4), are among other factors that accompany old age, albeit that deterioration in certain cognitive functions such as semantic memory and procedural memory are less obvious. Even in healthy older adults, reductions in muscle strength, co-ordination of force and grip, and general freedom of neck and limb movement all become more evident. More general health indices also show an increased susceptibility to and prevalence of heart disease, stroke, diabetes, and, importantly for elderly drivers, a slower or more limited recovery from similar levels of injury or damage than their younger counterparts. Against this panoply of decaying physical function, mental health also becomes more erratic (see Schwartz et al., 1998).

Dobbs, Heller, and Schopflocher (1998) contrasted the expert evaluations and errors made by three groups of drivers—normal young drivers, normal elderly drivers, and older drivers with clinically significant declines in mental abilities. The results show that hazardous errors were the single best indicator of membership in the group of older drivers with clinical impairment. This group also committed more errors than the two control groups in relation to turn positioning errors, minor positioning errors, and overcautiousness. All groups differed from each other on scanning errors. Furthermore, a regression analysis indicated that these five driving errors accounted for over 57% of the variance associated with global ratings provided by expert driving instructors.

McKnight and McKnight (1999), studying over 400 drivers aged 60 years and older, found reliable relationships between number of observed unsafe driving incidents and deficiencies in attentional, perceptual cognitive, and psychomotor performance. The test battery used by McKnight and McKnight was successful in discriminating "unsafe" elderly drivers from "safe" elderly drivers, correctly identifying 80% of those regarded as unsafe, and misidentifying 20% of "safe" drivers as "unsafe". Incidentally, in blind testing, the performance on the test battery was more reliable at distinguishing between drivers who had been involved in accidents and those who had not, than were examiners who drove with the individuals concerned. The nature of the accidents in which elderly drivers become involved appears to reflect the cognitive decline noted earlier.

McGwin, Owsley, and Ball (1998) present an overview of the characteristics of traffic crashes among young, middle-aged, and older drivers. The results suggest that the youngest and the oldest drivers were more likely to be considered at fault. With respect to crash characteristics, older drivers were less likely to have crashes involving driver fatigue, during the evening and early morning, on curved roads, during adverse weather, involving a single vehicle, and while travelling at high speeds. Conversely, older drivers were over-represented in crashes at intersections and/or involving failure to yield the right of way, unseen objects, and failure to heed stop signs or signals. Crashes occurring while turning and changing lanes were also more common among older drivers. Alcohol was less likely to be a factor in traffic crashes involving older adults. McGwin et al. suggest that these findings show the primary problem with the young is their increased exposure to higher-risk driving, lack of skill, but primarily inexperience. The safety advantage older drivers have lies in their tendency not to drive in higher-risk situations, but perceptual problems and difficulty in judging and responding to traffic flow often counteract this advantage. There is some evidence that older drivers seek to compensate for these increased difficulties by driving less.

Stutts (1998) set out to determine whether older drivers with poorer cognitive and/or visual function drive fewer miles or avoid driving in situations that pose higher crash risks, such as at night, in rush-hour traffic, or when weather conditions are bad. From a study of over 3200 elderly drivers applying for licence renewal in North Carolina (i.e. 65 years of age), Stutts showed a clear pattern of reduced driving exposure—lower annual miles and greater avoidance of high-risk driving situations—associated with lower levels of cognitive and visual function. In general, reduced driving exposure was greater where higher cognitive functions (including the Trail Making Test Parts A and B, the Short Blessed Orientation-Memory-Concentration test) were compromised than where visual functioning was reduced (e.g. measures of high- and low-contrast visual acuity, contrast sensitivity, and peripheral vision). Driving reduction was more likely among males than females. Men who scored in the lowest quartile of performance on one of the cognitive tests were six to seven times more likely to report driving fewer than 3000 miles a year than were men scoring in the highest quartile, and women with low scores were one-and-a-half to two times more likely to report driving less than 3000 miles than women with higher scores.

Although this suggests that some among the elderly realise that some of their abilities are less reliable than they used to be, there is substantial evidence that this is not the case for elderly drivers as a whole. Specifically, elderly drivers tend to forget the accidents in which they have been involved (McGwin et al., 1998), tend to have overly positive views of their ability to drive (Marottoli & Richardson, 1998), and are unaware of the level of functioning of their less elderly counterparts and of the types of performance deficits that increase as people grow older (Holland & Rabbitt, 1994). Because of this lack of information, feedback, and insight, elderly drivers are not, I believe, in a good position to determine for themselves when they should reduce or cease driving. I will return to the issue of driving cessation later, having discussed a number of types of damage and disease that also compromise driving ability.

## TRAUMATIC BRAIN INJURY AND DRIVING

Traumatic Brain Injury (TBI) or Closed Head Injury (CHI) results in disruption of neuronal activity and changes in the brain's ability to control the amount of oxygen in the blood, and in blood flow. The changes in neuroendocrine and neurotransmitter activity that result are associated with abnormalities in arousal, affect, cognition, and behaviour (Rose & Johnson, 1994). The prognosis for brain-injured individuals, as represented by some authors, is stark indeed: "recovery from TBI is always incomplete and deficits in remembering, organising, learning and planning create particular difficulties for those trying to return to work" (Grealy, Johnson, & Rushton, 1999, p. 661). What I am concerned with here is the likelihood that those with TBI might be able to resume driving after injury, and how we might assess their capacity to do so.

### Epidemiology

Jennett (1996) provides figures for a number of European countries and areas of Africa and North America for the incidence of head injury spanning the last three decades. Although there are striking differences in incidence, causes, and outcomes of head injury in different countries, I will restrict myself here to the situation as it pertains in Great Britain, not because the figures are especially good or bad, but because it serves to illustrate the points I want to make.

Estimating from the figures presented by Jennett (1996), about 4000 people per 100,000 receive medical attention for head injuries, or when surveyed report at least one day of disability because of a head injury. Between 210–404 per 100,000 of these are sufficiently badly injured to be admitted to hospital. Of these, some 80% are regarded as mildly injured (i.e. having a score of 13–15 on the Glasgow Coma Scale—which approximates to behaving responsively with

TABLE 9.1
Presentation and admission of adults at Accident & Emergency
departments with head injury per 100,000

| Causes | Attending A & E | Evidence of brain damage* | Coma lasting more than 6hrs | Death** |
|---|---|---|---|---|
| All causes: per 100,000 population | 1473 | 341 | | |
| All causes: per 100,000 men | 2180 | 537 | | |
| All causes: per 100,000 women | 831 | 163 | | |
| Falls: per 100,000 population | 459 | 118 | | |
| | *31%* | *35%* | *27%* | *25%* |
| Falls: per 100,000 men | 544 | 168 | | |
| Falls: per 100,000 women | 381 | 73 | | |
| Assaults: per 100,000 population | 399 | 147 | | |
| | *25%* | *43%* | *12%* | *2%* |
| Assaults: per 100,000 men | 677 | 171 | | |
| Assaults: per 100,000 women | 147 | 26 | | |
| Traffic accidents (RTA): | 222 | 70 | | |
| per 100,000 population | *15%* | *21%* | *50%* | *58%* |
| RTA: per 100,000 men | 306 | 77 | | |
| RTA: per 100,000 women | 144 | 39 | | |

Italicised percentages reflect proportion of damage categories attributable to specific causes.

* Regarded as any evidence of altered consciousness, before or after reaching hospital, or neurological signs such as brain contusion or intracranial haematoma.

** Death, includes death at scene, and applies to Great Britain rather than Scotland.

eyes, speech, and actions, or about 20 minutes coma), while between 5 and 10% are severely injured (i.e. 3–8 on the Glasgow Coma Scale—a score of 7 would reflect ability to make audible but intelligible sounds, opening eyes in response to pain, flexes body in response to pain, or in excess of six hours of coma). Since 1968, when the incidence of death was about 10 per 100,000, the United Kingdom death rate from head injury has been falling and is now estimated to be in the region of 6 per 100,000 (Jennett, 1996). About two-thirds of all of those admitted to hospital with head injuries are discharged within 48 hours (Jennett, 1996).

Irrespective of the age or the gender of the injured person, some 25% of all head injuries result from road accidents. Falls are a more prevalent cause for the young (less than 15 years of age 55%; 65 or older 40%; as opposed to 27% for those aged 15–64), while head injury is the result of assault for 32% of those aged between 15 and 64, compared with 5% and 3% for younger and older people respectively.

An extensive account of the incidence of head injury in Scotland based on data from 1985 is still among the best studies of the incidence of head injury anywhere in the world (Brookes et al., 1990). In Table 9.1 I have supplemented data from this study with national figures for deaths as the result of head injury for comparison for the year in question. A road accident may not be the most likely cause of attending at hospital with a suspected head injury, nor for finding evidence of head injury. However, head injuries sustained in road traffic accidents are much more likely to be severe, and are overwhelmingly more likely to lead to death.

Those who return to the community, even after mild head injury, may be left with some disability for several months. Kraus (1993) estimates that the number of new cases of head injury per year in the United States is in the region of 40 per 100,000, and the number per 100,000 of new cases of moderate or severe disability is 4 and 2 respectively. The prevalence of disability resulting from brain injury varies considerably across epidemiological studies (US 439 per 100,000, Kalsbeek, McLaurin, Harris, & Miller, 1980; Scotland, 100 per 100,000, Bryden, 1989). In the most recent, and perhaps authoritative study, Moscato, Trevisan, and Willer (1994) in a national household survey in Canada estimated the prevalence of disability resulting from head injury lasting more than six months as 54 per 100,000. Of those disabled as a result of head injury, some 36 per 100,000 report disability lasting for five years or more, and for 24 per 100,000 the disability had lasted more than 10 years after the injury.

There is a sad irony in the epidemiology of head injury: Those most likely to sustain injury, especially severe and hence long-lasting injury, are young males. Substantial numbers of these injuries result from road traffic accidents. That is, those who are most likely to have difficulties resuming driving, are those most likely to have been injured on the road in the first place.

## Outcomes of head injury

Most classifications of behaviour after a head injury do not address potential outcomes. More usually, approaches regard resultant behavioural problems as disorders (Eames, Haffey, & Cope, 1990; Rosenthal & Bond, 1990) and group them under neurological or recovery stages whose resolution determines the outcome (Jacobs, 1990; Wood, 1987). In particular, different approaches see the behavioural problems related to TBI as arising through personality changes (Prigatano, 1987) or as DSM-III psychiatric disturbances, such as schizophrenia, mood disorders, and personality disorders (Rosenthal & Bond, 1990; Varney, Martske, & Roberts, 1988; Yudofsky, Silver, & Schneider, 1987). Others have focused on cognitive and communication impairments, such as memory loss, disorientation, stuttering, aphasia, and attention problems (Lewis, Burke, & Carillo, 1987; McGuire & Rothenberg, 1986; Rousey, Arjunan, & Rousey, 1986). Here, I want to use the categorisation of head-injury consequences developed by Garcia (1994), because it clearly characterises the impact injuries have on the lives of the injured and those around them. Garcia categorises head injuries in terms of their expected potential outcome, identifying behaviours that are transient, modifiable, or chronic.

### Transient behavioural outcomes

Transient problem behaviours become evident soon after the patient emerges from a coma, and are most likely disappear with little or no systematic behavioural treatment. Other transient behaviours may emerge months later as the result of changes in the brain (swelling, intracranial bleeding, etc.) or to certain medical or "care" procedures (e.g. use of restraint, sedation). The more frequent transient behavioural problems include agitation, poor arousal, confabulation, screaming, verbal abuse, fighting with staff and others, enuresis, hallucinations, and delusions (Dunn, Umlauf, & Mermis, 1992; Eames et al., 1990; Jacobs, 1990). These may occur singly, but more usually several problem behaviours will be evident. Later, fears and consequent anxiety related to the sudden realisation of a dramatic change in self emerge (Rosenthal & Bond, 1990), and may again be accompanied by screaming, verbal abuse, constant pacing, and predatory and non-directed aggression (Cassidy, 1990). Both degree of neuropathological damage and environmental factors, such as the care regime available, contribute to the chronicity of these transient behaviours (Thomsen, 1990). Research suggests that the resolution of Post Traumatic Amnesia will frequently lead to disappearance of agitation, fighting (verbal or physical) or screaming, but these behaviours may re-emerge as anxiety and awareness of impairment grows (Nockleby & Deaton, 1987).

### Modifiable behavioural outcomes

The second class of behaviours that emerge following head injury are categorised as modifiable by Garcia (1994). When the individual with brain injury moves to a less restrictive environment, perhaps prior to or on re-entering the community or returning home, problem behaviours re-emerge partly because of the demands imposed by the requirement for increased functional independence. These behaviours differ from those in the transient category in aetiology and their resistance to change. Inconsistency in behaviour, verbal and physical abuse of others and self (Eames, 1988; Miller, 1990; Wood, 1987), inadequate social skills (Brotherton, Thomas, Wisotzek, & Milan, 1988; Turner, Green, & Braunling-McMorrow, 1990), and increased experience of anxiety or fears (Zenicus & Wesoloski, 1990) are characteristic of the emotional difficulties that arise. More cognitively, failure to follow instructions (Lewis & Bitter, 1991), difficulty in behaviour initiation (Pollens, McBratnie, & Burton, 1988; Sohlberg, Sprunk, & Metzelaar, 1988), and decreased ability to learn (Jacobs, 1990) are also widely reported. Obsessive behaviours (Eames et al., 1990; Wood, 1987), eating disorders (Jacobs, 1992), sexual problems (e.g. acting out or inhibition; Garde, Bontke, & Hoffman, 1990; Wood, 1987), and dependency and manipulative behaviour (Eames et al., 1990) are also acquired, maintained, or changed as a function of the sources of reinforcement, extinction, avoidance, and social modelling available to the head-injured person (Kazdin, 1988; Martin & Pear, 1988). Difficulties with memory, attention, arousal, or awareness of deficit, in addition to the intrinsic difficulties they pose, may also play a role as antecedents of behaviour and may become impediments for new learning (Horton & Barrett, 1988). Crucial for the modification of these problem behaviours is training in relaxation, de-sensitisation, role-playing, social skills, and operating in a controlled environment where the contingencies between actions and outcomes are consistent.

### Chronic behavioural outcomes

The final category of behaviours identified by Garcia are those described as chronic—being emotionally labile, lack of interest, irritability etc., perhaps lasting long after the initial injury (Thomsen, 1990). These problems may linger for several years, and continue long after physical restoration has reached a plateau (Kaplan, 1993). Psychosocial or behavioural problems, such as irritability, anxiety, indifference, and initiation of behaviour remain despite intervention. Severe impairment of frontal lobes results in deficits in goal-directed behaviour and loss of drive (Burke, 1993; Lewis & Bitter, 1991). Damage to the surfaces of the temporal lobes or to the limbic system can lead to perseverative behaviour, social and sexual disinhibition, impulsiveness, and episodic aggression (Lewis & Bitter, 1991), while damage to the hypothalamus may underlie lack of control in rage and fear (Seely, Stephens, & Tate, 1991).

The longevity of these effects is a function of the severity of the initial injury, especially for those with frontal lobe problems (Burke, 1993), where permanent neuropathology is believed to be at the root of these problems (Rosenbaum & Hoge, 1989). Among younger injured persons there is a higher risk of more severe sequelae (e.g. depression, Varney et al., 1988). Problems may also be increased through exaggeration of pre-morbid problem personality traits (e.g. anger management, drug or alcohol abuse), social maladjustment, and difficulty with authority figures (see Garcia, 1994).

There is a danger of catastrophising, but once again, because the young are more likely to survive an injury of given severity than the old, and because of the relationship between road traffic accidents and severity of head injuries, the young, inexperienced motorist is both at greater risk of being involved in a road accident, and more likely to suffer the severe injuries that would make driving again difficult and more dangerous.

## Resuming driving after Traumatic Brain Injury

The picture just offered of the consequences of brain injury may, I realise, exaggerate the difficulties those recovering from head injury may face when driving. However, I believe it is more dangerous to understate the difficulties involved.

In an important contribution to this debate, Brouwer and Withaar (1997, p. 179) offer a more optimistic note, suggesting that accounts in the literature of those who have suffered long periods of disturbed consciousness "who have been transferred to a rehabilitation hospital after the acute phase and who have made a good recovery" provide "an exaggerated impression of the problems CHI patients have . . . In the majority of cases, resuming driving occurs smoothly and without any medico-legal consideration". They reach this position by suggesting that assessment of fitness to drive should depend on ensuring that:

1. The probability of sudden and unpredictable lapses of control over behaviour is very low.
2. The perceptual, cognitive, and motor abilities necessary to be able to acquire and apply important driving skills are sufficient.
3. Social judgement and social responsibility are sufficient.

While agreeing wholeheartedly with these criteria, I do not believe that our current state of knowledge is sufficient to make such judgements reliably.

With respect to the first criterion, Brouwer and Whitaar suggest that lapses of attention are no more frequent in those who have suffered closed head injuries than in "normal healthy controls" (see also Van Zomeren & Brouwer, 1987) and that sustained attention is similar in both groups, (see also Parasuraman, Mutter, & Molloy, 1991). While it may be that in some cases, under assessment conditions, deficiencies in attentional control may not be evident, our concern must be with respect to situations that are less closely supervised, perhaps after an extended period of time on task, or where the task at hand is not the individual's primary goal. Specifically, Stablum, Mogentale, and Umilta (1996), showed that even two years after injury, people with mild traumatic brain injury were more subject to secondary task interference than age-, gender-, and education-matched controls. Interestingly, the patient and control groups did not differ when their visual selective attention abilities were assessed.

Regarding the second criterion, there is widespread recognition that those who have suffered traumatic brain injuries frequently have perceptual, cognitive and/or motor impairments (e.g. Schmidt, Brouwer, Vanier, & Kemp, 1996; Veltman, Brouwer, Van Zomeren, & van Woffelaar, 1996), and that performance slows still further and becomes more erratic as task complexity increases (Van Zomeren & Brouwer, 1994). However, Brouwer and Withaar (1997) claim that when this "slowness" is statistically controlled, impairment of higher-order aspects of information processing (e.g. planning, inhibition, flexibility, and divided attention) are less apparent. Recognising that "slow information processing may be a problem, particularly where it is extreme", they go on to suggest that "mild to moderate slowness can be well accommodated because the driving task has a lot of 'space' for compensatory behaviour through its hierarchical organisation and through its character of an over-learned cognitive and perceptual-motor skill" (1997, p. 189). The problem, however, is that we cannot assume that in every circumstance we as drivers can determine the pace at which we perform the task. Although the driving task is frequently forgiving of error, the clear association between human error and accident involvement underlines the fact that if we do trade off the possibility of error against an increase in the pace at which we perform, we do so in ways that can be catastrophically wrong. It is unlikely that people who suffer consistent or spasmodic failures of insight are well placed to make the accommodations required to avoid exposing themselves to the consequences of poor planning, inattention, and inability to initiate appropriate action, and to perform with flexibility.

Finally, with respect to the third criterion, Brouwer and Withaar claim that difficulties with social responsibility among those who have sustained traumatic brain injuries may be exaggerated. They do so on the basis of survey- and interview-based studies by Priddy, Johnson, and Lam (1990) and Brouwer, Van Zomeren, and van Woffelaar (1990), which show that in some circumstances people with traumatic brain injury become more responsible with regard to risk-taking and behaviours such as drinking and driving. Clearly we must avoid stigmatising people who have suffered injury, but self-reported behaviour, unreliable as it is for most of us, is a poor basis for doubting well-established clinical phenomena.

In short, such is the lasting damage to aspects of cognitive processing and emotional control that results from brain injury, damage to structures and processes that are intrinsically linked to driving, that I believe a safe resumption of driving is unlikely among those who have sustained severe brain injury. For those suffering mild brain injury the prospects are probably better, but extensive and rigorous empirical and clinical research must be at the basis of any such judgement. We are some way short of this position.

## DEMENTIA AND DRIVING

Increased longevity and a broader base of licence holding has led to a substantial increase in the average age of drivers. As those making up the rapid increace in levels of licence holding in the middle quarter of the twentieth century age, this trend will accelerate still further. Recent figures available in the United Kingdom,[1] for example, show that in 1997 there were almost six and a half million driving licence holders aged 60 and over (see Table 9.2). This is about a sixth of the current licence-holding population.

Over 40% of these licence holders were aged between 60 and 65 years of age, nearly 30% were aged between 66 and 70. Assuming there are no catastrophic changes in mortality rates, within a few years the UK will have well over one million licence holders in their eighties, some four million licence holders in their seventies, and an even larger number (circa 10 million) in their sixties. In other words, the number of drivers aged 60 and over will more than double

---

[1] Figures from UK Driver Licensing Vehicle Authority, records as at August 1997.

TABLE 9.2
UK driving licence holders aged 60 and over (1997)

| Age band | Males (% age band) | Females (% age band) | All (% total 60+) |
|----------|--------------------|-----------------------|--------------------|
| 60–65 | 1,609,849 (61%) | 1,021,417 (39%) | 2,631,266 (41%) |
| 66–70 | 1,171,082 (65%) | 634,834 (35%) | 1,805,916 (28%) |
| 71–75 | 722,341 (68%) | 340,302 (32%) | 1,062,643 (16%) |
| 76–85 | 621,342 (70%) | 265,230 (30%) | 886,572 (14%) |
| 86+ | 63,371 (75%) | 21,259 (25%) | 84,630 (1%) |
| All | 4,187,985 (65%) | 2,283,042 (35%) | 6,471,027 |

towards the end of the first decade of the twenty-first century, and will be more evenly distributed between males and females. It will increase by the same amount in the following decade, with some 40% of the driving population being over 60 by 2020, as opposed to the current level of 16%. These trends in the elderly driving population are similar in many other countries (e.g. Germany, Schlag, 1993; United States, Rowe & Kahn, 1997).

As discussed earlier, older drivers, while they are involved in comparatively fewer accidents than their younger counterparts, are involved in substantially more accidents than would be expected given the distance they drive per year. Estimates of this increased risk vary, but most suggest that drivers over 65 are twice as likely to be involved in an accident as drivers aged 25–64, per unit of distance driven (OECD, 1985). This is despite widespread reports that older drivers change their driving patterns, choosing slower roads, avoiding turning across traffic, etc. (see Holland & Rabbitt, 1994). There is increasing concensus that this rise in accident risk is not because of the ageing process per se, "but rather in age-related diseases and impairments affecting driving skills" (Lundberg et al., 1997, p. 28). Here I will group these under the general heading of dementia, which encompasses both cortical dementias (e.g. Dementia of the Alzheimer's Type, Pick's disease) and subcortical dementias (e.g. Parkinson's and Huntington's disease).

## Epidemiology

As a rough guide, and assuming no co-morbidity, about one in ten of the population in their sixties might be expected to be suffering from dementia of one form or another—that is, about two million people in the United Kingdom. Extrapolating to the driving population from this is very difficult. This is partly because the elderly are less likely to have ever driven than the young, and because it seems likely on a priori grounds that the more severely affected are unlikely to drive. Given these cautions, it is still reasonable to assume that perhaps several hundred thousand people with dementia hold current driving licences. This is an alarmingly high figure, all the more so when one realises that the incidence and impact of dementia both increase markedly beyond this age.

For convenience let me first consider the so-called cortical dementias. It is estimated that about 7% of all those aged over 65 suffer from the progressive degeneration of nerve cells in the cerebral hemispheres which is now referred to as Dementia of the Alzheimer's Type (Gurland & Cross, 1986), with its incidence doubling every five years (i.e. 14% of 70-year-old people, etc.; Bachman et al., 1993). Alzheimer's disease is accompanied by profound changes in cognitive performance functioning, but very substantial variation across cases and rates of deterioration in different functions is widely observed. Especially where onset is before 70 years of age, there is very substantial evidence of heredity, estimated to be in the region of 35–40% (Amaducci, Bocca, & Schoenberg, 1986) and still higher where the condition has appeared in successive generations. Recent research has localised Alzheimer's disease to chromosome 21, which is also the chromosome associated with Down's syndrome (Jarvik, 1988). Given the preceding sections, it is worth noting that head trauma is also strongly associated with increased likelihood of Alzheimer's disease (Mortimer & Pirozzolo, 1985). Such trauma are thought to weaken the immune system through breakdown of the blood–brain barrier following concussion, thus allowing greater access of viruses and toxins to the brain. Some studies have suggested that smoking, solvents, and aluminium are also associated with greater risk (US Congress, 1987). Loss of neurons, especially in the temporal lobes and brain stem nuclei (Rossor, 1987), and reduced production of associated neurotransmitters serves to disconnect temporal lobe structures from the remainder of the cerebral cortex and prefrontal from parietal structures. This damage may account for the memory deficits typically observed in Alzheimer's patients and their reduced ability to divide and switch attention (Parasuraman & Haxby, 1993).

Two other types of cortical dementia are widely reported, if rather less prevalent than Alzheimer's. Both have profound consequences for the functioning of the frontal lobes: Pick's disease typically has its onset in the person's fifties, while frontal lobe dementia typically has an earlier onset, but after the age of 40. Although Pick's disease has been known about for longer, the incidence of Pick's disease in the adult population is substantially lower (0.1%, see Lishman, 1987) than that estimated for frontal lobe dementia (circa 2%, see Neary & Sowden, 1991). Pick's disease is associated with autosomal dominant inheritance, in the region of 20–50% according to Cummings (1992), while in frontal lobe dementia the incidence of dementia in first-degree relatives is very high (some 50%, Neary & Sowden, 1991), thus showing that it too is transmitted as an autosomal dominant disease. The incidence of recent head injury appears to have a small effect, if any (see Mortimer & Pirozzolo, 1985).

In both cases deterioration in frontal areas of the brain is very marked, but both Pick's and frontal lobe patients do appear to have characteristically different patterns of damage. Thus, Pick's disease is marked by extensive atrophy in temporal and frontal neocortex, with the amygdala suffering deterioration early in the disease's onset. In most cases occipital and parietal lobes are unaffected, and the temporal gyrus, hippocampus, and cerebellum are also largely spared (Chui, 1989). The pattern of damage with frontal lobe dementia is similar in that frontal and temporal lobes sustain significant atrophy, while the corpus striatum, thalamus, cerebellum, and brain stem appear intact (Moss, Albert, & Kemper, 1992; Neary & Sowden, 1991). On the other hand, it is usual to find damage to parietal cortex, although the hippocampus and amygdala remain unaffected, despite damage to surrounding regions. Thus, perhaps the key neurological difference (in addition to the presence in one case of Pick's bodies, i.e. Pick's cells containing degraded protein), is that damage to the amygdala is almost universal in Pick's patients, but quite unusual in those with frontal lobe dementia. In later stages, both can be similar to Alzheimer's, and as with Alzheimer's, although not to the same extent, the nucleus basalis is reduced in size, and thalamic and basal ganglia atrophy is common.

By comparison with the cortical dementias, the incidence of subcortical dementias in the general population is relatively small—Huntington's disease (0.01%; Tobin, 1990), Parkinson's disease (0.02%; Granerus, 1990). The early focus on the motor aspects of Huntington's disease has tended to obscure the fact that patients also endure profound personality and cognitive difficulties. Importantly, from a diagnostic point of view, these motor, cognitive, and emotional changes may differ in severity and also as a function of when disease-onset occurs (Folstein, 1989). About one-quarter of all sufferers manifest the disease in their fifties, but the average age of onset is in the forties. However, this age-based onset pattern is somewhat misleading, as cases have even been detected before 5 years of age and after 70 years of age (Tobin, 1990). The disease is autosomal-dominant, with half of all offspring of the carrier parent eventually acquiring the disease, although onset is later and effects less severe when passed from mother to child. The faithful transmission from parent to child allows for very early and reliable diagnosis, with the possibility that the onset of the disease may be anticipated for many years before it takes effect.

The anatomical characterisation of Huntington's disease is of progressive atrophy of the caudate nucleus and the putamen, together with structures in the corpus striatum. There is some controversy as to whether the atrophy extends to cortical regions, with some authors suggesting deterioration in the cerebellum, thalamic nuclei, and other subcortical regions (Tobin, 1990). Deterioration of the corpus striatum brings about alterations in the levels of neurotransmitters in this region, which at normal levels exercise inhibitory effects. There is a concomitant increase in excitatory neurotransmitters, and together these changes provoke increases in the Huntington patient's characteristically tortuous involuntary movement spasms. Because the caudate nucleus projects to the prefrontal cortex, atrophy in this region effects a disconnection between the two, resulting in disease characteristics that share many similarities with frontal lobe disorders, even where patients have no prefrontal lesions (Cummings & Benson, 1990).

There are also pronounced motor aspects of Parkinson's disease. Specifically, Parkinsonian patients exhibit a characteristic "resting tremor" (i.e. rapid rythmical shaking of limbs, jaw, tongue, which disappears with voluntary movement), muscular rigidity, difficulties initiating movements (*akinesia*), and sometimes motor slowing (*bradykinesia*). Together these result in a characteristic expressionless stare, general loss of agility and fine co-ordination, and the typical shuffling gait with little steps. In all, Parkinson's disease is thought to affect some 0.20% of the general population (Granerus, 1990), but the incidence rises sharply among the over fifties (estimated to be 1%, Adams & Victor, 1981). There is little evidence that heredity is an important causal factor, but viral encephalitis and other post-viral conditions, effects of neuroleptic drugs and toxins are all thought to contribute (Tanner, 1989). Repeated head trauma, such as that arising in sports like boxing, are also thought to greatly increase the likelihood of developing Parkinson's disease (see Della Sala & Mazzini, 1989).

The anatomical characterisation of the disease is of progressive basal ganglia dysfunction, and a resulting failure to synthesise dopamine (Freedman, 1990). The dopamine depletion leads to frontal disconnections and thus to the presence and severity of motor problems. Cell loss also occurs in the locus coeruleus and basalis nucleus (Granerus, 1990), with a concomitant underproduction of non-dopaminergic neurotransmitters. Parkinsonian patients also tend to have abnormally long evoked potential latencies (Goodin, 1992). Adult patients whose onset is before 40 years of age tend to have a slower progression with fewer cognitive disorders, and less dementia (Levin, Tomer, & Rey, 1992). Older-onset patients experience a more rapid decline, cognitive impairment, and ten times the level of dementia of early-onset patients (Golbe, 1991).

## Deficits

The severity of the difficulties experienced by those suffering from dementias of different sorts depends in part on the age of onset of the disease.

### Alzheimer's disease

People suffering from Alzheimer's perform less well than age-matched normals on tests of visual discrimination, spatial judgement, and perceptual organisation (Cogan, 1985; Mendez et al., 1990), skills that one might reasonably expect to be involved in driving—especially in monitoring the environment for potential hazards. More severe cases also have impaired eye-movements, which has a collateral effect on these tasks. Among Alzheimer's sufferers, motor problems are rare (Adams, 1984; Cummings, 1988), although it may be that difficulties would emerge where motor tasks are more complex (Grafman et al., 1990). Thus, one might expect that difficulties in negotiating complex traffic situations may well be evident in more simple aspects of motor control. These circumstances will also prove difficult for Alzheimer's sufferers because attentional deficits are particularly prevalent. This, it has been found that immediate memory span is reduced (Morris & Baddeley, 1988), and that both focusing and shifting of attention (Nebes & Brady, 1989) and dividing of attention (Nebes, 1992) is defective. Choice reaction time is also slower than would be expected of people of similar age (Nestor, Parasuraman, & Haxby, 1991). It would appear that these deficits are more typical of later stages of the disease, as it has been shown that visual, verbal span, and sustained attention are satisfactory in its early stages (Schacter, Kaszniak, & Kihlstrom, 1989). Immediate memory also suffers (Morris & Baddeley, 1988), as does memory with even minimal delays (Albert, Moss, & Milberg, 1989). Such deficits are sometimes very severe in the early stages of the disease, with these difficulties propounded where transitory memory tasks are paired with an additional distractor task (Morris & Kopelman, 1986). Such difficulties are likely to give rise to confusion and loss of place errors when driving.

What might be termed long-term memory, and ability to learn and retain new material for an extended period of time, also suffers. The difficulty here appears to be a failure to benefit from the types of intervention that usually aid learning, such as repetition (Herlitz & Viitanen, 1991), organisation (Nebes, 1992), or imagery (Ober, Koss, Friedland, & Delis, 1985). Backman and Herlitz (1990) conclude that Alzheimer's disease is associated with a deficit in the ability to use task-relevant prior knowledge to enhance episodic remembering, and it is also clear from a number of studies that Alzheimer's sufferers have considerable difficulty in avoiding choosing familiar, but incorrect, distractors in recognition tasks (e.g. Eslinger & Damasio, 1986; Rapcsak, Kentros, & Rubens, 1990).

Mack, Patterson, Schnell, and Whitehouse (1993), summarise the range of cognitive difficulties encountered by Alzheimer's sufferers as comprising a visual perceptual factor, and factors for transient memory, enduring memory, and linguistic performance. There is also substantial evidence for emotional problems among Alzheimer's sufferers: ranging from reduced spontaneity, disinterest, passivity, and aimless wandering to bursts of violence and destructiveness, suspiciousness, and paranoia (Haley, Brown, & Levine, 1987). The incidence of depression is thought to decrease as the severity of dementia increases, only to be replaced by hallucinations and delusions in some 20–70% of cases (see Lopez et al., 1991). In its earlier stages some aspects of everyday life are continued with for longer than is in the interests of the sufferer's own safety and that of others. For example, although for their age a high proportion of Alzheimer's patients do give up driving, about 80% of those who continue get lost, and one in two or three become involved in car accidents (Kaszniak, 1991).

### Pick's disease

In both Pick's disease and frontal lobe dysfunction, personality and behaviour problems tend to emerge earlier than cognitive deficits (Moss et al., 1992). Frequently such difficulties emerge in social disinhibition, poor judgement and impulsivity, boorishness, apathy or impaired capacity for sustained motivation, compulsions, and meaningless tactile searching (Cummings, 1992). We might therefore expect driving to be compromised, albeit more by the erratic social interaction tendencies of Pick's sufferers than by the later-onset cognitive difficulties. Because of some of these changes, both groups of patients can be uncooperative in assessment situations and thus more detailed evidence of the cognitive decline that accompanies Pick's and frontal lobe dementia is relatively limited. That said, speech disorders are prominent, hyperorality (i.e. talking too much!), empty speech, or slowed dysfluent speech are reasonably typical, although memory deficits are not prominent (Albert et al., 1989; Neary & Sowden, 1991). However, the effects of the gross frontal damage common to both groups is evident in their disordered executive functions, limited abstraction abilities, and reasoning deficits (Moss et al., 1992). Such patients, even early in the disease, have great difficulty in remaining oriented and in maintaining routines, and thus would experience considerable difficulty in moderately demanding driving conditions, were they exposed to them.

## Huntington's disease

Among those with Huntington's disease, eye movements are slow to be initiated, and short and jerky rather than a smooth sweep on approach to a target, and patients also have difficulty maintaining their gaze on a target once it is located. Initiation of other movements is also slow, and motor co-ordination is poor, especially for the non-dominant hand (Bradshaw et al., 1992), which of course for most drivers would be used for gear changing.

Attention span deteriorates from normal levels to being particularly short, while difficulties in maintaining and shifting attention are also widely observed (Folstein, 1989). This would obviously compromise ability to drive. Huntington's patients are very vulnerable to interference effects, as shown by their poor performance on the Brown-Peterson task (Butters & Grady, 1977). Acquisition of new material is poor, and it has also been shown that retrieval can be enhanced where cueing or a recognition procedure is used to assess remembering (Massman et al., 1990). However, as the disease progresses, recognition performance also deteriorates, such that discrimination between information that the patient has attempted to learn and new information becomes increasingly difficult (Kremer et al., 1988). Huntington's patients show virtually normal priming even quite some time after onset (Heindel et al., 1989), showing that learning and implicit memory still function, although this should not be seen as an indication that procedural learning and memory, as might be required for driving, are intact.

Strategic use of memory resources is greatly impaired in Huntington's patients. Spontaneous use of rehearsal or imagery at encoding is very limited (Butters & Grady, 1977; Weingartner, Caine, & Ebert, 1979), while capitalising on the semantics of the to-be-learned materials does occur, but is also unreliable

(Weingartner et al., 1979). Serial learning is very difficult for Huntington's patients (Caine, Ebert, & Weingartner, 1977). Procedural learning is also impaired (Butters, Salmon, Heindel, & Graham, 1988; Paulsen, Salmon, Heindel, & Butters, 1991), as is generalisation of learned procedures (Bylsma, Brandt, & Strauss, 1990), although less so in the early stages of the disease (Saint-Cyr & Taylor, 1992). The fact that these deteriorations occur, as do deteriorations in speech production (e.g. articulation, rate, and intensity of delivery), even though vocabulary, syntax, and grammar aspects of speech do not falter until late into the course of the disease (Bayles, 1988), shows the differential impact of Huntington's disease on procedural and declarative aspects of memory. Together these deficits seem likely to have at first erratic but subsequently profound effects on driving performance.

Caine, Hunt, Weingartner, and Ebert, (1978, p. 381) suggest that patients are "acutely aware of their cognitive abilities". About 10% of patients present with mania (Folstein, 1989), while it has been estimated that up to 18% present with schizophrenic-like delusional symptoms, although bizarre hallucinations are rare. Irritability, suspiciousness, obsessionality, aggression, and sexual promiscuity in the early stages of the disease are all widely reported (Cummings, 1986). Some 50% of patients suffer from depression at some stage in the course of the disease, with one in five suffering from chronic depression (Folstein, 1989). Whether or not these emotional changes are a reaction to the commencement of what is in most cases a long-anticipated progressive and terminal deterioration of function, is not clear. The incidence of depression, for example, is higher than in Alzheimer's patients, although the level of self-awareness is probably not as acute throughout the course of the disease, and depression precedes the onset of motor and cognitive symptoms in many cases. The preoccupation that results from being aware of this slow decline of function is likely to undermine confidence, and make attention switching during a task difficult. The level of depression, and relative inertia that may result may lead to a reduction in driving, but an increased risk where the sufferer does drive.

### Parkinson's disease

Among Parkinsonian patients there is evidence of sensory deficits, most having a defective sense of smell (Doty, Deems, & Stellar, 1988), and about a third of patients complaining of sensory discomfort, pain, numbness, cold, or burning sensations (Bannister, 1992). Parkinsonian patients typically experience attentional deficits, although these are not always observed when attention is measured by digit span, being either within normal limits (Huber & Shuttleworth, 1990), or impaired (Sullivan & Sagar, 1988). Instead attentional deficits emerge in complex tasks requiring switching or sustained attention (Cummings, 1986; Wright, Burns, Geffen, & Geffen, 1990), or in making calculations that require mental tracking (as in the Paced Auditory Serial Addition Task; Huber & Shuttleworth,

1990). Passive reception and brief maintenance of information is relatively unimpaired, but performance deteriorates rapidly where a distractor task is introduced during the delay (Sullivan, Sagar, Cooper, & Jordan, 1993). However, as short-term recall of word lists or stories is impaired (Brown & Marsden, 1988), it is questionable whether transitory memory is in fact intact. In terms of more enduring memory, Parkinsonian patients perform relatively well in cued recall, paired associate, or recognition tasks (Beatty, 1992) and they also take advantage of categorisation where the to-be-learned material facilitates this, but patients are unlikely to initiate these retrieval strategies themselves (Brown & Marsden, 1988).

Parkinsonian patients experience profound procedural difficulties. This would appear to be more than a motor deficit, as sequencing and ordering tasks in general pose very great problems for the Parkinsonian patient (Vriezen & Moscovitch, 1990), as does performing procedural skills (Haarland & Harrington, 1990). Although dysfluencies in speech are widely observed, in Parkinsonian patients vocabulary, syntax, and grammatical knowledge appear to be intact (Bayles, 1988). With regard to the quality of speech, phrase length and overall output suffer, at least partly because of the motor control deficits such patients experience. However, it should be noted that in more discrete tasks, word-finding and retrieval are common (Beatty, 1992), while naming studies also provide equivocal results in different patient groups (Gurd & Ward, 1989).

Bondi and Kaszniak (1991) report a number of experiments that compare implicit and explicit memory in Alzheimer's and Parkinson's disease patients and healthy elderly subjects. Alzheimer's patients were impaired on all explicit tests and on word stem completion priming, but were intact on pursuit-rotor tracking and the skill learning component of the fragmented pictures test. Parkinson's patients were significantly better than Alzheimer's patients on all explicit memory tests, but were selectively impaired on the skill learning component of the fragmented pictures test. Finally, a mirror-reading test was given to Parkinson's patients and control subjects, with no significant differences found in performances between groups. Once again, because of the characteristically different damage suffered by these two groups of patients, this study suggests that different brain circuits underlie different implicit and explicit memory domains. Parkinson's patients consistently fail tests comprising both conceptual and executive functions. Errors normally arise when first required to formulate a strategy—once a solution is required, they perform at near normal levels (Saint-Cyr & Taylor, 1992). In fact, Parkinson's disease patients are similar in some respects to those with frontal lobe damage (Haarland & Harrington, 1990), with characteristics of prefrontal dysfunction such as difficulties in switching or maintaining a set, in initiating responses, in serial and temporal ordering, in generating strategies, in cognitive slowing, and diminished productivity (Cronin-Golumb, 1990; Dubois, Boller, Pillon, & Agid, 1991).

## CONTINUING DRIVING WITH NEUROLOGICAL
## DAMAGE AND DISEASE

All but the most severely head-injured people re-integrate into the community to a greater or lesser extent. How successfully they do so depends on the level of injury suffered, and on the care and rehabilitation they have had post-accident. In practice the provision of the latter is patchy and thus people with substantial, albeit invisible, deficits may rejoin the "normal" community. Because of this, and because of the absence of any systematic information, we cannot establish whether people with head injuries of different severity levels can reasonably be expected to drive safely after injury. However, on the basis of the foregoing review, I believe that the range and longevity of deficits suffered should encourage more caution about their prospects than is currently the case.

A number of studies have attempted to estimate the incidence of road traffic accidents involving drivers suffering from dementia. Whether risk is calculated in relation to a given period, or distance driven, crashes involving drivers suffering from dementia are at least twice as likely as for older drivers in general (Cooper, Tallman, Tuokko, & Beattie, 1993; Tuokko et al., 1995). There is also evidence that the degenerative aspects of dementia are also reflected in the accident involvement of these drivers. Waller, Trobe, and Olson (1993) and Drachman and Swearer (1993) show that accident involvement of age-matched controls and drivers in the early stages of dementia are little different—the difference thus emerges some time after disease onset, a three-year period being suggested by Drachman and Swearer (1993). These studies are, however, rather limited and serve as indications of where research is necessary rather than providing findings that are in themselves conclusive.

There are substantial overlaps in the functional deficits of some of those who have had head injuries or suffer from the types of dementia described earlier. These relate particularly to deficits in switching and maintaining attention, and temporary memory deficits, together with problems with self-monitoring and awareness of deficit, emotional stability, and control. There are also important differences between the typical head-injured person and dementia sufferer. Some of these differences, not least in the likely extent of their previous driving experience and their age, as well as in the particular deficits or combination of deficits, seem likely to lead to increased accident risk. The fact is that the available accident data indicate clearly that the incidence of accidents among those suffering from dementia is substantially higher than occurs in age-matched samples. It is important to recognise that whether for the typical head-injured driver, or those suffering from dementia, the age-matched samples themselves have substantially higher accident risk than the normal 30–50-year-old driver. This stresses the urgency of understanding the extent to which the deficits suffered by those with brain damage or disease impose limitations on the ability of those people to drive. Because we do not fully understand the relationship between standard psychometric tests and driving performance, I believe that this requires that assessments of driving capability are made on tasks as similar to real driving conditions as is practicable. It also requires us to attempt to assess driving within a cognitively plausible model or framework, rather than in the somewhat atheoretical way we currently do. In the final chapter of this book I will attempt to summarise many of the important elements of previous chapters which suggest to me a particular type of framework.

# CHAPTER TEN

# Towards a cognitive account of driver behaviour

*The foregoing chapters have described the driving task, and the cognitive processes on which it depends. In this final chapter, I try to sketch a cognitive theory of how people drive, which attempts an integration of the previous chapters. In doing so, I address some aspects of a future research agenda, which might provide a basis for formally testing aspects of this theory, and a future agenda for application, which has implications for training, licensing, and assessing the psychological fitness of people to drive.*

Although any rational analysis would surely place preservation of one's own personal safety at the heart of the concerns of a driver, I believe it is but one of the goals a driver has, and most of the time is not especially influential. Instead the driver's aspirations are to reach destinations, avoid obstacles, minimise delay and driving time, enjoy driving, feel in control, etc. These proximal goals are in some cases related to wider safety issues, but I believe it is their concrete expression or realisation, in the situation in which the driver finds him or herself, rather than more abstract principles such as safety, that has a real impact on behaviour. As experts, when investigating accidents or attempting to account for aberrant behaviour, we wonder why someone drove riskily, or took a particular risk. However, just because we as investigators have understanding safety as a goal, it does not mean that the driver had safety as a primary goal, or ever had sufficient knowledge of possible outcomes available on which to base a deliberate action. In the framework I am about to outline, I try to capture the importance of the multiplicity of driver goals and how they sometimes find expression in behaviour.

**_E N V I R O N M E N T_**

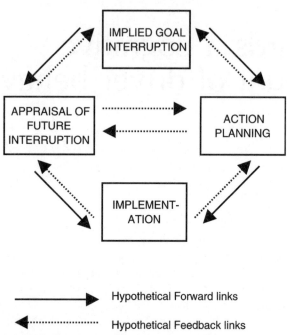

Hypothetical Forward links

Hypothetical Feedback links

**Figure 10.1.**   Four elements of driver behaviour.

## A FRAMEWORK FOR UNDERSTANDING
## THE DRIVING TASK

In 1995, as a putative way of understanding the influences on drivers' responses to risk, I proposed four hypothetical processes that underlie driver behaviour: (1) a process that detects changes which imply some discontinuity in currently active goals; (2) a process that appraises this threat; (3) a process that selects and constructs the most appropriate form of action in the circumstances; and (4) a process responsible for the implementation of any changes in current activity that this may require. Figure 10.1 summarises the relationships between these four processes. Later, with my colleagues Sean Hammond and David Field, Graham Grayson and Geoff Maycock, and funding from the United Kingdom Department of Environment Transport and the Regions, over a period of three or so years I have had the opportunity to explore this approach and its psychometric reliability and validity more fully.

Over 400 drivers were tested as part of the development, testing, and validation of this four-facet hypothetical framework. In advance, we predicted which of a range of computer-based and computer versions of standard psychological tests and specially constructed tests related to driving (e.g. steering and braking control, self-assessment of driving skills, etc.) would measure the functioning of the four putative aspects of driving.[1] As will be shown later, the predicted four-facet framework strongly emerged from a confirmatory factor analysis using all of the measures taken. This confirmed the statistical integrity of the hypothetical framework. Furthermore, the actual driving speeds and driving ability, as assessed by an accompanying driving examiner, of 100 or so of these drivers during a supervised assessment drive were very reliably predicted by elements of the four-facet framework.[2] This element of the validation study will also be described in a little more detail later, after I describe the role and function of each facet of the framework in turn, how it was operationalised in the validation study, and the way I now see each facet as it relates to driver behaviour in general.

## Implied goal interruption

As discussed earlier, I assume that a number of goals may simultaneously influence driving, and only when they are satisfied do they relinquish control over behaviour. These will include: achieving the purpose of the journey, and probably remaining safe and/or deriving pleasure from driving. Having goals, rather than general aspirations, implies for me that our past experience, or general problem-solving ability in situations quite unlike those previously encountered, is capable of specifying how progress towards the goal might be achieved.[3] Past experience, in the form of automatically retrieved memories, which matches the current situation increases our sensitivity to similarities previously associated with goal interruption. By "increases our sensitivity", and it may be an unfortunate phrase, I do not mean to imply that we, necessarily, become conscious of the memory, nor of the direct effect its retrieval may have on our actions and evaluations. Instead such priming from such implicit memories may bring about physiological changes, or changes in action, which we may subsequently interpret as having been brought about by some environmental event.

For example, suppose my car closes on a vehicle ahead unexpectedly quickly. The sense of surprise I may feel in this circumstance must have been preceded by some monitoring of that vehicle's current position and how it has recently changed. It may be the "updating" I become aware of, but it is almost certainly not the process of determining some discontinuity in the rate of change of closure on the vehicle ahead. Sudden closure is one signal that is predictive of goals being interrupted—it may convey delay, and perhaps danger. With regard to detecting hazards, which covers some but not all of what implied goal interruption is

---

[1] Full details of the tests, testing arrangements, and results are provided in Groeger et al. (1998a, b).

[2] In fact 30% of the variability in speed over the 20-mile route was predicted by the model, and 47% of the variability in the examiner's blind ratings of care, attention, skill, and ability.

[3] The parallel here between Logan's (1988) ideas of what constitutes automaticity is deliberate.

involved in, some discrepancy or discontinuity is detected which is predictive of being endangered, even though the individual may not be conscious of it, or subsequently be able to report it. For the most part such predictive relationships are learned through experience. Not all need to be learned as part of the driving task (e.g. ducking when a stone hits the windscreen of your vehicle as you drive along probably reflects transfer from learning as a child), but some (e.g. anticipating the presence of child pedestrians near parked cars) require instruction, if not direct experience, before they can be acquired. This is particularly the case where a number of different cues are needed to discriminate between hazardous and non-hazardous circumstances, such multiple-cue probability learning being notoriously difficult even in laboratory tasks (see Brehmer, 1990). An individual's propensity to evaluate situations as threatening to some current goal, which might be the case with someone who has high trait anxiety, and the range and attractiveness of response options available will all influence hazard detection. Detection of implied goal interruptions, dependent as it is on retrieval from prior experience, is likely to be better among those with substantial and varied actual experience of driving.

As originally conceptualised, this facet was seen in the context of hazard detection, and as a result many of the tests used reflected concerns with hazard perception, evaluations of traffic scenes, judgement of trajectories, and time-to-arrival, as well as a number of measures of decision-making quality—as qualities such as thoroughness, perfectionism, etc. seemed likely to influence the extent to which people interrogate their environment and interpret discrepancies between what they expect and what they find. Despite this intended bias towards risk-related evaluations, I believe the tests reflect processes that are also more generally involved in aspects of driving where other goals and expectations might be threatened.

A principal components analysis of the measures related to this first facet from the validation study referred to earlier, resulted in a 5-factor solution accounting for 51.34% of the total variance, with an overall simplicity of 0.90. These factors and the tests that load on them are presented graphically in Figure 10.2. The first factor includes a number of scales from Robert West's Decision Making Style measure—loading positively on instinctiveness and social resistance and negatively on idealism and hesitancy. This combination imples a "readiness to respond", meaning the individual's tendency to act in a fashion that might seem hasty or on the basis of less information than others might require before acting. The second factor relates directly to how drivers evaluate traffic scenes, in terms of the control they have in such circumstances, and the dangers evident therein (scene assessment). The third factor that emerged involved the driver's tendency to be thorough, requirement for being in control, and tendency to regard driving situations as difficult. This I interpret as reflecting a behavioural standard, i.e. the driver's expectations of their own performance and that of others, something like the driver's level of task involvement. Spatial reasoning emerged as a

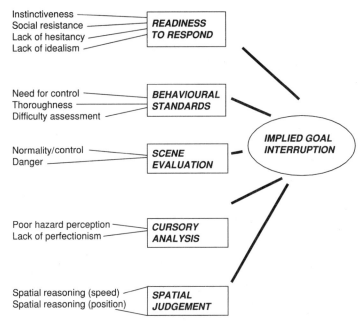

**Figure 10.2.**    Elements of implied goal interruption.

reliable and separate factor, suggesting that ongoing assessment of trajectory and potential collision is a key feature of how implied goal interruptions might be detected. Finally, poor performance on the hazard perception test used and lack of perfectionism combined in the final factor, perhaps suggesting more cursory analysis than is desirable.

Considering these facets as the basis for how drivers determine whether current goals might be under threat, the way factors emerge suggests that what is involved are processes that determine possible interactions with other road users, obstacles, etc., the extent and criteria the driver has for analysing the currect situation, their general tendency to wish to be proactive or reactive, and the standards they have for that action.

## Appraisal of future interruption

Once detected, the threat implicit in the future interruption of some current goal is evaluated. It is at this stage that beliefs about one's self, propensities to belief that negative events are likely to occur (i.e. confidence), the extent of threat present, the seriousness of the consequences, the value of such negative consequences to the individual, and the inherent controllability of the threat are all combined to yield some determination to act. I have discussed how such efficacy beliefs develop and influence both action and emotional reaction in Chapter 8.

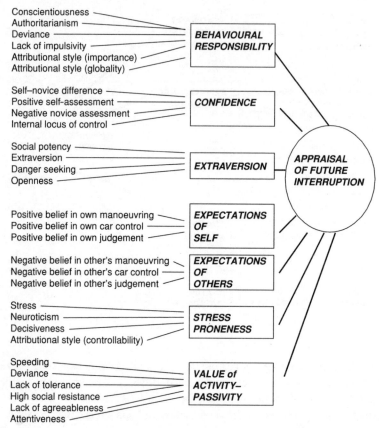

**Figure 10.3.** Elements of appraisal of future interruption.

Groeger and Grande (1996) have demonstrated that control beliefs strongly influence male drivers' self-assessments but not those of female drivers, whereas mood states play a greater role in female drivers' views of their own ability than they do in males. Appraisal therefore involves a range of both temporary and more enduring "personality" factors, but is also influenced by the knowledge that reflects the task experience the driver has had. Although it is likely that many hazards invoke some appraisal prior to an action being undertaken, this is not necessarily the case with simple, well-learned risks. It is therefore predicted that appraisal processes may be differentially influential in drivers' capacities to detect and respond appropriately to hazards at different levels of experience (see Figure 10.3).

Of course the goal that is threatened with interruption may not relate to personal safety, but instead to the progress one is attempting to make, or the pleasure one requires of the driving experience. In such circumstances, the frustration that results from a goal being interrupted may result in an increase in hostility, where the individual has a tendency to believe that what has provoked the interruption is specific to that particular circumstance and due to external causes. Where the individual's appraisal of the situation leads him or her to believe that more than that circumstance will be affected, e.g. the delay is not because of one person driving slowly and but the result of some more general log-jam, then the anticipated regret in having to relinquish some goal or fail to achieve it in spite of one's best efforts may lead to increased sadness and deflation rather than hostility.

As originally conceived, this facet of driver behaviour was thought likely to involve one's appraisal of one's self, expectations of others, the desirability of being active or passive, the importance of different consequences of action or inaction, and so forth. In the validation study, what emerged from a principal components analysis of the measures, which were a priori predicted to comprise this facet, was a 7-factor solution that has an overall Kaiser simplicity index of 0.89 (Kaiser, 1974), and accounts for 55% of the variance.

The first factor emerging I now think of as behavioural responsibility, as it comprised loadings from an impulsivity score as well as danger seeking, and negative loadings from conscientiousness. It reflects the individual's desire to take responsibility for what happens. The second factor comprised loadings from the Self Assessment Scales, but particularly the difference between self and novice, and a loading that reflects a tendency for the individuals who see themselves as similar to the novice to manifest low externality of control. This might thus be labelled confidence. The third factor reflects extraversion, comprising loadings from extraversion and social potency tests as well as danger seeking, openness to experience, and impulsivity. The fourth and fifth factors clearly relate to belief in own ability and belief in other's ability. We labelled the next factor to emerge stress proneness, as it was loaded on by neuroticism and stress scales, and negatively by conscientiousness, which is suggestive of the typically chaotic nature of highly stressed individuals. Finally, a number of Robert West's driving style scales combined to form a factor I now consider reflects an "activity–passivity" continuum. It comprises loadings from the driver's self-reported tendency to speed, and his or her tendency to be intolerant, and resistant to social pressure and norms. As such, not unlike extraversion, it reflects a wish to engage energetically with the task or a preference for less demand.

## Action planning

In the course of driving a whole range of actions are routinely prepared and performed under the control of a hierarchy of different goals. For example, a driver may be trying to locate a particular address, allowing other traffic to turn across him or her, and holding the clutch and accelerator at the engine biting point, all simultaneously (see Grayson, 1991). I envisage that action planning is implicated where people have to determine how to achieve some newly established goal, or to identify some action that will circumvent some temporary goal interruption. For example, detecting an upcoming hazard implies a discontinuity in the current or "normal" control structure, the extent of which depends on the outcome of threat appraisal processes and the ease with which a "satisfactory" (i.e. in terms of established or new goals) course of action can be determined. A threat appraised as being of minor importance will perturb the normal control of activity relatively little and may not be responded to. A threat that is appraised as very important will cause a reallocation of attention and the interruption, perhaps the forgetting, and consequent need for re-planning of the goals currently operating. Where the threat is sufficiently great the attention allocated to it may even prevent the selection of an appropriate, perhaps even any, course of action. Thus one important aspect of what governs an individual's response selection is his or her attentional capacity as well as the ability to re-orient attention effectively in complex situations.

For example, when another vehicle is approaching on a collision course—a hazard that is easily detectable perceptually—the threat may be "reduced" by looking away from it (a naturally overlearned response which must be overcome in this case), by slowing down (and relying on the oncoming driver acting in order to avoid a collision), or by changing course (which may be optimal in most cases, but also requires a judgement of what the other driver will do, and of what other hazards may be entailed in doing so). Selecting appropriately between these alternatives is not as trivial as it might first seem. In the first place the extent to which the different courses of action have been practised will vary markedly. This probably does not matter where all actions have been highly practised, but this may not be the case with novice drivers, which may explain why drivers with different experience levels respond differently to similar hazards (see Malaterre, 1990). It is also unlikely that knowledge of the outcomes of different courses of action will be comparable, and thus it may be difficult to envisage which of a number of candidates is the most desirable. It should also be noted that having a large range of equally practised possible courses of action may not in itself be desirable, as decision time tends to increase with the range of alternatives available. It may be that appraisal processes are also involved in the selection of action as well as in the allocation of attention. Prospect theory, for example, suggests that where individuals perceive themselves to be in high potential loss situations more extreme decision options are favoured. For example, a driver, in a situation that is not intrinsically dangerous, having been slowed down more than he would wish by traffic ahead, may eventually through frustration overtake the slower traffic. In doing so he may deliberately underplay the risk involved and continue to drive, perhaps even faster than he had planned, as a way of resolving frustration and restoring the lost excitement. I know I have done this, on countless occasions, not because of the possibility of being late, but deliberately as a way of asserting myself over the situation, restoring my sense of power and excitement.

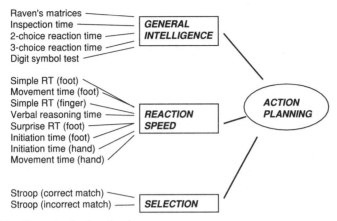

**Figure 10.4.**  Elements of action planning.

Initially I expected that action planning would depend on factors such as attentional control, selection between alternatives, inhibition, intellectual capacity, etc.; in other words the sorts of executive processes usually seen as dependent on the frontal lobes (see Chapter 5). Because of this, the tests used included Raven's matrices, choice reaction time, simple reaction, digit–symbol conversion, Stroop interference, and information-processing speed. Three factors emerged from the principal components analysis of the action planning tests. These account for 54% of the common variance, and provide a reliable and simple structure—the Kaiser simplicity index was (0.95).

These factors seemed to conveniently organise themselves into tests that assess general intelligence, notably including measures that are culture fair (such as Raven's matrices), information-processing speed (i.e. which of a set of three rapidly masked lines was the longest), choice reaction time, and the rapidity with which one set of symbol codes can be converted into another (see Figure 10.4). Each test has clear temporal dependencies, but requires the speeded application of some reasonably complex principle that is contingent on the information present in the scene. The second factor is a simple speed of response measure, and although this may seem more like the performance of a simple action, i.e. more characteristic of what is defined as implemetation, knowledge of how quickly one can perform is a crucial aspect of knowing whether performing one action or an alternative is best in a given situation. The appearance of the Stroop test as a single factor indicates that selecting between information and response inhibition are also coherent with these other aspects of action planning.

## Implementation

Implementation refers to the way the action selected is performed, although it also covers cases in which the decision taken is to "do nothing" or more probably "maintain current activity". As such, within this scheme, implementation relates

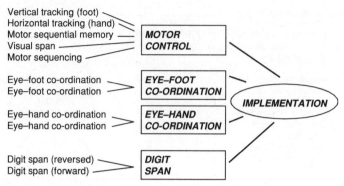

**Figure 10.5.** Elements of implementation.

to repertoires of movements associated with particular fingers, hands, or feet, motions of head and eyes required for checking mirrors, blind spots, etc. It would also include the sequencing and co-ordination of these actions, where those involved are routinely performed together in parallel or in an interdependent fashion. Although implementation is the basis of what might be termed behavioural routines, I envisage that where activities must be combined in order to satisfy the criteria action planning has determined for the course of action appropriate in a given situation, there are processing capacity limitations that, as they approach being exceeded, begin to require more conscious control than implementation would otherwise have. Thus, for unusual combinations, transfer to a new vehicle or configuration of controls, or where the driver is very experienced, the implementation may be a much more deliberate process. Furthermore, I envisage that the feedback that naturally arises from performance serves to augment the information available to action planning, by yielding information about outcomes. Implementation may also feed back to appraisal, further bolstering or undermining the performer's view of their own ability, as has been demonstrated by Groeger and Grande (1996), and in the longer term may also influence control beliefs.

When initially proposing the four-facet framework, I believed that implementation would be reflected in performance on tests that involved tracking of objects travelling vertically or horizontally, using braking or accelerating pedal actions or a steering motion respectively; eye–hand and eye–foot co-ordination, again using the steering wheel or foot pedals; together with measures of memory span for verbal and spatial information as well as actions. Principal components analysis of the data from our validation study identified four components as the optimal solution (see Figure 10.5). These jointly accounted for 74.6% of the common test variance, and had a Kaiser simplicity index of 0.99, which is particularly good. These four factors resulted from combinations of tests which tapped eye–hand co-ordination, eye–foot co-ordination, digit, span, and motor control (which incorporated the tracking measures as well as visuo-spatial memory, especially for sequential operations). Eye–hand and eye–foot co-ordination seem both obvious and reasonable measures of how well drivers might implement the actions they have selected, and reflect relatively simple co-ordination rather than lengthy integration of such activities over time, which is essentially what the motor control factor reflects. Understood in this way, it is clear why visuo-spatial sequential memory would play an important role in successful implementation. Finally, although it may be surprising, the inclusion of digit span, which requires series of digits to be remembered in the order in which they were heard or in the reverse order, suggests the involvement of some general capacity for information intake, organisation, and output (see Groeger et al., 1999).

## EVALUATING THE FOUR-FACET FRAMEWORK

Although the tests used to operationalise the different elements of this framework do appear to suggest a degree of coherence and reality, David Field, Sean Hammond, and I decided to formally test the coherence of the framework, and assess its validity in terms of its ability to predict actual driving behaviour.

### Statistical integrity of the four-facet framework

A multiple group method of confirmatiory factor analysis demonstrated that the elements of the four facets described earlier fitted the predicted structure very well. As all the parameters of the model were given the freedom to vary within the constraints of a general model, we were able to examine the complexity of each component in order to explore the degree of overlap between facets. This also applies to the relationships between facets and so an oblique structure was posited. In this way a naturally occurring orthogonal structure should emerge if it is applicable and should not be imposed as a model artefact.

Table 10.1 shows the extent to which each element fits each of the four facets, the coherence of each facet and of the overall solution. This analysis shows that the indices of factor fit range between 0.92 and 0.75. These indices are essentially signal to noise ratios for the true and error variances identified by the model. As such they may be interpreted in much the same way as Cronbach's alpha coefficients, in which a coefficient of 0.70 is generally held to be minimal for a useful test. The overall index of fit emerges at 0.89 which tells us that there is a good fit of the data to the four-facet model.

However, there are one or two cautions that need to be raised. First, the action planning factor has an index of fit of only 0.75. While this is certainly adequate, it is not high. One explanation for this is that implementation components, especially motor control and digit span, also produce small salient loadings on this factor, action planning. This might be explained by the ubiquitous presence of psychometric "g" which tends to emerge whenever tests of speed

TABLE 10.1
Confirmatory factor analysis (all parameters free) oblique factor fit

| | Implied goal interruption | Appraisal | Planning | Implementation | Fit |
|---|---|---|---|---|---|
| *Implied goal interruption* | — | | | | |
| Readiness to respond | 0.48 | −0.13 | −0.07 | 0.03 | 0.90 |
| Behavioural standards | 0.50 | 0.02 | −0.12 | 0.04 | 0.93 |
| Scene analysis | 0.46 | 0.09 | −0.02 | −0.04 | 0.94 |
| Spatial judgement | 0.47 | −0.00 | 0.13 | 0.08 | 0.90 |
| Cursory analysis | 0.37 | 0.01 | 0.08 | −0.11 | 0.86 |
| *Appraisal* | *0.06* | | | | |
| Responsibility | 0.03 | 0.35 | −0.17 | −0.10 | 0.74 |
| Confidence | 0.02 | 0.38 | 0.19 | −0.02 | 0.79 |
| Extraversion | 0.13 | 0.31 | −0.19 | −0.14 | 0.57 |
| Expectations of self | −0.05 | 0.38 | 0.05 | 0.13 | 0.86 |
| Expectations of others | −0.05 | 0.43 | 0.10 | 0.21 | 0.75 |
| Stress proneness | −0.18 | 0.33 | 0.05 | 0.07 | 0.73 |
| Activity–passivity | 0.09 | 0.31 | −0.04 | −0.14 | 0.75 |
| *Planning* | *0.22\*\** | *0.06* | | | |
| General IQ | −0.07 | 0.09 | 0.66 | 0.10 | 0.94 |
| Reaction speed | 0.06 | 0.00 | 0.62 | −0.10 | 0.96 |
| Selection | 0.00 | −0.10 | 0.64 | 0.00 | 0.97 |
| *Implementation* | *0.13\*\** | *−0.04* | *0.30\*\** | | |
| Motor control | 0.04 | −0.13 | 0.37 | 0.38 | 0.48 |
| Eye–foot | −0.09 | 0.05 | −0.03 | 0.54 | 0.95 |
| Eye–hand | 0.00 | 0.09 | −0.05 | 0.65 | 0.97 |
| Digit span | 0.04 | −0.02 | −0.29 | 0.28 | 0.48 |
| Factor fit | 0.92 | 0.92 | 0.75 | 0.84 | 0.89 |

Italicised entries reflect correlations between facets; $*p < .05$, $**p < .01$.

and general ability are integrated. The strong correlation between the implementation and action planning factors (0.30) tends to bear this out. However, there is clearly sufficient distinction between the two factors to justify their independence. A second area of caution is the fact that the digit span and motor control components manifest low fit to the model and this is due to the fact that they load on action planning as well as their designated implementation factor. However, as we have seen, this is in accordance with expectation based on the theory of psychometric "g".

The extraversion component also manifests a poor fit although it is most salient with appraisal and does not manifest any other salient loading. It would appear that extraversion variance is spread across the remaining three factors fairly evenly. Again, it might be expected from the factor-analytic literature on personality tests that extraversion would emerge as an ubiquitous factor in much the same way as "g" emerges with performance tests. This may simply serve to validate the component and, given the fact that it is salient only on appraisal, it does not compromise the integrity of the model as a whole.

## Validity of the four-facet framework

The research project in which the four-facet framework was developed also afforded the opportunity to measure the actual driving performance of some 100 drivers who were tested as part of the original development of the computerised test battery. This study, which is reported more fully elsewhere (Grayson et al., 1998), required drivers to drive their own vehicle along a mixed 20-mile suburban–rural route, while accompanied by a retired state driving examiner. The driver was requested to drive normally, and while they did so, the examiner assessed the driver's performance on a range of dimensions (safety, speed choice, anticipation, speed appropriateness, attention, and skill), using a 5-point scale. The driver's speed along sections of the route was later derived from a video recording of each drive. Our concern here is to assess the extent to which the four facet parameters can predict objective measures of a driver's performance.

Driver performance was assessed in a variety of ways. The examiner's ratings of behaviour are strongly correlated with each other, to such an extent that a principal components analysis of the six ratings revealed just two factors, one that accounted for 17% of the variance in ratings and on which just one scale (speed choice) loaded, while all other examiner judgements were heavily loaded on the first factor (in excess of 0.85 in each case), which accounted for 68% of the variance. Factor scores were calculated for each factor, and these became two of the indices of driver performance (speed choice and driver ability). The third index of performance was an objective measurement of the driver's speed at each site, when contrasted with the speed of the rest of the sample at that site, averaged over all 20 observation points. This is referred to as "relative speed".

We then used a multiple regression approach to determine whether, and to what extent, the elements of the four-facet framework predicted driver behaviour. The results were very promising. Ignoring demographics such as age and gender, 41% of the variability in driver ability ratings were predictable from four elements of the four-facet framework: High levels of motor control and general IQ, and lower levels of cursory analysis and impulsivity were associated with higher driving ability. If all the model parameters are considered first and then the driver's age is taken into account, the model (good eye–foot co-ordination, lower cursory analysis, lower impulsivity and age) now accounts for 47% of the variance in driving ability. Where age is considered first, an almost identical model emerges. These analyses suggest that "age" is in part a combination of those facets of behaviour that are measured by motor control and general IQ, which were themselves found to be related in the confirmatory analysis of variance reported earlier. However, the key point is that the model components perform well in predicting how a driver's driving will be assessed by an accompanying examiner.

As mentioned earlier, a second factor also emerged from the driving examiner's ratings of behaviour. This loaded heavily on just one scale—speed choice. Once again the model elements were used as potential predictors of this assessment, and once again these fared quite well. Three model components (motor control, reaction time, and compliance) together predict 41% of the variance in how speed choice is rated by the examiner. Where the impact of age is assessed by taking its effects into account first, or after all model parameters have been considered, no more variance is accounted for, nor is there any change in the model components.

Finally, 30% of the variance in actual relative speed over sections of the route was also predicted by three elements of the four-facet framework: higher levels of motor control, more cursory analysis and activity–passivity. This was so whether age was accounted for first, last, or excluded from the analyses.

In summary, depending on how we choose to measure driver behaviour, i.e. through subjective assessments, by an experienced observer, or that driver's actual speed in relation to other drivers taking part in the study, model components account for between 40% and 30% respectively. The components that do so are broadly similar: Motor control and activity–passivity feature in both solutions, and reaction time and cursory analysis in the rating and ratio measurement respectively. Quality indices of driving, as indexed by the ratings the experienced observer makes, are also very well predicted by the computerised tests, with motor control and cursory analysis featuring in the optimal solution, this time with general IQ and impulsivity. Although some of these variables do indeed relate to age, and effects are weakened if the effects of age are first taken into account, the model parameters still have very considerable explanatory power. Taken together, the results reported in this section offer a partial, but I think very promising, validation of the four-facet framework of driver behaviour. In the remainder of this chapter I want to try to apply this framework to some of the major theoretical and practical problems those of us seeking to understand, measure, and improve driver behaviour have to face.

## THE FOUR-FACET FRAMEWORK AND BEYOND

Some of the practical problems posed by driving which require solutions have always been present. For the past 100 years, we have had to train and assess drivers' competence and we have always had to consider incremental increases in the technological sophistication of the vehicle. Providing solutions has, arguably, never been as possible or as pressing.

The consequences of affluence, more cost-effective manufacturing, and the aspirational inflation that has resulted from wider access to education, have all contributed to the increases in the proportion of young people seeking to drive.

As discussed earlier, younger drivers are more likely to be accident-involved, and when damaged or killed impose a huge emotional and economic cost. The increased longevity of the population underlies the rapidly increasing number of elderly motorists. This, for reasons discussed earlier, has the potential to lead to a consequent increase in the volume of accidents. If we are to meet this increased demand for motoring safely, we need to develop ways of training and assessing the competence of motorists who will have a far broader range of general abilities than has hitherto been the case.

The virtue of understanding how general cognitive abilities underlie driver performance is that it would enable us to design training and competence testing that is appropriate to those we train and test, and the driving they wish to do. The road safety community already recognises that this is necessary because, for example, we train and test commercial and public service drivers differently. A second virtue of understanding how cognition underpins driving is that we can more reliably identify those technological changes in the vehicle that would enhance driving comfort and safety, and those that would detract from it. Furthermore, it would enable us to identify the particular critical driving scenarios in which safety of new in-vehicle devices must be assured, and how we might measure any decrements in performance that might result. This would be safer for users, and more cost effective for manufacturers, than adopting a more general, and I believe less sensitive, manner of evaluating new devices.

The four-facet framework I have advanced here is coherent with the theorising and findings reviewed in earlier chapters of the book. I believe that it provides a reasonable account of how drivers drive and the cognitive abilities and processes they rely on for doing so. I do not expect that it will be any more than a staging post along the track to a better understanding. To test it, and ultimately move beyond it, I believe we will need a range of different types of empirical data. Partly for their practical importance and partly for the theoretical advances they will allow us to make, let me identify three areas of work specifically. First, the operationalisation of the four-facet framework as depicted earlier depends on reasonably large numbers of tests. We have not sought to optimise the tests used, in terms of their length or capacity to discriminate between drivers, or the clarity with which they relate to mainstream cognitive theories. There are also other types of ability and faculty which I believe we would profit from assessing. Second, it is important to see how well the four-facet framework accounts for more carefully specified aspects of driver performance, and whether, with sufficiently large numbers of drivers of different types (e.g. learning drivers, newly qualified novices, elderly drivers, massively experienced commercial drivers), the same facets of the model would predict the behaviour of each group of motorists in different driving scenarios. Finally, linking the patterns of driving difficulties of those motorists, or would-be motorists, who have well specified acquired neurological deficits would provide a way of assessing the plausibility of the framework in neurological terms, which I believe is an essential constraint on any psychological theory. It would also provide the basis of more appropriate assessments of the safe driving potential of those with disability.

Throughout this book I have sought to present driving as a complex cognitive task. I have done so because of the range of activities involved in driving, the multiplicity of ways in which these activities must interact, and the varying circumstances in which they must be deployed. A framework that could genuinely explain and predict driver behaviour would be as complex as cognition itself. There is no single model of cognition that approaches the required explanatory power. This might imply that we who seek to understand the cognitive underpinnings of everyday tasks, such as driving, should wait in the theoretical wings until a sufficiently powerful and well specified model emerges. I believe we must take on more responsibility than this. The genuine complexity of driving, that which makes it most difficult to understand and predict, is precisely the problem models of cognition must resolve. We in applied cognitive psychology will probably never be centre-stage, partly because of the methodological difficulties involved in having sufficient control over complex behaviour in real environments. But we can and should be more than bit-part players. To be so we must try to grasp, study, and apply the subtleties of current cognitive approaches, and I have tried to lay the groundwork for that in this book.

# References

Adams, R.D. (1984). Aging and human locomotion. In M.L. Albert (Ed.), *Clinical neurology of aging*. New York: Oxford University Press.

Adams, R.D., & Victor, M. (1981). *Principles of neurology*. New York: McGraw-Hill.

Adelson, E.H., & Bergen, J.R. (1985). The plenoptic function and the elements of early vision. In M.S. Landy & J.A. Movshon (Eds.), *Computational models of visual processing*. Cambridge, MA: MIT Press.

Ajzen, I., & Fishbein, M. (1977). Attitude–behavior relations: A theoretical analysis and a review of empirical research. *Psychological Bulletin, 84*, 888–918.

Ajzen, I., & Fishbein, M. (1980). *Understanding attitudes and predicting social behavior*. Englewood Cliffs, NJ: Prentice-Hall.

Albert, M.S., Moss, M.B., & Milberg, W. (1989). Memory testing to improve the differential diagnosis of Alzheimer's disease. In K. Igbal, H.M. Wisniewski, & B. Winblad (Eds.), *Alzheimer's disease and related disorders*. New York: Alan R. Liss.

Alexander, G.J., & Lunenfeld, H. (1972). Satisfying motorists' need for information. *Traffic Engineering, 43*, 46–70.

Allard, F., & Starkes, J.L. (1991). Motor skill experts in sports, dance and other domains. In K.A. Ericsson & J. Smith (Eds.), *Towards a general theory of expertise, prospects and limits* (pp. 126–152). Cambridge: Cambridge University Press.

Allport, D.A., Antonis, B., & Reynolds, P. (1972). On the division of attention: A disproof of the single channel hypothesis. *Quarterly Journal of Experimental Psychology, 24*, 225–235.

Amaducci, L.A., Bocca, W.A., & Schoenberg, B.S. (1986). Origin of the distinction between Alzheimer's disease and senile dementia: How history can clarify nosology. *Neurology, 36*, 1497–1499.

Anderson, J.R. (1982). Acquisition of cognitive skill. *Psychological Review, 89*, 369–406.

Anderson, J.R. (1983). *The architecture of cognition*. Cambridge, MA: Harvard University Press.

205

Anderson, J.R. (1987). Methodologies for studying human knowledge. *Behavioral and Brain Sciences, 10*, 467–505.

Anderson, J.R. (1993). *Rules of the mind.* Hillsdale, NJ: Erlbaum.

Anderson, J.R. (1995). *Learning and memory: An integrated approach.* New York: Wiley & Sons.

Anderson, J.R., & Fincham, J.M. (1994). Acquisition of procedural skills from examples. *Journal of Experimental Psychology: Learning, Memory and Cognition, 20*(6), 1322–1340.

Anderson, M.C., Bjork, R.A., & Bjork, E.L. (1994). Remembering can cause forgetting—retrieval dynamics in long-term memory. *Journal of Experimental Psychology: Learning, Memory and Cognition, 20*(5), 1063–1087.

Anderson, M.C., & McCulloch, K.C. (1999). Integration as a general boundary condition on retrieval-induced forgetting. *Journal of Experimental Psychology: Learning, Memory and Cognition, 25*, 608–629.

Andrade, J. (1995). Learning during anaesthesia: A review. *British Journal of Psychology, 86*(4), 479–506.

Annett, J., & Kay, H. (1957). Knowledge of results and skilled performance. *Occupational Psychology, 31*, 69–79.

Antes, J.R., & Pentland, J.G. (1981). Picture context effects on eye movement patterns. In D.F. Fisher, R.A. Monty, & J.W. Senders (Eds.), *Eye movements: Cognition and visual perception.* Hillsdale, NJ: Erlbaum.

Bachman, D.L., Wolf, P.A., Linn, R.T., Knoefel, J.E., Cobb, J.L., Belanger, A.J., White, L.R., & Dagostino, R.B. (1993). Incidence of dementia and probable Alzheimer's disease in general population: The Framingham study. *Neurology, 43*, 515–519.

Backman, L., & Herlitz, A. (1990). The relationship between prior knowledge and face recognition memory in normal aging and Alzheimer's disease. *Journals of Gerontology, 45*, 94–100.

Baddeley, A.D. (1968). A three-minute reasoning test based on grammatical transformations. *Psychonomic Science, 10*, 341–342.

Baddeley, A.D. (1986). *Working memory.* Oxford: Oxford University Press.

Baddeley, A.D. (1990). *Human memory: Theory and practice.* Hove, UK: Lawrence Erlbaum Associates Ltd.

Baddeley, A.D. (1998). Recent developments in working memory. *Current Opinion in Neurobiology, 8*(2), 234–238.

Baddeley, A.D., Emslie, H., Kolodny, J., & Duncan, J. (1998). Random generation and the executive control of working memory. *Quarterly Journal of Experimental Psychology, 51*(4), 819–852.

Baddeley, A.D. & Hitch, G. (1974). Working memory. In G.A. Bower (Ed.), *The psychology of learning and motivation* (pp. 47–89). New York: Academic Press.

Baddeley, A.D., Lewis, V.J., & Nimmo-Smith, I. (1978). When did you last . . . ? In M.M. Gruneberg, P.E. Morris, & R.N. Sykes (Eds.), *Practical aspects of memory* (pp.77–83). London: Academic Press.

Badgaiyan, R.D., & Posner, M.I. (1996). Priming reduces input activity in right posterior cortex during stem completion. *NeuroReport, 7*, 2975–2978.

Bandura, A. (1988). Self-efficacy conception of anxiety. *Anxiety Research, 1*, 77–98.

Bandura, A. (1989). Human agency in social cognitive theory. *American Psychologist, 44*, 1175–1184.

Bandura, A. (1997). *Self-efficacy: The exercise of control.* New York: W.H. Freeman.

Bannister, R. (1992). *Brain and Bannister's clinical neurology.* Oxford: Oxford University Press.

Bargh, J.A. (1992). The ecology of automaticity: Towards establishing the conditions needed to produce automatic processing effect. *American Journal of Psychology, 105,* 181–199.

Barone, P., & Joseph, J.P. (1989). Prefrontal cortex and spatial sequencing in macaque monkey. *Experimental Brain Research, 78,* 447–464.

Baumhart, R. (1968). *An honest profit.* New York: Prentice-Hall.

Bayles, K.A. (1988). Dementia: The clinical perspective. *Archives of Neurology, 48,* 155–159.

Beatty, W.W. (1992). Memory disturbances in Parkinson's disease. In S.J. Huber & J.L. Cummings (Eds.), *Parkinson's disease.* New York: Oxford University Press.

Bekerian, D.A., & Baddeley, A.D. (1980). Saturation advertising and the repetition effect. *Journal of Verbal Learning and Verbal Behavior, 19,* 17–25.

Benson, P., & Perrett, D. (1992). Face to face with the perfect image. *New Scientist, 133*(1809), 32–35.

Bentler, P.M., & Spechart, G. (1979). Models of attitude–behavior relations. *Psychological Review, 86,* 452–64.

Berry, D.C., & Broadbent, D.E. (1984). On the relationship between task performance and associated verbalizable knowledge. *Quarterly Journal of Experimental Psychology: Human Experimental Psychology, 36A,* 209–231.

Bilodeau, E.A., and Bilodeau, I.M. (1958). Variable frequency knowledge of results and the learning of simple skill. *Journal of Experimental Psychology, 55,* 379–383.

Bloom, B.S. (1974). Time and learning. *American Psychologist, 29,* 682–688.

Bohannon, J.N., & Symons, V.L. (1992). Flashbulb memories: Confidence, consistency, and quantity. In E. Winograd & U. Neisser (Eds.), *Affect and accuracy in recall: Studies of "flashbulb" memories* (pp. 65–91). New York: Cambridge University Press.

Boldovici, J.A. (1987). Measuring transfer in military settings. In S.M. Cormier & J.D. Hagman (Eds.), *Transfer of learning* (pp. 239–260). San Diego, CA: Academic Press.

Bondi, M.W., & Kaszniak, A.W. (1991). Implicit and explicit memory in Alzheimer's disease and Parkinson's disease. *Journal of Clinical and Experimental Neuropsychology, 13,* 339–358.

Bondi, M.W., Kaszniak, A.W., Rapcsak, S.Z., & Butters, M.A. (1993). Implicit and explicit memory following anterior communicating artery aneurysm rupture. *Brain and Cognition, 22*(2), 213–229.

Borst, A., & Bahde, S. (1988). Spatio-temporal integration of motion. *Naturwissenschaften, 75,* 265–267.

Bourke, P.A. (1997). Measuring attentional demand in continuous dual-task performance. *Quarterly Journal of Experimental Psychology: Human Experimental Psychology, 50A*(4), 821–840.

Bourke, P.A., Duncan, J., & Nimmo-Smith, I. (1996). A general factor involved in dual-task performance decrement. *Quarterly Journal of Experimental Psychology: Human Experimental Psychology, 49A*(3), 525–545.

Boyce, S.J., & Pollatsek, A. (1992). Identification of objects in scenes: The role of scene background in object naming. *Journal of Experimental Psychology: Learning, Memory and Cognition, 18,* 531–543.

Brackstone, M., & McDonald, M. (2000). Car following: A historical review. *Transportation Research: Traffic Psychology and Behavior*, *F*, *2*(4), 181–196.

Bradburn, N.M., Rips, L.J., & Shevell, S.K. (1987). Answering autobiographical questions: The impact of memory and inference on surveys. *Science*, *236*, 157–161.

Bradshaw, J.L., & Mattingley, J.B. (1995). *Clinical neuropsychology: Behavioral and brain science*. Sydney: Academic Press.

Bradshaw, J.L., Philips, J.G., Dennis, C., Mattingley, J.B., Andrews, D., Chiu, E., Pierson, J.M., & Bradshaw, J.A. (1992). Initiation and execution of movements in those suffering from and at risk of developing Huntington's disease. *Journal of Clinical and Experimental Neuropsychology*, *14*, 179–192.

Breckler, S.J. (1984). Empirical validation of affects, behavior and cognition as distinct components of attitude. *Journal of Personality and Social Psychology*, *47*, 1191–1205.

Brehmer, B. (1990). Variable errors set a limit to adaptation. *Ergonomics*, *33*(10/11), 1231–1239.

Broadbent, D.E. (1977). Levels, hierarchies, and the locus of control. *Quarterly Journal of Experimental Psychology*, *29*, 181–201.

Brookes, M., MacMillan, R., Culley, S., Anderson, E., Murray, S., & Mendelow, A.D. (1990). Head injuries in accident/emergency departments. How different are children from adults. *Journal of Epidemiology and Community Health*, *44*, 147–151.

Brotherton, F.A., Thomas, L.L., Wisotzek, I.E., & Milan, M.A. (1988). Social skills training in the rehabilitation of patients with traumatic closed head injury. *Archives of Physical and Medical Rehabilitation*, *69*, 827–832.

Brouwer, W.H., van Zomeren, A.H., & van Woffelaar, P.C. (1990). Traffic behaviour after severe traumatic brain injury. In B.G. Deelman, R.J. Saan, & A.H. van Zomeren (Eds.), *Traumatic brain injury, clinical, social and rehabilitational aspects*. Lisse: Swets & Zeitlinger.

Brouwer, W.H., & Withaar, F.K. (1997). Fitness to drive after traumatic brain injury. *Neurorehabilitation*, *7*(3), 177–193.

Brown, A.L. (1990). Domain-specific affect learning and transfer in children. *Cognitive Science*, *14*, 107–133.

Brown, G.D.A., & Hulme, C. (1995). Modelling item length effects in memory span: No rehearsal needed? *Journal of Memory and Language*, *34*(5), 594–621.

Brown, I.D. (1982). Exposure and experience are a confounded nuisance in research on driver behaviour. *Ergonomics*, *14*, 345–352.

Brown, I.D., & Groeger, J.A. (1988). Risk perception and decision taking during the transition between novice and experienced driver status. *Ergonomics*, *31*(4), 585–598.

Brown, I.D., Groeger, J.A., & Biehl, B. (1987). Is driver training contributing enough towards road safety? In J.A. Rothengatter & R.A. de Bruin (Eds.), *Road users and traffic safety* (pp. 135–156). Assen, The Netherlands: van Gorcum.

Brown, I.D., Tickner, A.H., & Simmonds, D.C.V. (1969). Interference between concurrent tasks of driving and telephoning. *Journal of Applied Psychology*, *53*, 419–424.

Brown, J.D. (1986). Evaluations of self and others: Self-enhancement biases in social judgements. *Social Cognition*, *4*, 353–376.

Brown, N.R., Rips, L.J., & Shevell, S.K. (1985). The subjective dates of natural events in very long-term memory. *Cognitive Psychology*, *17*, 139–177.

Brown, R.G., & Marsden, C.D. (1988). "Subcortical dementia": The neuropsychological evidence. *Neuroscience*, *25*, 363–387.

Bruce, V., Green, P.R., & Georgeson, M.A. (1996). *Visual perception: Physiology, psychology, and ecology.* Hove, UK: Psychology Press.

Bryan, L.B., & Harter, N. (1897). Studies on the telegraphic language: The acquisition of a hierarchy of habits. *Psychological Review, 6,* 345–375.

Bryden, J. (1989). How many head injured? The epidemiology of post head injury disability. In R.L.L. Wood & P. Eames (Eds.), *Models of brain injury rehabilitation.* London: Chapman & Hall.

Burke, W.H. (1993). The tough case: Life care plan for a behaviorally challenging patient. *Headlines,* March/April, 18–19.

Butters, N., & Grady, M. (1977). Effect of pre-distractor delays on the short-term memory performance of patients with Korsakoff's and Huntington's disease. *Neuropsychologia, 15,* 701–706.

Butters, N., Salmon, D.P., Heindel, W., & Graham, E. (1988). Episodic, semantic, and procedural memory: Some comparisons of Alzheimer's and Parkinson's patients. In R.D. Terry (Ed.), *Aging and the brain.* New York: Raven Press.

Bylsma, F.W., Brandt, J., & Strauss, M.E. (1990). Aspects of procedural memory are differentially impaired in Huntington's disease. *Archives of Clinical Neuropsychology, 5,* 287–297.

Byrne, R.W. (1979). Memory for urban geography. *Quarterly Journal of Experimental Psychology, 31,* 147–154.

Byrne, R.W. (1982). Geographical knowledge and orientation. In A. Ellis (Ed.), *Normality and pathology in cognitive functions* (pp. 239–264). New York: Academic Press.

Caine, E.D., Ebert, M.H., & Weingarten, H. (1977). An outline for the analysis of dementia. *Neurology, 23,* 1087–1092.

Caine, E.D., Hunt, R.D., Weingartner, H., & Ebert, M.H. (1978). Huntington's dementia. *Archives of General Psychiatry, 35,* 377–384.

Caird, J.K., & Hancock, P.A. (1994). The perception of arrival time for different oncoming vehicles at an intersection. *Ecological Psychology, 6,* 83–109.

Carlson, V.R., & Tassone, E.P. (1971). Familiar size and unfamiliar size: A theoretical derivation and test. *Journal of Experimental Psychology, 87,* 109–115.

Cassidy, J.W. (1990). Pharmacological treatment of post-traumatic behavioral disorders: Aggression and disorders of mood. In R.L. Wood (Ed.), *Neurobehavioral sequelae of traumatic brain injury.* New York: Taylor & Francis.

Catalano, J.F., & Kleiner, B.M. (1984). Distant transfer in coincident timing as a function of variability of practice. *Perceptual and Motor Skills, 58,* 851–856.

Cavallo, V., & Laurent, M. (1988). Visual information and skill-level in time-to-collision estimation. *Perception, 17,* 623–632.

Cavallo, V., Mestre, D., & Berthelon, C. (1997). Time-to-collision judgements: Visual and spatio-temporal factors. In J.A. Rothengatter & E. Carbonell Vaya (Eds.), *Traffic and transport psychology: Theory and application* (pp. 97–112). Amsterdam: Elsevier.

Chapman, P.R., & Underwood, G. (1998). Visual search of dynamic scenes: Event types and the role of experience in viewing driving situations. In G. Underwood (Ed.), *Eye guidance in reading and scene perception* (pp. 369–394). Oxford: Elsevier.

Charness, N. (1979). Components of skill in bridge. *Canadian Journal of Psychology, 33,* 1–16.

Chase, W.G., & Ericsson, K.A. (1981). Skilled memory. In J.R. Anderson (Ed.), *Cognitive skills and their acquisition* (pp. 141–189). Hillsdale, NJ: Erlbaum.

Chase, W.G., & Simon, H.A. (1973). Perception in chess. *Cognitive Psychology, 4*, 55–81.

Chi, M.T.H., & Van Lehn, K.A. (1991). The content of physics self-explanations. *Journal of the Learning Sciences, 1*, 69–105.

Christianson, S.A. (1992a). Emotional stress and eyewitness memory: A critical review. *Psychological Bulletin, 112*, 284–309.

Christianson, S.A. (1992b). *The handbook of emotion and memory: Research and theory.* Hillsdale, NJ: Lawrence Erlbaum.

Christianson, S.A. (1997). On emotional stress and memory: We need to recognize threatening situations and we need to "forget" unpleasant experiences. In D.G. Payne & F.G. Conrad (Eds.), *Intersections in basic and applied memory research* (pp. 133–156). Mahwah, NJ: Erlbaum.

Christianson, S.A., Loftus, E.F., Hoffman, H., & Loftus, G. (1991). Eye fixations and memory for emotional events. *Journal of Experimental Psychology: Learning, Memory and Cognition, 17*, 693–701.

Christianson, S.A., & Nilsson, L.G. (1989). Hysterical amnesia: A case study of aversively motivated isolation of memory. In T. Archer & L.G. Nilsson (Eds.), *Aversion, avoidance, and anxiety: Perspectives on aversively motivated behavior* (pp. 289–310). Hillsdale, NJ: Lawrence Erlbaum Associates Inc.

Christianson, S.A., Nilsson, L.G., & Silfvenius, H. (1987). Initial memory deficits and subsequent recovery in two cases of head trauma. *Scandinavian Journal of Psychology, 28*, 267–280.

Chui, H.C. (1989). Dementia: A review emphasising the clinicopathologic correlation and brain–behaviour relationships. *Archives of Neurology, 46*, 806–814.

Churchland, P.S., Ramachandran, V.S., & Sejnowski, T.J. (1994). A critique of pure vision. In C. Koch & J.L. Davis (Eds.), *Large-scale neuronal theories of the brain: Computational neuroscience* (pp. 23–60). Cambridge, MA: MIT Press.

Cleeremans, A., Destrebecqz, A., & Boyer, M. (1998). Implicit learning: News from the front. *Trends in Cognitive Sciences, 2*(10), 406–416.

Clegg, B.A., DiGirolamo, G.J., & Keele, S.W. (1998). Sequence learning. *Trends in Cognitive Sciences, 2*(8), 275–281.

Cogan, D.G. (1985). Visual disturbances with focal progressive dementing disease. *American Journal of Opthamology, 100*, 68–72.

Cohen, A.S. (1981). Car drivers' pattern of eye fixations on the road and in the laboratory. *Perceptual and Motor Skills, 52*, 515–522.

Cohen, A.S., & Studach, H. (1977). Eye movements while driving cars around curves. *Perceptual and Motor Skills, 44*, 683–689.

Conway, M.A. (1990). *Autobiographical memory.* Buckingham, UK: Open University Press.

Cooper, P.J., Tallman, K., Tuokko, H., & Beattie, B.L. (1933). Vehicle crash involvement and cognitive deficits in older drivers. *Journal of Safety Research, 24*, 9–17.

Cope, D.N. (1990). Pharmacology for behavioral deficits: Disorders of cognition and affect. In R.L. Wood (Ed.), *Neurobehavioral sequelae of traumatic brain injury.* New York: Taylor & Francis.

Courtney, S.M., Petit, L., Maisog, J.M., Ungerleider, L.G., & Haxby, J.V. (1998). An area specialized for spatial working memory in human frontal cortex. *Science, 279*(5355), 1347–1351.

Courtney, S.M., Ungerleider, L.G., Keil, K., & Haxby, J.V. (1996). Object and spatial visual working memory activate separate neural systems in human cortex. *Cerebral Cortex, 6*(1), 39–49.

Cowan, N. (1994). *Attention and memory.* Oxford: Oxford University Press.

Craik, F.I.M., & Anderson, N.D. (1999). Applying cognitive research to problems of aging. *Attention and Performance, 17,* 583–615.

Craik, F.I.M., & Lockhart, R.S. (1972). Levels of processing: A framework for memory research. *Journal of Verbal Learning and Verbal Behavior, 11,* 671–684.

Craik, F.I.M., & Lockhart, R.S. (1986). CHARM is not enough: Comments on Eich's model of cued recall. *Psychological Review, 93,* 360–364.

Craver-Lemley, C., Arterberry, M.E., & Reeves, A. (1997). Effects of imagery on vernier acuity under conditions of induced depth. *Journal of Experimental Psychology: Human Perception and Performance, 23*(1), 3–13.

Craver-Lemley, C., Arterberry, M.E., & Reeves, A. (1999). "Illusory" illusory conjunctions: The conjoining of features of visual and imagined stimuli. *Journal of Experimental Psychology: Human Perception and Performance, 25*(4), 1036–1049.

Craver-Lemley, C., & Reeves, A. (1992). How visual imagery interferes with vision. *Psychological Review, 99*(4), 633–649.

Cronin-Golumb, A. (1990). Abstract thought in aging and age-related neurological disease. In F. Boller & J. Grafman (Eds.), *Handbook of neuropsychology (Vol. 3).* Amsterdam: Elsevier.

Crossman, E.R.F.W. (1959). A theory of acquisition of speed skill. *Ergonomics, 2,* 153–166.

Cummings, J.L. (1986). Subcortical dementia: Neuropsychology, neuropsychiatry and pathophysiology. *British Journal of Psychiatry, 149,* 682–697.

Cummings, J.L. (1988). Dementia of the Alzheimer type: Challenges of definition and clinical diagnosis. In H.A. Whitaker (Ed.), *Neurological studies of nonfocal brain damage: Dementia and trauma.* New York: Springer-Verlag.

Cummings, J.L. (1992). Neuropsychiatric aspects of Alzheimer's disease and other dementing illnesses. In S.C. Yudofsky & R.E. Hales (Eds.), *American Psychiatric Press textbook of neuropsychiatry.* Washington, DC: American Psychiatric Press.

Cummings, J.L., & Benson, D.F. (1990). Subcortical mechanisms and human thought. In J.L. Cummings (Ed.), *Subcortical dementia.* New York: Oxford University Press.

Cutting, J.T. (1986). *Perception with an eye for motion.* Cambridge, MA: MIT press.

Da Silva, J.A., & Da Silva, C.B. (1983). Scaling apparent size in a large open field: Some new data. *Perceptual and Motor Skills, 56,* 135–138.

Da Silva, J.A., & Dos Santos, R.A. (1982). Scaling apparent size in a large open field: Presence of a standard does not increase the exponent of the power function. *Perceptual and Motor Skills, 55,* 267–274.

Deakin, J.M., & Allard, F. (1991). Skilled memory in expert figure skaters. *Memory and Cognition, 19,* 79–86.

Deffenbacher, J.L., Oetting, E.R., & Lynch, R.S. (1994). Development of a driving anger scale. *Psychological Reports, 74*(1), 83–91.

DeGraef, P. (1992). Scene-context effects and models of real world perception. In K. Rayner (Ed.), *Eye movements and visual cognition: Scene perception and reading.* New York: Springer Verlag.

DeGraef, P., Christiaens, D., & d'Ydewalle, G. (1990). Perceptual effects of scene context on object identification. *Psychological Research, 52*, 317–329.

de Groot, A.D. (1966). Perception and memory versus thought: Some old ideas and recent findings. In B. Kleinmuntz (Ed.), *Problem solving*. New York: Wiley.

Deiber, M.P., Passingham, R.E., Colebatch, J.G., Friston, K.J., Nixon, P.D., & Frackowiak, R.S.J. (1991). Cortical areas and the selection of movement. A study with positron emission tomography. *Experimental Brain Research, 84*, 393–402.

Delis, D.C., Massman, P.J., & Butters, N. (1991). Profiles of demented and amnesic patients on the California Verbal Learning Test: Implications for the assessment of memory disorders. *Psychological Assessment, 3*, 19–26.

Della Sala, S., & Mazzini, L. (1989). Post-traumatic extrapyramidal syndrome: Case report. *Italian Journal of Neurosciences, 11*, 65–69.

DeLucia, P.R. (1991). Pictorial and motion-based information for depth perception. *Journal of Experimental Psychology: Human Perception and Performance, 17*, 738–748.

Denton, G.G. (1966). A subjective scale of speed when driving a motor vehicle. *Ergonomics, 9*(3), 203–210.

D'Esposito, M., Detre, J.A., Alsop, D.C., & Shin, R.K. (1995). The neutral basis of the central executive system of working memory. *Nature, 378*(6554), 279–281.

Detterman, D.K., & Sternberg, J.R. (Eds.) (1992). *Transfer on trial: Intelligence, cognition and instruction*. Norwood, NJ: Ablex Publishing Co.

di Pellegrino, G., Fadiga, L., Fogassi, L., Gallese, V., & Rizzolatti, G. (1992). Understanding motor events: A neurophysiological study. *Experimental Brain Research, 91*, 176–180.

Doane, S.M., Alderton, D.L., Sohn, Y.W., & Pellegrino, J.W. (1996). Acquisition and transfer of skilled performance: Are visual discrimination skills stimulus specific? *Journal of Experimental Psychology: Human Perception and Performance, 22*(5), 1218–1248.

Dobbs, A.R., Heller, R.B., & Schopflocher, D. (1998). A comparative approach to identify unsafe older drivers. *Accident Analysis and Prevention, 30*(3), 363–370.

Donges, E. (1978). A two-level model of driver steering behavior. *Human Factors, 20*(6), 691–707.

Doty, R.L., Deems, D.A., & Stellar, S. (1988). Olfactory dysfunction in Parkinsonianism: A general defect unrelated to neurologic signs, disease stage, or disease duration. *Neurology, 38*, 1237–1244.

Drachman, D.A., & Swearer, J. (1993). Driving and Alzheimer's disease: The risk of crashes. *Neurology, 43*, 2448–2456.

Dubois, B., Boller, F., Pillon, B., & Agid, Y. (1991). Cognitive deficits in Parkinson's disease. In F. Boller & J. Grafman (Eds.), *Handbook of neuropsychology (Vol. 5)*. Amsterdam: Elsevier.

Duffy, C.J., & Wurtz, R.H. (1991). Sensitivity of MST neurons to optic flow stimuli: I. A continuum of response selectivity to large field stimuli. *Journal of Neurophysiology, 65*, 1329–1345.

Duncan, J., Williams, P., & Brown, I. (1991). Components of driving skill: Experience does not mean expertise. *Ergonomics, 34*, 919–937.

Duncan, J., Williams, P., Nimmo-Smith, I., & Brown, I.D. (1992). The control of skilled behavior: Learning, intelligence and distraction. In D.E. Meyer & S. Kornblum (Eds.), *Attention and performance XIV*. Cambridge, MA: MIT Press.

Dunn, M.E., Umlauf, R.L., & Mermis, B.J. (1992). The rehabilitation situations invent-
ory: Staff perception of difficult behavioral situations in rehabilitation. *Archives of
Physical and Medical Rehabilitation, 73,* 316–319.

Dunning, D., Meyerowitz, J.A., & Holzberg, A.D. (1989). Ambiguity and self-evaluation:
The role of idiosyncratic trait definitions in self-serving assessments of ability. *Journal
of Personality and Social Psychology, 57*(6), 1082–1090.

Eames, P. (1988). Behavior disorders after severe head injury: Their nature and causes,
and strategies for management. *Journal of Head Trauma Rehabilitation, 3,* 1–6.

Eames, P., Haffey, W.J., & Cope, W. (1990). Treatment of behavioral disorders. In M.
Rosenthal, E.R. Griffith, M.R. Bond, & J.D. Miller (Eds.), *Rehabilitation of the adult
and child with a traumatic brain injury.* Philadelphia: F.A. Davis.

Ebbinghaus, H. (1885/1964). *Memory: A contribution to experimental psychology.* New
York: Dover Publications. [Translation from the 1885 edition of *Uber das Gedachtnis.*
Leipzig: Dunker]

Egan, D.E., & Schwartz, B.J. (1979). Chunking in recall of symbolic drawings. *Memory
and Cognition, 7,* 149–158.

Einstein, G.O., & Hunt, R.R. (1980). Levels of processing and organization: Additive
effects of individual item and relational processing. *Journal of Experimental Psychology: Human Learning and Memory, 6,* 588–598.

Eiser, J.R., & van der Pligt, J. (1988). *Attitudes and decisions.* London: Routledge.

Ekman, P. (1973). Cross-cultural studies of facial expression. In P. Ekman (Ed.),
*Darwin and facial expression: A century of research in review.* New York: Academic
Press.

Elander, J., West, R., & French, D. (1993). Behavioral correlates of individual differences in road-traffic crash-risk: An examination of methods and findings. *Psychological Bulletin, 113,* 279–294.

Endsley, M.R. (1995). Toward a theory of situation awareness in dynamic systems.
*Human Factors, 37,* 32–64.

Ericsson, K.A., & Charness, N. (1994). Expert performance—its structure and acquisition.
*American Psychologist, 49*(8), 725–747.

Ericsson, K.A., & Kintsch, W. (1995). Long term working memory. *Psychological Review,
102,* 211–245.

Ericsson, K.A., & Lehmann, A.C. (1996). Expert and exceptional performance: Evidence of maximal adaptation to task constraints. *Annual Review of Psychology, 47,*
273–305.

Erikson, B., & Horberg, U. (1980). *Eye movements of drivers in urban traffic. Uppsala
Psychological Reports 283.* University of Uppsala, Sweden.

Eslinger, P.J., & Damasio, A.R. (1986). Preserved motor learning in Alzheimer's disease:
Implications for anatomy and behavior. *Journal of Neuroscience, 6,* 3006–3009.

ETSC. (1999). *Reducing the severity of road injuries through post impact care.* Brussels:
European Transport Safety Council.

Evans, L. (1970). Speed estimation from a moving vehicle. *Ergonomics, 13*(2), 219–230.

Evans, L. (1991). *Traffic safety and the driver.* New York: Van Nostrand Reinhold.

Fairclough, S.H., May, A.J., & Carter, C. (1997). The effect of time headway feedback
on following behaviour. *Accident Analysis and Prevention, 29*(3), 387–397.

Farah, M.J. (1988). Is visual imagery really visual? Overlooked evidence from neuropsychology? *Psychological Review, 95,* 307–317.

Fazio, R.H. (1986). How do attitudes guide behavior? In R.M. Sorretino & E.T. Higgins (Eds.), *Handbook of motivation and cognition: Foundations of social behavior.* New York: Guilford Press.

Fendrich, D.W., Gesi, A.T., Healy, A.F., & Bourne, L.E. (1995). The contribution of procedural re-instatement to implicit and explicit memory effects in a motor task. In A.F. Healy & L.E. Bourne (Eds.), *Learning and memory of knowledge and skills.* Thousand Oaks, CA: Sage.

Fendrich, D.W., Healy, A.F., & Bourne, L.E. (1991). Long-term repetition effects for motoric and perceptual procedures. *Journal of Experimental Psychology: Learning, Memory and Cognition, 17,* 137–151.

Fiez, J.A., Raife, M.E., Balota, D.A., Tallal, P., & Schwartz, D. (1996). PET activation of posterior temporal regions during auditory word presentation and verb generation. *Cerebral Cortex, 6*(1), 1–10.

Finn, P., & Bragg, B.W.E. (1986). Perception of risk of an accident by young and older drivers. *Accident Analysis and Prevention, 18,* 289–298.

Fisher, R.P., & Geiselman, R.E. (1992). *Memory enhancing techniques for investigative interviewing.* Springfield, IL: Thomas.

Fisk, A.D., & Jones, C.D. (1992). Global versus local consistency: Effects of degree of within-category consistency on performance and learning. *Human Factors, 34,* 693–705.

Fisk, A.D., Lee, M.D., & Rogers, W.A. (1991). Recombination of automatic processing components: The effects of transfer, reversal and conflict situations. Special issue: Training theory, methods, and technology. *Human Factors, 33,* 267–280.

Fisk, A.D., Oransky, N.A., & Skedsvold, P.R. (1988). Examination of the role of "higher-order" consistency in skill development. *Human Factors, 30,* 567–581.

Fitts, P.M. (1962). Factors in complex skill training. In R. Glaser (Ed.), *Training research and education.* Pittsburgh: Pittsburgh University Press.

Fitts, P.M. (1964). Perceptual-motor skill learning. In A.W. Melton (Ed.), *Categories of human learning.* New York: Academic Press.

Fitts, P.M., & Posner, M.I. (1967). *Human performance.* Monterey, CA: Brooks-Cole.

Fletcher, P.C., Frith, C.D., Grasby, P.M., Shallice, T., Frackowiak, R.S.J., & Dolan, R.J. (1995). Brain systems for auditory-verbal memory: An in vivo study in humans, *Brain, 118,* 401–406.

Folstein, S.E. (1989). *Huntington's disease.* Baltimore, MD: The Johns Hopkins University Press.

Freedman, M. (1990). Parkinson's disease. In J.L. Cummings (Ed.), *Subcortical dementia.* New York: Oxford University Press.

Friedman, A. (1979). Framing pictures: The role of knowledge in automized encoding and memory for gist. *Journal of Experimental Psychology: General, 108,* 316–355.

Frith, C.D., Friston, K., Liddle, P.F., & Frackowiak, R.S.J. (1991). Willed action and the prefrontal cortex in man. *Proceedings of Royal Society, 244,* 241–246.

Fuller, R. (1984). A conceptualization of driving behaviour as threat avoidance. *Ergonomics, 27*(11), 1139–1155.

Garcia, J. (1994). Behavior after a traumatic brain injury: Toward a classification based on three outcome categories. *Rehabilitation Education, 8*(3), 259–274.

Garde, F.H., Bontke, C.F., & Hoffman, M. (1990). Sexual functioning and marital adjustment after traumatic brain injury. *Journal of Head Trauma Rehabilitation, 5,* 52–59.

Gathercole, S. (1996). *Models of short term memory.* Hove, UK: Psychology Press.

Geiselman, R.E., & Fisher, R.P. (1997). Ten years of cognitive interviewing. In D.G. Payne & F.G. Conrad (Eds.), *Intersections in basic and applied memory research* (pp. 291–310). Hillsdale, NJ: Erlbaum.

Gibson, J.J. (1979). *The ecological approach to visual perception*. Boston, MA: Houghton Mifflin.

Godthelp, H. (1986). Vehicle control during curve driving. *Human Factors, 28*(2), 211–221.

Golbe, L.I. (1991). Young-onset Parkinson's disease: A clinical review. *Neurology, 41,* 168–173.

Goldman-Rakic, P.S. (1995). Architecture of the prefrontal cortex and the central executive. In J. Grafman, K. Holyoak, & F. Boller (Eds.), Structure and function of the human prefrontal cortex. *Annals of New York Academy of Sciences, 279,* 71–83.

Goodin, D.S. (1992). Electrophysiological correlates of dementia in Parkinson's disease. In S.J. Huber & J.L. Cummings (Eds.), *Parkinson's disease: Neurobehavioural aspects.* New York: Oxford University Press.

Gottsdanker, R.M. (1956). The ability of human operators to detect the acceleration of target motion. *Psychological Bulletin, 53,* 477–487.

Gottsdanker, R.M., Frick, J., & Lockherd, R. (1961). Identifying the acceleration of visual targets. *British Journal of Psychology, 52,* 31–42.

Graesser, A.C., Singer, M., & Trabasso, T. (1994). Constructing inferences during narrative text comprehension. *Journal of Memory and Language, 26,* 69–83.

Graf, P., & Schachter, D.L. (1985). Implicit and explicit memory for new associations in normal and amnesic subjects. *Journal of Experimental Psychology: Learning, Memory and Cognition, 13,* 45–53.

Grafman, J. (1991). Plans, actions and mental sets. Managerial knowledge units in the frontal lobes. In E. Perceman (Ed.), *Integrative theory and practice in clinical neuropsychology.* Hillsdale, NJ: Erlbaum.

Grafman, J. (1995). Similarities and distinctions among current models of prefrontal cortical functions. In J. Graffman, K.J. Holyoak, & F. Boller (Eds.), The structure and functions of the human prefrontal cortex. *Annals of New York Academy of Sciences, 769,* 337–395.

Grafman, J., Weingarter, H., Newhouse, P.A., Thompson, K., Lalonde, F., Litvan, I., Molchan, S., & Sunderland, T. (1990). Implicit learning in patients with Alzheimer's disease. *Pharmacopsychiatry, 23,* 94–101.

Granerus, A.K. (1990). Update on Parkinson's disease: Current considerations and geriatric aspects. In M. Beringer & S.I. Finkel, (Eds.), *Clinical and scientific psychogeriatrics: Vol. 2. The interface between psychiatry and neurology.* New York: Springer.

Grasby, P.M., Frith, C.D., Friston, K.J., & Simpson, J. (1994). A graded task approach to the functional mapping of brain areas implicated in auditory verbal memory. *Brain, 117*(6), 1271–1282.

Grayson, G. (1998). *Risk, hazard perception and perceived control: Vol. 4. Behavioural study* (Unpublished Project Report No. PR/TT/124/98). Crowthorne, UK: Transport Research Laboratory.

Grayson, G.B. (1991). Driver behaviour. In *SAFETY 91.* Crowthorne, UK: Transport Research Laboratory.

Grayson, G.B., Maycock, G., Groeger, J.A., Hammond, S., & Field, D. (1998). *Risk, hazard perception and perceived control: Vol. 1. Summary* (Unpublished Project Report No. TT /124/98; DPU 9/31/14). Crowthorne, UK: Transport Research Laboratory.

Grealy, M.A., Johnson, D.A., & Rushton, S.K. (1999). Improving cognitive function following brain injury: The use of exercise and virtual reality. *Archives of Physical Medicine and Rehabilitation, 80*(6), 661–667.

Grimes, J. (1996). On the failure to detect changes in scenes across saccades. In K. Akins (Ed.), *Perception* (pp. 89–110). New York: Oxford University Press.

Groeger, J.A. (1997). *Memory and remembering: Everyday memory in context.* Harlow, UK: Addison-Wesley-Longman.

Groeger, J.A. (1998). Close, but no cigar: Assessment of a headway warning device. *Proceedings of Institute of Electrical Engineers, 230*(5), 1–4.

Groeger, J.A. (2000). *Distance, speed and time estimation in simulated driving conditions.* Manuscript submitted for publication.

Groeger, J.A., & Brady, S. (1998). *Differential effects of formal and informal driver training.* London: Department of Environment, Transport and the Regions.

Groeger, J.A., & Brady, S.J. (1999). The relationship between training, practice and license requirements. *Journal of International Association of Traffic and Safety Sciences, 23*(1), 1–9.

Groeger, J.A., & Brady, S.J. (in press). Tau-det or not? Visual information and control of car following. In A.G. Gale (Ed.), *Vision in vehicles VII.* Amsterdam: Elsevier.

Groeger, J.A., & Brown, I.D. (1989). Assessing one's own and others' driving ability: Influences of sex, age, and experience. *Accident Analysis and Prevention, 21*(2), 155–168.

Groeger, J.A., Carsten, O.M.J., Blana, E., & Jamson, H. (1999). Speed and distance estimation under simulated conditions. In A.G. Gale, I.D. Brown, C.M. Haslegrave, & S.P. Taylor (Eds.), *Vision in vehicles VII.* Amsterdam: Elsevier.

Groeger, J.A., & Chapman, P.R. (1996). Judgement of traffic scenes: The role of danger and difficulty. *Applied Cognitive Psychology, 10,* 349–364.

Groeger, J.A., & Chapman, P.R. (1997). Normative influences on decisions to offend. *Applied Psychology: An International Review, 46*(3), 265–286.

Groeger, J.A., Chapman, P.R., & Clegg, B.A. (2000). *Developing an understanding of danger and difficulty.* Manuscript in preparation.

Groeger, J.A., Chapman, P.R., & Stove, A.G. (1994). Following more safely: Effects of the DETER in-car headway advisory system. In S.A. Robertson (Ed.), *Contemporary ergonomics* (pp 199–204). London: Taylor & Francis.

Groeger, J.A., & Clegg, B.A. (1998). Automaticity and driving: Time to change gear conceptually. In J.A. Rothengatter & E. Carbonell Vaya (Eds.), *Traffic and transport psychology: Theory and application* (pp. 137–146). Amsterdam: Elsevier.

Groeger, J.A., & Clegg, B.A. (2000a). *Instruction and the power law of practice.* Manuscript submitted for publication.

Groeger, J.A., & Clegg, B.A. (2000b). *Practice and instruction when learning to drive.* London: The Stationery Office.

Groeger, J.A., & Comte, S. (1999). Time estimation in the time-to-collision task: The impact of a simultaneous secondary task. In A.G. Gale, I.D. Brown, C.M. Haslegrave, & S.P. Taylor (Eds.), *Vision in vehicles VII* (pp. 363–372). Amsterdam: Elsevier.

Groeger, J.A., Field, D., & Hammond, S. (1998a). *Risk, hazard perception and perceived control. Vol. 2: Computerised assessments of drivers' skills: relationships between measures* (Unpublished Project Report No. TT /124/98; DPU 9/31/14). Crowthorne, UK: Transport Research Laboratory.

Groeger, J.A., & Grande, G.E. (1996). Self-preserving judgements of skill. *British Journal of Psychology*, *87*, 61–79.

Groeger, J.A., Hammond, S., & Field, D. (1998b). *Risk, hazard perception and perceived control: Vol. 3. Computerised testing of drivers' skills and the development of the IATH model of responses to risk* (Unpublished Project Report No. TT/124/98; DPU 9/31/14). Crowthorne, UK: Transport Research Laboratory.

Groeger, J.A., Hammond, S., & Field, D. (1999). Measuring memory span. *International Journal of Psychology*, *34*(5/6), 359–363.

Groeger, J.A., & Maycock, G. (1999). *The role of professional instruction and private tuition when learning to drive*. Confidential report to Department of Environment Transport and the Regions, August.

Groeger, J.A., & Rothengatter, J.A. (1998). Psychology in traffic. *Transportation Research: Traffic Psychology and Behaviour*, *1*, 1–12.

Gurd, J.M., & Ward, D.D. (1989). Retrieval from semantic and letter-initial categories in patients with Parkinson's disease. *Neuropsychologia*, *27*, 743–746.

Gurland, B.J., & Cross, P.S. (1986). Public health perspectives on clinical memory testing of Alzheimer's disease and related disorders. In L.W. Poon (Ed.), *Clinical memory assessment of older adults*. Washington, DC: American Psychological Association.

Haarland, K.Y., & Harrington, D.L. (1990). Complex movement behaviour: Towards understanding cortical and subcortical interactions in regulating control processes. In G.R. Hammond (Ed.), *Advances in psychology: Cerebral control of speech and limb movements*. Amsterdam: Elsevier.

Haley, W.E., Brown, S.L., & Levine, E.G. (1987). Family caregiver appraisals of patient behavioural disturbance in senile dementia. *International Journal of Aging and Humane Development*, *25*, 25–34.

Hancock, P.A., & Manser, M.P. (1997). Time-to-contact: More than tau alone. *Ecological Psychology*, *9*(4), 265–297.

Hancock, P.A., & Scallen, S.F. (1999). The driving question. *Transportation Human Factors*, *1*, 47–55.

Hayes, A.E., Davidson, M.C., Keele, S.W., & Rafal, R.D. (1998). Toward a functional analysis of the basal ganglia. *Journal of Cognitive Neuroscience*, *10*(2), 178–198.

Hayman, C.A.G., MacDonald, C.A., & Tulving, E. (1993). The role of repetition and associative interference in new semantic learning in amnesia: A case experiment. *Cognitive Neuroscience*, *5*(4), 375–389.

Heckhausen, H., & Beckmann, J. (1990). Intentional action and action slips. *Psychological Review*, *97*(1), 36–48.

Heider, F. (1946). Attitudes and cognitive organization. *Journal of Psychology*, *21*, 107–112.

Heindel, W.C., Salmon, D.P., & Butters, N. (1991). The biasing of weight judgments in Alzheimer's and Huntington's disease: A priming or programming phenomenon? *Journal of Clinical and Experimental Neuropsychology*, *13*, 189–203.

Heindel, W.C., Salmon, D.P., Shults, C.W., Walicke, P.A., & Butters, N. (1989). Neuropsychological evidence for multiple implicit memory systems—a comparison of Alzheimer's, Huntington's, and Parkinson's-disease patients. *Journal of Neuroscience*, *9*(2), 582–587.

Helander, M., & Soderberg, S. (1972). Driver visual behavior and electrodermal response during highway driving. *Goteborg Psychological Reports*, *2*, 4.

Henderson, J.M. (1992). Identifying objects across saccades: Effects of extrafoveal preview and flanker object context. *Journal of Experimental Psychology: Learning, Memory, and Cognition, 18,* 521–530.

Henderson, J.M., & Ferreira, F. (1993). Eye movement control in reading: Fixation measures reflect foveal but not parafoveal processing difficulty. *Canadian Journal of Experimental Psychology, 47,* 201–211.

Henderson, J.M., & Hollingworth, A. (1998). Eye movements during scene viewing. In G. Underwood (Ed.), *Eye guidance in reading and scene perception* (pp. 269–293). Oxford: Elsevier.

Herlitz, A., & Viitanen, M. (1991). Semantic organisation and verbal episodic memory in patients with mild and moderate Alzheimer's disease. *Journal of Clinical and Experimental Neuropsychology, 7,* 305–313.

Heuer, F., Reisberg, D., & Rios, C. (1997). The memory effects of thematically induced emotion. In D.G. Payne & F.G. Conrad (Eds.), *Intersections in basic and applied memory research* (pp. 113–131). Mahwah, NJ: Erlbaum.

Hildreth, E.C. (1984). *The measurement of visual motion.* Cambridge, MA: MIT Press.

Hildreth, E.C., Beusmans, J.M.H., Boer, E.R., & Royden, C.S. (1998). *From vision to action: Experiments and models of steering control during driving.* Cambridge Basic Research, Technical Report 98–2. Cambridge, MA.

Hintzman, D.L. (1986). "Schema abstraction" in a multiple-trace memory model. *Psychological Review, 93,* 411–428.

Hintzman, D.L., Curran, T., & Oppy, B. (1992). Effects of similarity and repetition on memory: Registration without learning? *Journal of Experimental Psychology: Learning, Memory and Cognition, 18,* 667–680.

Hirtle, S.C., & Jonides, J. (1985). Evidence of hierarchies in cognitive maps. *Memory and Cognition, 13,* 208–217.

Hoffman, E.R. (1994). Estimation of time to vehicle arrival—effects of age on use of available visual information. *Perception, 23,* 947–955.

Hoffman, E.R., & Mortimer, R.G. (1994). Drivers' estimates of time to collision. *Accident Analysis and Prevention, 26,* 511–520.

Holland, C.A., & Rabbitt, P.M.A. (1994). The problems of being an older driver: Comparing the perceptions of an expert group and older drivers. *Applied Ergonomics, 25*(1), 17–27.

Holyoak, K.J., & Mah, W.A. (1982). Cognitive reference points in judgements of symbolic magnitude. *Cognitive Psychology, 14,* 328–352.

Horneman, C. (1993). *Driver education and training: A review of the literature.* TRA Driver Education Unit, Armidale, Australia.

Horton, A.M., & Barrett, D. (1988). Neuropsychological assessment and behavior therapy: New directions in head trauma rehabilitation. *Journal of Head Trauma Rehabilitation, 3,* 57–64.

Huber, S.J., & Shuttleworth, E.C. (1990). Neuropsychological assessment of subcortical dementia. In J.L. Cummings (Ed.), *Subcortical dementia.* New York: Oxford University Press.

Hull, C.L. (1943). *Principles of behavior.* New York: Appleton Century Crofts.

Hull, M., & Christie, R. (1992). *Hazard Perception Test: The Geelong trial and future development. National Road Safety Seminar, Vol. 2.* The Official Committee on Road Safety and Road Traffic Safety Research Council, Wellington, New Zealand.

Huttenlocher, J., Hedges, L., & Prohaska, V. (1988). Hierarchical organization in ordered domains: Estimating the dates of events. *Psychological Review, 95,* 471–484.

Huttenlocher, J., Hedges, L.V., & Bradburn, N.M. (1990). Reports of elapsed time: Bounding and rounding processes in estimation. *Journal of Experimental Psychology: Learning, Memory and Cognition, 16,* 196–213.

Hyde, T.S., & Jenkins, J.J. (1973). Recall of words as a function of semantic, graphic and syntactic orienting tasks. *Journal of Verbal Learning and Verbal Behavior, 12,* 471–480.

Idzikowski, C., & Baddeley, A.D. (1983). Fear and dangerous environments. In G.R.J. Hockey (Ed.), *Stress and fatigue in human performance.* Chichester, UK: John Wiley.

Idzikowski, C., & Baddeley, A.D. (1987). Fear and performance of novice parachutists. *Ergonomics, 30,* 1463–1474.

Immink, M.A., & Wright, D.L. (1998). Contextual interference: A response planning account. *Quarterly Journal of Experimental Psychology, 51*(4), 735–754.

Jacobs, H.E. (1990). Identifying and describing neurobehavioral sequelae. In R.L. Wood (Ed.), *Neurobehavioral sequelae of traumatic brain injury.* New York: Taylor & Francis.

Jacobs, H.E. (1992). *Behavior analysis guidelines and brain injury rehabilitation: People, principles and programs.* Aspen: Aspen Publishing Company.

Jarvik, L.F. (1988). Aging of the brain: How can we prevent it? *The Gerontologist, 28,* 739–747.

Jeannerod, M. (1997). *The cognitive neuroscience of action.* Oxford: Blackwell.

Jennett, B. (1996). Epidemiology of head injury. *Journal of Neurology, Neurosurgery and Psychiatry, 60,* 362–369.

Johnston, A., & Clifford, C.W.G. (1995). A unified account of three apparent motion illusions. *Vision Research, 35,* 1109–1123.

Johnston, E.B., Cumming, B.G., & Landy, M.S. (1994). Integration of stereopsis and motion shape cues. *Vision Research, 34,* 2259–2275.

Jonah, B.A. (1997). Sensation seeking and risky driving: A review and synthesis of the literature. *Accident Analysis and Behavior, 29*(5), 651–665.

Jonides, J., Smith, E.E., Koeppe, R.A., Awh, E., Minoshima, S., & Mintun, M.A. (1993). Spatial working memory in humans as revealed by PET. *Letters to Nature, 363,* 623–625.

Judd, C.H. (1908). The relation of special training to general intelligence. *Educational Review, 36,* 28–42.

Jueptner, M., Stephan, K.M., Frith, C.D., Brooks, D.J., Frackowiak, R.S.J., & Passingham, R.E. (1997). Anatomy of motor learning. 1. Frontal cortex and attention to action. *Journal of Neurophysiology, 77*(3), 1313–1324.

Kahneman, D. (1973). *Attention and effort.* Englewood Cliffs, NJ: Prentice-Hall.

Kaiser, H.F. (1974). An index of factorial simplicity. *Psychometrika, 39,* 401–415.

Kalsbeek, W.D., McLaurin, R.L., Harris, B.S.H., & Miller, J.D. (1980). The national head and spinal cord injury survey: Major findings. *Journal of Neurosurgery, 53,* S19–31.

Kaplan, S. (1993). 5-year tracking of psychosocial changes in people with severe traumatic brain injury. *Rehabilitation Counseling Bulletin, 36,* 151–159.

Kappe, B., & Korteling, H. (1997). Time to contact estimation is based upon inferential and direct visual information [Cited in Cavallo, V., Mestre, D., & Berthelon, C. (1997). *Time-to-collision judgements: Visual and spatio-temporal factors*]. In J.A. Rothengatter

& E. Carbonell Vaya (Eds.), *Traffic and transport psychology: Theory and application*. Amsterdam: Elsevier.

Kassin, S.M., Ellsworth, P.C., & Smith, V.L. (1989). The "general acceptance" of psychological research on eyewitness testimony: A survey of experts. *American Psychologist, 44,* 1089–1098.

Kaszniak, A.W. (1991). Dementia and the older driver. *Human Factors, 33,* 527–537.

Kazdin, A.E. (1988). *Behavior modification in applied settings.* Pacific Grove, CA: Brooks-Cole.

Keele, S.W. (1968). Movement control in skilled performance. *Psychological Bulletin, 70,* 387–403.

Keele, S.W. (1986). Movement control in skilled motor performance. *Psychological Bulletin, 70,* 387–403.

Kincade, R.G. (1963). *A differential influence of augmented feedback on learning and performance.* AMRL-TDR-63-12. Dayton, OH: Aerospace Medical Research Laboratory.

Kirschbaum, C., & Hellhammer, D.H. (1994). Salivary cortisol in psychoneuroendocrine research: Recent developments and applications. *Psychoneuroendocrinology, 19*(4), 313–333.

Kline, D.W., & Fuchs, P. (1993). The visibility of symbolic highway signs can be increased among drivers of all ages. *Human Factors, 35*(1), 25–34.

Koch, C., & Ullman, S. (1985). Shifts in selective visual attention: Towards the underlying neural circuitry. *Human Neurobiology, 4,* 219–227.

Koenderink, J.J. (1986). Optic flow. *Vision Research, 26,* 161–180.

Koenderink, J.J., & van Doorn, A.J. (1976). Local structure of movement parallax of the plane. *Journal of the Optical Society of America, 66,* 717–723.

Koh, K., & Meyer, D.E. (1991). Function learning: Induction of continuous stimulus–response relations. *Journal of Experimental Psychology: Learning, Memory and Cognition, 17,* 811–836.

Kolers, P., & Roediger, H.L. (1984). Procedure of mind. *Journal of Verbal Learning and Verbal Behavior, 23,* 425–449.

Kolers, P.A., & Duchnicky, R.L. (1985). Discontinuity in cognitive skill. *Journal of Experimental Psychology: Learning, Memory and Cognition, 4,* 655–674.

Kosslyn, S.M. (1994). *Image and brain: The resolution of the imagery debate.* Cambridge, MA: MIT Press.

Kraus, J.F. (1993). Epidemiology of head injury. In P.R. Cooper (Ed.), *Head injury.* Baltimore: William Wilkins.

Kremer, J.H., Delis, D.C., Blusewicz, M.J., Brandt, J., Ober, B.A., & Strauss, M. (1988). Verbal memory errors in Alzheimer's and Huntington's dementias. *Developmental Neuropsychology, 4,* 1–15.

Kroemer, K.H.E. (1971). Foot operation of controls. *Ergonomics, 14,* 333–361.

Kruysse, H.W., & Christie, R. (1992). Why are experts not better in judging the danger of filmed traffic conflicts. *Accident Analysis and Prevention, 24,* 227–235.

Land, M.F., & Horwood, J. (1995). Which parts of the road guide steering? *Nature, 377,* 339–340.

Land, M.F., & Lee, D.N. (1994). Where we look we steer. *Nature, 369,* 742–744.

Lane, D.M., & Robertson, L. (1979). The generality of the levels of processing hypothesis: An application to memory for chess positions. *Memory and Cognition, 7,* 253–256.

Lane, N.E. (1987). *Skill acquisition: Rates, patterns, issues and training implications.* New York: Springer Verlag.

Larwood, L. (1978). Swine flu: A field study of self-serving biases. *Journal of Applied Social Psychology, 18*, 283–289.

Lazarus, R.S., & Folkman, S. (1984). *Stress, coping and appraisal.* New York: Springer.

Lazarus, R.S., Kanner, A.D., & Folkman, S. (1980). Emotions: A cognitive phenomenal analysis. In R. Plutchik & H. Kellerman (Eds.), *Emotion, theory, research and experience.* New York: Academic Press.

Lazarus, R.S., & Smith, C.A. (1988). Knowledge and appraisal in the cognition–emotion relationship. *Cognition and Emotion, 2*, 281–300.

Lee, D.N. (1976). A theory of visual control of braking based on information about time to collision. *Perception, 5*, 437–459.

Lee, D.N. (1980). The optic flow field: The foundation of vision. *Philosophical Transactions of the Royal Society of London, B, 290*, 169–179.

Lee, D.N., & Lishman, J.R. (1977). Visual proprioceptive control of stance. *Scandinavian Journal of Psychology, 18*, 224–230.

Lee, D.N., & Reddish, P.E. (1981). Plummeting gannets: A paradigm of ecological optics. *Nature, 293*, 293–294.

Lee, D.N., & Young, D.S. (1985). Visual timing of interceptive action. In D. Ingle, M. Jeannerod, & D.N. Lee (Eds.), *Brain mechanisms and spatial vision* (pp. 1–30). Dordrecht: Martinus Nijhoff.

Lee, T.D., & Magill, R.A. (1983). The locus of the contextual interference effect in motor skill acquisition. *Journal of Experimental Psychology: Learning, Memory and Cognition, 9*, 730–746.

Lee, T.D., & Magill, R.A. (1985). Can forgetting facilitate skill acquisition? In D. Goodman, R.B. Wilberg, & I.M. Franks (Eds.), *Differing perspectives in motor learning and control* (pp. 3–22). Amsterdam: North Holland.

Levin, B.E., Tomer, R., & Rey, G.J. (1992). Clinical correlates of cognitive impairment in Parkinson's disease. In S.J. Huber & J.L. Cummings (Eds.), *Parkinson's disease.* New York: Oxford University Press.

Lewis, C.H. (1988). Why and how to learn why: Analysis-based generalization of procedures. *Cognitive Science, 12*, 211–256.

Lewis, F.D., & Bitter, C.F. (1991). Applied behavior analysis and work adjustment training. In B.T. McMahon & L.R. Shaw (Eds.), *Work worth doing: Advances in brain injury rehabilitation.* Orlando, FL: Paul M. Deutsch.

Lewis, F.D., Burke, W.H., & Carillo, R. (1987). Model for the rehabilitation of head injured adults in the post-acute setting. *Journal of Applied Rehabilitation Counseling, 18*, 39–45.

Lezak, M.D. (1995). *Neuropsychological assessment.* New York: Oxford University Press.

Lishman, W.A. (1987). *Organic psychiatry.* Oxford: Blackwell.

Liu, A. (1998). What the driver's eye tells the car's brain. In G. Underwood (Ed.), *Eye guidance in reading and scene perception* (pp. 431–452). Oxford: Elsevier.

Liu, A., Veltri, L., & Pentland, A. (1996). *Modelling changes in eye fixation patterns while driving* (Technical Report CBR- TR96-1). Cambridge, MA: Nissan Cambridge Basic Research.

Liu, A., Veltri, L., & Pentland, A.P. (1997). Modelling changes in eye fixation patterns while driving. In A.G. Gale (Ed.), *Vision in vehicles VI.* Amsterdam: Elsevier.

222    UNDERSTANDING DRIVING

Livingstone, M.S., & Hubel, D.H. (1988). Segregation of form, colour, movement and depth. *Science, 240*, 740–749.

Loftus, E.F. (1980). *Memory.* Reading, MA: Addison-Wesley.

Loftus, E.F., Loftus, G.R., & Messo, J. (1987). Some facts about "weapon focus". *Law and Human Behavior, 11*, 55–62.

Loftus, E.F., & Marburger, W. (1983). Since the eruption of Mt. St. Helens, has anyone beaten you up? Improving the accuracy of retrospective reports with landmark events. *Memory and Cognition, 11*, 114–120.

Logan, G.D. (1988). Towards an instance theory of automatization. *Psychological Review, 95*, 492–527.

Logie, R.H. (1995). *Visuo-spatial working memory.* London: Lawrence Erlbaum Associates Ltd.

Lopez, O.I., Becker, J.T., Brenner, R.P., Rosen, J., Bajulayie, O.I., & Reynolds, C.F. (1991). Alzheimers-disease with delusions and hallucinations—neuropsychological and electroencephalic correlates. *Neurology, 41*(6), 906–912.

Lorge, I., & Thorndike, E.L. (1935). The influence of delay in the after-effect of a connection. *Journal of Experimental Psychology, 18*, 187–194.

Lundberg, C., Johansson, K., Ball, K., Bjerre, B., Blomqvist, C., Braekhus, A., Brouwer, W.H., Bylsma, F.W., Carr, D.B., Englund, L., Friedland, R.P., Hakamies-Blomqvist, L., Klemetz, G., O'Neill, D., Odenheimer, G.L., Rizzo, M., Schelin, M., Seideman, M., Tallman, K., Viitanen, M., Waller, P.F., & Winblab, B. (1997). Dementia and driving: An attempt at concensus. *Alzheimer Disease and Associated Disorders, 11*(1), 28–37.

Lunenfeld, H., & Alexander, G. (1990). *A users guide to positive guidance* (3rd Ed.). Report No. FHWA-SA-90-017. Federal Highway Administration, US Department of Transportation, Washington, DC.

Luoma, J. (1986). *The acquisition of visual information by the driver: Interaction of relevant and irrelevant information.* Reports from Liikenneturva 32/1986. Helsinki: Central Organisation for Traffic Safety.

Luria, A.R. (1966). *The higher cortical functions in man.* New York: Basic Books.

Mack, J.L., Patterson, M.B., Schnell, A.H., & Whitehouse, D.J. (1993). Performance of subjects with probable Alzheimer's disease and normal elderly controls on the Gollin Incomplete Pictures test. *Perceptual and Motor Skills, 77*, 951–969.

MacKay, D.G. (1982). The problem of flexibility, fluency, and speed–accuracy trade-off in skilled behavior. *Psychological Review, 89*, 483–506.

Magill, R.A., & Hall, K.G. (1990). A review of the contextual interference effect in motor skill acquisition. *Human Movement Science, 9*, 241–299.

Mahoney, J.V., & Ullman, S. (1988). Image chunking defining spatial blocks for scene analysis. In Z. Pylyshyn (Ed.), *Computational processes in human vision: An interdisciplinary perspective.* Norwood, NJ: Ablex.

Malaterre, G. (1990). Error analysis and in-depth accident studies. *Ergonomics, 33*(10/11), 1403–1421.

Mangels, J.A., Ivry, R.B., & Shimizu, N. (1998). Dissociable contributions of the prefrontal and neocerebellar cortex to time perception. *Cognitive Brain Research, 7*(1), 15–39.

Manser, M.P., & Hancock, P.A. (1996). The influence of approach angle on estimates of time-to-collision. *Ecological Psychology, 8*, 71–99.

Marcel, A.J. (1983). Conscious and unconscious perception: Experiments on visual masking and word recognition. *Cognitive Psychology, 15*, 197–237.

Markus, H., & Nurius, P. (1986). Possible selves. *American Psychologist, 41*(9), 954–969.

Marottoli, R.A., & Richardson, E.D. (1998). Confidence in, and self-rating of, driving ability among older drivers. *Accident Analysis and Prevention, 30*(3), 331–336.

Martin, G., & Pear, J. (1988). *Behavior modification: What it is and how to do it.* Englewood Cliffs, NJ: Prentice Hall.

Massman, P.J., Delis, D.C., & Butters, N. (1993). Does impaired primacy recall equal impaired long-term storage? Serial position effects in Huntington's disease and Alzheimer's disease. *Developmental Neuropsychology, 9,* 1–15.

Massman, P.J., Delis, D.C., Butters, N., Levin, B.E., & Salmon, D.P. (1990). Are all subcortical dementias alike—verbal learning and memory in Parkinson's and Huntington's disease patients. *Journal of Clinical and Experimental Neuropsychology, 12*(5), 729–744.

Massman, P.J., Delis, D.C., Salmon, D.P., Butters, N., & Demadura, T.L. (1991). Spatial cognition in Alzheimers disease—subtypes of impairment in visual hierarchical processing. *Journal of Clinical and Experimental Neuropsychology, 13*(1), 51.

Masson, M.E.J. (1986). Identification of typographically transformed words: Instance-based skill acquisition. *Journal of Experimental Psychology: Learning, Memory and Cognition, 12,* 479–488.

Masson, M.E.J. (1990). Cognitive theories of skill acquisition. *Human Movement Science, 9,* 221–239.

Mathews, M.L., & Moran, A.R. (1986). Age differences in male drivers' perception of accident risk: The role of perceived driving ability. *Accident Analysis and Prevention, 18,* 299–313.

Maycock, G., Lockwood, C.R., & Lester, J.F. (1991). *The accident liability of car drivers.* Department of TRL Research Report 315. Crowthorne, UK: Transport Research Laboratory.

Mazur, J.E., & Hastie, R. (1978). Learning as accumulation: A re-examination of the learning curve. *Psychological Bulletin, 85*(6), 1256–1274.

McCormick, I.A., Walkey, F.H., & Green, D.E. (1986). Comparative perceptions of driver ability—a confirmation and expansion. *Accident Analysis and Prevention, 18,* 205–208.

McGuire, T.L., & Rothenberg, M.B. (1986). Behavioral and psychosocial sequelae of pediatric head injury. *Journal of Head Trauma Rehabilitation, 1,* 1–6.

McGuire, W.J. (1961). A multiprocess model for paired associate learning. *Journal of Experimental Psychology, 62,* 335–347.

McGwin, G., Owsley, C., & Ball, K. (1998). Identifying crash involvement among older drivers: Agreement between self-report and state records. *Accident Analysis and Prevention, 30*(6), 781–791.

McKee, S.P., Silverman, G.H., & Nakayama, K. (1986). Precise velocity discrimination despite random variations in temporal frequency and contrast. *Vision Research, 26,* 609–619.

McKeithen, K.B., Reitman, J.S., Rueter, H.H., & Hirtle, S.C. (1981). Knowledge organization and skill differences in computer programs. *Cognitive Psychology, 13,* 307–325.

McKenna, F., & Crick, J.L. (1991). Experience and expertise in hazard perception. In G.B. Grayson & J.F. Lester (Eds.), *Behavioural research in road safety.* Crowthorne, UK: Transport Research Laboratory.

McKenna, F.P. (1993). It won't happen to me: Unrealistic optimism or illusion of control? *British Journal of Psychology*, *84*, 39–50.

McKenna, F.P., & Crick, J.L. (1994). *Hazard perception in drivers: A methodology for testing and training*. TRL Contractor Report 313. Crowthorne, UK: Transport Research Laboratory.

McKenna, F.P., & Horswill, M.S. (1997). Differing conceptions of hazard perception. In G.B. Grayson (Ed.), *Behavioural research in road safety: VII* (pp. 74–81). Crowthorne, UK: Transport Research Laboratory.

McKenna, F.P., Stanier, R.A., & Lewis, C. (1991). Factors underlying illusory self-assessment of driving skill in males and females. *Accident Analysis and Prevention*, *23*(1), 45–52.

McKnight, A.J., & Adams, R.D. (1970). *Driver education task analysis: Vol. I. Task descriptions*. Alexandria, VA: Human Resources Research Organization.

McKnight, A.J., & McKnight, A.S. (1999). Multivariate analysis of age-related driver ability and performance deficits. *Accident Analysis and Prevention*, *31*(5), 445–454.

McLeod, P., McLaughlin, C.M., & Nimmo-Smith, I. (1985). Information encapsulation and automaticity: Evidence from the visual control of finely timed actions. In M.I. Posner & O.S.M. Marin (Eds.), *Attention and performance XI* (pp. 391–406). Hillsdale, NJ: Erlbaum.

McLeod, R.W., & Ross, H.E. (1983). Optic flow and cognitive factors in time-to-collision estimates. *Perception*, *12*, 417–423.

McWalter, G.J., Montaldi, D., & Bhutani, G.E. (1991). Paired associate learning in dementia of the Alzheimer's type. *Neuropsychology*, *5*, 205–211.

Means, B., Mingay, D.J., Nigam, A., & Zarrow, M. (1988). A cognitive approach to enhancing health survey reports of medical visits. In M.M. Gruneberg, P.E. Morris, & R.N. Sykes (Eds.), *Practical aspects of memory: Current research and issues, Vol. 1: Memory in everyday life* (pp. 536–542). Chichester, UK: John Wiley & Sons.

Meiran, N. (1996). Reconfiguration of processing mode prior to task performance. *Journal of Experimental Psychology: Learning, Memory, and Cognition*, *22*(6), 1423–1442.

Mendez, M.F., Mendez, M.A., Martin, R., Smyth, K.A., & Whitehouse, P.J. (1990). Complex visual disturbances in Alzheimer's disease. *Neurology*, *40*, 439–443.

Merat, N., & Groeger, J.A. (2000). *Working memory and auditory localization: Demand for central resources impairs performance*. Manuscript submitted for publication.

Merat, N., Groeger, J.A., & Withington, D. (1999). Localising localisation: The role of working memory in auditory localisation. *International Journal of Psychology*, *34*(5/6), 317–321.

Merigan, W.H., & Maunsell, J.H.R. (1993). How parallel are the primate visual pathways? *Annual Review of Neuroscience*, *16*, 369–402.

Meyer, R.E. (1989). Models of understanding. *Review of Educational Research*, *72*, 43–64.

Michon, J.A. (1985). A critical review of driver behavior models: What do we know, what should we do? In L. Evans & R.C. Schwing (Eds.), *Human behavior and traffic safety*. New York: Plenum Press.

Miller, L. (1990). Major syndromes of aggressive behavior following head injury: An introduction to evaluation and treatment. *Cognitive Rehabilitation*, *6*, 14–19.

Milosevic, S. (1986). Perception of vehicle speed. *Revija za psihologiju*, *16*, 11–19.

Milosevic, S., & Milic, J. (1990). Speed perception in road curves. *Journal of Safety Research*, *21*, 19–23.

Miura, T. (1990). Active function of eye movement and useful field of view in a realistic setting. In R. Groner, G. d'Ydewalle, & R. Parham (Eds.), *From eye to mind: Information acquisition in perception, search and reading* (pp. 119–127). Amsterdam: Elsevier.

Morris, C.D., Bransford, J.D., & Franks, J.J. (1977). Levels of processing versus transfer appropriate processing. *Journal of Verbal Learning and Verbal Behavior, 16,* 519–533.

Morris, R.D., & Baddeley, A.D. (1988). Primary and working memory functioning in Alzheimer-type dementia. *Journal of Clinical and Experimental Neuropsychology, 10,* 279–296.

Morris, R.G., & Kopelman, M.D. (1986). The memory deficits in Alzheimer-type dementia: A review. *The Quarterly Journal of Experimental Psychology, 38A,* 575–602.

Morrison, J.E. (1991). *Training for performance: Principles of applied human learning.* Chichester, UK: Wiley.

Mortimer, J.A., & Pirozzolo, F.J. (1985). Remote effects of head trauma. *Developmental Neuropsychology, 1,* 215–229.

Moscato, B.S., Trevisan, M., & Willer, B.S. (1994). The prevalence of traumatic brain injury and co-occurring disabilities in a national household survey of adults. *Journal of Neuropsychiatry and Clinical Neuroscience, 6,* 134–142.

Moscovitch, M. (1995). Recovered consciousness—a hypothesis concerning modularity and episodic memory. *Journal of Clinical and Experimental Neuropsychology, 17*(2), 276–290.

Moss, M.B., Albert, M.S., & Kemper, T.L. (1992). Neuropsychology of frontal lobe dementia. In R.F. White (Ed.), *Clinical syndromes in adult neuropsychology: The practitioner's handbook.* Amsterdam: Elsevier.

Mourant, R.R., & Rockwell, T.H. (1970). Mapping eye-movement patterns to the visual scene in driving: An exploratory study. *Human Factors, 12,* 81–87.

Mourant, R.R., & Rockwell, T.H. (1972). Strategies of visual search by novice and experienced drivers. *Human Factors, 14,* 325–335.

Mourant, R.R., Rockwell, T.H., & Rackoff, N.J. (1969). Drivers' eye movements and visual workload. *Highway Research Record, 292,* 1–10.

Myles-Worsley, M., Johnston, W.A., & Simons, M.A. (1988). The influence of expertise on x-ray image processing. *Journal of Experimental Psychology: Learning, Memory and Cognition, 14,* 553–557.

Naatanen, R., & Summala, H. (1972). *Road-user behavior and traffic accidents.* Amsterdam: North Holland.

Nairne, J.S. (1990). A feature model of immediate memory. *Memory and Cognition, 18*(3), 251–269.

Naveh-Benjamin, M., & Jonides, J. (1984). Maintenance rehearsal: A two component analysis. *Journal of Experimental Psychology: Learning, Memory and Cognition, 10,* 369–385.

Naveh-Benjamin, M., & Jonides, J. (1986). On the automaticity of frequency coding: Effects of competing task load, encoding strategy and intention. *Journal of Experimental Psychology: Learning, Memory and Cognition, 12,* 378–386.

Navon, D., & Gopher, D. (1979). On the economy of the human-information processing system. *Psychological Review, 86,* 214–255.

Nawrot, M., & Sekuler, R. (1990). Assimilation and contrast in motion perception: Explorations in co-operativity. *Vision Research, 30,* 1439–1451.

Neary, D., & Sowden, J.S. (1991). Dementia of the frontal lobe type. In H.S. Levin, H.M. Eisenberg, & A.L. Benton (Eds.), *Frontal lobe function and dysfunction.* New York: Oxford University Press.

Nebes, R.D. (1992). Cognitive dysfunction in Alzheimer's disease. In F.I.M. Craik & T.A. Salthouse (Eds.), *The handbook of aging.* Hillsdale, NJ: Erlbaum.

Nebes, R.D., & Brady, C.B. (1989). Focused and divided attention in Alzheimer's disease. *Cortex, 25,* 305–315.

Nestor, P.G., Parasuraman, R., & Haxby, J.V. (1991). Speed of information processing and attention in early Alzheimer's dementia. *Developmental Neuropsychology, 7,* 242–256.

Newcomb, T.M. (1981). Heiderian balance as a group phenomenon. *Journal of Personality and Social Psychology, 27,* 154–165.

Newell, A. (1990). *Unified theories of cognition.* Cambridge, MA: Harvard University Press.

Newell, A., & Rosenbloom, P.S. (1981). Mechanisms of skill acquisition and the law of practice. In J.R. Anderson (Ed.), *Cognitive skills and their acquisition.* Hillsdale, NJ: Erlbaum.

Newsome, W.T., Shadlen, M.N., Zohary, E., Britten, K.H., & Movshon, J.A. (1995). Visual motion: Linking neuronal activity to psycho-physical performance. In M.S. Gazzaniga (Ed.), *The cognitive neurosciences* (pp. 401–414). Cambridge, MA: MIT Press.

Nissen, M.J., & Bullemer, P. (1987). Attentional requirements of learning: Evidence from performance measures. *Cognitive Psychology, 19,* 1–32.

Nissen, M.J., Willingham, D., & Hartman, M. (1989). Explicit and implicit remembering: When is learning preserved in amnesia? *Neuropsychologia, 27,* 341–352.

Nockleby, D.M., & Deaton, A.V. (1987). Denial versus distress: Coping patterns in post head trauma patients. *International Journal of Clinical Neuropsychology, 9,* 145–148.

Norman, D.A. (1981). Categorization of action slips. *Psychological Review, 88,* 1–15.

Norman, D.A., & Shallice, T. (1986). Attention to action: Willed and automatic control of behavior. In R.J. Davidson, G.E. Schwartz, & D. Shapiro (Eds.), *Consciousness and self-regulation: Advances in research and theory, Vol. 4.* New York: Plenum Press.

Norman, D.A., & Shallice, T. (1980). *Attention to action: Willed and automatic control of behavior.* CHIP Document No. 99. Centre for Human Information Processing, University of California, San Diego, La Jolla.

Norman, G.R., Brooks, L.R., & Allen, S.W. (1989). Recall by expert medical practitioners as a record of processing attention. *Journal of Experimental Psychology: Learning, Memory and Cognition, 15,* 1166–1174.

Oatley, K., & Johnson-Laird, P.N. (1987). Towards a cognitive theory of emotions. *Cognition and Emotion, 1,* 29–50.

Ober, B.A., Koss, E., Friedland, R.P., & Delis, D.C. (1985). Processes of verbal memory failure in Alzheimer-type dementia. *Brain and Cognition, 4,* 90–103.

OECD. (1985). *Traffic safety of elderly road users.* Paris: Author.

Olson, P.L., Battle, D.S., & Aoki, T. (1989). *Driver eye fixations under different operating conditions.* Technical Report UMTRI-89-3. Ann Arbor, MI: University of Michigan Transportation Research Institute.

Olson, P.L., & Sivak, M. (1986). Perception-response time to unexpected roadway hazards. *Human Factors, 28*(1), 91–96.

Osaka, N. (1988). Speed estimation through restricted visual field during day and night: Nasotemporal hemi-field differences. In A.G. Gale, M.A. Freeman, & C.M. Haselgrave (Eds.), *Vision in vehicles II*. Amsterdam: Elsevier.

Owsley, C., & McGwin, G. (1999). Vision impairment and driving. *Survey of Opthmatology, 43*(6), 535–550.

Pandya, D.N., van Hoesen, G.W., & Mesulam, M.-M. (1981). Efferent connections of the cingulate gyrus in the rhesus monkey. *Experimental Brain Research, 42*, 319–330.

Parasuraman, R., & Haxby, J.V. (1993). Attention and brain function in Alzheimer's disease: A review. *Neuropsychology, 7*, 242–272.

Parasuraman, R., Mutter, S.A., & Molloy, R. (1991). Sustained attention following mild head injury. *Journal of Clinical and Experimental Neuropsychology, 13*(5), 789–811.

Parker, D., Lajunen, T., & Stradling, S. (1998). Attitudinal predictors of interpersonally aggressive violations on the road. *Transportation Research: Traffic Psychology and Behaviour, F*(1), 11–24.

Pashler, H.E. (1998). *The psychology of attention*. Cambridge, MA: MIT Press.

Patrick, J. (1992). *Training: Research and practice*. London: Academic Press.

Paulesu, E., Frith, C.D., & Frackowiak, R.S. (1993). The neural correlates of the verbal component of working memory. *Nature, 362*(6418), 342–345.

Paulsen, J.S., Butters, N., & Salmon, D.P. (1993). Prism adaptation in Alzheimer's and Huntington's disease. *Neuropsychology, 14*, 1–9.

Paulsen, J.S., Salmon, D.P., Heindel, W., & Butters, N. (1991). The utility of the Wisconsin card sorting test and the selective reminding test in the detection and discrimination of dementia. *Journal of Clinical and Experimental Neuropsychology, 13*(1), 65–66.

Payne, D.G. (1986). Hypernesia for pictures and words: Testing the recall level hypothesis. *Journal of Experimental Psychology: Learning, Memory and Cognition, 12*, 16–29.

Pelz, D.C., & Krupat, E. (1974). Caution profile and driving record of undergraduate males. *Accident Analysis and Prevention, 6*, 45–58.

Pennington, N., Nicolich, R., & Rahm, J. (1995). Transfer of training between cognitive sub-skills: Is knowledge use specific? *Cognitive Psychology, 28*, 175–224.

Pentland, A.P. (1987). A new sense for depth of field. *IEEE Transactions PAMI, 9*, 523–531.

Peterson, C. (1991). The meaning and measurement of explanatory style. *Psychological Inquiry, 2*, 1–10.

Petrides, M., Alivisatos, B., Evans, A.C., & Meyer, E. (1993). Functional activation of the human frontal cortex during performance of verbal working memory tasks. *Proceedings of the National Academy of Science, 90*, 873–877.

Poggio, G., & Poggio, T. (1984). The analysis of stereopsis. *Annual Review of Neuroscience, 7*, 379–412.

Pollens, R.D., McBratnie, B.P., & Burton, P.L. (1988). Beyond cognition: Executive functions in closed head injury. *Cognitive Rehabilitation, 6*, 26–32.

Posner, M.I., & Peterson, S.E. (1990). The attention system of the human brain. *Annual Review of Neuroscience, 13*, 25–42.

Posner, M.I., & Raichle, M.E. (1994). *Images of mind*. New York: Scientific American Library.

Posner, M.J., DiGirolamo, G.J., & Fernandez-Duque, D. (1997). Brain mechanisms of cognitive skills. *Consciousness and Cognition, 6*, 267–290.

Predebon, J. (1990). Relative distance judgements of familiar and unfamiliar objects viewed under representatively natural conditions. *Perception and Psychophysics, 47,* 342–348.

Priddy, D.A., Johnson, P., & Lam, C.S. (1990). Driving after severe head injury. *Brain Injury, 4*(3), 267–272.

Prigatano, G.P. (1987). Personality and psychosocial consequences after brain injury. In M.J. Meier, A.L. Benton, & L. Diller (Eds.), *Neuropsychological rehabilitation.* New York: Guilford Press.

Radavansky, G.A., & Zacks, R.T. (1997). The retrieval of situation-specific information. In M.A. Conway (Ed.), *Cognitive models of memory* (pp. 173–214). Hove, UK: Psychology Press.

Ragland, J.D., Glahn, D.C., Gur, R.C., & Censits, D.M. (1997). PET regional cerebral blood flow during working and declarative memory: Relationship with task performance. *Neuropsychology, 11*(2), 222–231.

Raichle, M.E. (1993). The scratch-pad of the mind. *Nature, 363*(6430), 583–584.

Rapcsak, S.Z., Kentros, S.A., & Rubens, A.B. (1990). Impaired recognition of meaningful sounds in Alzheimer's disease. *Journal of Clinical and Experimental Neuropsychology, 14,* 801–821.

Rausecker, J.P., von Grunau, M.W., & Poulin, C. (1987). Centrifugal organization of direction preferences in the cat's lateral suprasylvian visual cortex and its relation to flow field processing. *Journal of Neuroscience, 7,* 943–958.

Reason, J.T. (1984). Lapses of attention in everyday life. In R. Parasuraman & D.R. Davies (Eds.), *Varieties of attention* (pp. 515–549). Orlando, FL: Academic Press.

Recarte, M.A., & Nunes, L.M. (1996). Perception of speed in an automobile: Estimation and production. *Journal of Experimental Psychology: Applied, 2*(4), 291–304.

Regan, D., & Beverley, K.I. (1978). Looming detectors in the human visual pathway. *Vision Research, 18,* 415–421.

Reid, L.D. (1983). A survey of recent driver steering behavior models suited to accident studies. *Accident Analysis and Prevention, 15*(1), 23–40.

Reitman, J.S. (1976). Skilled perception in Go: Deducing memory structures from inter-response times. *Cognitive Psychology, 8,* 336–356.

Restle, F., & Greeno, J.G. (1970). *Introduction to mathematical psychology.* Reading, MA: Addison-Wesley.

Richardson-Klavehn, A., & Bjork, R.A. (1988). Measures of memory. *Annual Review of Psychology, 39,* 475–543.

Richer, F., Decary, A., Lapierre, M.-P., Rouleau, I., & Saint-Hilaire, J.-M. (1993). Target detection deficits in frontal lobectomy. *Brain and Cognition, 21,* 203–211.

Rizzolatti, G., & Craighero, L. (1998). From spatial attention to attention to objects: An extension of the premotor theory of attention. *Revue de Neuropsychologie, 8*(1), 155–174.

Roediger, H.L., & Blaxton, T.A. (1987). Retrieval modes produce dissociations in memory for surface information. In D.S. Gorfein & R.S. Hoffman (Eds.), *Memory and learning: The Ebbinghaus centennial conference.* Hillsdale, NJ: Erlbaum.

Rogers, R.D., Baker, S.C., Owen, A.M., Frith, C.D., Dolan, R.J., Frackowiak, S.J., & Robbins, T.W. (1994). Frontal and parietal activations in a test of planning: A PET study with the Tower of London. *Society for Neuroscience Abstracts, 20,* 353.

Rogers, R.D., & Monsell, S. (1995). Costs of a predictable switch between simple cognitive tasks. *Journal of Experimental Psychology: General, 124*(2), 207–231.

Rogers, T.B., Kuiper, N.A., & Kirker, W.S. (1977). Self-reference and the encoding of personal information. *Journal of Personality and Social Psychology, 35*(9), 677–688.

Rose, F.D., & Johnson, D.A. (1994). Virtual reality in brain damage rehabilitation. *Medical Science Research, 22*, 1.

Rosenbaum, A., & Hoge, S. (1989). Head injury and marital aggression. *American Journal of Psychiatry, 146*(7), 1048–1051.

Rosenthal, M., & Bond, M.R. (1990). Behavioral and psychiatric sequelae. In M. Rosenthal, E.R. Griffith, M.R. Bond, & J.D. Miller (Eds.), *Rehabilitation of the adult and child with traumatic brain injury*. Philadelphia: F.A. Davis.

Rossor, M. (1987). The neurochemistry of cortical dementias. In S.M. Stahl, S.D. Iversen, & E.C. Goodman (Eds.), *Cognitive neurochemistry*. Oxford: Oxford University Press.

Roth, E.C., & Hellige, J.B. (1998). Spatial processing and hemispheric asymmetry: Contributions of the transient/magnocellular visual system. *Journal of Cognitive Neuroscience, 10*(4), 472–484.

Rousey, C.G., Arjunan, K.N., & Rousey, C.L. (1986). Stressful treatment of stuttering following closed head injury. *Journal of Fluency Disorders, 11*, 257–261.

Rowe, J.W., & Kahn, R.L. (1997). Successful aging. *Gerontologist, 37*(4), 433–440.

Rubin, D.C., & Baddeley, A.D. (1989). Telescoping is not time compression: A model of the dating of autobiographical events. *Memory and Cognition, 17*, 653–661.

Rubin, D.C., Wetzler, S.E., & Nebes, R.D. (1986). Autobiographical memory across the life-span. In D.C. Rubin (Ed.), *Autobiographical memory* (pp. 202–221). Cambridge: Cambridge University Press.

Rumelhart, D.E., & McClelland, J.L. (Eds.). (1986). *Parallel distributed processing*. Cambridge, MA: MIT Press.

Runeson, S. (1975). Visual prediction of collision with natural and unnatural motion functions. *Perception and Psychophysics, 18*, 261–266.

Rutley, K.S., & Mace, D.G.W. (1968). *A preliminary investigation into the frequency of driver motor actions and eye movements*. RRL Report LR 162. Crowthorne, UK: Road Research Laboratory.

Sadalla, E.K., Burroughs, W.J., & Staplin, L.J. (1980). Reference points in spatial cognition. *Journal of Experimental Psychology: Human Learning and Memory, 5*, 516–528.

Sagberg, F. (1998). *Month-by-month changes in accident risk*. Paper presented at the International Congress of Applied Psychology, San Fransisco, 9–14 August.

Saint-Cyr, J.A., & Taylor, A.E. (1992). The mobilization of procedural learning: The "key signature" of the basal ganglia. In L.R. Squire & N. Butters (Eds.), *Neuropsychology of memory*. New York: Guilford Press.

Salame, P., & Baddeley, A.D. (1989). Effects of background music on phonological short-term store. *Quarterly Journal of Experimental Psychology, 41*, 107–122.

Salas, E., Driskell, J.E., & Hughes, S. (1996). The study of stress and human performance. In J.E. Driskell & E. Salas (Eds.), *Stress and human performance* (pp. 1–46). Mahwah, NJ: Erlbaum.

Schacter, D.L. (1964). The interaction of cognitive and physiological determinants of emotional state. In L. Berkowitz (Ed.), *Advances in experimental social psychology, Vol. 1*. New York: Academic Press.

Schacter, D.L. (1994). Priming and multiple memory systems: Perceptual mechanisms of implicit memory. In D.L. Schacter & E. Tulving (Eds.), *Memory systems 1994* (pp. 233–268). Cambridge, MA: MIT Press.

Schacter, D.L. (1996). *Searching for memory: The brain, the mind, and the past.* New York: Basic Books.

Schacter, D.L., Alpert, N.M., Savage, C.R., Rauch, S.L., & Albert, M.S. (1996a). Conscious recollection and the human hippocampal formation: Evidence from positron emission tomography. *Proceedings of the National Academy of Science, 93,* 321–325.

Schacter, D.L., Reiman, E., Curran, T., Yun, L.S., Bandy, D., McDermott, K.B., & Roediger, H.L., III (1996b). Neuroanatomical correlates of veridical and illusory recognition memory: Evidence from positron emission tomography. *Neuron, 17*(2), 267–274.

Schacter, D.L., & Tulving, E. (Eds.). (1994). *Memory systems 1994.* Cambridge, MA: MIT Press.

Schacter, D.L., Kaszniak, A.W., & Kihlstrom, J.F. (1989). Models of memory and the understanding of memory disorders. In T. Yanagihara & R.C. Petersen (Eds.), *Memory disorders: Research and clinical practice.* New York: Marcel Dekker.

Schiff, W., & Detwiler, M. (1979). Information used in judging impending collisions. *Perception, 8,* 647–658.

Schiff, W., & Oldak, R. (1990). Accuracy of judging time-to-arrival: Effects of modality, trajectory, and sex. *Journal of Experimental Psychology: Human Perception and Performance, 16,* 303–316.

Schiff, W., Oldak, R., & Shah, V. (1992). Ageing persons' estimates of vehicular motion, *Psychology and Ageing, 7,* 518–525.

Schlag, B. (1993). Elderly drivers in Germany: Fitness and driving behavior. *Accident Analysis and Prevention, 25*(1), 47–55.

Schmidt, I.W., Brouwer, W.H., Vanier, M., & Kemp, F. (1996). Flexible adaptation to changing task demands in severe closed head injury patients: A driving simulator study. *Applied Neuropsychology, 3*(3 & 4), 155–165.

Schmidt, R.A. (1975). A schema theory of discrete motor skill learning. *Psychological Review, 82,* 225–260.

Schmidt, R.A. (1982). *Motor control and learning: A behavioral emphasis.* Champaign, IL: Human Kinetics Publishers.

Schmidt, R.A. (1988). *Motor control and learning: A behavioral emphasis* (2nd Ed.). Champaign, IL: Human Kenetics Publishers.

Schmidt, R.A., & Bjork, R.A. (1992). New conceptualisations of practice—common principles in three paradigms suggest new concepts in training. *Psychological Science, 3*(4), 207–217.

Schmidt, R.A., Young, D.E., Swinnen, S., & Shapiro, D.C. (1989). Summary knowledge of results for skill acquisition: Support for the guidance hypothesis. *Journal of Experimental Psychology: Learning, Memory and Cognition, 15,* 352–359.

Schneider, W. (1985). Training high performance skills: Fallacies and guidelines. *Human Factors, 27,* 285–300.

Schneider, V.I., Healy, A.F., Ericsson, K.A., & Bourne, L.E. (1995). The effects of contextual interference on the acquisition and retention of logical rules. In A.F. Healy & L.E. Bourne (Eds.), *Learning and memory of knowledge and skills: Durability and specificity* (pp. 95–131). Thousand Oaks, CA: Sage.

Schneider, W., Dumais, S.T., & Shiffrin, R.M. (1984). Automatic and controlled processing and attention. In R. Parasuraman & D.R. Davies (Eds.), *Varieties of attention.* Orlando, FL: Academic Press.

Schwartz, M.F. (1995). Re-examining the role of executive functions in routine action production. In J. Graffman, K.J. Holyoak, & F. Boller (Eds.), The structure and functions of the human prefrontal cortex, *Annals of New York Academy of Sciences*, *769*, 321–335.

Schwartz, N., Park, D.C., Knauper, B., & Sudman, S. (1998). *Cognition, aging and self-reports*. Philadelphia, PA: Psychology Press.

Seely, R.R., Stephens, T.D., & Tate, P. (1991). *Essentials of anatomy and physiology*. St. Louis: Mosby Year Book.

Sellen, A.J., & Norman, D.A. (1992). The psychology of slips. In B.J. Baars (Ed.), *Experimental slips and human error. Exploring the architecture of volition*. New York: Plenum Press.

Sereno, M.E. (1993). *Neural computation of pattern motion: Modelling stages of motion analysis in the primate visual cortex*. Cambridge, MA: MIT Press.

Shallice, T. (1982). Specific impairments in planning. *Philosophical Transactions of the Royal Society of London, B29*, 199–209.

Shallice, T., & Burgess, P.W. (1991). Deficits in strategy application following frontal lobe damage in man. *Brain, 114*, 727–741.

Shallice, T., Fletcher, P., Frith, C.D., & Grasby, P. (1994). Brain regions associated with acquisition and retrieval of verbal episodic memory. *Nature, 368*(6472), 633–635.

Shallice, T., Fletcher, P., Frith, C.D., Grasby, P., Frackowiak, R.S.J., & Dolan, R.J. (1995). Brain regions associated with acquisition and retrieval of verbal episodic information. *Nature, 368*(6472), 633–635.

Shea, J.B., & Morgan, R.B. (1979). Contextual interference effects on the acquisition, retention and transfer of a motor skill. *Journal of Experimental Psychology: Human Learning and Memory, 5*, 179–185.

Shea, J.B., & Zimny, S.T. (1983). Context effect in memory and learning movement information. In R.A. Magill (Ed.), *Memory and control of action* (pp. 145–166). Amsterdam: North Holland.

Shea, J.B., & Zimny, S.T. (1988). Knowledge incorporation in motor representation. In O.J. Meijer & K. Roth (Eds.), *Complex movement behaviour: The motor-action controversy* (pp. 289–314). Amsterdam: North Holland.

Shiffrin, R.M., & Schneider, W. (1977). Controlled and automatic human information processing: Perceptual learning, automatic attending, and a general theory. *Psychological Review, 84*, 127–190.

Shinar, A., McDowell, E.D., & Rockwell, T.H. (1977). Eye movements in curve negotiation. *Human Factors, 19*, 63–71.

Shinar, D. (1998). Aggressive driving: The contribution of the drivers and the situation. *Transportation Research: Traffic Psychology and Behaviour, 1F*(2), 137–159.

Shinar, D., Meir, M., & Ben-Shoham, I. (1998). How automatic is manual gear shifting? *Human Factors, 40*(4), 647–654.

Sidaway, B., Fairweather, M., Sekiya, H., & McNitt-Gray, J. (1996). Time to collision estimation in a simulated driving task. *Human Factors, 38*, 1227–1244.

Simpson, J.I. (1984). The accessory optic system. *Annual Review of Neuroscience, 7*, 13–41.

Singley, M.K., & Anderson, J.R. (1989). *The transfer of cognitive skill*. Cambridge, MA: Harvard University Press.

Sirigu, A., Zalla, T., Pillon, B., Grafman, J., Dubois, B., & Agid, Y. (1995). Planning and script analysis following frontal lobe lesions. In J. Grafman, K. Holyoak, & F. Boller

(Eds.), Structure and function of the human prefrontal cortex. *Annals of New York Academy of Sciences, 279,* 277–288.

Sivak, B., & MacKenzie, C.L. (1992). The contributions of peripheral vision and central vision to prehension. In L. Proteau & E. Digby (Eds.), *Vision and motor control: Advances in psychology, No. 85* (pp. 233–259). Amsterdam: North-Holland.

Slameka, N.J., & Graf, P. (1978). The generation effect: Delineation of a phenomenon. *Journal of Experimental Psychology: Human Learning and Memory, 14,* 223–239.

Sloman, S.A., Hayman, C.A.G., Ohta, N., Law, J., & Tulving, E. (1988). Forgetting in primed fragment completion. *Journal of Experimental Psychology: Learning, Memory and Cognition, 14,* 223–239.

Smallman, H.S., & MacLeod, D.I.A. (1994). Size-disparity correlation in stereopsis at contrast threshold. *Journal of Optical Society of America, A11,* 1940–1948.

Smiley, A., Reid, L.D., & Fraser, M. (1980). Changes in driver steering control with learning. *Human Factors, 22*(4), 401–416.

Smith, A.T., & Edgar, G.K. (1994). Antagonistic comparison of temporal frequency filter outputs as a basis for speed perception. *Vision Research, 34,* 253–265.

Smith, E.E., & Jonides, J. (1997). Working memory: A view from neuroimagery. *Cognitive Psychology, 33,* 5–42.

Smith, E.E., Jonides, J., Koeppe, R.A., & Awh, E. (1995). Spatial versus object working memory: PET investigations. *Journal of Cognitive Neuroscience, 7*(3), 337–356.

Snoddy, G.S. (1926). Learning and stability. *Journal of Applied Psychology, 10,* 1–36.

Sohlberg, M.M., Sprunk, H., & Metzelaar, K. (1988). Efficacy of external cueing system in an individual with severe frontal lobe damage. *Cognitive Rehabilitation, 6,* 36–41.

Somonov, P.V., Frolov, M.V., Evtushenko, V.F., & Sviridov, E. (1977). Effect of emotional stress on the recognition of visual patterns. *Aviation, Space and Environmental Medicine,* 856–858.

Spears, W.D. (1983). *Processes of skill performance: A foundation for the design and use of training equipment.* NAVTRAEQUIPCEN 78-C-0013-4. Orlando, FL: Naval Training Equipment Center.

Spears, W.D. (1985). Measurement of learning and transfer through curve fitting. *Human Factors, 27,* 251–266.

Spurr, R.T. (1969). Subjective aspects of braking. *Automobile Engineer, 59,* 58–61.

Stablum, F., Mogentale, C., & Umilta, C. (1996). Executive functioning following mild closed head injury. *Cortex, 32*(2), 261–278.

Steblay, N.M. (1992). A meta-analytic review of the weapon focus effect. *Law and Human Behavior, 16*(4), 413–424.

Stelmach, G.E., Castiello, U., & Jeannerod, M. (1994). Orienting the finger opposition space during prehension movements. *Journal of Motor Behavior, 26*(2), 178–186.

Sternberg, S., Knoll, R.L., & Turock, D.L. (1990). Hierarchical control in the execution of action sequences: Tests of two invariance properties. In M. Jeannerod (Ed.), *Attention and performance XIII* (pp. 3–55). Hillsdale, NJ: Erlbaum.

Stevens, J.C., & Savin, H.B. (1962). On the form of learning curves. *Journal of Experimental Analysis of Behavior, 5*(1), 15–18.

Stewart, D., Cudworth, C.J., & Lishman, J.R. (1993). Misperception of time-to-collision by drivers in pedestrian accidents. *Perception, 22*(10), 1227–1244.

Stewart, D., Cudworth, C.J., & Lishman, J.R. (1997). Response to the critical note "Correcting some misperceptions of time-to-collision" by James Tresilian. *Perception*, *26*, 237–241.

Stuss, D.T., & Benson, D.F. (1983). Frontal lobe lesions and behavior. In A. Kertesz (Ed.), *Localization in neuropsychology*. New York: Academic Press.

Stuss, D.T., & Benson, D.F. (1986). *The frontal lobes*. New York: Raven Press.

Stuss, D.T., Benson, D.F., Kaplan, E.F., Weir, W.S., & Della Malva, C. (1981). Leucotomized and nonleucotomized schizophrenics: Comparison on tests of attention. *Biological Psychiatry*, *16*, 1085.

Stuss, D.T., Shallice, T., Alexander, M.P., & Picton, T.W. (1995). A multi-disciplinary approach to anterior attentional functions. In J. Grafman, K. Holyoak, & F. Boller (Eds.), Structure and function of the human prefrontal cortex. *Annals of New York Academy of Sciences*, *279*, 191–211.

Stutts, J.C. (1998). Do older drivers with visual and cognitive impairments drive less? *Journal of the American Geriatrics Society*, *46*(7), 854–861.

Sullivan, E.V., & Sagar, H.J. (1988). Nonverbal short-term impairment in Parkinson's disease. *Journal of Clinical and Experimental Neuropsychology*, *10*, 34.

Sullivan, E.V., Sagar, H.J., Cooper, J.A., & Jordan, N. (1993). Verbal and nonverbal short-term memory impairment in non-treated Parkinson's disease. *Neuropsychology*, *7*, 396–405.

Summala, H. (1981). Drivers' steering reaction to a light stimulus on a dark road. *Ergonomics*, *24*(2), 125–131.

Sun, H.J., Carey, D.P., & Goodale, M.A. (1992). A mammalian model of optic-flow utilization in the control of locomotion. *Experimental Brain Research*, *91*, 171–175.

Svenson, O. (1981). Are we all less risky and more skilful than our fellow drivers? *Acta Psychologica*, *47*, 143–148.

Taira, M., Mine, S., Georgopoulous, A.P., Murata, A., & Sakata, H. (1990). Parietal cortex neurons on the monkey related to the visual guidance of hand movements. *Experimental Brain Research*, *83*, 29–36.

Tanaka, H., & Saito, H. (1989). Analysis of motion of the visual field by direction, expansion/contraction and rotation cells clustered in the dorsal part of the medial superior temporal area of the macaque monkey. *Journal of Neurophysiology*, *62*, 626–641.

Tanner, C.M. (1989). The role of environmental toxins in the etiology of Parkinson's disease? A critical review. *Neurology*, *40*, 17–31.

Taylor, D.H. (1964). Driver's galvanic skin response and the risk of accident. *Ergonomics*, *7*, 439–451.

Teghtsoonian, R. (1973). Range effects in psychophysical scaling and a revision of Steven's law. *American Journal of Psychology*, *86*(1), 3–27.

Teghtsoonian, R., & Teghtsoonian, M. (1970). Scaling apparent distance in a natural outdoor setting. *Psychonomic Science*, *21*, 215–216.

Teigen, K.H. (1994). Yerkes-Dodson: A law for all seasons. *Theory and Psychology*, *4*, 525–547.

Thompson, C.P., Skowronski, J.J., & Lee, D.J. (1988). Telescoping in dating naturally occurring events. *Memory and Cognition*, *16*, 461–468.

Thomsen, I.V. (1990). Recognizing the development of behavior disorders. In R.L. Wood (Ed.), *Neurobehavioral sequelae of traumatic brain injury*. New York: Taylor & Francis.

Thorndike, E.L. (1906). *Principles of teaching*. New York: A.G. Seiler.

Thorndike, E.L. (1932). *The fundamentals of learning*. New York: Bureau of Publications, Teachers College.

Thurstone, L.L. (1919). The learning curve equation. *Psychological Monographs, 26*, 114.

Thurstone, L.L. (1930). The learning function, *Journal of General Psychology, 3*, 469–493.

Tillman, W.A., & Hobbs, G.E. (1949). The accident prone automobile driver: A study of the psychiatric and social background. *American Journal of Psychiatry, 106*, 321–331.

Tobias, B.A., Kihlstrom, J.F., & Schacter, D.L. (1992). Emotion and implicit memory. In S.A. Christianson (Ed.), *The handbook of emotion and memory research and theory* (pp. 167–192). Hillsdale, NJ: Erlbaum.

Tobin, A.J. (1990). Genetic disorders: Huntington's disease. In A.L. Pearlman & R.C. Collins (Eds.), *Neurobiology of disease*. New York: Oxford University Press.

Tolman, E.C. (1918). Nerve process and cognition. *Psychological Review, 25*(6), 423–442.

Tolman, E.C. (1919). English and mathematical abilities of a group of college students. *Journal of Educational Psychology, 10*(2), 95–103.

Toyama, K., Komatsu, Y., Kasai, H., Fujii, K., & Umetani, K. (1985). Responsiveness of Clare-Bishop neurons to visual cues associated with motion of a visual stimulus in three-dimensional space. *Vision Research, 25*, 407–414.

Tresilian, J.R. (1991). Empirical and theoretical issues in the perception of time-to-contact. *Journal of Experimental Psychology: Human Perception and Performance, 17*, 865–876.

Tresilian, J.R. (1995). Perceptual and cognitive processes in time-to-contact estimation: Analysis of prediction motion and relative judgement tasks. *Perception and Psychophysics, 57*, 231–245.

Tresilian, J.R. (1997). Correcting some misperceptions of time-to-collision: A critical note. *Perception, 26*, 229–236.

Triggs, T., & Berenyi, J.S. (1982). Estimation of automobile speed under day and night conditions. *Human Factors, 24*, 111–114.

Tulving, E., Schacter, D.L., & Stark, H.A. (1982). Priming effects in word-fragment completion are independent of recognition memory. *Journal of Experimental Psychology: Learning, Memory and Cognition, 8*, 336–342.

Tuokko, H., Tallman, K., Beattie, B.L., Cooper, P., & Weir, J. (1995). An examination of driving records in a dementia clinic. *Journal of Gerontology, 550*, 173–181.

Turner, J.M., Green, G., & Braunling-McMorrow, D. (1990). Differential reinforcement of low rates of responding (DRL) to reduce dysfunctional social behaviors of a head injured man. *Behavioral Residential Treatment, 5*, 7–9.

Tversky, B. (1981). Distortions in memory for maps. *Cognitive Psychology, 13*, 407–433.

Tversky, B. (1997). Memory for pictures, maps, environments and graphs. In D.G. Payne & F.G. Conrad (Eds.), *Intersections in basic and applied memory research* (pp. 257–278). Mahwah, NJ: Erlbaum.

Tzelgov, J. (1997). Specifying the relations between automaticity and consciousness: A theoretical note. *Consciousness and Cognition, 6*, 441–451.

Tzeng, O.J.L. (1976). A precedence effect in the processing of verbal information. *American Journal of Psychology*, *89*, 577–599.

Underwood, G. (1998). *Eye guidance in reading and scene perception*. Oxford: Elsevier.

Underwood, G., Chapman, P., Wright, S., & Crundall, D. (1999). Anger while driving. *Transportation Research: Traffic Psychology and Behaviour*, *2F*(1), 55–68.

Underwood, G., & Everatt, J. (1996). Automatic and controlled information processing: The role of attention in the processing of novelty. In O. Neumann & A.F. Sanders (Eds.), *Handbook of perception and action: Vol. 3. Attention*. London: Academic Press.

US Congress, Office of Technology Assessment. (1987). *Losing a million minds: Confronting the tragedy of Alzheimer's disease and other dementias* (OTA-BA-323). Washington, DC: US Government Printing Office.

Vandenberghe, R., Duncan, J., Dupont, P., Ward, R., Poline, J.B., Bormans, G., Michiels, J., Mortelmans, L., & Orban, G.A. (1997). Attention to one or two features in left or right visual field: A positron emission tomography study. *Journal of Neuroscience*, *17*(10), 3739–3750.

van der Horst, A.R.A. (1990). *A time-based analysis of road user behaviour in normal and critical encounters*. PhD thesis. TNO Institute for Perception, Soesterberg, The Netherlands.

van Rossum, J.H. (1990). Schmidt's schema theory: The empirical basis of the variability of practice hypothesis: A critical analysis. Special Issue: The learning, memory and perception of perceptual-motor skills. *Human Movement Science*, *9*, 387–435.

van Winsum, W. (1996). *From adaptive control to adaptive driver behaviour*. PhD thesis. Traffic Research Centre VSC, University of Groningen, The Netherlands.

van Winsum, W., & Brouwer, W. (1997). Time headway in car following and operational performance during unexpected braking. *Perceptual and Motor Skills*, *3*(2), 1247–1257.

van Zomeren, A.H., & Brouwer, W.H. (1987). Head injury concepts and attention. In H. Levin & J. Grafman (Eds.), *Neurobehavioral recovery from head injury*. New York: Oxford University Press.

van Zomeren, A.H., & Brouwer, W.H. (1994). *Clinical neuropsychology of attention*. New York: Oxford University Press.

Varney, N.R., Martske, J.S., & Roberts, R.J. (1988). Major depression in patients with closed head injury. *Neuropsychology*, *1*, 7–9.

Veltman, J., Brouwer, W.H., Van Zomeren, A.H., & van Woffelaar, P.C. (1996). Central executive aspects of attention in subacute severe and very severe closed head injury patients: Planning, inhibition, flexibility and divided attention. *Neuropsychology*, *10*(3), 357–367.

Verfaellie, M., Bauer, R.M., & Bowers, D. (1991). Autonomic and behavioural evidence of implicit memory in amnesia. *Brain and Cognition*, *15*, 10–25.

Verwey, W.B. (1991). *Towards guidelines for in-car information management: Driver workload in specific driving situations*. Report IZF 1991 C-13. Soesterberg, The Netherlands: Institute of Perception.

Verwey, W.B. (1994). *Mechanisms of skill in sequential motor behavior*. PhD thesis, TNO Soesterberg.

Verwey, W.B. (1996). Buffer loading and chunking in sequential key-pressing. *Journal of Experimental Psychology: Human Perception and Performance*, *22*, 544–562.

Vriezen, E.R., & Moscovitch, M. (1990). Memory for temporal order and conditional associative-learning in patients with Parkinson's disease. *Neuropsychologia, 28,* 1283–1293.

Wagenaar, W.A. (1986). My memory: A study of autobiographical memory over six years. *Cognitive Psychology, 18,* 225–252.

Wagner, H. (1982). Flow-field variables trigger landing in flies. *Nature, 297,* 147–148.

Wallace, S.A., & Weeks, D.L. (1988). Temporal constraints in the control of prehensile movement. *Journal of Motor Behavior, 20*(2), 81–105.

Wallace, W.P. (1965). Review of the historical, empirical, and theoretical status of the von Restorff phenomenon. *Psychological Bulletin, 63*(6), 410–424.

Waller, P.F. (1991). The older driver. *Human Factors, 33,* 499–505.

Waller, P.F., Trobe, J.D., & Olson, P.L. (1993). *Crash characteristics associated with early Alzheimer's disease.* Presented at the 37th annual meeting of the Association for the Advancement of Automotive Medicine, San Antonia, Texas.

Wang, Y., & Frost, B.J. (1992). Time to collision is signalled by neurons in the nucleus rotundus of pigeons. *Nature, 356,* 236–238.

Wann, J.P. (1996). Anticipating arrival: Is the tau margin a specious theory? *Journal of Experimental Psychology: Human Perception and Performance, 22,* 1031–1048.

Watts, G.R., & Quimby, A.R. (1979). *Design and validation of a driving simulator.* TRRL Report LR907. Crowthorne, UK: Transport and Road Research Laboratory.

Weiner, B. (1979). A theory of motivation for some classroom experiences. *Journal of Educational Psychology, 71,* 3–25.

Weingartner, H., Caine, E.D., & Ebert, M.H. (1979). Imagery, encoding and retrieval of information from memory: Some specific encoding changes in Huntington's disease. *Journal of Abnormal Psychology, 88,* 52–58.

Weingartner, H., Eckardt, M., & Grafman, J. (1993). The effects of repetition on memory performance in cognitively impaired patients. *Neuropsychology, 7,* 385–395.

Weinstein, N.D. (1980). Unrealistic optimism about future life events. *Journal of Personality and Social Psychology, 39,* 806–820.

Weinstein, N.D. (1982). Unrealistic optimism about susceptibility to health problems. *Journal of Behavioral Medicine, 5,* 441–460.

Weist, W.M., & Bell, B. (1985). Stevens's exponent for psychophysical scaling of perceived, remembered and inferred distance. *Psychological Bulletin, 98*(3), 457–470.

Welford, A.T. (1986). Note on the effects of practice on reaction times. *Journal of Motor Behavior, 18*(3), 343–345.

Welford, A.T. (1988). Acquiring skills: Some experiences. *Journal of Motor Behavior, 20,* 458–461.

West, R., Elander, J., & French, D. (1992). *Decision making, personality and driving style as correlates of individual risk.* TRL Report CR309. Crowthorne, UK: Transport Research Laboratory.

Wickens, C.D. (1976). The effects of divided attention on information processing in tracking. *Journal of Experimental Psychology: Human Perception and Performance, 2,* 1–13.

Wickens, C.D. (1980). The structure of attentional resources. In R. Nickerson (Ed.), *Attention and performance VIII* (pp. 239–257). Hillsdale, NJ: Erlbaum.

Wickens, C.D. (1984). Processing resources in attention. In R. Parasuraman & R. Davies (Eds.), *Varieties of attention* (pp. 63–101). New York: Academic Press.

Wickens, C.D. (1992). *Engineering psychology and human performance.* New York: Harper Collins.

Wickens, C.D., Sandry, D., & Vidulich, M. (1983). Compatibility and resource competition between modalities of input, central processing and output: Testing a model of complex task performance. *Human Factors, 25,* 227–248.

Wicker, A.W. (1969). Attitudes versus actions: The relationship of overt and behavioral responses to attitude objects. *Journal of Social Issues, 25,* 41–78.

Wierwille, W.W., Casali, J.G., & Repa, B.S. (1983). Driver steering reaction time to abrupt-onset of crosswinds as measured in a moving-base simulator. *Human Factors, 25,* 103–116.

Wilde, G.J.S. (1982). The theory of risk-homeostasis: Implications for safety and health. *Risk Analysis, 2,* 209–255.

Wilde, G.J.S., Gerszke, D., & Paulozza, L. (1998). Risk optimization and transfer. *Transportation Research: Traffic Psychology and Behaviour, F*(1), 77–93.

Williams, A.F. (1997). *Graduated licensing and other approaches to controlling young driver risk taking.* Paper presented at Risk-Taking and Traffic Safety, Chatham, MA, 19–22 October.

Willingham, D.B. (1998). A neuropsychological theory of motor skill learning. *Psychological Review, 105*(3), 558–584.

Wills, T.A. (1981). Downward comparison principles in social psychology. *Psychological Bulletin, 90,* 245–271.

Wing, A.M., & Fraser, C. (1983). The contribution of the thumb to reaching movements. *Quarterly Journal of Experimental Psychology, 35,* 297–260.

Wing, A.M., Turton, A., & Fraser, C. (1986). Grasp size and accuracy of approach in reaching. *Journal of Motor Behavior, 18*(3), 245–260.

Wolfe, J.M., & Bennett, S.C. (1997). Pre-attentive object files: Shapeless bundles of basic features. *Vision Research, 37,* 25–43.

Wood, L. (1987). *Brain injury rehabilitation: A neurobehavioral approach.* London: Croom Helm.

Wright, M.J., Burns, R.J., Geffen, G.M., & Geffen, L.B. (1990). Covert orientation of visual attention in Parkinson's disease: An impairment in the maintenance of attention. *Neuropsychologia, 28,* 151–159.

Wulf, G., Schmidt, R.A., & Deubel, H. (1993). Reduced feedback frequency enhances generalized motor program learning but not parametrization learning. *Journal of Experimental Psychology: Learning, Memory and Cognition, 19,* 1134–1150.

Yarbus, A.L. (1967). *Eye movements and vision.* New York: Plenum Press.

Yarmey, A.D. (1990). Accuracy and confidence of duration estimates following marked and unmarked modifiers. *Journal of Applied Social Psychology, 20,* 1139–1149.

Yerkes, R.M., & Dodson, J.D. (1908). The relation of strength of stimulus to rapidity of habit-formation. *Journal of Comparative Neurology and psychology, 18,* 459–482.

Yilmaz, E.H., & Warren, W.H. (1995). Visual control of braking: A test of the tau hypothesis. *Journal of Experimental Psychology: Human Perception and Performance, 21*(5), 996–1014.

Yudofsky, S.C., Silver, J.M., & Schneider, S.E. (1987). Pharmacologic treatment of aggression. *Psychiatric Annals, 17,* 397–407.

Zeki, S. (1993). *A vision of the brain.* Oxford: Blackwell Scientific Publications.

Zenicus, A.H., & Wesoloski, M.D. (1990). Using stress management to decrease inappropriate behavior in a brain injured adult. *Behavioral Residential Treatment, 5,* 61–64.

Zuckerman, M., & Lubin, B. (1985). *Manual for the Multiple Affect Adjective Checklist.* San Diego, CA: Educational & Industrial Testing Service.

Zwann, R.A. (1994). Effect of genre expectations on text comprehension. *Journal of Experimental Psychology: Learning, Memory, and Cognition, 20,* 920–933.

# Author Index

Adams, R.D., 76, 181
Adelson, E.H., 9
Agid, Y., 185
Ajzen, I., 144
Albert, M.S., 105, 180, 182, 183
Alderton, D.L., 27, 94
Alexander, M.P., 56, 57, 62, 63, 67, 74
Alivisatos, B., 108
Allard, F., 101
Allen, S.W., 101
Allport, D.A., 73
Alpert, N.M., 105
Alsop, D.C., 108
Amaducci, L.A., 179
Anderson, E., 172
Anderson, J.R., 55, 65, 66, 80, 88, 89,
    91, 92
Anderson, M.C., 60
Anderson, N.D., 168
Andrade, J., 99
Andrews, D., 183
Annett, J., 95
Antes, J.R., 134
Antonis, B., 73
Aoki, T., 51
Arjunan, K.N., 173
Awh, E., 108

Bachman, D.L., 179
Backman, L., 182
Baddeley, A.D., 57, 65, 70, 73, 100,
    107, 110, 111, 116, 117, 128, 182
Badgaiyan, R.D., 105
Bahde, S., 18
Bajulayie, O.I., 182
Baker, S.C., 108
Ball, K., 168, 170, 171, 178
Balota, D., 108, 110
Bandura, A., 143, 160
Bandy, D., 105
Bannister, R., 184
Bargh, J.A., 67
Barone, P., 31
Barrett, D., 175
Battle, D.S., 51
Bauer, R.M., 104
Baumhart, R., 145
Bayles, K.A., 184, 185
Beattie, B.L., 186
Beatty, W.W., 185
Becker, J.T., 182
Beckmann, J., 64
Bekerian, D.A., 100
Belanger, A.J., 179
Bell, B., 6

Ben-Shoham, I., 69
Bennett, S.C., 135
Benson, D.F., 57, 60, 180
Benson, P., 138
Bentler, P.M., 145
Berenyi, J.S., 11
Bergen, J.R., 9
Berthelon, C., 7, 21, 22
Beusmans, J.M.H., 51
Beverley, K.I., 9
Biehl, B., 75
Bilodeau, E.A., 95
Bilodeau, I.M., 95
Bitter, C.F., 174, 175
Bjerre, B., 178
Bjork, E.L., 60
Bjork, R.A., 60, 81, 104, 145
Blana, E., 199
Blaxton, T.A., 104
Blomqvist, C., 178
Bloom, B.S., 96
Blusewicz, M.J., 183
Bocca, W.A., 179
Boer, E.R., 51
Bohhanon, J.N., 127
Boldovici, J.A., 96
Boller, F., 185
Bond, M.R., 173, 174
Bondi, M.W., 185
Bontke, C.F., 174
Bormans, G., 60
Borst, A., 18
Bourke, P.A., 69
Bourne, L.E., 86, 106, 137
Bowers, D., 104
Boyce, S.J., 134
Brackstone, M., 46
Bradburn, N.M., 116, 117
Bradshaw, J.A., 183
Bradshaw, J.L., 27, 183
Brady, C.B., 182
Brady, S., 82, 84, 154
Brady, S.J., 47
Braekhus, A., 178
Bragg, B.W.E., 146
Brandt, J., 183, 184
Bransford, J.D., 100

Braunling-McMorrow, D., 174
Breckler, S.J., 145
Brehmer, B., 192
Brenner, R.P., 182
Britten, K.H., 8
Broadbent, D.E., 90
Brookes, M., 172
Brooks, D.J., 28
Brooks, L.R., 101
Brotherton, F.A., 174
Brouwer, W.H., 175, 176, 177, 178
Brown, A.L., 92
Brown, G.D.A., 107
Brown, I., 36, 38, 68, 70
Brown, I.D., 65, 66, 67, 68, 70, 75, 110, 111, 145
Brown, J.D., 147
Brown, N.R., 115
Brown, R.G., 185
Brown, S.L., 182
Bruce, V., 6
Bryan, L.B., 84
Bryden, J., 173
Bullemer, P., 105
Burke, W.H., 173, 175
Burns, R.J., 184
Burroughs, W.J., 113
Burton, P.L., 174
Butters, N., 183, 184
Bylsma, F.W., 178, 184
Byrne, R.W., 112

Caine, E.D., 183, 184
Caird, J.K., 21, 22
Carey, D.P., 18
Carillo, R., 173
Carlson, V.R., 7
Carr, D.B., 178
Carsten, O.M.J., 12, 13, 16, 199
Carter, C., 45
Casali, J.G., 35, 36
Cassidy, J.W., 174
Castiello, U., 31
Catalano, J.F., 93
Cavallo, V., 7, 21, 22
Censits, D.M., 108
Chapman, P., 162

Chapman, P.R., 45, 51, 52, 121, 125, 130, 132, 136, 140
Charness, N., 80, 101
Chase, W.G., 101
Chi, M.T.H., 92
Chiu, E., 183
Christiaens, D., 134
Christianson, S.A., 126, 127
Christie, R., 136
Chui, H.C., 180
Churchland, P.S., 134
Clegg, B.A., 68, 75, 82, 84, 106, 130, 132, 138
Cobb, J.L., 179
Cogan, D.G., 181
Cohen, A.S., 52
Comte, S., 12, 13, 16, 21, 23, 112
Conway, M.A., 115, 144
Cooper, J.A., 185
Cooper, P., 186
Cooper, P.J., 186
Cope, W., 173, 174
Courtney, S.M., 108
Cowan, N., 73, 74
Craighero, L., 27
Craik, F.I.M., 100, 168
Craver-Lemley, C., 111
Crick, J.L., 136, 137, 139
Cronin-Golumb, A., 185
Cross, P.S., 179
Crossman, E.R.F.W., 76
Crundall, D., 162
Cudworth, C.J., 7, 22
Culley, S., 172
Cumming, B.G., 10
Cummings, J.L., 179, 180, 181, 183, 184
Curran, T., 100, 105
Cutting, J.T., 6

Da Silva, C.B., 6
Da Silva, J.A., 6
Dagostino, R.B., 179
Damasio, A.R., 182
Davidson, M.C., 28
de Groot, A.D., 101
Deakin, J.M., 101

Deaton, A.V., 174
Decary, A., 60
Deems, D.A., 184
Deffenbacher, J.L., 126, 162
Degraef, P., 134
Delis, D.C., 182, 183
Della Malva, C., 60
Della Sala, S., 181
DeLucia, P.R., 21
Demadura, T.L., 183
Dennis, C., 183
Denton, G.G., 12, 14
D'Esposito, M., 108
Detre, J.A., 108
Detwiler, M., 21, 22
Deubel, H., 96
di Pellegrino, G., 27
DiGirolamo, G.J., 56, 88, 91, 104, 106
Doane, S.M., 27, 94
Dobbs, A.R., 169
Dodson, J.D., 126
Dolan, R.J., 61, 108
Donges, E., 48
Dos Santos, R.A., 6
Doty, R.L., 184
Drachman, D.A., 186
Driskell, J.E., 122
Dubois, B., 185
Duchnicky, R.L., 81, 82
Duffy, C.J., 19
Dumais, S.T., 66, 67
Duncan, J., 36, 38, 60, 67, 68, 69, 70, 107, 111
Dunn, M.E., 174
Dunning, D., 145, 146, 147
Dupont, P., 60
d'Ydewalle, G., 134

Eames, P., 173, 174
Ebbinghaus, H., 80
Ebert, M.H., 183, 184
Edgar, G.K., 9
Egan, D.E., 101
Einstein, G.O., 86
Eiser, J.R., 145
Ekman, P., 159
Elander, J., 76, 158

Ellsworth, P.C., 126
Elmslie, H., 70, 107
Endlsey, M.R., 140
Englund, L., 178
Ericsson, K.A., 80, 86, 101, 102
Erikson, B., 51
Eslinger, P.J., 182
ETSC, xv
Evans, A.C., 108
Evans, L., xv, 11, 12, 166
Everatt, J., 66
Evtushenko, V.F., 128

Fadiga, L., 27
Fairclough, S.H., 45
Fairweather, M., 21
Farah, M.J., 111
Fazio, R.H., 145
Fendrich, D.W., 106, 137
Fernandez-Duque, D., 56, 88, 91, 104
Ferreira, F., 134
Field, D., 111, 140, 149, 151, 152, 153,
        156, 191, 201
Fiez, J.A., 108, 110
Fincham, J.M., 89
Finn, P., 146
Fishbein, M., 144
Fisher, R.P., 128
Fisk, A.D., 60, 137
Fitts, P.M., 88
Fletcher, P., 61, 109
Fogassi, L., 27
Folkman, S., 159
Folstein, S.E., 180, 183, 184
Frackowiak, R.S., 108, 110
Frackowiak, R.S.J., 28, 61
Frackowiak, S.J., 108
Franks, J.J., 100
Fraser, C., 31
Freedman, M., 181
French, D., 76, 158
Frick, J., 46
Friedland, R.P., 178, 182
Friedman, A., 134
Frith, C.D., 28, 61, 108, 109, 110
Frolov, M.V., 128
Frost, B.J., 18

Fuchs, P., 3
Fujii, K., 19
Fuller, R., 121

Gallese, V., 27
Garcia, J., 173, 174, 175
Garde, F.H. 174
Gathercole, S., 107
Geffen, G.M., 184
Geffen, L.B., 184
Geiselman, R.E., 128
Georgeson, M.A., 6
Georgopoulous, A.P., 31
Gerszke, D., 121
Gesi, A.T., 106, 137
Gibson, J.J., 22
Glahn, D.C., 108
Godthelp, L.I., 48, 49
Golbe, L.I., 181
Goodale, M.A., 18
Goodin, D.S., 181
Gopher, D., 72
Gottsdanker, R.M., 46
Grady, M., 183
Graesser, A.C., 114
Graf, P., 104, 144
Grafman, J., 65, 66, 181
Graham, E., 184
Grande, G.E., 143, 146, 148, 149, 152,
        155, 194, 198
Granerus, A.K., 180, 181
Grasby, P., 61, 109
Grayson, G., 133, 140
Grayson, G.B., 151, 153, 156, 195, 201
Grealy, M.A., 171
Green, D.E., 146, 147
Green, G., 174
Green, P.R., 6
Greeno, J.G., 80
Grimes, J., 134
Groeger, J.A., 6, 7, 12, 13, 16, 21, 23,
        45, 47, 68, 71, 75, 81, 82, 84, 85,
        97, 105, 107, 108, 111, 112, 115,
        121, 125, 127, 128, 130, 132, 138,
        140, 143, 144, 145, 146, 148, 149,
        151, 152, 153, 154, 155, 156, 160,
        162, 163, 191, 194, 198, 199, 201

Gur, R.C., 108
Gurd, J.M., 185
Gurland, B.J., 179

Haarland, K.Y., 185
Haffey, W.J., 173, 174
Hakamies-Blomqvist, L., 178
Haley, W.E., 182
Hammond, S., 111, 140, 149, 151, 152, 153, 156, 191, 201
Hancock, P.A., 18, 21, 22, 96
Harrington, D.L., 185
Harris, B.S.H., 173
Harter, N., 84
Hastie, R., 77, 78, 79, 81, 84
Haxby, J.V., 108, 179, 182
Hayes, S.E., 28
Hayman, C.A.G., 104
Healy, A.F., 86, 106, 137
Heckhausen, H., 64
Hedges, L., 116, 117
Hedges, L.V., 117
Heider, F., 144
Heindel, W., 184
Heindel, W.C., 183
Helander, M., 50
Heller, R.B., 169
Hellhammer, D.H., 122
Hellige, J.B., 9
Henderson, J.M., 133, 134
Herlitz, A., 182
Heuer, F., 126, 127
Hildreth, E.C., 10, 51
Hintzman, D.L., 100, 114
Hirtle, S.C., 101, 113
Hitch, G., 107
Hobbs, G.E., 165
Hoffman, E.R., 20, 46, 137
Hoffman, H., 127
Hoffman, M., 174
Hoge, S., 175
Holland, C.A., 171, 178
Hollingworth, A., 133, 134
Holyoak, K.J., 113
Holzberg, A.D., 146, 147
Horberg, U., 51
Horneman, C., 76

Horswill, M.S., 139
Horton, A.M., 175
Horwood, J., 49, 50
Hubel, D.H., 9
Huber, S.J., 184
Hughes, S., 122
Hull, C.L., 77, 80
Hull, M., 136
Hulme, C., 107
Hunt, R.D., 184
Hunt, R.R., 86
Huttenlocher, J., 116, 117
Hyde, T.S., 100

Idikowski, C., 128
Immink, M.A., 87
Ivry, R.B., 27

Jacobs, H.E., 173, 174
Jamson, H., 12, 13, 16, 199
Jarvik, L.F., 179
Jeannerod, M., 26, 30, 31, 32
Jenkins, J.J., 100
Jennett, B., 171, 172
Johansson, K., 178
Johnson, D.A., 171
Johnson, P., 177
Johnson-Laird, P.N., 159
Johnston, E.B., 10
Johnston, W.A., 102
Jonah, B.A., 166
Jones, C.D., 60, 137
Jonides, J., 67, 108, 113
Jordan, N., 185
Joseph, J.P., 31
Judd, C.H., 91
Jueptner, M., 28

Kahn, R.L., 178
Kahneman, D., 73
Kaiser, H.F., 195
Kalsbeek, W.D., 173
Kanner, A.D., 159
Kaplan, E.F., 60
Kaplan, S., 175
Kasai, H., 19
Kassin, S.M., 126

Kaszniak, A.W., 182, 185
Kay, H., 95
Kazdin, A.E., 174
Keele, S.W., 28, 67, 106
Keil, K., 108
Kemp, F., 176
Kemper, T.L., 180, 182, 183
Kentros, S.A., 182
Kihlstrom, J.F., 128, 182
Kincade, R.G., 96
Kintsch, W., 101, 102
Kirker, W.S., 144
Kirschbaum, C., 122
Kleiner, B.M., 93
Klemetz, G., 178
Kline, D.W., 3
Knauper, B., 168, 169
Knoegel, J.E., 179
Knoll, R.L., 90
Koch, C., 134
Koenderink, J.J., 18
Koeppe, R.A., 108
Koh, K., 93
Kolers, P., 81, 82, 106
Kolodny, J., 70, 107
Komatsu, Y., 19
Kopelman, M.D., 182
Koss, E., 182
Kosslyn, S.M., 26
Kraus, J.F., 173
Kremer, J.H., 183
Kroemer, K.H.E., 35, 43
Krupat, E., 136
Kruysse, H.W., 136
Kuiper, N.A., 144

Lajunen, T., 162
Lalonde, F., 181
Lam, C.S., 177
Land, M.F., 36, 49, 50
Landy, M.S., 10
Lane, D.M., 101
Lane, N.E., 94
Lapierre, M.-P., 60
Larwood, L., 145
Laurent, M., 21, 22
Law, J., 104

Lazarus, R.S., 159
Lee, D.J., 116, 117
Lee, D.N., 17, 18, 22, 36, 42, 46, 47, 49
Lee, M.D., 137
Lee, T.D., 87
Lehmann, A.C., 80
Lester, J.F., 115, 119, 167
Levin, B.E., 181
Levine, E.G., 182
Lewis, C., 146, 147
Lewis, C.H., 92
Lewis, F.D., 173, 174, 175
Lewis, V.J., 116
Lezak, M.D., 61
Linn, R.T., 179
Lishman, J.R., 7, 22, 46, 47
Lishman, W.A., 179
Litvan, I., 181
Liu, A., 51, 52
Livingstone, M.S., 9
Lockhart, R.S., 100
Lockherd, R., 46
Lockwood, C.R., 115, 119, 167
Loftus, E.F., 117, 127, 128
Loftus, G., 127
Loftus, G.R., 127
Logan, G.D., 67, 80, 88, 90, 121, 139, 191
Logie, R.H., 73, 107, 112
Lopez, O.I., 182
Lorge, I., 95
Lubin, B., 160
Lundberg, C., 178
Luoma, J., 51
Luria, A.R., 63, 64
Lynch, R.S., 126, 162

MacDonald, C.A., 104
Mace, D.G.W., 51
Mack, J.L., 182
MacKay, D.G., 65, 88, 89
MacKenzie, C.L., 31
MacLeod, D.I.A., 5, 8
MacMillan, R., 172
Magill, R.A., 87
Mah, W.A., 113
Mahoney, J.V., 133

Malaterre, G., 196
Mangels, J.A., 27
Manser, M.P., 18, 21, 22
Marburger, W., 117
Marcel, A.J., 67
Markus, H., 149
Marottoli, R.A., 171
Marsden, C.D., 185
Martin, G., 174
Martin, R., 181
Martske, J.S., 173, 175
Massman, P.J., 183
Masson, M.E.J., 93
Mathews, M.L., 146
Mattingley, J.B., 27, 183
Maunsell, J.H.R., 9
May, A.J., 45
Maycock, G., 97, 115, 119, 151, 153,
    156, 167, 201
Mazur, J.E., 77, 78, 79, 81, 84
Mazzini, L., 181
McBratnie, B.P., 174
McClelland, J.L., 89
McCormick, I.A., 146, 147
McDermott, K.B., 105
McDonald, M., 46
McDowell, E.D., 50
McGuire, T.L., 84, 173
McGwin, G., 168, 169, 170, 171
McKeithen, K.B., 101
McKenna, F., 136, 137, 139
McKenna, F.P., 139, 146, 147
McKnight, A.J., 76, 170
McKnight, A.S., 170
McLaughlin, C.M., 67
McLaurin, R.L., 173
McLeod, P., 67
McLeod, R.W., 17, 21, 22
McNitt-Gray, J., 21
Means, B., 117
Meir, M., 69
Mendelow, A.D., 172
Mendez, M.A., 181
Mendez, M.F., 181
Merat, N., 71, 107, 112
Merigan, W.H., 9
Mermis, B.J., 174

Messo, J., 127
Mestre, D., 7, 21, 22
Mesulam, M.-M., 59
Metzelaar, K., 174
Meyer, D.E., 93
Meyer, E., 108
Meyer, R.E., 92
Meyerowitz, J.A., 145, 146, 147
Michiels, J., 60
Michon, J.A., 65
Milan, M.A., 174
Milberg, W., 182, 183
Milic, J., 12
Miller, J.D., 173
Miller, L., 174
Milosevic, S., 11, 12
Mine, S., 31
Mingay, D.J., 117
Minoshima, S., 108
Mintun, M.A., 108
Miura, T., 51
Mogentale, C., 176
Molchan, S., 181
Molloy, R., 176
Monsell, S., 62
Moran, A.R., 146
Morgan, R.B., 85, 86
Morris, C.D., 100
Morris, R.D., 182
Morris, R.G., 182
Mortelmans, L., 60
Mortimer, J.A., 179
Mortimer, R.G., 20, 137
Moscato, B.S., 173
Moscovitch, M., 60, 185
Moss, M.B., 180, 182, 183
Mourant, R.R., 48, 50
Movshon, J.A., 8
Murata, A., 31
Murray, S., 172
Mutter, S.A., 176
Myles-Worsley, M., 102

Naatanen, R., 121
Nairne, J.S., 100
Naveh-Benjamin, M., 67
Navon, D., 72

Nawrot, M., 10
Neary, D., 179, 180, 183
Nebes, R.D., 115, 182
Nestor, P.G., 182
Newcomb, T.M., 144
Newell, A., 76, 78, 79, 80
Newhouse, P.A., 181
Newsome, W.T., 8
Nicolich, R., 92
Nigam, A., 117
Nilsson, L.G., 127
Nimmo-Smith, I., 67, 68, 70, 111, 116
Nissen, M.J., 105
Nockleby, D.M., 174
Norman, D.A., 57, 63, 64, 66, 101
Nunes, L.M., 12, 13
Nurius, P., 149

Oatley, K., 159
Ober, B.A., 182, 183
Odenheimer, G.L., 178
OECD, 178
Oetting, E.R., 126, 162
Ohta, N., 104
Oldak, R., 21, 22
Olson, P.L., 35, 51, 186
O'Neill, D., 178
Oppy, B., 100
Orban, G.A., 60
Owen, A.M., 108
Owsley, C., 168, 170, 171

Pandya, D.N., 59
Parasuraman, R., 176, 179, 182
Park, D.C., 168, 169
Parker, D., 162
Pashler, H.E., 61, 91
Passingham, R.E., 28
Patrick, J., 96
Patterson, M.B., 182
Paulesu, E., 108, 110
Paulozza, L., 121
Paulsen, J.S., 184
Payne, D.G., 126
Pear, J., 174
Pellegrino, J.W., 27, 94
Pelz, D.C., 136

Pennington, N., 92
Pentland, A.P., 4, 51
Pentland, J.G., 134
Perrett, D., 138
Peterson, C., 161, 162
Peterson, S.E., 56, 58
Petrides, M., 108
Philips, J.G., 183
Picton, T.W., 56, 57, 62, 63, 67, 74
Pierson, J.M., 183
Pillon, B., 185
Pirozzolo, F.J., 179
Poggio, G., 5
Poggio, T., 5
Poline, J.B., 60
Pollatsek, A., 134
Pollens, R.D.E., 174
Posner, M.I., 56, 58, 88, 105
Posner, M.J., 88, 91, 104
Poulin, C., 19
Predebon, J., 6, 7
Priddy, D.A., 177
Prigatano, G.P., 173
Prohaska, V., 116, 117

Quimby, A.R., 140

Rabbitt, P.M.A., 171, 178
Radavansky, G.A., 113, 114
Rafal, R.D., 28
Ragland, J.D., 108
Rahm, J., 92
Raichle, M.E., 56
Raife, M.E., 108, 110
Ramachandran, V.S., 134
Rapcsak, S.Z., 182
Rauch, S.L., 105
Rausecker, J.P., 19
Reason, J.T., 63, 64
Recarte, M.A., 12, 13
Reddish, P.E., 18
Reeves, A., 111
Regan, D., 9
Reid, L.D., 48
Reiman, E., 105
Reisberg, D., 126, 127
Reitman, J.S., 101

Repa, B.S., 35, 36
Restle, F., 80
Rey, G.J., 181
Reynolds, C.F., 182
Reynolds, P., 73
Richardson, E.D., 171
Richardson-Klavehn, A., 104, 145
Richer, F., 60
Rios, C., 126, 127
Rips, L.J., 115, 116
Rizzo, M., 178
Rizzolatti, G., 27
Robbins, T.W., 108
Roberts, R.J., 173, 175
Robertson, L., 101
Rockwell, T.H., 48, 50
Roediger, H.L., 104, 105, 106
Rogers, R.D., 62, 108
Rogers, T.B., 144
Rogers, W.A., 137
Rose, F.D., 171
Rosen, J., 182
Rosenbaum, A., 175
Rosenbloom, P.S., 76, 78, 79, 80
Rosenthal, M., 173, 174
Ross, H.E., 17, 21, 22
Rossor, M., 179
Roth, E.C., 9
Rothenberg, M.B., 173
Rouleau, I., 60
Rousey, C.G., 173
Rousey, C.L., 173
Rowe, J.W., 178
Royden, C.S., 51
Rubens, A.B., 182
Rubin, D.C., 115, 116, 117
Rueter, H.H., 101
Rumelhart, D.E., 89
Runeson, S., 46
Rushton, S.K., 171
Rutley, K.S., 51

Sadalla, E.K., 113
Sagar, H.J., 184, 185
Sagberg, F., 166
Saint-Cyr, J.A., 184, 185
Saint-Hilaire, J.-M., 60

Saito, H., 19
Sakata, H., 31
Salame, P., 107
Salas, E., 122
Salmon, D.P. 183, 184,
Sandry, D., 73
Savage, C.R., 105
Savin, H.B., 79, 81
Scallen, S.F., 96
Schacter, D.L., 104, 105, 128, 159, 182
Schelin, M., 178
Schiff, W., 21, 22
Schlag, B., 178
Schmidt, I.W., 176
Schmidt, R.A., 32, 65, 81, 94, 95, 96
Schneider, S.E., 173
Schneider, V.I., 86
Schneider, W., 55, 66, 67, 78, 138
Schnell, A.H., 182
Schoenberg, B.S., 179
Schopflocher, D., 169
Schwartz, B.J., 101
Schwartz, D., 108, 110
Schwartz, M.F., 64, 65
Schwartz, N., 168, 169
Seely, R.R., 175
Seideman, M., 178
Sejnowski, T.J., 134
Sekiya, H., 21
Sekuler, R., 10
Sellen, A.J., 64, 66
Sereno, M.E., 9
Shadlen, M.N., 8
Shah, V., 21, 22
Shallice, T., 56, 57, 61, 62, 63, 67, 74, 109
Shapiro, D.C., 95
Shea, J.B., 85, 86
Shevell, S.K., 115, 116
Shiffrin, R.M., 55, 66, 67, 138
Shimizu, N., 27
Shin, R.K., 108
Shinar, A., 50, 162
Shinar, D., 69
Shults, C.W., 183
Shuttleworth, E.C., 184
Sidaway, B., 21

Silfvenius, H., 127
Silver, J.M., 173
Simmonds, D.C.V., 70, 110
Simon, H.A., 101
Simons, M.A., 102
Simpson, J.I., 18
Singer, M., 114
Singley, M.K., 91, 92
Sivak, B., 31
Sivak, M., 35
Skowronski, J.J., 116, 117
Slameka, N.J., 144
Sloman, S.A., 104
Smallman, H.S., 5, 8
Smith, A.T., 9
Smith, C.A., 159
Smith, E.E., 108
Smith, V.L., 126
Smyth, K.A., 181
Snoddy, G.S., 76
Soderberg, S., 50
Sohlberg, M.M., 174
Sohn, Y.W., 27, 94
Somonov, P.V., 128
Sowden, J.S., 179, 180, 183
Spears, W.D., 78
Spechart, G., 145
Sprunk, H., 174
Spurr, R.T., 42
Stablum, F., 176
Stanier, R.A., 146, 147
Staplin, L.J., 113
Starkes, J.l., 101
Steblay, N.M, 127
Stellar, S., 184
Stelmach, G.E., 31
Stephan, K.M., 28
Stephens, T.D., 175
Sternberg, S., 90
Stevens, J.C., 79, 81
Stewart, D., 7, 22
Stove, A.G., 45
Stradling, S., 162
Strauss, M., 183
Strauss, M.E., 184
Stuss, D.T., 56, 57, 60, 62, 63, 67, 74

Stutts, J.C., 170
Sudman, S., 168, 169
Sullivan, E.V., 184, 185
Summala, H., 36, 121
Sun, H.J., 18
Sunderland, T., 181
Svenson, O., 145
Sviridov, E., 128
Swearer, J., 186
Swinnen, S., 95
Symons, V.L., 127

Taira, M., 31
Tallal, P., 108, 110
Tallman, K., 178, 186
Tanaka, H., 19
Tanner, C.M., 181
Tassone, E.P., 7
Tate, P., 175
Taylor, A.E., 184, 185
Taylor, D.H., 125
Teghtsoonian, M., 6
Teghtsoonian, R., 6, 7
Teigen, K.H., 126
Thomas, L.L., 174
Thompson, C.P., 116, 117
Thompson, K., 181
Thomsen, I.V., 174, 175
Thorndike, E.L., 91, 95
Thurstone, L.L., 76, 77
Tickner, A.H., 70, 110
Tillman, W.A., 165
Tobias, B.A., 128
Tobin, A.J., 180
Tolman, E.C., 80
Tomer, R., 181
Toyama, K., 19
Trabasso, T., 114
Tresilian, J.R., 17, 21, 22, 23, 47
Trevisan, M., 173
Triggs, T., 11
Trobe, J.D., 186
Tulving, E., 104, 105
Tuokko, H., 186
Turner, J.M., 174
Turock, D.L., 90
Turton, A., 31

Tzersky, B., 112, 138, 140
Tzelgov, J., 67
Tzeng, O.J.L., 116

Ullman, S., 133, 134
Umetani, K., 19
Umilta, C., 176
Umlauf, R.L., 174
Underwood, G., 48, 51, 52, 66, 136, 140, 162
Ungerleider, L.G., 108
US Congress, Office of Technology Assessment, 179

van der Horst, A.R.A., 43
van der Pligt, J., 145
van Doorn, A.J., 18
van Hoesen, G.W., 59
Van Lehn, K.A., 92
van Rossum, J.H., 94
van Winsum, W., 43, 44
van Woffelaar, P.C., 176, 177
van Zomeren, A.H., 176, 177
Vandenberghe, R., 60
Vanier, M., 176
Varney, N.R., 173, 175
Veltman, J., 176
Veltri, L., 51
Verfaellie, M., 104
Verwey, W.B., 30, 71
Victor, M., 181
Vidulich, M., 73
Viitanen, M., 178, 182
von Grunau, M.W., 19
Vriezen, E.R., 185

Wagner, H., 18
Walicke, P.A., 183
Walkey, F.H., 146, 147
Wallace, S.A., 31
Wallace, W.P., 127
Waller, P.F., 178, 186
Wang, Y., 18
Wann, J.P., 18
Ward, D.D., 185
Ward, R., 60
Warren, W.H., 45

Watts, G.R., 140
Weeks, D.L., 31
Weingarter, H., 181
Weingartner, H., 183, 184
Weinstein, N.D., 145
Weir, J., 186
Weir, W.S., 60
Weist, W.M., 6
Welford, A.T., 65, 67
Wesoloski, M.D., 174
West, R., 76, 158
Wetzler, S.E., 115
White, L.R., 179
Whitehouse, D.J., 182
Whitehouse, P.J., 181
Wickens, C.D., 66, 73, 109
Wicker, A.W., 144
Wierwille, W.W., 35, 36
Wilde, G.J.S., 121
Willer, B.S., 173
Williams, A.F., 76
Williams, P., 36, 38, 67, 68, 70, 111
Willingham, D.B., 28, 33, 104
Wills, T.A., 147
Winblab, B., 178
Wing, A.M., 31
Wisotzek, I.E., 174
Withaar, F.K., 175, 176
Withington, J., 107
Wolf, P.A., 179
Wolfe, J.M., 135
Wood, L., 173, 174
Wright, D.L., 87
Wright, M.J., 184
Wright, S., 162
Wulf, G., 96
Wurtz, R.H., 19

Yarbus, A.L., 134
Yarmey, A.D., 117
Yerkes, R.M., 126
Yilmaz, E.H., 45
Young, D.E., 95
Young, D.S., 18
Yudofsky, S.C., 173
Yun, L.S., 105

Zacks, R.T., 113, 114
Zarrow, M., 117
Zeki, S., 26, 31
Zenucus, A.H., 174

Zimny, S.T., 86
Zohary, E., 8
Zuckerman, M., 160
Zwann, R.A., 114

# Subject Index

Accelerator-to-brake movement, 35
Accidents
  child pedestrians, 7, 21–22
  in dementia sufferers, 186
  and driver age, 166–168, 170, 171,
    178
  and driver experience, 166–167
  and driver training, 75–76
  financial costs of, xv–xvi
  head injuries resulting from,
    172–173
  memory for, 114–119
  statistics, xv
Accommodation, 4
ACT*/ACT-R theory, 88–89, 90
Action Disorganization Syndrome,
  65
Action plans, 195–197
Action point, 46
Acts of Parliament, xiv
Age, see Driver age; Elderly drivers
Aggression, 162–163
Alzheimer's disease, 179, 181–182
Anger, 162–163
Arousal
  and danger, 122–125
  and memory, 126–131

Attention, 56–63
  schemata, 57–63
  setting, 58, 59
  shared, 59, 60–61
  sustained, 58–59
  switching, 59, 61–62
Attitudes, 143–145
Attributional style, 161–162
Automaticity, 65–69, 138–139
Autonomic responses, 122–125

Basal ganglia, 27–28
Behaviour and attitudes, 144–145
Blur, 4
Brain injury, see Traumatic brain injury
Braking
  accelerator-to-brake movement, 35
  collision avoidance, 42–45

Car following, 45–48
Central executive, 107, 108, 109, 110
Cerebellum, 27
Chess, 101
Child pedestrian accidents, 7, 21–22
Cingulate cortex, 26, 31, 61
Closed head injury, see Head injury
COBALT model, 28–29

Collision avoidance, 42–45
Collision time, 17–23
Concentration, 59
Cones, 2
Contention scheduling, 57
Context neurons, 31
Contextual interference, 85–87
Controlled processing, 66

Danger, 121–141
    driver assessment of, 132–133
    memory for, 125–131
    physiological response to, 122–125
Date recall, 115–119
Declarative knowledge, 88, 89
Dementia, 177–185
    road accidents involving sufferers of,
        186
Depth of field, 4
Depth perception, 4–6
Disparity, 4–5
Distance estimation, 6–8
Distractions when driving, 69–74
Downward comparison, 147
Driver age, 166–171
    accident involvement, 166–168, 170,
        171, 178
    reaction time, 34–35
    self-assessment of ability, 153,
        171
    see also Elderly drivers
Driver experience
    accident involvement, 166–167
    distraction-induced effects on driving,
        71, 72
    gaze patterns, 48
    gear changing, 68, 69
    hazard perception, 135, 136
    self-assessment of ability, 152–153
    speed estimation, 16
    time-to-collision estimation, 22
Driver training, 75–76, 82–85, 94–95,
    96–97, 138
Driving
    distractions during, 69–74
    four facet theory of, 190–204
    historical aspects, xiii–xiv

learning to, 82–85, 94–95, 96–97
    self-assessment of ability, 145–152
Driving scene assessment, 132–136
Driving tests
    for experienced drivers, 160–162
    outcome and self-belief in driving
        ability, 154–155
Dual tasks, 69–74

Elderly drivers, 168–171
    accident involvement, 168, 170, 171,
        178
    dementia in, 178
    numbers of, 177–178
    reaction time, 34, 35
    self-assessment of ability, 153, 171
    time-to-collision estimation, 22
    visibility problems in, 3
Emotions, 159–163
Endocrine responses, 122
Everyday errors, 64–65
Experience and learning, 101–103,
        see also Driver experience
Explicit memory, 104–106
Extra-pyramidal system, 26
Eye movements
    gaze patterns, 48–53
    vergence, 4

Fatality rates, xv
Fear, see Danger
Feedback, 95–96
Flicker, 9
Fog, 3, 11
Following behaviour, 45–48
Foot reaction time, 34–35
Four facet theory of driving, 190–204
Frontal lobe dementia, 179, 180, 182–183

Gaze patterns, 48–53
Gear changing, 29–32, 36–38
    automaticity of, 67–69
    changing-up and changing-down,
        37–38, 68
Gender-related differences
    speed adjustment, 16
    time-to-collision estimation, 22

Goal interruption, 191–193
Grasp, 31

Hand reaction time, 34, 35–36
Hazard perception, 135, 136–141
Head injury, 171–177
    and Alzheimer's disease, 179
    behavioural outcomes, 174–175
    driving resumption after, 175–177,
        186
    epidemiology, 171–173
    outcomes, 173–175
    and Parkinson's disease, 181
    from road accidents, 172–173
Hierarchical systems, 89–90
Huntington's disease, 180, 183–184

Image blur, 4
Implementation, 197–199
Implicit memory, 104–106
Instance theory, 90–91
Instruction, 95–96

Knowledge, declarative, 88, 89
Knowledge of results, 95

Lateral geniculate nucleus, 9
Learner drivers, self-assessment of
        ability, 153–154, 158–159
Learning, 76–88
    curves, 76–80
    to drive, 82–85, 94–95, 96–97
    and experience, 101–103
    feedback effects, 95–96
    and memory, 100–101
    and practice, 76–88
    transfer, 91–95
Light, 1–3
Linear perspective, 5
Logistic functions, 78–79
Looming detectors, 9

Magnocellular (M) pathways, 9
Markov modelling, 53
Memory, 99–119
    for accidents, 114–119
    under anaesthesia, 99–100

and arousal, 126–131
for dangerous situations, 125–131
for dates, 115–119
for driving situations, 128–131
explicit/implicit, 104–106
and learning, 100–101
measurement, 104
redintegration, 100
"skilled", 101–103
spatial, 112–114
working, 107–112
Motion parallax, 10
Motion perception, 8–11
Motor Car Act (1903), xiv
Motor chunks, 30
Motor control, 26–29, 32–33
Motor cortex, 27
Motor dominant neurons, 31
Multiple Affect Adjective Checklist,
    160

Object-oriented actions, 26–33
Old age, see Elderly drivers
Optic flow, 18–19
Orbitofrontal connections, 60

Parietal cortex, 27
Parkinson's disease, 181, 184–185
Parvocellular (P) pathways, 9
Phonological loop, 107, 108
Physiological response to danger,
    122–125
Pick's disease, 179–180, 182–183
Power functions, 76–78, 79–80
Practice, 76–88
    and driving skill development, 82–85
    massed/distributed, 80–82, 85–87
    and performance, 76–80
Prefrontal cortex, 27, 31
Premotor cortex, 27
Primary visual cortex, 5
Procedural reinstatement, 106
Prospect theory, 196
Pyramidal system, 26

Reaching, 31
Reaction time, 34–36

Retina, 2
Retrieval-induced forgetting, 60
Road accidents
    child pedestrians, 7, 21–22
    in dementia sufferers, 186
    and driver age, 166–168, 170, 171, 178
    and driver experience, 166–167
    and driver training, 75–76
    financial costs of, xv–xvi
    head injuries resulting from, 172–173
    memory for, 114–119
    statistics, xv
Road fatalities, xv
Road network, extent of, xiv–xv
Road rage, 162–163
Road safety training, 137, 138
Road Traffic Act (1930), xiv
Rods, 2
Routine actions, 63–65

Salience, 133–134
Scene perception, 132–136
Schemata, 57–63
    brain control, 59
    sharing across, 59, 60–61
    suppression, 59, 60
    switching, 59, 61–62
Self-assessment of driving ability,
    145–152
    and actual ability, 156–159
    and age, 153, 171
    and driving test outcome, 154–155
    and experience, 152–153
    in learner drivers, 153–154, 158–159
Self-efficacy, 152–156
    and actual ability, 156–159
Self-enhancement, 147
Self-paced activity, 66
Sex differences
    speed adjustment, 16
    time-to-collision estimation, 22
Shading, 5
Situation models, 113–114
Skill acquisition, 76, 88–91, 95–96
Skill transfer, 91–95

"Skilled" memory, 101–103
Spatial frequency, 2–3
Spatial memory, 112–114
Speed adjustment, 14–17
Speed estimation, 11–13, 16
Speedometer use, 11–12
Steering behaviour, 35–36, 48–53
Stress, 122
Supervisory Attention System, 57

Tau, 17–18, 20–21
    global/local, 17–18
Tau-dot, 42–43, 45
Telescoping of events, 116, 117
Threat, see Danger
Time-to-collision, 17–23
Traffic scene assessment, 132–136
Training
    of drivers, 75–76, 82–85, 94–95,
        96–97, 138
    in road safety, 137, 138
Traumatic brain injury, 171–177
    and Alzheimer's disease, 179
    behavioural outcomes, 174–175
    driving resumption after, 175–177,
        186
    epidemiology, 171–173
    outcomes, 173–175
    and Parkinson's disease, 181
    from road accidents, 172–173
Two second rule, 45

Velocity adjustment, 14–17
Velocity estimation, 11–13, 16
Vergence eye movements, 4
Vigilance, 58–59
Visual cortex, 5
Visuo-spatial sketchpad, 107, 108,
    111–112
von Restorff effect, 127

Wisconsin Card Sorting Test, 61
Working memory, 107–112

Yerkes-Dodson law, 126